# Healing and Power in Ghana

## STUDIES IN
## WORLD CHRISTIANITY

*The Nagel Institute for the Study of World Christianity*
*Calvin College*
Joel A. Carpenter
*Series Editor*

## OTHER BOOKS IN THE SERIES

*A Spirit of Revitalization*
Kyama M. Mugambi

*John Song*
Daryl R. Ireland

*Christianity and Catastrophe in South Sudan*
Jesse A. Zink

*The Rise of Pentecostalism in Modern El Salvador*
Timothy H. Wadkins

*Global Christianity and the Black Atlantic*
Andrew E. Barnes

*The Making of Korean Christianity*
Sung-Deuk Oak

*Converts to Civil Society*
Lida V. Nedilsky

*Evangelical Christian Baptists of Georgia*
Malkhaz Songulashvili

*China, Christianity, and the Question of Culture*
YANG Huilin

*The Evangelical Movement in Ethiopia*
Tibebe Eshete

# Healing and Power in Ghana

*Early Indigenous Expressions of Christianity*

*Paul Glen Grant*

BAYLOR UNIVERSITY PRESS

*Cover Design* by Kasey McBeath
*Cover image*: As part of the Odwira festival, a young woman, possessed by an ancestral spirit and accompanied by members of her clan, delivers food to the family shrine. Akropong-Akuapem, Ghana, October 2015. Photo by Paul Glen Grant.
*Series design* by Diane Smith

Hardcover ISBN: 978-1-4813-1267-7
Library of Congress Control Number: 2020943944

NATIONAL
ENDOWMENT
FOR THE
HUMANITIES

*Healing and Power in Ghana* has been made possible in part by a major grant from the National Endowment for the Humanities: NEH CARES. Any views, findings, conclusions, or recommendations expressed in this book do not necessarily represent those of the National Endowment for the Humanities.

Printed in the United States of America on acid-free paper with a minimum of thirty percent recycled content.

Dedicated to the memory of Paul Jeasene and Joseph Kwaku Dako: fiery and unafraid
Hebrews 11:39-40

# Series Foreword

It used to be that those of us from the global North who study world Christianity had to work hard to make the case for its relevance. Why should thoughtful people learn more about Christianity in places far away from Europe and North America? The Christian religion, many have heard by now, has more than 60 percent of its adherents living outside of Europe and North America. It has become a hugely multicultural faith, expressed in more languages than any other religion. Even so, the implications of this major new reality have not sunk in. Studies of world Christianity might seem to be just another obscure specialty niche for which the academy is infamous, rather like an "ethnic foods" corner in an American grocery store.

Yet the entire social marketplace, both in North America and in Europe, is rapidly changing. The world is undergoing the greatest transregional migration in its history, as people from Africa, Asia, Latin America, and the Pacific region become the neighbors down the street, across Europe and North America. The majority of these new immigrants are Christians. Within the United States, one now can find virtually every form of Christianity from around the world. Here in Grand Rapids, Michigan, where I live and work, we have Sudanese Anglicans, Adventists from the Dominican Republic, Vietnamese Catholics, Burmese Baptists, Mexican Pentecostals, and Lebanese Orthodox Christians—to name a few of the Christian traditions and movements now present.

Christian leaders and institutions struggle to catch up with these new realities. The selection of a Latin American pope in 2013 was in some respects the culmination of decades of readjustment in the Roman Catholic Church.

Here in Grand Rapids, the receptionist for the Catholic bishop answers the telephone first in Spanish. The worldwide Anglican communion is being fractured over controversies concerning sexual morality and biblical authority. Other churches in worldwide fellowships and alliances are treading more carefully as new leaders come forward and challenge northern assumptions, both liberal and conservative.

Until very recently, however, the academic and intellectual world has paid little heed to this seismic shift in Christianity's location, vitality, and expression. Too often, as scholars try to catch up to these changes, says the renowned historian Andrew Walls, they are still operating with "pre-Columbian maps" of these realities.

This series is designed to respond to that problem by making available some of the coordinates needed for a new intellectual cartography. Broad-scope narratives about world Christianity are being published, and they help to revise the more massive misconceptions. Yet much of the most exciting work in this field is going on closer to the action. Dozens of dissertations and journal articles are appearing every year, but their stories are too good and their implications are too important to be reserved for specialists only. So we offer this series to make some of the most interesting and seminal studies more accessible, both to academics and to the thoughtful general reader. World Christianity is fascinating for its own sake, but it also helps to deepen our understanding of how faith and life interact in more familiar settings.

So we are eager for you to read, ponder, and enjoy these Baylor Studies in World Christianity. There are many new things to learn, and many old things to see in a new light.

Joel A. Carpenter
Series Editor

# Contents

# Acknowledgments

He doesn't know, he's a foreigner
—*Twi Proverb*

This book began its life when I met Kwasi Cornelius, who died more than a century ago. He was so unlike anyone I had ever encountered—and yet I somehow knew him. It was then that I fell in love with the drama unfolding in the Akuapem hills, where Cornelius had spent a few passing years. Aside from one passing anecdote, he was too idiosyncratic to fit into this book: too restless, too disrespectful to the missionaries, and too challenging a research topic, but he led me to some of the other Ghanaian Christians whose ideas constitute the focus of this book. His descendants in the UK and Ghana have provided some encouragement. Neal Kodesh encouraged me to embark upon a needle in a haystack exercise, and Jim Sweet showed me how to keep elegant theories submitted to messy human realities and stories.

Much of the research behind this book was done for a dissertation written under Rudy Koshar, who laid down a crucial challenge to me: that I could and should push myself to learn to read the missionaries' abysmal handwriting. Koshar was right, and one of the key discoveries here–that the missionaries were increasingly internalizing Ghanaian religious paradigms, while the home office was censoring them–owes to Koshar's insistence on doing the hard work.

Florence Bernault warned me not to misconstrue the religious story in Akuapem's hills as a cultural or even charitable one, as if the foreign missionaries had been willing to suffer lifetimes of diseases, terrifying supernatural encounters, loneliness, and, all too often, a painful death for the sake of a cultural exchange project. These particular missionaries were clearly motivated by something deeper, she said, and if this research was not going to be about anything less than blood sacrifice—and above all the cross of Jesus that lay at the heart of the missionaries' message, and which the people of Akuapem understood in sacrificial and ritual terms—it would be missing the main point. Thank you, Florence, for believing in me.

Andrew Walls bluntly insisted that this project ought only to be done in conversation with Akuapem's Odwira festival. He could not have known that the next Odwira would also be the first in four decades to call a late king into the ranks of the ancestors. I owe my understanding of the moral imagination to Richard Werbner, who invited me to his Satterthwaite Colloquium of African Ritual and Religion. Paul Jenkins' enthusiasm helped bring to life the full humanity of long-dead missionaries. His decades of archival indexing and microfilming made the project possible. Henk Bosch corrected my Hebrew and convinced me to think more deeply about indigenous use of the Old Testament. Kwabena Asamoah-Gyadu and David Owusu-Ansah have let me ask questions I would be too embarrassed to ask otherwise and treated me seriously. Only over time did I realize that I was dealing with giants in their respective fields. Bright Obeng spent two days in Elmina with me; we did not find Cornelius' house, but I learned so much else.

The last thing Ghana—or Africa in general—needs is yet another foreigner synthesizing nationals' research. While I am confident that I have acknowledged my debts and my sources, I am well aware that so many others could have written this book with the kind of resources that were available to me. This research was funded in part by a Doris Quinn dissertation fellowship, a David M. Stowe research fellowship at Yale Divinity School, a John Hope Franklin research grant from Duke University, a Central European History Society research grant, and various travel grants from the University of Wisconsin. A generous Kaplan Award in the History of Social Justice made a big difference—not only in material terms, but in Michael Kaplan's ongoing encouragement and human touch, long after the term of the award itself. The staff at the University of Wisconsin's Memorial Library kindly retrieved Basel Mission annual reports for me when the library was closed for the coronavirus (and told me not to tell anyone).

The faculty, librarians and students at the Akrofi-Christaller Institute in Akropong have shown so much tolerance and hospitality—I thank you all. Alison Howell connected me with the human-intellectual resources of the institute and made time for me to ask my ignorant questions. Ernestina Afriyie drove up to Akropong from Tema just to explain Odwira protocol to me—only later did I understand how radical of an innovator she herself was. Ernest

Nyarko took me to the feeding of the ancestors procession, explaining spirit possession and rescuing me from a drunk young man who had stolen my hat to enforce my respect for the dead. Jonah Kwotua warned me against thinking like an American, told me to let the locals do their rituals, and prophesied over my children.

Bob Frykenberg has been a mentor for over a dozen years. When I declined his invitation to switch to South Asian history, he continued to guide and inculcate the task of combining gravity in research with human decency. Ron Morgan's parting words of encouragement in Mexico City gave me the push I needed to finish the manuscript. Joel Carpenter believed in me before he believed in the project itself and continued to prod it along until I finally sent him my prospectus, and he read through three drafts. At just the right moment, he bought me breakfast during yet another bummer of an AHA.

To the extent that the best ideas come in conversation with others, I owe an enormous debt to Andrew Barnes for ten years of encouragement, mentoring, challenging, personal advice, and invitations to join in with others. More than anyone else, Andrew has told me I belong in the field.

I had known Joshua Settles in a previous career. I have fond memories of staying up late along the blood-soaked banks of the Chattahoochee, wondering if human reconciliation could ever be possible. What a surprise to reconnect, years later, in Akuapem, of all places. Pauline and Joshua's recurring hospitality, which I have only been able to repay with suitcases full of Tylenol and curry paste, helped me get my sea legs in Ghana.

Fabu Carter taught me to view ancestry as love rather than blood. Brian Russell taught me that loyalty can be an act of the will. Dwight Perry reminded me that the people in the story matter more than the theories. Alex Gee's encouragement over more than two decades has given me a sense of how much we can change as we become new people.

Matt Zabel offered deep joy and encouragement at a disheartening moment, along with several pounds of Belarussian chocolate and a gas card.

Chris and Tricia, Katie and Jeff, Jackie and Park, who have never judged—at least to my face—the wisdom or practical utility of embarking on an academic career in my mid-thirties: thank you for the love. Bob and Patty had their doubts about letting their daughter marry an eccentric, and I hope this book brings some relief.

Kay Grant, otherwise known as Mom, told me to quit my ministry job before it was too late. I am not sure I did so in time, but her life-long belief in risk taking has been an ongoing source of inspiration. As a nurse with a background in travel medicine, she was able to explain several West African diseases to me. Brian Grant (Dad) read large portions of this research and connected countless dots I had not seen.

Becca knows better than anyone else how much this has cost. Weeping may last through the night, but joy comes in the morning.

Josiah, Silas, and Lydia: sing the chains off!

# Introduction

## *The Moral Imagination*

"Jesus is the Son of God," said the Christian evangelist.
"My shrine-spirit is also a child of God," said the traditionalist.
What is the next line in the discussion?[1]

—*Kwame Bediako, Congress of the World Evangelical Fellowship,
June 1992, in Manila, Philippines*

Not all historical ruptures have been necessary, and not all can be healed. Sometimes, however, healing begins with rupture. This book tells one such story. In the final years before colonial rule in what is now Ghana, African men and women in search of healing, belonging, and spiritual power created a new kind of Christianity commensurate with their own needs. In order to do this, since the Christians with whom they were acquainted were foreign, they needed to make the message their own. This they did in two ways.

First, they imposed an indigenous cosmological framework upon the message, experimenting with Christian ceremonies, buildings, and stories for practical solutions to real-world problems. Along the way they developed vehicles for prosperity, protection, and healings from the raw materials of missionary Christianity. In hindsight, the unfinished product of their nineteenth-century work looks conspicuously contemporary—akin to the Pentecostal

---

[1]  Kwame Bediako, "The Unique Christ in the Plurality of Religions," in *The Unique Christ in our Pluralist World*, ed. Bruce J. Nicholls (Grand Rapids: Baker, 1994), 47.

impulse that has come to infuse much of twenty-first-century Africa's social-political ecosystems. Second, and indistinguishable from the first because Christianity had arrived in the flesh and blood and minds of foreigners, the process of reformulating the message entailed incorporating the missionaries themselves into this homegrown project. Against their own wishes, which tended toward ascetic attention to duty, German missionaries became shrine priests, tasked with calling upon heaven's armies to drive away enemies and heal those possessed by spirits. To the extent that they complied with indigenous demand, these missionaries were hearing their own message with new ears, growing progressively alienated from home in the process.

Similar dynamics have played out repeatedly around the world for centuries. The story unfolding in the late precolonial years in the southeast Gold Coast stands out in one important regard: the locals' unwavering insistence on seizing hermeneutical control both over the written message—the Bible, translated into the vernacular, and the songs, prayers, and rituals of Christian worship—and the messengers themselves. The preachers, evangelists, and congregants at the center of this story were profoundly successful at reformulating the message—so much so as to demand serious questions about recent scholarship on West African Pentecostalism in the present day. In its performative aesthetics the Ghanaian Christianity created a century and a half ago anticipated the born-again variant, which exploded upon the scene after independence in 1957. Regarded alongside the former, the latter appears much less like a foreign import, regardless of its institutional genealogy. Indeed, the intellectual framework of importing, reformulating, and redeploying foreign religions has been a defining characteristic of the West African intellectual history for centuries. Imperialist attempts at enforcing ethnic, linguistic, and ritual purity have rarely prevailed against an ancient and sustained moral imagination capable of turning strangers into neighbors. This is one of Ghana's supreme contributions to world civilization.

However, if the simple fact of a nineteenth-century homegrown prefiguration of twenty-first-century Pentecostalism resolves an important question—the stunning success of born-again Christianity despite its foreign lineage—a second question immediately arises. This is the question of rupture. Why was there a gap of several decades between these early Pentecostal-like manifestations and their reappearance in the 1920s as African-Initiated Churches—and another gap until the 1960s with global Pentecostalisms imported from overseas? Why did so much time pass between these expressions of an indigenous Christian vision? I propose that the answer lies in Ghanaian Christian failure to convert the missionaries or, put another way, missionary failure to receive the indigenous vision as it was created before their eyes. At the very moment of breakthrough in the 1870s, after decades of futile efforts, the missionaries withdrew into the arms of imperialist supremacy. Over a short half decade, the German missionaries performed a stunning and deeply upsetting about-face, accepting and colluding with Britain's program of indirect rule. Meanwhile, the two key Germans, Johann Georg Widmann and Johannes Zimmermann, both died in late 1876 and were replaced by a prouder young generation. Increasingly willing to sideline indigenous Christian leaders in the interest of access to British funding for the mission—funding that required the Germans to assume an attitude of civilizing mission—the missionaries began quashing indigenous intellectual and practical initiatives within the congregations under their purview. It would fall to African-Initiated Churches of the 1920s to rekindle the entrepreneurial and magical spirit of a half century earlier, and it would not be until the 1960s and 1970s that that same spirit would reemerge in its present form. In other words, while a thread of intention and vision unites indigenous Christianity of the 1870s and 1970s, its institutional and practical lineage was ruptured by colonialism.

On the other hand, the continuities are so great that one cannot fail to study Ghana's nineteenth-century church history without sensing continuities with the Pentecostal present. From the perspective of an unbroken West African moral framework and ontological vision, missionary collusion with imperialism seems less than successful. As a dehumanizing religious imposition, missionary imperialism was not the equal of the enduring indigenous vision; the former turned out to be little more than a colonial interlude.

∿

This book makes three central claims. First, I argue that a form of Christianity, epistemologically and ontologically contiguous with Pentecostalism despite having few institutional continuities, emerged a half century before that movement's customary birthdate in the first decade of the twentieth century; second, that this indigenous Christianity was an autochthonous product of West African intellectual history; and third, that the indigenous project of reformulating Christianity expressed itself, in part, as a pervasive and sustained attempt at incorporating the foreign messengers into the emergent program. In marked contrast both with the German missionaries, who insisted on thinking in European categories of ethnicity and thus struggled to imagine foundations for social cohesion other than nations, and the British, whose missionaries in the precolonial Gold Coast rarely stayed long enough to learn indigenous languages, the indigenous Christians of Akuapem thought in transnational terms from the very beginning.

Across Africa, most people who became Christians after 1840 did so in conversation with other Africans, and at least since the late 1960s, historians have recognized that narratives of African Christianity focused on missionary thoughts and deeds are rarely of much use in explaining the sweeping changes.[2] The reverse is also true: especially for the nineteenth century, narratives of West African Christianity that omit missionaries are incomplete at best, because that story usually unfolded in cross-cultural contexts. However, West Africa, especially in the nineteenth century, had its own particular histories of encounter with global processes—both the Muslim north and the Christian Atlantic—and thus cannot represent African Christian history in general.[3] Writing about early twentieth-century East Africa, Derek Peterson could credibly speak of "ethnic patriotism" among Kenyan Christians.[4] Such a logic does not readily transfer to the Gold Coast, where European-derived definitions of ethnicity break down amid a complex cast of linguistic, social, cultural, and religious pluralism.[5] Ghanaians have learned that, although neither money nor politics nor military might can be expected to endure, relationships might.

Put another way, although Ghanaians have always sought to apply Christianity to their own problems and priorities—quite often against the wishes of the missionaries—only rarely have they asked the missionaries to go away, even when no longer needed. Rather, they have consistently hoped the missionaries would join them in developing a new Christianity. Consequently, a historically honest approach demands the robust treatment both of the foreigners and the locals, and of the ways both changed and became new people

---

[2]   Kwame Bediako, *Christianity in Africa: The Renewal of a Non-Western Religion* (Maryknoll, N.Y.: Orbis, 1996); David Jacobus Bosch, *Transforming Mission: Paradigm Shifts in Theology of Mission* (Maryknoll, N.Y.: Orbis, 1991); Robin Horton, "African Conversion," *Africa* 41, no. 2 (1971): 85–108; Robert L. Montgomery, *The Lopsided Spread of Christianity: Toward an Understanding of the Diffusion of Religions* (Westport, Conn.: Praeger, 2002); J. D. Y. Peel, *Christianity, Islam, and Orișa Religion: Three Traditions in Comparison and Interaction* (Berkeley: University of California Press, 2016); Dana L. Robert, *Christian Mission: How Christianity Became a World Religion* (Hoboken: Wiley, 2009); Lamin Sanneh, *Translating the Message: The Missionary Impact on Culture*, 2nd ed. (Maryknoll, N.Y.: Orbis, 2008); Andrew Walls, *The Cross-Cultural Process in Christian History: Studies in the Transmission and Appropriation of Faith.* (Maryknoll, N.Y.: Orbis, 2002).

[3]   Lamin Sanneh, *The Crown and the Turban: Muslims and West African Pluralism* (Boulder, Colo.: Westview, 1996).

[4]   Derek R. Peterson. *Ethnic Patriotism and the East African Revival: A History of Dissent, c. 1935 to 1972* (Cambridge: Cambridge University Press, 2012).

[5]   Sara Berry, *No Condition is Permanent: The Social Dynamics of Agrarian Change in Sub-Saharan Africa* (Madison: University of Wisconsin Press, 1993).

as they lived and died with one another, and as they articulated the message back and forth to one another.

From the 1840s, when locals of the southeast Gold Coast endowed their missionaries with the title of *asɔfoɔ* (shrine priests), through the bitter years of colonialism to the 1920s, when their descendants initiated forgiveness and reconciliation with estranged and deported former missionaries, Ghanaian Christians have never ceased to invite. Few of the missionaries have ever fully accepted the invitation. Nevertheless, a core argument advanced here holds that the indigenous Ghanaian urge to incorporate foreigners into fellowship derives from an ancient West African moral tradition that predates widespread conversion to Christianity by centuries.

Today, several generations after the events discussed in the present study, Ghana's religious economy has been thoroughly suffused by spiritual impulses variously described as Pentecostal or born-again, and the trend shows no signs of slowing. Most Ghanaian Pentecostal churches are younger than their founders. Many others are a half century old or younger, and a few others trace their roots to the second decade of the twentieth century. Nearly all, however home-grown they may be, can trace their institutional genealogy to foreigners, be they Nigerian, American, or European. That they do so, often with pride—as an assertion of their pastors' global connectedness—does not necessarily mean that these churches are genuine imports. With a few important exceptions, the emerging historical consensus holds that West African Pentecostalism is something of an exotic plant, however deep its roots may have grown since its arrival.[6] One of this book's claims is that questions of institutional lineage are beside the point. Long before the formal, institutional arrival of a form of Christianity now termed Pentecostal, Ghanaian men and women were already imposing Pentecostal-like demands on the missionary Christianity they had on hand. Even an exotic plant requires good soil in which to thrive, and in West Africa, that soil was a human willingness to imagine a better world in the face of such brutal concussions as the transatlantic slave trade and colonial rule. The tumultuous half century or so between these twin impositions was anything but tranquil. Throughout various wars and economic interruptions,

---

[6]   Important exceptions include J. Kwabena Asamoah-Gyadu. "The Church in the African state—The Pentecostal/Charismatic Experience in Ghana," *Journal of African Christian Thought* 1, no. 2 (1998), 51–57; Paul Gifford, *Ghana's New Christianity: Pentecostalism in a Globalizing African Economy* (Bloomington: Indiana University Press, 2004); P. White, "Centenary of Pentecostalism in Ghana (1917–2017): A case study of Christ Apostolic Church International," *HTS Teologiese Studies/Theological Studies* 75, no. 4 (2019), a5185, https://doi.org/10.4102/hts.v75i4.5185.

some men and women of the southeast Gold Coast identified in Christianity a vehicle for mastery over their most pressing challenges.

Given the turmoil of the times, these challenges were quite diverse. Along with the rest of coastal West Africa in the middle of the nineteenth century, the Gold Coast was undergoing painful political and economic reconfigurations. Even as several kingdoms fell, putting thousands of refugees to flight, a sustained cognitive framework for problem solving continued to operate unbroken. This was a moral imagination capable of forging enduring relationships across human divides, and of importing, reformulating, improvising upon, and redeploying whatever intellectual and spiritual resources were uncovered in the process. Christianity had been present in the region for centuries, largely confined to the persons of European residents of coastal forts, slave dungeons and trading posts, including the Euro-African descendants of foreign soldiers' unions with indigenous women. However, from the late 1820s, a new type of Christian had appeared, unbidden, in the southeast of the Gold Coast: a multiracial cast of foreigners—a mixture of West Indians and Germans, together with a few Africans from elsewhere in the continent—who came as settlers and missionaries. After a few failed starts in the 1820s and 1830s, these newcomers definitively established themselves in the mountain kingdom of Akuapem north of Accra in the early 1840s, thence sending their successors deeper into the interior toward the east, the north, and the west. From the very beginning, the locals and the refugees among whom these foreigners were living set themselves to the creative work of seeking pragmatic uses for these world travelers and their religion.

Over the ensuing four decades, numerous locals arrived at the conviction that the message contained more power than its messengers realized. The missionaries, after all, had failed to bring wealth to Akuapem, had failed to protect the kingdom from British aggression, and had been unwilling to produce the protective amulets that were the stock trade of most other religious entrepreneurs. They were, moreover, consistently sick for months and years on end—sometimes in their bodies, and sometimes in their minds. They died at astonishing rates. Indeed, for the first decade of its existence, the missionaries' graveyard grew faster than their congregation did. Small wonder, then, that by 1860—twenty-five years after the missionaries' first arrival in Akropong—the entire body of the Christian community in Akuapem's royal city of Akropong measured 241 in number and consisted mainly of children attending missionary schools. Within ten years, everything had changed. By 1870, the congregation had tripled in size, to 748, with much of the growth coming in a three-year period late in the decade.[7] What had changed during that decade? It was not the missionaries, who continued to struggle to survive, and whose effectiveness was undercut by constant turnover of personnel. Nevertheless, the number of Akuapem's Christians grew spectacularly during the late 1860s.

Among the various factors to the growth of the church in Akropong from 1867, I focus on two; both are products of indigenous intellectual history. The first was a consistent insistence by refugees and the poor, the enslaved, the handicapped, and the otherwise marginalized that Christianity could, and therefore should, heal and protect. During the middle years of the century, tremendous overseas demand for West African palm oil (used during those years to lubricate industrial machinery in Britain) induced several small polities to lay claim to vast tracts of bottomland forest heretofore of little economic significance. Wars and smaller-scale conflicts broke out, and Akuapem was flooded with refugees. The religious change of the 1860s was driven, in part, by hundreds of displaced persons who sought protection and social incorporation into Christian congregations.

The second factor was an explosive new resource. This was the Bible in vernacular translation: *Anyamesɛm*, or the "words of *Onyame*." The translators (a German-Ghanaian team) identified the supreme indigenous deity with the God of Christian scripture. *Onyame*, heretofore inaccessible and silent because he was too lofty, now spoke for the first time, and spoke in words which most of the missionaries, in-country for only a few years, could barely master. Having translated and promulgated Onyame's words, the missionaries subsequently struggled to control and contain indigenous biblical hermeneutics. More subtly, several of the missionaries, especially the handful of seniors of the group—those who had spent more of their lives in Akuapem than in the rural German villages of their upbringing—relearned the message as the indigenous people spoke it back to them. This dialectic process persisted long after the establishment of an indigenous clergy, because the indigenous Christians insisted on incorporating the missionaries, even after they no longer needed them. Then and now, the underlying moral logic of the land prioritized the human in human structures.

These twin impulses—a violent economic transition paired with a politically electric new message from God—constituted the stage for cross-cultural religious experimentations and urgent biblical hermeneutics. The raw material for these experiments was not Christianity in general, or in theory, or a set of

---

[7]　These numbers are compiled from the Basel Mission's annual reports, the so-called *Jahresberichte*, henceforth abbreviated *JB*. Each number reflected the status as of January 1 of the year, and thus represents the change over the previous year.

metaphysical propositions. To the contrary: to most of the midcentury people of Akuapem, the religious message was indistinguishable from the messengers living among them, in their towns—men and women who had learned their languages, who got sick, had babies, laughed, sang, argued, made mistakes, and died in the villages. These people were, for the most part, Germans. However, again, they were not Germans in general, but a particular variety of lower-middle-class enthusiasts called *Pietists*, in the employ of an organization formally named the *Evangelische Missionsgesellschaft* but universally known as the "Basel Mission" after the city of its home office, located across the German frontier in Switzerland.

As the men and women of Akuapem began reformulating Christianity to plumb its social-political potential for resolving intractable problems, they did so in conversation with these Pietist missionaries. They did this in quotidian interactions, such as conversations at market or while working together (the Basel Mission had sent rural German peasants to Akuapem—people who understood livestock, seeds, and tools, and enjoyed talking about them for hours). They did it in moments of crisis, such as dying children or palace intrigue. They did it during rituals and ceremonies, such as when laying foundations for new houses. The pedestrian quality of these interactions is important for what followed later in the century. For nearly a half century the men and women of Akuapem encountered the men and women of the Basel Mission at a deeper, more genuine, and more authentic fashion than nearly any other Africans did with their European or American guests.

Furthermore, indigenous understanding of these foreign Christians included awareness that the missionaries were considered odd by their own neighbors back in Germany. Before the 1870s, when the Basel Mission put an end to the practice, several young men and at least one woman of Akuapem traveled to Basel. There they discovered to their tremendous surprise that the lands of the upper Rhine were anything but prosperous, lagging far behind Britain. They also discovered that the Pietists of the Basel Mission were increasingly alienated from their own city as many Swiss natives, along with millions of other Europeans, were abandoning the God of their fathers. This knowledge of the missionaries' homeland constituted real power to the intellectual leaders of the emergent indigenous Christian churches, who understood that because Christianity was fiercely contested in Europe, there was corresponding room for flexibility and thus practical and hermeneutical innovation in Africa.

And herein lies the contradiction. Having established an indigenous Ghanaian church, having translated the Bible, and having trained several cohorts of preachers to interpret the same from the original Hebrew and Greek texts, the Basel Mission had effectively ceded control of the message before deciding, a few years later, that they wanted it back. Especially after its 1874 war with the regional great power Asante, Britain was imposing a new kind of political economy on the Gold Coast, and the Basel Mission (which had always taken directions from the home office in Switzerland) yielded to British assumptions and definitions. The cost was broken relationships with indigenous Christians. Missionary paternalism might have stunted religious innovation within the local churches, but could not forestall the inevitable: the rise of African-Initiated Churches, typically led, during the late nineteenth and early twentieth centuries, by charismatic leaders asserting ownership of some kind of supernatural message.

∿

Christianity has grown faster in West Africa than nearly all sober expectations made at the end of the colonial period. Observers of Ghana and Nigeria regularly publish astonished and often sensationalist and alarmist analyses of independent, Pentecostal, and kindred "born-again" movements and autonomous congregations contending with one another for members. These religious innovations have proven enduring because they were so natural and obvious to participants. Nevertheless, few Western scholars writing at the dawn of independence anticipated the scale of Christian growth that would follow throughout the continent. During the colonial period, many imperial officers had taken for granted that Christianity was a European religion. That assumption was simplistic at best, but it was—and continues to be—shared by more than a few European and American missionaries, who, unaware of the creative work their own medieval ancestors had done in translating a West Asian message into European contexts, have seen false consciousness in African innovations.

During the last two centuries in the Ghanaian kingdoms of Akuapem and Akyem Abuakwa, and indeed much of West Africa, religious change has been the engine of fundamental reconfigurations of social and family relations—reconfigurations that predated colonialism and continue to this day. At a broader level, African Christianity, which predates its northwestern European variant by centuries and yet still seeks an indigenous foundation, has become the heartbeat of today's world Christianity. However, that story—for all its sweepingly transnational dynamics—is radically and dangerously incomplete if it is not anchored in daily life experience. A despondent German missionary burying his wife with his own hands, as David Eisenschmid of the Basel Mission did in the town of Kyebi in 1867, was healed as he was enveloped

10 — Healing and Power in Ghana

in his grief by people who stood by him and took up his tears as their own, as Eisenschmid's neighbors did: Africans converting their missionary.[8]

The following study, then, is about missionary subjectivity to African religious innovations. It is about the ways men and women of the pre- and early-colonial Gold Coast imposed their wishes, dreams, and fears upon the missionaries living among them, and about missionaries' varied responses. More specifically, it is about the ways the people of Akuapem, and of a few neighboring kingdoms, strategized to incorporate the foreign (Germans, mostly, of the Switzerland-based Basel Mission) missionaries into autochthonous ways of thinking and making community and healing social ruptures. This book, in other words, tells the story of two parallel religious transformations wrapped up in one extended encounter: the missionary reception of Ghanaian Christianity. To a degree unmatched in Africa, these missionaries, German speakers of the Basel Mission, became different people in their eighty-year tenure in Akuapem, which ended violently at British hands during the First World War. Throughout that entire time, but especially after the missionaries, in partnership with locals, had translated the Bible into the Twi language, Ghanaians—Christians and non-Christians alike—had constantly imposed upon the Basel missionaries their own homegrown priorities.

These priorities rarely aligned precisely with those of the foreigners, even when the natives could read them straight out of their Bibles. Take the Eucharist, for example: the Christian ritual, done in remembrance of Jesus' death on the cross. Indigenous seminarians, literate in Greek and Hebrew, whose keen interest in the Old Testament arose out of their intuitive understanding of the ancient Hebrew sacrificial economy, consistently understood that ritual in ecclesiological terms. That is, they understood Jesus' sacrifice as creative of a new kind of community. This was not an original insight of theirs: it has been part of Christian teaching since the beginning. However, it was not an emphasis of the Basel missionaries. As the latter approached the Eucharist, they were inclined to think primarily in terms of atonement, of forgiveness of sin. This also was a biblically feasible doctrine, because the Scriptures were hermeneutically pluripotent on these matters. The missionaries could listen to the message spoken back to them and receive the message like never before—or they could refuse to listen. Many African Christians of the twenty-first century, only a few generations removed from the rupture, have a visceral understanding of the problem presented by the Christian message for communal cohesion. This is even more so when the social scars of the religious encounter remain, as they have in Akuapem. Kwame Bediako once asked: "How can one

8    David Eisenschmid, "Zweierlei Sterben," *Heidenbote* (henceforth *HB*) 1867, 216.

keep the Christian revelation intact, yet vindicate for the Christian conscience a place to feel at home in the common culture shared with non-Christians?"[9] It is a deep problem, and one that might possibly have no definitive answers; its impossibility gets to the heart of the human condition.

This geographic center of this story is the Akuapem ridge of southeastern Ghana, where several decades of attempts at forging a lasting community out of an eclectic mixture of refugees and displaced people had already taken place before the first Basel missionary arrived in 1835. The most successful of these attempts had come only seven years earlier in 1828, when Akuapem's army managed to defeat the Asante Empire's army in open battle. It was a humiliating, but temporary, setback to the Asante, who would go on to other wars and diplomatic adventures in the region. But to the small Akuapem, a peripheral player in regional politics, this battle was—and remains—the single most glorious moment in memory. It had, moreover, an outsized religious outcome: Akuapem's soldiers captured a talisman, the *Odwira*, which the Asante had carried into battle. The Odwira now became the property of the Akuapem, or perhaps the other way around—the Akuapem now belonged to the Odwira. Either way, Akuapem's annual Odwira festival, built around the nexus of the yam harvest and ancestral veneration, with the office of the king at the fulcrum of the spiritual and temporal worlds, subsequently became the defining ritual of Akuapem's kings—their supreme annual responsibility, and the cornerstone to their legitimacy in a kingdom bitterly divided by language and lineage.

Akuapem's Odwira was only seven years old when the first Basel missionary—an idiosyncratic Dane by the name of Andreas Riis—asked the king for permission to settle in the royal town of Akropong. Akuapem was then a two days' march north of the coastal kingdom of Accra, where an entirely different language—Gã—was spoken, and several days to the southeast of Asante, whose language and culture were very close to that of Akuapem's. The people of Akuapem spoke two languages: Twi, the language of the Akyem ruling family and several thousand other migrants from various Twi states, and Guan, the language of the native peoples, who in the early nineteenth century were slowly becoming a minority in their own country. The Twi-speakers were, and are, mostly matrilineal, and the Guan are patrilineal.[10] Akuapem is, therefore, a small kingdom built immediately atop a ridge describing one

---

[9] Kwame Bediako, *Theology and Identity: The Impact of Culture Upon Christian Thought in the Second Century and in Modern Africa* (Oxford: Regnum, 1992), 440.

[10] To complicate matters, there are a few Guan towns on the central ridge that have adopted the language of the Akyem—Twi—while remaining patrilineal in ancestral structure. This twist serves to demonstrate how little language has to do with ethnicity in the region. The German missionaries, who generally understood language as utterly important

of West Africa's most socially and religiously meaningful frontiers. Together with the Akyem, the Asante, and several other small kingdoms extending to the west, the Twi-speakers of Akuapem belong to a broader ethnic grouping called the Akan, although they did not think of themselves in those terms in the nineteenth century. "Akan" is an imprecise ethnic denominator centered on matriliny and language (Twi, plus related dialects, the most important of which is Fante, spoken along the coast to the west of Accra), but to most people who have historically fallen under those lines, ancestral clan and village have been the only meaningful denominators of belonging.

The missionaries who came to Akuapem from the 1830s were mostly Germans and Swiss of the Basel Mission. As they worked in the Gold Coast, they came to reflect upon their own people's past, and to recognize that they, too, had once been heathens. Andrew Walls was a professor at a college in Sierra Leone in the 1960s, when he realized that his students intuitively understood the Christian communities of the first century—people whom Walls, of Scotland, only knew from book learning. A century earlier in 1859, a German missionary had made a similar observation. The real advance of Christianity in the interior of the Gold Coast, Johannes Zimmermann said, was not made by missionaries but by Africans themselves, and above all by such as were "uncontrolled by missionaries." This autochthonous initiative, Zimmermann continued, led to a situation "not unlike that of Germany in the Middle Ages."[11] The longer German missionaries lived in the Gold Coast, the more they recognized the gap between the biblical social context and the world of their own upbringings. Like the Africans among whom they were working, the Germans were once heathens.

Basel missionaries went deep into indigenous societies, often gaining greater facility in the languages than any other Europeans, and gradually becoming more and more African in their outlook. As a result, many of them grew estranged from their homelands, and exactly at a time of unprecedented social upheaval. Johann Widmann, for example, departed for Akuapem in 1843, and died in 1877, taking only two furloughs during that time. His career in Africa thus began prior to the revolutions of 1848 and came to its mortal conclusion after Akuapem's incorporation into Britain's Gold Coast Colony. Widmann's intellectual development is utterly fascinating. While his eccentric peer and close friend Johannes Zimmermann has always attracted more

---

as a social denominator, misunderstood Guan adaptation of Twi as evidence of that people's imminent disappearance from history.

[11] Zimmermann quoted in Albert Ostertag, "Die Goldküste und die basler Mission daselbst," *Evangelisches Missions-Magazin* (henceforth *EMM*) 1859, 47.

historical attention (a small-town baker by training, Zimmermann married an Angolan missionary and composed hundreds of songs in two indigenous languages, even as he quoted Goethe), Widmann traveled a greater distance in his own worldview. At the beginning of his career, after three months in the field, he saw African spirituality as "untenable superstition."[12] Over time, he came to think like his neighbors and parishioners, going as far as calling down armies from heaven in 1869, asserting that he thereby had blocked the Asante army from its intended invasion.[13] The home office, however, increasingly sensitive to educated opinion back home, did not publish these remarks.

Other Germans, especially those who came later in the century, had a harder time identifying with the natives. Incrementally but inexorably, Britain imposed indirect rule in Akuapem in the third quarter of the century; Germany became a (minor) colonial power in 1885; and the missionaries increasingly struggled to distinguish their faith from nationalism, progress, science (especially biomedicine and immunizations), and commerce. As a result, the Basel Mission in Ghana at the threshold of the First World War in 1914 was far less identified with Ghanaian life than it had been fifty years earlier. If the mission's early years contain a story of unparalleled missionary entrance, by way of equally unparalleled missionary suffering, into an African culture, the later years saw an ugly self-segregation, a refusal to be incorporated—a heartbreaking paternalism—replace the genuine meeting that had taken place earlier. Much of this trajectory, moreover, was taken in response to events far away, back in Europe.

But not all Ghanaian Christians have seen things that way: while fully aware of the missionaries' faults (personal, theological, and otherwise), many churches of the Gold Coast, even those not descended from the Basel Mission, retain affectionate memories of many of the missionaries, honoring them (some of them, at any rate) with the very loaded word of "ancestors." In 1944, speaking of Basel missionary Johann Christaller, who had died a half century earlier, philosopher-lawyer-patriot J. B. Danquah said in the acknowledgments to one of his books:

> Christaller . . . appears to me . . . the ancestor of the thought that informs these pages. In that sense, the spiritual sense, this book must be taken as

---

[12] Johannes Widmann, journal entry from October 2, 1843, published in *Jahresbericht* (annual report; henceforth *JB*) 1844, which in that year was printed in the *EMM* 1844, 190. Widmann had arrived in Akuapem on June 17 of that year (page 178 of the same report).

[13] Johannes Widmann, letter to Basel dated August 4, 1869 (BMA D-1.26 item 41, 1869).

having been written by him, or, not to be unnecessarily mysterious, with his spiritual cooperation.[14]

Likewise, the theological institute at which I did much of my fieldwork, which was founded in the 1980s with a robustly Afrocentric vision, is named in part for Christaller, and its research facility is called the Johannes Zimmermann Library. Within the moral imagination of these scholars, Afrocentrism need not conflict with honoring foreigners as ancestors. Quite the opposite, in fact: the latter is an expression of the former—West African religious aesthetics have never prioritized ethnic purity.

Indeed, in some key respects, the ideas behind this book have taken shape as I have meditated on the problem of life together in a pluralistic world. My goal has been to look at a thoroughly cross-cultural religious encounter, involving Africans and Europeans, through the lens of contemporary African religious questions. And, of course, the first step toward that goal is to recognize that distinctions between religion and politics, or between individual conscience and collective duty, or between the natural and supernatural, are historically contingent and did not originate in West Africa. The historian's appropriate response to claims of the miraculous, or of possession by spirits, or of forest monsters, or of gods speaking in dreams, is not to ask whether it happened, or how it happened, but how participants changed course accordingly.[15] The supernatural grows even more politically salient as a historical lens when the missionaries themselves disavowed or ignored miracles performed by indigenous Christians, which were of real, tangible political consequence—especially those which might aggravate conflicts between shrine priests and the king. In Akuapem, conflict between king and priests usually had to do with disagreements on the division of labor in the unseen realm, rather than with one party or the other intruding upon the other's exclusive jurisdiction. But to the extent that the missionaries entered the conversation, they needed to do so on the intellectual terms of the locals, and in ways educated Germans back home would find laughable. The arc of Johann Widmann's intellectual growth, from

[14] J. B. Danquah, *The Akan Doctrine of God: A Fragment of Gold Coast Ethics and Religion* (London: Lutterworth, 1944), 185.

[15] For this reason, I do not find mid-twentieth-century anthropological speculation on the metaphysics or psychic machinery of possession, as attempted, for example, by Mary Field, to be historically relevant: "The possessed person is in a state of dissociated personality. . . . It is the total banishment of all but one stream [of consciousness] which is the essential feature of dissociation. It is not true of the possessed person that, as Africans have it, "something has come to him"; rather it is that something has gone from him." M. J. Field, "Spirit Possession in Ghana," in *Spirit Mediumship and Society in Africa*, ed. John Beattie and John Middleton (London: Routledge & K. Paul, 1969), 164.

skeptic to partisan of spiritual warfare, largely reflects his internalization of African presumptions. The point is not to exoticize, but to explore the ways some of these foreigners learned to live in a bigger universe.

~

In the first two chapters I define the felt needs against which men and women in the precolonial Gold Coast evaluated the Christian message. These needs corresponded with very old social values and were not identical with the missionary message. The Akan-speaking kingdoms of Akuapem and adjacent Akyem Abuakwa were under tremendous political, economic, and social strain throughout the three centuries preceding the Basel Mission's arrival. These forces included slave raids by Europeans and Africans alike and, after abolition, a violent reordering of the political economy.

Chapter 1 sets what follows in its broader social-political setting, arguing that the large mid-nineteenth-century movement to Christianity (developed in chapters 5 through 7) must be understood against the backdrop of local frustrations with the indigenous ritual toolkit's capacity to heal the frayed social and family fabric. Chapter 2 catalogs the religious and ritual tools by which Akuapem's political and religious leadership addressed social problems from rebellions to divorces and unwanted spirit possessions. It focuses on three: *Odwira*, a harvest festival paired with (matrilineal) ancestral veneration; sacrifice to spirits, a class of techniques for acquiring control over the unseen world; and sanctuary shrines, institutions of last resort when the first two failed. Chapter 2 furthermore argues that Christianity became an attractive option only once locals could satisfactorily position the initial cohort of indigenous Christian preachers and teachers within these extant categories.

Chapters 3 and 4 introduce a foreign religion. Christianity had three and a half centuries of history in the Gold Coast when the German missionaries arrived—primarily as the house religion of European (slave) trading forts—and many indigenous kings and priests were solidly familiar with Atlantic Christianity. In order to ask why so few Ghanaians converted during those long years, chapter 3 contrasts the religion of the European trading companies and slave forts with patterns of pragmatic indigenous religious experimentation introduced in chapter 2, ultimately arguing that for much of its history in the Gold Coast, most natives have found Atlantic Christianity irrelevant—not because it was foreign, but because it was impotent to meet local needs (and, indeed, was generally a noxious presence as the religious currency of the slave trade).

Although there were a few missionary efforts in the Gold Coast before the nineteenth century, a turning point in Ghana's religious history came with the arrival of the Basel Mission in a few rounds in the 1820s. Chapter 4 introduces these men and women in their homeland context and establishes the basis of their capacity for cross-cultural learning. I focus less on belief and doctrine, because these so-called Pietists did not hold radically different beliefs than most of their German Protestant neighbors, and more on the social life of the missionary-minded youthful subset of the same in rural southwestern Germany and northwestern Switzerland. The Basel Mission began as the city was under French bombardment and was being protected by Russian armies that included pagan and Muslim troops from central Asia and Caucasia. It was a youth movement at first, characterized by spiritual experimentation and daydreaming (and complemented by reading missionary newsletters from all around the world). Focusing on a short-lived but very influential 1840s wave of exorcisms and faith healings, I argue that the Pietist missionary form of Christianity that arrived in the Gold Coast at that time did not so much sprout from ancient Germanic soil as emerge in cross-cultural conversation. Having settled in Akuapem, the Basel Mission was more malleable in indigenous hands—more receptive to indigenous reformulations of the message—than other missionary societies. This chapter engages extensively with Birgit Meyer's notion of "translating the devil," arguing that the discrepancy between official missionary statements and practical activities in the field reveals that before the consolidation of British colonial rule, German missionaries acted with neither the conviction nor the explicit message of European supremacy; the missionaries in Akuapem, in particular, adapted an experimental approach to spiritual power encounters.

Chapters 5 through 7, which focus on the years between 1842 and 1874, constitute the core of my argument. Most of the foundational intellectual developments toward the indigenization of the Basel-Mission-derived churches were laid during these thirty years. Chapter 5 is about local non-Christians' efforts at finding an indigenous category by which they might make optimal use of the foreigners. Several years before there was a single indigenous convert in Akuapem, the men and women of Akuapem had already identified the Basel missionaries as a new class of shrine priests, demanding comparable services from them. The missionaries, on the other hand, initially considered shrine priests to be nothing more than charlatans. This chapter identifies patterns in indigenous non-Christian attempts at making use of the foreign missionaries, and the ways the missionaries came to reimagine their project in response to indigenous demand.

Chapter 6 narrows the theme of indigenous engagement with the foreign religion to focus on the Bible in translation. The Basel Mission began its work of translating the Bible early on, publishing sections as soon as they were available, with the combined Old and New Testaments appearing in Twi in 1872. From the very beginning, indigenous preachers and teachers advanced a hermeneutical agenda at odds with that of the missionaries. The former made far more sense within the ideological and ontological frameworks of Ghanaian political life. The Basel Mission's translation and subsequent publication of Scripture, grounded in years of study both in the original languages and in Twi, effectively stripped the missionaries of hermeneutical control over the message. Developing ideas from J. D. Y. Peel, I argue that as indigenous Ghanaians and German missionaries looked at the same scriptures, they saw very different things. The Germans read in their Bibles a call to self-effacement, of death to self and of duty, while their Ghanaian fellow laborers saw words of power and healing.

Chapter 7 narrows the focus even further, making two arguments. As indigenous preachers went out among the people—and therefore among jealous priests and rival political leaders—they did not shy away from power confrontations with hostile shrines. Much of the move toward conversion after the 1850s took place in the aftermath of such displays of supernatural power. However, not only did this tend to happen when the missionaries were not present, but the missionaries did not seem to see it when it did. After an indigenous preacher raised a child from the dead, most of the missionaries (Widmann excepted) never mentioned the spectacular event, which would enter the indigenous Christian community's memory as a watershed. To the contrary, two missionaries, visiting that town a few weeks later, expressed almost willful surprise at the locals' greater interest in missionary street preaching. There was a second reason for missionary obliviousness to indigenous experimentation with the message: the foreign agents were sick and dying at rates surpassing other missionary societies. This chapter looks at the lessons the Basel Mission drew from lifetimes of sickness and grief.

The conclusion makes two longitudinal arguments. The first is that the creative space, within which indigenous Christians associated with the Basel Mission were able to interpose hermeneutical innovations, collapsed after Britain's imposition of indirect rule in Akuapem in the mid-1870s. Indigenous Christian innovations did not cease, however, but moved beyond the missionaries' gaze, emerging in the 1920s as what would later be called African-Initiated Churches. Recent scholarship has demonstrated an unbroken thread between heterodox independent evangelists of the 1920s and the Pentecostal movement, which rose in southern Ghana in the 1970s, despite those two religious waves sharing little to no institutional overlap. This line of thinking owes much—both to the published research and to ongoing informal teaching at academic conferences—to Kwabena Asamoah-Gyadu. Developing his arguments, I go further back in time to the precolonial encounter in the Akuapem hills. The 1920s constituted a renewal of indigenous Christian patterns of innovation—centered on healing and protection—briefly interrupted by colonialism. Despite its globally interconnected aesthetics, twenty-first century Ghanaian Pentecostalism is a fundamentally African religion.

The second concluding argument returns to the small-town scale in Akropong in the present day. In the past decade, after nearly two centuries of stalwart animosity to Akuapem's annual indigenous harvest festival (which includes spirit possession and ancestral veneration), the Christian churches have embraced and begun attending and participating in the festivities. This section builds on oral interviews conducted during 2015's Odwira, asking questions about the nature and limits of the indigenization of Christianity, not only in Ghana, but anywhere in the world.

～

My sources draw largely from those of the Basel Mission itself, whose home office, and whose field missionaries, wrote and published in meticulous detail. Missionaries mailed home quarterly reports, along with ethnographic, spiritual, and economic observations, and brought every important decision before the mission board, the "committee." This correspondence survives in the Basel Mission archives and has been microfilmed, a format that makes possible the slow-going task of reading the missionaries' nearly illegible German handwriting. Occasionally, the home office edited and published extracts of this correspondence in one or the other of three different in-house periodicals. These were:

1. The *Evangelische Heidenbote* (abbreviated HB), the "Heathen Messenger," a monthly magazine of Basel Mission stories from the field, intended for donors and friends of the mission. Here ran missionaries' obituaries and accounts of their troubles; here ran anecdotes of conversions (never, however, of miracles) and of heathen depravity (the tyranny of chiefs being a favorite). The *Heidenbote* was devout, moralistic, and emotional, and tended to focus on the missionaries. It also represented something of a providentialist vision of history, in which God's veiled will was understood to control time itself.[16]

---

[16] Michael Kannenberg, *Verschleierte Uhrtafeln: Endzeiterwartungen im württembergischen Pietismus zwischen 1818 und 1848* (Göttingen: Vandenhoeck & Ruprecht, 2007).

2. Annual reports—*Jahresberichte* (sing. *Jahresbericht*, abbreviated JB)—
distributed at the Basel Mission's festive annual meetings. In addition
to business and accounting ledgers, lists of personnel, and profiles of
indigenous congregations (all organized with Swiss attention to detail),
these annual reports also contained various reports and correspondence
not published elsewhere, including eulogies for the deceased, synopses
of worship services and sermons for the deputation of new missionaries, and the lyrics to songs written for the occasion of the annual meetings. If the *Heidenbote* partially served to recruit new donors and inspire
the devout, the *Jahresberichte* were intended for a readership of mission
insiders and stakeholders. Here, accordingly, appeared the only hints of
the missionaries' engaging with locals on the latter's religious terms (and
even then, most examples were toned down or redacted altogether).

3. The *Evangelisches Missions-Magazin* (abbreviated EMM), a scholarly
quarterly, intended to speak into the German-speaking world's theological, ethnographic, and linguistic academic circles. The *EMM* ran Basel
missionaries' analyses of indigenous cosmologies, compilations of native
proverbs, and similar studies from other missionary societies.

To these periodicals the Basel Mission regularly added various books,
atlases, hymnals, pamphlets, and other publications, some meant as history,
and some meant as inspiration. The mission published histories every few
decades, and some of these contradict one another. The Basel Mission Archives
also hold several invaluable artifacts of ethnographic interest: school essays
by locals, often on questions about indigenous history and customs; lists of
jokes and riddles; collections of proverbs; royal genealogies, and so on, including unpublished essays by missionaries, probably submitted for inclusion in a
Basel Mission publication.

Additionally, several missionaries, especially the ones who retired from
the field with their health still intact, published memoirs and other books
with external publishers, where no mission imprimatur was needed. In other
cases, descendants of missionaries have published their missionary forebears'
diaries, and I have used these, to the extent that they seem reliable. Several
indigenous Christians also wrote memoirs and opinion pieces, and in the
1940s and 1950s, Ghanaian churches published a number of interviews and
memories of elderly church leaders; these provide an especially valuable
source in respect to the spiritual vision behind the native-missionary relationships, as they occasionally recount events which the missionaries had
seen in decidedly different ways.

The Basel Mission also operated within a transnational network of likeminded missionary societies, sometimes as friends, and sometimes as rivals. If some missionaries nursed personal grudges with members of other agencies, they usually affirmed, at least superficially, the same goals and aspirations, and were, accordingly, aware of each other. Many of the missionaries subscribed to another periodical, the unaffiliated *Calwer Missionsblatt*, which abstracted missionary newsletters from around the world. This journal allowed workers deep in the African interior to drop references to India or the South Pacific or the American Civil War into their correspondence. On occasion, then, I resort to missionary sources from that transnational network, as I trace ideas circulating the globe with no bearing on colonial politics. To the Basel Mission record, I have added a few archival sources of other agencies—like those of the Wesleyan Methodist Missionary Society, active in territory overlapping with that of the Baslers. Like those of the Basel Mission, WMMS archives, which reside at the School of Oriental and African Studies in England, have been filmed and distributed widely (and in handwriting that is much easier to decipher). I have also drawn on British colonial correspondence, especially at a few moments at which my story intersected with empire: especially the Second British-Ashanti war (1873–1874). Much of this material resides in British Government publications found in various research libraries in the United States.

Finally, I have had recourse to three archival sources in Ghana: the Furley Collection at the Balme Library of the University of Ghana at Legon, the Johannes Zimmermann Library at the Akrofi-Christaller Institute in Akropong, and the Public Records and Archives Administration Department in Accra. The Furley Collection is an incomparable set of precolonial European and African archival sources on the history of the Gold Coast and West Africa. It is especially strong in Danish West African history. Smaller and specialized but highly valuable, the special collections at the Zimmermann Library focus on the history of autonomous Ghanaian theology and biblical hermeneutics, mostly of the twentieth century.

The pages that follow, then, attempt to apply an African architecture to a cross-cultural encounter, which has so often been treated as an overture to colonialism. But it is not my goal to produce some kind of reverse historical ethnography, whereby Europe is made strange in order to render Africa less so; nor am I trying use the missionary sources to write African history. Rather, the deeper I have looked into the personal motivations and changed minds which emerged in cross-cultural dialogue, the more I have realized that something profoundly transnational had developed here, in which race, and tribe, and tongue, and nation, and class, and disability lost so much of their power to divide, even as new, and perhaps equally divisive, denominators of loyalty and belonging took their place. This process began before colonialism and long before the arrival of institutional Pentecostalism from overseas. The eighty-year encounter that unfolded in the Akuapem hills and in the adjacent lowlands, then, resolved in a profound reimagining of Christianity according to an enduring social and cosmic vision.

What emerged was foolishness to the missionaries, perhaps, but constitutes a feat of the moral imagination of global importance. It is perhaps West Africa's outstanding contribution to the world, and certainly to world Christianity.

# 1

# Primal Globalization

On his way home from an expedition to an outlying district in the north-ern end of the mountainous Akuapem Kingdom, a traveling evange-list named Kwasi Badu Cornelius—also known as David Cornelius—passed through a deep kettle of a valley, densely wooded and surrounded by moun-tains. It was September 1875, a year and a half since the conclusion of hostili-ties in a complicated regional war largely remembered for Britain's sacking of the Asante Empire's royal city of Kumasi. The focus of that war had been the collision of two superpowers, but the geopolitical whirlwind had pulled the entire region into ancillary conflicts. In the process, thousands of people had needed to flee for their lives. Many found safe haven by placing themselves under the protection of a local king, a local shrine priest, or some other patron. Many others hid. On that September day, Cornelius met some of them. He had little to report back to his German employers with the Basel Mission. The ref-ugees had come from Anlo (near the delta of the Volta River, a few days to the east) and were generally receptive to his evangelistic message, but not enough to turn from "their idols."[1] Cornelius offered no further details, and like refu-gees anywhere, then or now, the people camping in that secluded ravine seem to have disappeared into the mists of time.

The seventy years preceding Britain's invasion had seen profound social, economic, political, and religious turmoil throughout the Gold Coast. A dis-torted economy, mainly integrated into global capitalism through the trans-atlantic slave trade, was yielding to industrial commerce—above all in the production of palm oil. The slave trade was one of history's great evils, but

---

[1] Basel Mission Archives (BMA), D-1.27 (1875), Akropong item 218: David Cornelius to Committee, report from December 20, 1875.

West African societies had innovated various political (and therefore inextricably religious) techniques for managing the damage. The trade's abrupt
end, imposed unilaterally from Europe, was something less than an unmiti-
gated blessing. Centuries' worth of trade infrastructure, wealth relations, and
sources of political legitimacy evaporated, and new ones were still in their
infancy. Put simply, during the middle of the nineteenth century, the coastal
regions of West Africa were undergoing as violent a social-political-economic
disruption as anywhere in the world—including the American Civil War or
Europe's industrial revolutions. The unnamed refugees hiding in the forest,
whose stories became little more than footnotes in a traveler's report, were
only a few among millions throughout the region for whom the changing
times represented great danger.

The men and women of Ghana had plenty of ideas for addressing this
emergency. This book proceeds from two interrelated assumptions: that political, social, and religious changes cannot be disentangled from one another, and
that religious changes are both cause and effect of the historical moments in
which they take place. Relative to mid-nineteenth century Ghana, this means
that humans shaped their times by means of religious tools. Faced with great
danger—from disease to war—at every turn, Ghanaians sifted through whatever religious or ritual tools were at hand, as they sought healing and power.
Some of these tools they imported wholesale from foreigners, and others they
invented on the spot. More frequently, they repurposed or tweaked existing
tools, or used them in new ways, to get what they needed. In short, religious
change did not simply happen: it was the outcome of much experimentation
and innovation. It was fundamentally cross-cultural, as was the human reality
of the times. The people of the early and mid-nineteenth century Gold Coast
had little to gain by insisting on ethnic purity or ideological authenticity, when
practical experience told them that what mattered most was what worked.

To return to Kwasi Badu Cornelius: later that year, the evangelist engaged
in a power showdown with the head priest of an unnamed village over rain-
making. In response to a dare from the priest, Cornelius prayed for rain and
received it, and the local chief needed to shelter under his umbrella.[2] To Cornelius, the encounter was part and parcel of his work, and it was scarcely
more remarkable than other adventures, such as confrontations with mocking
crowds, an escape without incident from accidentally stepping on a venom-
ous snake, or the inability of an angry god to harm him after demonstratively
removing and eating fish from a sacred pond.[3] Cornelius was no German

[2] Basel Mission Archives (BMA), D-1.27 (1875), Akropong item 218: David Cornelius
to Committee, report from December 20, 1875.
[3] BMA, D-1.27 (1875), Akropong item 185, David Cornelius, "Reise von Akropong
nach Begoro," May 13, 1875.

missionary, and he would soon be dismissed for insubordination. In his reckoning, Christianity was about healing, protection, wealth, and power as surely as it was about forgiveness of sins. Christianity was not the property of the missionaries, and having introduced a highly malleable variant of the Christian message into the indigenous ecosystem, the missionaries could not control its subsequent reformulation.

Europeans had been present, at least on the coast, for well over three hundred years before the Basel Mission arrived. Most, but not all, of these foreigners were Christians (at least some were Jews), and few had given much thought to the religious lives of the locals. The missionaries, when they arrived, were unclear about what they were doing and why; imagining themselves to be offering some kind of reparations for the slave trade, these men and women left behind a complicated legacy. On the one hand, they learned indigenous languages like few Europeans before or after, and they translated the Bible into vernacular languages. On the other hand, they could not imagine assimilating into the people among whom they lived. Persisting in social distance, indulging in the ubiquitous European conflation of diverse indigenous peoples as "negroes," the missionaries struggled to gain much of an audience.

All this changed within a few short years in the late 1860s. The reasons had little to do with a missionary breakthrough. Rather, two things had happened. First, the tumultuous social and political conditions of the middle of the century began to spiral out of anyone's control, and the existing ritual toolkit for healing social ruptures began to fail: too many people were falling through the cracks. Second, men and women of Akuapem, who had been quietly observing the missionaries for years, looking for ways to make the message useful, began to meet with success. Accepting the message on rather different terms than it was offered, they came to view Christianity as a vehicle for defeating the oppressive powers of the world, healing the sick, and casting out possessing spirits.

Divorced from the historical setting in which it took place, this indigenous religious change could easily appear a subset of European intellectual history—as if Africans had no past or present, no thoughts of their own or conflicts or rivalries. That European fallacy, shared with merchants and colonial officials, filled the pages of missionary writings, which were often meant for an audience of supporters, for generations. However, neither the perpetrators nor the victims of the Gold Coast's internal conflicts shared in the preposterous European conceit that Africans had no history. Belligerents and refugees alike knew who they were, where they came from, and who their rivals were—and they evaluated the Christian message, and its messengers, against the background of those needs. These needs, of course, reflected the human condition. Some needed shelter or protection. Others, whose basic needs were secured, sought wealth and power, or advantage over rivals, for themselves or their children.

The fears, goals, and aspirations (both corporate and individual) against which the men and women of Akuapem and the Gold Coast heard, received, rejected, and reconfigured the missionaries' message were as diverse as that mountain kingdom, perched as it was astride numerous ethnic, linguistic, and religious frontiers, and filled with the incompletely incorporated refugees of regional warfare and the children and children's children of foreign slaves. Which is to say: the horizons of the moral imagination in nineteenth-century Akuapem were historically contingent. Much of this book revolves around the cross-cultural process of conversion, but that dynamic can only be understood in light of the particular conditions of social marginalization in Akuapem, which formed the potential energy toward the reception of a new message. My central argument in this chapter is that mid-nineteenth-century social marginalization in Akuapem reflected, in part, the coexistence of two rival sacrificial traditions in this small kingdom, corresponding to a major West African cultural frontier, which the Akuapem ridge happened to straddle. At a time of widespread warfare and displacement, much of it driven by the transatlantic slave trade, two very different approaches to the ritual incorporation of people into clans and communities emerged, each with its own strengths and weaknesses. Akuapem's spiritual toolkit relied on different kinds of sacrifice—to shrine spirits and to ancestral spirits, respectively—for this work. Each functioned in different ways and with different outcomes.

The upshot of Akuapem's bifurcated religious economy was the existence of a class of doubly marginalized people: those who could not be incorporated anywhere. These people were the lowest of the low: slaves, for the most part, and the sons and daughters of slaves, but also the disabled, refugees from elsewhere, people who seemed to be cursed, and people whose moral choices had seen them expelled from their clans. These people were beyond the healing reach of Akuapem's sacrificial apparatus.

I develop my argument as follows. First, I survey the broader geographical historical conditions, which gave rise to the religious and political clash in the Akuapem kingdom. While the story of Akuapem's religious changes would reverberate throughout the entire Gold Coast and beyond, those changes were also products of a singular local history. In other words, the story involves the interplay between the local and the global or, more accurately, the rise of the local within a framework of global or regional conditions—a dynamic I am calling *primal globalization*. Next, I turn to the most important political innovation to emerge from that global-local conversation: the Akan forest kingdoms, of which Akuapem was the southeastern-most exemplar, and the social upheavals and concomitant political-military innovations of the Atlantic slaving era—devastating changes, which continued well into the nineteenth century. I pay especial attention to the spiritual epistemologies and practices, which derived in part from historical experience. Finally, I turn to the immediate context of religious innovation in early nineteenth-century Akuapem. As in much of non-Muslim West Africa, Akuapem's was a spiritual-political economy dominated by sacrifice and spiritual patronage. The men and women of Akuapem only embraced the missionaries' message after they had found ways to intelligibly incorporate the foreigners into existing social and religious categories.

This chapter thus spans a thousand years and involves people groups from both Africa and Europe. This is because the history of the southeast Gold Coast is inextricably global—and not merely at the level of trade, whereby an archaeologist might find artifacts from multiple cultures.[4] Distinct people groups have been living alongside one another in Akuapem for centuries, and to an extent have arisen in multiethnic contexts. German-speaking missionaries, arriving in the nineteenth century, sought to establish ethnic churches, analogous to their own state churches. They were destined for frustration, because their hosts were not keen on aggravating ethnic tensions within a pluralistic setting. The people of Akuapem had various felt needs corresponding with personal circumstance, cultural priorities, and the political-economic climate, but these needs rarely corresponded with what the missionaries had on offer.

This chapter concludes with a discussion of those felt needs as of the early nineteenth century. The whirlwind of global capitalist disruption had not dissipated with abolition, although it had become something less bloody. Well into the century, social emergencies proliferated, and the existing religious infrastructure grew ever less able to manage the problems. Locals sought tools for healing social wounds but rarely sought isolation from the rest of the world. In its peoples' felt needs and moral imagination, Akuapem was thus globally interconnected from the start.

PRIMAL GLOBALIZATION

The Akuapem hills are not high, rising about five hundred meters from their southern base on the rolling coastal plains. To the traveler approaching from

---

[4]  Brempong Osei-Tutu, "Mound Makers and Brass Casters from the Akwapem Ridge," *Journal des Africanistes* 75, no. 2 (2005), 54–63.

the coast, however, they begin quite abruptly, so that the railroad line from Accra to Kumasi, built in the 1920s, needed to detour to the west around the hills' southern terminus. The hills continue for a few hundred kilometers in a north-by-northeasterly direction, with a stunning break in the middle where the Volta River slices through. Today that rocky gorge lies beneath a massive hydroelectric reservoir, which sends power to sprawling Accra. The artificial lake behind the dam constitutes a barrier separating the booming coastal cities from the sleepy interior, but for hundreds of years the reverse was the case: the Volta Gorge was the principal highway by which migrants, merchants, and slaves, speaking many languages, reached the coastal plains from the east and, more importantly, from the distant north.[5] Perched immediately above and to the southwest of the gorge is the mountain kingdom of Akuapem—too close to be isolated from regional and Atlantic warfare and commerce, but just separate enough, and just inconvenient enough, and just poor enough, for successive empires to regard the kingdom as little more than a source of food and slaves. In the eighteenth and nineteenth centuries, Akuapem was thus both a crossroads and a dead end. The hills are made of a mixture of quartzite and slate and bear no minerals worth mining. Crucially for a political economy such as the Gold Coast's, there was no gold to be found in Akuapem's rocks or streams.[6] Gold was an all-important denominator of wealth in much of the region, and this mineral poverty pushed Akuapem's kings and, later, the educated class that emerged from mission schools into commercial agriculture. Ghana's twentieth-century cocoa boom began here, in part because there were few other possibilities for accumulating wealth in the colonial cash economy. For centuries, however, the people of the ridge have produced an agricultural surplus—and have accordingly drawn the attention of invading armies in need of food security. An English observer, Henry Meredith, had this to say in 1811, shortly after Akuapem was ravaged in a punitive Asante expedition under General Opoku Ferefere:

> Agriculture is their chief support, and before the present war, they supplied Accra and Adampe with almost all the necessities of life: Akuapim [sic] was in fact the granary of these countries. . . . Their chief trade consisted of agricultural productions which always meet with a ready sale, and for which they received in return, salt, dried fish, gunpowder, iron, guns and cotton manufactures.[7]

---

[5]  Timothy Lenoch, "Beneath a Fluid Surface: The Volta Valley, the Dente Shrine and Kete-Krachi, Ghana" (master's thesis, University of Wisconsin-Madison, 2005).

[6]  J. Byer, "Geology," in *Akwapim Handbook*, ed. David Brokensha (Tema: Ghana Pub. Corp., 1972), 2.

[7]  Henry Meredith, *An Account of the Gold Coast of Africa, with a Brief History of the African Company* (London: Longman, Hurst, Rees, Orme, and Brown, 1812), 227.

However slight the hills' elevation, their slopes are steep and the ravines deep. The soils are shallow and well-drained. Despite the hills' higher levels of precipitation than on the plains, there are no large rivers or lakes, most water immediately running off to either side of the ridge, to the northwest or the southeast. These two geological features—the elevation and the scarcity of standing water—combine for a subtle but very important ecological contrast with Accra and the coast: it is a healthy place. The towns strung along the narrow top of the ridge are several degrees cooler than the coast, with thick morning fog helping to keep the crops green during the dry season. More importantly, there are far fewer mosquitos and, accordingly, fewer cases of yellow fever and malaria. It was this quality to Akuapem's geography that brought the Basel Mission to Addo Dankwa's court. Having suffered from various tropical diseases during its first decade in the Gold Coast, the Basel Mission was pleased to have won the king's permission for its people to settle in Akuapem's healthier climate. Andreas Riis arrived in 1835, remaining for a few years before returning to Basel to recruit others. He returned in 1842 with a mixed group of European and West Indian settlers, thus beginning a seventy-year span of continuous Basel Mission presence. During that time, a deep and reciprocal cross-cultural encounter matured into one of West Africa's oldest Protestant communities. However, early missionaries seem to have had very little grasp of the kingdom's particular social dynamics, imagining Akuapem to be a mere stepping stone toward a bigger prize: the conversion of the Asante.

To understand the political powder keg in which the early indigenous Christian communities operated, it is vital to appreciate the pluralistic context of encounter in the Akuapem hills. Akuapem was then, and remains today, a linguistically and culturally pluralistic state, in which political unity has rarely come easy. Henry Meredith (1811) and Andreas Riis (1835), arriving at the Akuapem royal city of Akropong, were dealing with what was, in fact, a relatively new kingdom, ruled by lords whose Twi-speaking ancestors had only arrived in the previous century. Royal subjects spoke two different languages and multiple dialects of each. Some (including the royal family) organized themselves in matrilineal, and others in patrilineal, fashion—a very important distinction in a religious situation revolving around ancestral veneration. They worshiped a mixture of territorial and clan deities, some of which deities were rivals. Moreover, the situation was constantly churning in response to the global violence of the transatlantic slave trade and, by the second quarter of the nineteenth century, regional conflicts big and small erupting in response to economic change in the slave trade's aftermath. Akuapem's combustive social politics gave shape to the Basel Mission's subsequent career in the entire Gold

Coast. For their part, these politics, which were inextricable from ritual and religion, reflected the kingdom's long struggles for unity and sovereignty.

In such a context, the very notion of "indigenous" is fraught. This much is clear: the royal house did not have deep roots in Akuapem. The king ruled over subjects who had been there long before him. The latter people were the heirs of a long and complicated history of migrations and social change, much of which is lost. They fell into two main groups by dialect: Kyerepong and Guan (also spelled Guaŋ or Guang, and sometimes called Kyerepong-Guan and Late-Guan, because the two dialects are mutually intelligible).[8] Some have resided in the hills for many centuries: at least some of them have farmed yams in the hills since around 500 CE, having at a much earlier time (ca. 1300 BCE) begun migrating south as the Sahara expanded.[9] The earliest pioneers seem to have arrived in small groups that, over the centuries, absorbed several waves of newcomers into their clans and villages. Consequently, Akuapem's genealogical inheritance reflects constant change: there has never been a time of ethnic or religious homogeneity. For at least a millennium, then, and probably much longer, the people of the Akuapem hills have cultivated moral and intellectual tools for turning strangers into neighbors. The challenge of life together with others has nearly always been high on indigenous political-religious agendas. Few Europeans before or during the colonial period appreciated the depth of this need and the sophistication of homegrown ethical thought, preserved in proverbs and storytelling, viewing the medium of oral transmission to be incapable of truth or depth.

At the very least, early Guan settlers were regularly joined by refugees displaced by migrants from the east, including the ancestors of today's Ewe and (possibly) Gã peoples.[10] Another possibility, advanced during the 1920s by Enoch Azu, a Basel Mission-educated Krobo man (from the lowlands immediately to the east of the Akuapem ridge) who collected the stories of the elderly priests in his community, was that the Guan emerged together with those people groups before eventually splintering off as a distinctive people group.[11] In the 1950s, Eva Meyerowitz collected several Guan traditions of origin within her broader study of Akan origins, finding a muddy scheme of

---

[8]  M. A. Kwamena-Poh, *Government and Politics in the Akuapem State, 1730–1850*, Legon History Series (Evanston, Ill.: Northwestern University Press, 1973), 8.

[9]  Colin Painter, "The Guang and West African Historical Reconstruction," *Ghana Notes and Queries* 9 (November 1966), 58–65.

[10]  Kwamena-Poh, *Government and Politics*, 13.

[11]  Noa Akunor Aguae Azu, *Adangbe (Adangme) History*, trans. Enoch Azu (Accra: Govt. Print Office, 1929).

origins somewhere to the northeast, arriving in migrations occurring either in waves or in a back-and-forth pattern, or both.[12] It seems likely that the Guan emerged, and have always lived, in multilingual and multireligious settings. Michelle Gilbert has argued that the kind of complex pluralism that characterized nineteenth-century Akuapem and the surrounding region cannot be adequately subsumed into the European logic of *ethnicity*:

> The situation is complex, though one may choose to frame it over-simply in terms of hegemony (Akan vis-a-vis the Guan) . . . to propagandise a position rather than appeal to the authority of the "traditional" arbitrations, destoolment, ancestral shrines and gods.[13]

Gilbert's difficulty in reducing the conflict to paper certainly helps explain the missionaries' nineteenth-century confusion over—and occasionally hostility to—Guan distinctiveness. Coming of age in the middle of the nineteenth century in a part of the German-speaking world in which dialect was growing increasingly political, the Basel missionaries struggled to comprehend a social situation in which families could be multilingual.[14] The missionaries' confusion may be read from a map of Akuapem, published by the Basel Mission in 1857 (Akropong is near the center of the excerpt). The missionaries drew a line through the middle of the kingdom, demarking two linguistic communities—the Twi (here spelled *Otschi*) and the Kyerepong (*Kjerepon*). No such stark line existed on the ground, however, as the linguistic communities in question overlapped considerably. To the locals in the middle of the nineteenth century, patterns of family lineage were more important than language. Thus, the patrilineal people of Mamfe (the first town south of Akropong) were universally identified as Guan, despite their having switched languages to Twi early in the century. Guan identity, then, was not anchored in language—a reality the missionaries found baffling because of their insistence in regarding language as the essence of belonging.

At the time that the missionaries created this map, most people of Akuapem were bilingual, and clan lineage and religion—rather than language—were the most meaningful social divisions.

The missionaries discounted that distinction, prioritizing language as human denominator. As if to emphasize the supreme importance of language,

---

[12]  Eva Meyerowitz, *Akan Traditions of Origin* (London: Faber and Faber, 1952), 76–79.

[13]  Michelle Gilbert, "No Condition Is Permanent: Ethnic Construction and the Use of History in Akuapem," *Africa: Journal of the International African Institute* 67, no. 4 (1997), 501.

[14]  Alfred Senn, "Verhältnis von Mundart und Schriftsprache in der Deutschen Schweiz," *Journal of English and Germanic Philology* 34, no. 1 (1935), 42–58.

Akuapem in 1857. Note the tidy linguistic divide just north of Akropong;
the mapmaker has displaced Akropong (which actually sits at the bend in
the road) to the south. Joseph Josenhans, *Atlas der evangelischen Missions-
Gesellschaft zu Basel* (Basel, 1857), plate 4 (detail).

the mapmakers displaced the dots for Akropong and Abirew (spelled here
"Abru") away from one another. In fact, the two towns are both situated at
the bend in the road through which the mapmakers have drawn the linguistic
line. Today the towns are contiguous, but even in 1857 were only a few hundred meters apart. Akropong's ancestral mausoleum is even closer—halfway
between the two towns.

The missionaries' map, therefore, is less than useful as a representation of
Akuapem. However, as a depiction of the political imaginaries of the mapmakers, the distortions imposed upon the map are profoundly revealing, and shed
light on the possibilities for pluralistic belonging in nineteenth-century western Europe. Put simply, the missionaries understood human belonging—and
thus the nature of a church—in decidedly different ways than the people
among whom they were living. If the missionaries, in entering Akuapem, had
hoped for a neat gateway into Asante and the broader Twi- and Akan-speaking
world, they had entered the wrong kingdom.

## CULTURE HACKED FROM NATURE

Akuapem was founded in 1730 and has been ruled by Twi-speaking kings for nearly its entire existence as a distinct state. Akuapem's kings had arrived from elsewhere, tracing their roots to the nearby kingdom of Akyem Abuakwa. It was with these people, the Twi-speaking peoples of Akuapem, rather than the indigenous Guan, that the Basel Mission had its deepest encounter. In the nineteenth century, people speaking Twi or similar dialects and languages—collectively called Akan—were organized in several kingdoms, of which the most important was Asante. The distinctive cultural background of these people groups was of great importance in shaping the nineteenth-century parameters of religious conversion. Beginning in the fifteenth century or earlier, larger groups of migrating peoples, among whom several spoke an earlier version of Akan, began a sustained effort at conquering the forest from the north. This migration from the savannahs and grasslands entered the nationalistic imagination in the early twentieth century, as anticolonial leaders attempted to give their new country an ancient past—endowing the embryonic republic with the name of the medieval empire of Ghana. Whether or not the forest pioneers were actually from Ghana is immaterial for the present: the point is that the people who managed to build kingdoms in the forests had originally come from elsewhere. They had learned to live in a dangerous ecosystem, had built a social order from the experience, and had eventually invented a new kind of political-military state capable of sustaining the concussions of the transatlantic slave trade, while so many other kingdoms failed. The Akan pioneers in the northern forests hoped to carve out a place to live and produce food, in which they might be spared from molestation by the empires of the western Sudan.[15]

Akuapem's ridgetop forest was an eastern outpost of the much bigger and wider woodlands of the regions to the west, which were so formative in Akan consciousness. That belt of barely traversable wet woodlands, with a canopy ranging between one hundred and two hundred feet above the ground, effectively separated the coast from the rich savannahs and grasslands of the upper Volta valley.[16] In 1824, British Consul Joseph Dupuis described the forest thus:

> We suddenly found ourselves in a forest as magnificent as it was dense and intricate. Numerous plants and creepers of all dimensions chained tree to tree, and branch to branch, clustering the whole in entanglement. . . . The opacity of this forest communicated . . . a semblance of twilight; no ray of

---

[15] Ivor Wilks, *Forests of Gold: Essays on the Akan and the Kingdom of Asante* (Athens: Ohio University Press, 1993), 68–69.

[16] Wilks, *Forests of Gold*, 41–44.

sunshine penetrated the cheerless gloom, and we were in idea entombed in foliage of a character novel and fanciful.[17]

It was a very difficult environment, but not impossible: the rainforest, infested with yellow fever, guinea worm, malaria, and other diseases, with wild animals great and small, and haunted by monsters and evil spirits, could be life-giving if appropriately tamed.[18] And this required a great deal of accumulated knowledge: by trial and error, migrants gradually learned what snails could be eaten, how diseases could be contained, and how territorial spirits could be appeased. Dupuis' journey through the forest, otherwise made in "death-like silence," was punctuated "by the occasional shouting of the negroes, to put to flight, as they termed it, the evil spirits of the forest."[19]

The key to the Akan states' success at building large societies in the forest belt lay in their joining this acquired knowledge to a clan-based social order centered on food production. In the first instance, this meant rewarding individual initiative in ongoing forest clearing for agrarian purposes. This was a backbreaking task. It needed to be done by hand with axes and machetes and without draft animals, which succumbed to tsetse flies within days of entering the forest. By one estimate, clearing a one-hectare field from virgin forest would involve the removal of some 1,250 tons of vegetation.[20] This work consisted of clearing brush, then felling the trees and burning or otherwise removing the waste, and stumping. The colonial census office in 1931 estimated ninety-six man-days per acre of secondary forest, but virgin forest was exponentially harder to clear.[21] These estimates furthermore fail to account for the nutritional demands on laborers thus engaged: someone would need to be growing crops and raising livestock, and someone else hunting or fishing, to fuel the enterprise. Forest clearing was an altogether massive undertaking.

This kind of manual labor did not immediately result in profit, or even food: it was an investment undertaken for the long haul, which is to say, for future generations. It represented a matrician (or a man's) assent that the

---

[17] Joseph Dupuis, *Journal of a Residence in Ashantee* (London: Henry Colburn, 1824), 15–16.

[18] T. C. McCaskie, *State and Society in Pre-Colonial Asante*, African Studies Series (Cambridge: Cambridge University Press, 1995), 25–26.

[19] Dupuis, *Journal of a Residence*, 16.

[20] John F. V. Phillips, *Agriculture and Ecology in Africa, a Study of Actual and Potential Development South of the Sahara* (London: Faber and Faber, 1960), 160–61, cited in Wilks, *Forests of Gold*, 58.

[21] A. W. Cardinall, *The Gold Coast, 1931* (Accra, Gold Coast: Census Office, Government Printer, 1931), 86–87.

social—and therefore religious—order was legitimate.[22] The cumulative experience helped establish enduring cultural priorities relating to industriousness, fruitfulness, increase, abundance, cleanliness, and accumulation—values that older generations continued to impress upon their heirs through proverbs. These values outlasted the political and economic conditions behind the forest migrations, as well as the even greater interruptions which followed—not the least of which was the progressively escalating slave trade centered on the Atlantic coast.

Europeans had largely ceased trading in slaves by the time Basel missionaries found their way to Akuapem, and more than one interior kingdom had risen and fallen. Innumerable wars had run their course, large-scale migrations had unfolded, languages had changed, and local religions had changed beyond recognition—but daily experience in the forest belt continued to legitimate a social vision grounded in a drive for prosperity against an unpredictable political, economic, and ecological environment. In T. C. McCaskie's words, "the security of the hard-won cultural niche was understood to be fragile, requiring unremitting vigilance in its defense against a vast and anarchically irruptive nature."[23] Fields could return to forest within a single rainy season. This struggle against nature, which was not distinct from the unseen and often capricious spiritual realm with which it interacted, depended on the reproductive increase of the people themselves, and this in turn depended on the viability of the agricultural enterprise.

The principal impediment to the effective establishment of this agrarian order in the forest was a deficit of human labor: slaves and captives, in the main.[24] Specifically, slaves were needed to aid the ambitions of young men pioneering ever deeper into the forest, who could aspire to wealth and rank within their respective clans by developing forestlands into croplands. This demand for slaves had as a peculiar consequence that some of the earliest European commerce in African slaves in this region went in the opposite direction than elsewhere: northward from the Atlantic, away from the coast. The Portuguese

---

[22]  Specifically, accumulation of wealth through strategic labor was a generally recognized means by which an aspirational young man could become a "big man." T. C. McCaskie developed this argument over a study published in two parts between 1983 and 1986: "Accumulation, Wealth and Belief in Asante History. I. To the Close of the Nineteenth Century," *Africa: Journal of the International African Institute* 53, no. 1 (1983), 23–43, 79; "Accumulation, Wealth and Belief in Asante History: II. The Twentieth Century," *Africa: Journal of the International African Institute* 56, no. 1 (1986): 3–23. See also Emmanuel Akyeampong and Pashington Obeng, "Spirituality, Gender, and Power in Asante History," *International Journal of African Historical Studies* 28, no. 3 (1995): 486.

[23]  McCaskie, *State and Society*, 74.

[24]  Akosua Adoma Perbi, *A History of Indigenous Slavery in Ghana: From the 15th to the 19th Century* (Accra: Sub-Saharan Publishers, 2004), 17–20.

named the "Gold Coast" the strip of the Atlantic littoral, centered on São Jorge da Mina, (today's Elmina, about 150 km west of Accra), where locals might be willing to exchange gold for slaves.[25]

One early observer was João de Barros (1496–1570), commander of da Mina from 1522 to 1525. In 1552, thirty years after his term, de Barros published a book on "the deeds which the Portuguese performed" in Africa and the Indian Ocean. In speaking of commerce on the West African littoral, he wrote:

> As [the] kingdom of Beny [Benin, in today's southeastern Nigeria] was near the Castle of S. Jorge da Mina and as the negroes who brought gold to that marketplace were ready to buy slaves to carry their merchandize, the King [of Portugal] ordered the building of a factory in a port of Beny, called Gato, whither there were brought for sale a great number of those slaves who were bartered very profitably at the Mina, for the merchants of gold gave twice the value obtainable for them in the Kingdom.[26]

De Barros added that some of the slaves were passed on all the way to the "province of Mandinga" where they "either remained in their original [pagan] condition or became Moors [Muslims]." Intriguingly, de Barros expressed moral revulsion at the slave trade on account of the "pagans who were in our possession" passing "into the hands of infidels once more."[27] In the sixteenth century, most of these slaves were put to work on small gangs, clearing forest, and later they were directed to small alluvial gold mines of the forest.[28]

Success at mastering the forest was central to the Akan states' vision of social order, and thus it cannot be understated as culturally formative experience. Likewise, religious practices cannot be distinguished from the technical mastery of survival in one of the world's most biologically dangerous environments. Not only did foreign slaves bring their own gods into the mix, but they also reimagined their clan-based gods as forest gods. Richard Werbner has argued that nineteenth- and twentieth-century migrations of gods built upon a long history of the same, predating Atlantic commerce.[29] This point is very important for what follows: the people of the Gold Coast have many centuries'

---

[25] Walter Rodney, "Gold and Slaves on the Gold Coast," *Transactions of the Historical Society of Ghana* 10 (1969).

[26] João de Barros, "Asia," in *The Voyages of Cadamosto and Other Documents on Western Africa in the Second Half of the Fifteenth Century*, ed. G. R. Crone (1552; London: Hakluyt Society, 1937), 124.

[27] de Barros, "Asia," 125.

[28] Wilks, *Forests of Gold*, 72–78.

[29] Richard P. Werbner, *Ritual Passage, Sacred Journey: The Process and Organization of Religious Movement* (Manchester, England: Manchester University Press, 1989), 226.

experience at hearing new spiritual ideas and practices, rejecting some and making others their own. The religious, the political, and the social cannot be disentangled within this complicated dynamic of migrations and ethnic mixing. It was neither natural nor accidental, but an artifact of intellectual history. In McCaskie's words:

> The entire thrust of the historical record points to a sophisticated working-out or elaboration over time of discrete principles and imperatives that were identified as being the instruments of maximization and the guarantors of order. . . . There is in Asante history a unity of knowledge and belief, of understanding and purpose, that implies very considerable levels of reflective or meditative self-consciousness.[30]

Although McCaskie developed this argument in regards to the Asante kingdom, it held equally for the two adjacent Akyem kingdoms, one of which later came to rule Akuapem. The fundamental social understanding derived from many years' experience at polyglot work gangs developing subsistence agriculture in a harsh forest ecosystem: "Culture was, quite literally, hacked out of nature," he concluded with characteristic grandeur.[31] The entire system depended on the development and consistent implementation of a mechanism for incorporating outsiders, which is to say, absorbing slaves and foreigners (including whatever religious innovations they might add) into an existing network of matrilineal clans. It was a system geared toward the accumulation of wealth in people. Within the bounds of an older, and sustained, commitment to matrilineage (whereby a man's children belonged to his wives' respective clans), it rewarded ambitious young men with the prospect of rank, fame, and fortune.

No responsible account of Ghanaian Christianity can afford to skip past this foundational human experience of endurance, in pursuit of healing and prosperity, against all range of human and spiritual aggression. Long before the postcolonial explosion of born-again Christianity, and even before the arrival of European missionaries toward the end of the slave trade years, generations of men and women had established and tested their own criteria defining the good life and the meaning of experience. Indigenous efforts to make strategic use of foreign religious messengers must be viewed in this context.

### MILITARY STATES AND THE ATLANTIC TRADE

However, the social and cultural background alone cannot suffice as context for the indigenous reception and rejection of Christianity, absent at least a

---

[30] McCaskie, *State and Society*, 74.
[31] McCaskie, *State and Society*, 74.

cursory discussion of an important political innovation: the ɔman—a new kind of military state originating among the Akan states of the forest belt. By the beginning of the seventeenth century, a degree of agrarian stability had been reached in the forests to the west of today's Akuapem, at which point surplus food production could be achieved with much smaller inputs of labor.[32] This maturing of the agrarian economy allowed gold to emerge as an increasingly important factor in the regional economy. During the forest-clearing days, labor was indispensable and thus relatively more valuable, and the central Gold Coast was a net importer of slaves; when agricultural stability was reached, laborers became more dispensable and gold emerged as the most important denominator of wealth.[33] Since this development began taking place during the same years that the European demand for slave labor was growing rapidly, the maturing of the agrarian forest economy had as a fateful consequence the reversal of the flow of the slave trade back toward the Atlantic—people exchanged for gold.

The emergence of the Atlantic trade instigated social turmoil, new kinds of warfare, and political innovations deep into the interior. Foremost among these, at least for the purposes of understanding the political dynamic into which the Basel Mission would stumble in the nineteenth century, was the reconfiguration of political authority along military lines. This military state was called an ɔman, and its chief the ɔmanhene. Various local or district heads—often rendered in English as chiefs—doubled as leaders in a tightly organized military hierarchy. The rallying point in war was no longer the akyeneboa or clan-insignia, but the royal stools—above all those belonging to the late kings. In an ɔman, political structures were conceived as bureaucratic facsimiles of military formations, with major -hene sub-chieftaincies named for battlefield positions or "wings."[34] The key ingredient to the system's endurance was balance; authorities built up various -hene wings from geographically scattered villages so as make insurrection very difficult to achieve.[35] It was an efficient way of raising and organizing an army without a standing class of officers, and it ensured a degree of loyalty, as young soldiers (as warrior

---

[32] Running some calculations upon John Phillips' numbers from 1960, Wilks concluded that clearing a one-hectare field that had been fallowed for fifteen years would involve the removal of one hundred tons of vegetation—a steep drop-off from the 1,250 tons needing to be cleared from primal forests. Wilks, *Forests of Gold*, 56.

[33] Kwame Arhin, "Monetization and the Asante State," in *Money Matters: Instability, Values and Social Payments in the Modern History of West African Communities*, ed. Jane I. Guyer (Portsmouth, N.H.: Heinemann, 1995). Also see McCaskie, *State and Society*, 38.

[34] Kwamena-Poh, *Government and Politics*, 159.

[35] M. J. Field, *Akim-Kotoku: An Oman of the Gold Coast* (London: Crown Agents for the Colonies, 1948), 6.

societies called *asafo*) acquired battlefield experience with men of other clans and localities.[36] However—and this point is important for nineteenth-century Akuapem—the clan system did not go away entirely, and "the continued existence of the two systems led inevitably to complicated arrangements," which is to say, compromises.[37]

The first of the Akan states to transition to a military order was Akwamu, before 1600.[38] Akwamu developed a confederation of towns into a kingdom, organizing them without respect to clan affiliation. Akwamu overran and annexed what would later be called Akuapem sometime around 1649, thus consolidating its control over the coastal plains, including Accra, which had fallen to Akwamu sometime earlier.[39] Neither the ridge nor the coast—which were populated by very different people groups and organized as loose confederations of small city-states—could match Akwamu's superior military organization.

The timing of this conquest had brutal consequences for the conquered, corresponding as it did with the entrance into the Atlantic economy of several new European countries. Only one year before Akwamu had annexed the ridge into its empire, peace had returned to Europe after the devastating Thirty Years' War. In the aftermath of the Peace of Westphalia, Europeans with access to credit began scrambling to (re-)enter global commerce sooner than the competition. The Swedes, the Dutch, and the English all established permanent trading posts in the Accra area in 1649. They were not the first Europeans: the Portuguese had maintained an outpost in Accra a century earlier, which the local Gã had destroyed in the 1570s.[40] More recently, the Dutch had built a cabin nearby in 1642, eventually developing it into Fort Crèvecœur (renamed Ussher after being taken over by the British in the nineteenth century).[41] The project with the greatest religious consequences for Akuapem in the interior was the Scandinavian one. Shortly after Westphalia, Swedish merchants, led by a Dutchman living in Swedish-owned Bremen (now in Germany) organized

[36] Anshan Li, "Social Protest in the Gold Coast: A Study of the Eastern Province in the Colonial Period" (PhD diss., University of Toronto, 1993), 130–31.

[37] Eva Meyerowitz, *The Sacred State of the Akan* (London: Faber and Faber, 1951), 34.

[38] Carl Christian Reindorf, *The History of the Gold Coast and Asante: Based on Traditions and Historical Facts Comprising a Period of More Than Three Centuries from about 1500 to 1860*, 2nd ed. (1889; Accra: Ghana Universities Press, 1966), 58–63.

[39] Ivor Wilks, *Akwamu 1640–1750: A Study of the Rise and Fall of a West African Empire* (1958; Trondheim, Norway: Dept. of History, Norwegian University of Science and Technology, 2001), 7.

[40] M. E. Kropp Dakubu, *Korle Meets the Sea: A Sociolinguistic History of Accra* (New York: Oxford University Press, 1997), 147.

[41] Ghana Information Services Department, *Ghana Official Handbook* (Accra: Information Services, 1971), 220.

the Swedish Africa Company.[42] Like most other speculative new European ventures of that time, the Swedish effort was neither focused nor well-organized, and its managers had nearly no knowledge of political or economic conditions in West Africa. Their business plan was unfocused—it was simply to establish a trading presence on the coast at a moment of commercial scramble between different European companies; its managers were prepared to experiment.

Having landed on the southeastern Gold Coast at the town of Osu (located an hour's walk east of Accra and today a downtown neighborhood in that sprawling city), the Swedes solicited Akwamu permission, readily granted, to establish a trading post (before ceding it to the Danes a few years later).[43] Initially, slavery was not the foremost export from the fortified post, which they called "Christiansborg." The point was to experiment in trade, ascertaining in practice what would be profitable. An inventory of two of the first Swedish ships back to Europe (impounded in Plymouth in 1652 in an intra-European trade dispute) included the following cargo:

The ship *Christina*:

- "596 marks of gold or thereabouts, packed in 20 bags, marked,"

- "6 or 7000 of elephant teeth."

The ship *Norcoping*:

- "4, 5, or 6000 elephant teeth."[44]

However, during the next several decades, transatlantic slavery grew exponentially, and it eventually came to dominate the southeastern Gold Coast's Atlantic trade. The monetization of captive humans at the coast, of course, coincided with the simultaneous incorporation of nearly the entirety of Atlantic coastal Africa into the slave trade. The emergence of the transatlantic slave economy coincided in Akuapem with foreign occupation, with predictable consequences. And since the earliest stages of Nordic mercantile presence in the Gold Coast unfolded in the context of a European continent recovering

---

[42] R. Porter, "The Crispe Family and the African Trade in the Seventeenth Century," *Journal of African History* 9, no. 1 (1968), 69.

[43] Eric Schnakenbourg, "Sweden and the Atlantic: The Dynamism of Sweden's Colonial Projects in the Eighteenth Century," in *Scandinavian Colonialism and the Rise of Modernity*, ed. Magdalena Naum and Jonas M. Nordin, Contributions to Global Historical Archaeology (New York: Springer, 2013), 229–42.

[44] Thomas Birch, ed., "State Papers, 1653: January," in *A Collection of the State Papers of John Thurloe, Volume 1, 1638–1653* (London: Fletcher Gyles, 1742), 222–24, *British History Online*, accessed June 27, 2019, http://www.british-history.ac.uk/thurloe-papers/vol1/pp222-224.

from one of the worst wars in its history, there was little oversight, and thus little strategy, aside from profit in trade. For at least a century, Danish merchants operated in Accra in the near absence of supervision from European colonial or trading institutions, and by the grace of local kings; a saying circulated that "Heaven is high and Europe far away."[45] Consequently, on the ground in the Gold Coast, European actors found themselves pulled into a complicated geopolitical theater they barely understood.

The eighty years of subjugation to Akwamu rule were very difficult for Akuapem's indigenous people. An oral tradition, committed to paper in the 1880s in Twi—probably by David Asante, who was the Basel Mission's first indigenous missionary—related this graphic tale of cruelty committed by an Akwamu lord:

> One day Ansa Sasraku[46] ordered the Akuapem people to cut down brush, and they did as he ordered. But instead of thanking them . . . he had an *aserdowa* bird [the smallest bird in West Africa] and pepper brought and when it was cooked gave it to them. When the Akuapems did not eat it, he was angry, bound some of them and killed them, some he sold, and many more Akuapem women . . . he made his slaves.[47]

If the author was indeed David Asante, the anecdote might need to be taken with a grain of salt, as he was a member of Akuapem's ruling family, the legitimacy of which derived from its central role in expelling Akwamu in the 1730s. Nevertheless, Akwamu's brutal rule over the Akuapem hills was undoubtedly interconnected with the Atlantic slave trade then on the ascendant in Accra. The Guan residents, who had no gold and were therefore mainly useful to their overlords as producers of food, suddenly became commodities in their own right.[48]

Akwamu armies began raiding the hills extensively for captives to sell to Europeans on the coast. In 1703, Akwamu went so far as to relocate its capital city from the plains northwest of Accra, whence they had been able to

---

[45] Pernille Ipsen, *Daughters of the Trade: Atlantic Slavers and Interracial Marriage on the Gold Coast* (Philadelphia: University of Pennsylvania Press, 2015), 24.

[46] According to Kwamena-Poh, this was the title of the stool, not the name of the king himself. Kwamena-Poh, *Government and Politics*, 27, n. 5.

[47] Bernhard Struck, "Geschichliches über die östlichen Tschi-Länder (Goldküste): Aufzeichnungen eines Eingeborenen," *Anthropos* 18 (1923).

[48] Johannes Rask, *A Brief and Truthful Description of a Journey to and from Guinea*, in *Two Views from Christiansborg Castle*, trans. and ed. Selena Axelrod Winsnes (Accra: Sub-Saharan Publishers, 2009), 81.

command the gold trade, to the top of the ridge, near today's Aburi.[49] This willingness to relocate an entire city for the purpose of commercial gain testified to the radical changes to the pattern of trade in those years. Although many slaves came from the far north and were marched along the ridge, through Aburi and down toward Accra (while others, including runaways and refugees, took shelter in the hills), many Guan locals were also captured. Ludvig Rømer wrote in 1760 (that is, thirty years after Akwamu's collapse), that "[Akwamu King] Aqvando . . . permitted his people to steal and plunder both among themselves and the mountain negroes. . . . Thus the precious slave trade in Accra flourished."[50]

The hills' violent incorporation into the slave trade also had religious consequences, as people on the run flooded the region, running this way and that and hiding in ravines. A major shrine to the god Dente, situated at the Volta cataracts at Kete-Krachi, seems to have been established by Dente's priests who abandoned the village of Larteh in today's Akuapem, taking their shrine and associated ritual tools with them.[51]

AKUAPEM: THE THOUSAND ARMIES

Akuapem was born of resistance to foreign occupation by a slave-trading kingdom. However intolerable Akwamu rule may have been, the occupied peoples of the ridge were unable to mount effective resistance until 1729. At that time, Akwamu fell into a civil war, which began as a succession dispute and progressively drew in neighboring states, and culminated in the sacking of Akwamu's capital city, when its population was put to flight, its shrines desecrated, and its armies enslaved.[52] The war had two important consequences for the nineteenth-century religious encounter involving the Basel Mission. One was the unification of the hill people into an independent state called Akuapem. The war's other outcome was the fledgling kingdom's subjugation to a Twi-speaking dynasty, newly arrived from the adjacent kingdom of Akyem Abuakwa. The initial uprising was a military disaster. Akwamu crushed the rebels, sold hundreds into slavery, and stole great numbers of women.[53] The

[49]  Wilks, *Akwamu 1640–1750*, 43.

[50]  Ludvig Ferdinand Rømer, *A Reliable Account of the Coast of Guinea (1760)*, trans. Selena Axelrod Winsnes (Oxford: Published for the British Academy by the Oxford University Press, 2000), 132 (orig. 144).

[51]  Donna Maier Weaver, "Kete-Krachi in the Nineteenth Century: Religious and Commercial Center of the Eastern Asante Borderlands" (PhD diss., Northwestern University, 1975).

[52]  Ivor Wilks' meticulous sleuthing work on the Akwamu civil war is definitive: *Akwamu 1640–1750*.

[53]  Kwamena-Poh, *Government and Politics*, 33.

next year, however, as the Akwamu civil war was escalating into a regional conflict, a joint campaign by the Akyem, the Gã, and other peoples eastward toward the Volta defeated the Akwamu, who fled to the north and established a small successor kingdom.

The Guan residents of the ridge had never been able to unify, except for during the recently concluded war, when they (rather grandiosely) called themselves Aku-Apem, or "a thousand armies."[54] But the clock could not be rewound: as of 1730, at a time of extensive regional warfare fueled by the Atlantic slave trade, the Akuapem could not expect to once again scatter to their respective fields and disparate villages without a king to protect them. Three years later, accordingly, the Guan villages swore loyalty to a foreign ɔhene, a prince from the Akyem Abuakwa kingdom, asking him to build them into a state. Akuapem's origins as an autonomous state, in which a Twi-speaking and matrilineal foreign dynasty ruled over a mostly Guan and patrilineal populace, are thus matters of tremendous contention. Was the Akyem dynasty invited in, or did it push its way in? Was the oath of loyalty—the so-called Abotakyi Accord, taken in Obosomase before the god Kyenku—made under duress?[55] Conflicting accounts, preserved by confused Europeans (Danish officers and, later, missionaries), present the historian with a valuable lens on the contested nature of power in Akuapem—they reveal the shady circumstances of conquest and the pain of remembering the past.[56]

In 1733, Akuapem's new kings thus found themselves faced with the challenge of building a state out of a diverse and traumatized populace. The problem was compounded by the intellectual framework the Akyem rulers were importing into the new state. The political legitimacy of the ɔman rested on two basic social assumptions, neither of which applied to the fledgling state, with its unique cultural demographics. The first of these was the Akan paradigm—and concomitant praxis—of matrilineal ancestry, which greatly shaped the king's ritual responsibilities (and therefore his legitimacy), and which was intricately tied to religion.[57] The second was the Akan tradition of separation of powers. In the ɔman system, political and military leaders (chiefs and kings, whose offices are designated by the suffix -hene) and priests of abosom spirits were almost always different people. Arriving in Akuapem's second century of existence, European missionaries misread this separation of powers

---

[54] Kwamena-Poh, *Government and Politics*, 34.

[55] Kwamena-Poh, *Government and Politics*, 135.

[56] Michelle Gilbert, "Disguising the Pain of Remembering in Akwapim," *Africa* 80, no. 3 (2010), 426–52.

[57] Meyerowitz, *The Sacred State*, esp. chapter 5, p. 84ff. Caution is needed here, because Meyerowitz tended to posit a cohesive philosophical structure on what may be in fact inherited praxis.

as analogous to separation of church and state, with the implication that they could work with the king but not with the priests. In the Basel Mission's first visit to Akuapem (in January 1835), Andreas Riis set the pattern for his successors: he approached the king in an attitude of reverential protocol, seeking his permission to enter the royal city. On the other hand, he had no reluctance to speaking contemptuously to the priests. "I told him [a 'fetish-priest'] that his work is all lies and deception," Riis wrote, adding that he was speaking through an interpreter.[58]

In contrast with the division of labor Riis encountered in Akropong, these offices were typically united in one man in Guan society—a theocratic way of organizing political authority. In practical terms during the kingdom's early history, this difference seems not to have been reconcilable, and Akuapem's kings came to feel that the Guan king-priests could not be incorporated into the royal state. The solution was to impose a parallel authority upon the Guan villages, in the form of -hene sub-chiefs.[59] In marked contrast with other Akan states, the Akuapem king's control on his kingdom was thus perpetually tenuous. Akuapem's social pluralism was not limited to religion: linguistic diversity on the Akuapem ridge also constituted a striking social difference from that of Akyem Abuakwa, whence the royal family had come.

This is not to say that the Akan states were homogenous. Rather, it was that kings' success at bridging social and cultural differences hinged on their capacity to assimilate religious structures into an orderly framework of politics and military office. Greater Asante, which was profoundly segmented by class, had little trouble handling ethnic difference: most outsiders were slaves, and could accordingly be assimilated into a caste system that was efficient at individuating aspirations and diluting discontent.[60] The reason the Asante state could impose such a comprehensive system of "belief" (to use McCaskie's term) on unhappy subjects was because of that state's success in all other areas of life.[61] Tiny Akuapem could never aspire to impose internal hegemony, but this basic limit did not stop its kings from trying. As a result, Akuapem's king—the Okuapemhene—was never able to fully subject all of his villages. His practical authority never grew commensurate with his ritual assertions.

---

[58] Andreas Riis, HB 1835, 62 (published August 15, 1835, from a letter dated February 27, 1835).

[59] Eric Okyere Ayisi, "The Basis of Political Authority of the Akwapem Tribes (Eastern Ghana) (Social Change: A Sociological Study)" (PhD diss., University of London, 1965), 137–39.

[60] Kwame Arhin, "Rank and Class among the Asante and Fante in the Nineteenth Century," Africa: Journal of the International African Institute 53, no. 1 (1983), 2–22.

[61] McCaskie, State and Society, 74.

The missionaries did not fail to observe insubordination taking place before their eyes, especially in their visits to the Larteh and Kyerepong villages. In 1843, for example, in his report on a day trip from Akropong to the nearby town of Abirew, Johann Widmann ascertained that the latter still had not appointed an *ɔhene* after eleven decades of Akropong's rule, remaining instead faithful to their priest-king.[62] But the missionaries tended to view linguistic diversity as the root of communal division. From the 1840s on, the Basel Mission divided its congregations into synods defined by language: the Gã (Accra and region) and the Twi (the name of the Akan dialect spoken by the Akyem communities of Akuapem) districts, with the Guan simply lumped in with the Twi. In this regard, the missionaries got it wrong: language did not make a people, as it did in German-speaking Europe, but kinship in ancestral cults did. The most important fault line between Guan and their Akan neighbors was not language, but kinship—specifically, visions of ancestry, to which I now turn.

Long after Akuapem's founding as an ɔman, the Guan communities continued to practice a kind of theocracy, whereby, according to Otutu Bagyire VI, the chief of (Kyerepong-Guan) Abiriw in 1967, "every Guan stool was attached to an ancestral *akpe*," or god.[63] The key difference here with Akan cosmology is that the Guan gods were formerly-living male ancestors, while the Akan *abosom* spirits, although themselves created beings, had an existence preceding and independent of human affairs.[64] As a consequence, "the office of a Guan chief was indistinguishable from that of a priest."[65] "The chief at Adukrom is simultaneously the fetish priest," Johann Widmann wrote in 1861, by which time he had been living in Akropong for eighteen years.[66] Widmann's engagement with the Guan was a fascinating story in its own right, but along with Christaller and other missionaries, Widmann persisted in siding with the Akan authorities against the Guan. This missiological decision would reverberate for generations.

[62]  Widmann's letter excerpted in *JB* 1844, 191.
[63]  Abiriwhene Otutu Bagyire VI, "The Guans: A Preliminary Note," *Ghana Notes and Queries* 7 (1967), 23.
[64]  Bagyire VI, "The Guans," 23. For comparison with Akan cosmology, see Charles Sarpong Aye-Addo, *Akan Christology: An Analysis of the Christologies of John Samuel Pobee and Kwame Bediako in Conversation with the Theology of Karl Barth* (Eugene, Ore.: Pickwick, 2013). Aye-Addo makes the additional claim that the *abosom* were held to have been created by *Nyame*, which is to say, did not have an independent existence. There is not universal agreement on this matter, and in some respects, the debate might be less than enlightening, especially if historical questions are being asked.
[65]  Bagyire VI, "The Guans."
[66]  Widmann's letter excerpted in *JB* 1861, 163.

The German missionaries settling in Akropong had arrived in an incredibly complicated country—even by West African standards—in which language, domestic relations, politics, and culture all overlapped in not entirely coterminous boundaries. This diversity touched on everything. Kwame Labi has explored the Akan-Guan conflict in Akuapem, which played out over a century, through the lens of regalia and arts. His helpful insight is that confusing and contradictory oral traditions concerning the Akanization of Akuapem might be winnowed by the use of historically dateable objects. "The introduction of the Akan political system, chieftaincy, in Akuapem," Labi says, "gradually separated priestly and political roles."[67] Art and regalia produced during this period reflect the changes, because the "new art and regalia projected the image, power, and glory of chiefship contrary to the priestly regalia which was based on the dictates of the gods." The art and regalia of the kings and chiefs were subject to improvisation, while those of the priests were not. The latter reveal continuity in structures of authority, while the former display multi-ethnic appropriations. These differences must be understood in only the most relative of terms. Akan kingship was anything but religiously agnostic or disinterested: the mere conversion to Christianity of the Akyem Abuakwa king's royal drummer in the 1870s was sufficient to provoke a constitutional crisis in that state. Theirs was not a secular politics, but a delicate division of labor with the priests. Akan kingship was legitimized by religious rituals, but this was still a radical break from Guan theocratic system.[68] Kwamena-Poh summarizes of the Akyem kings of Akuapem:

> These strangers superimposed upon the Guan communities, among whom they settled, a new political conception, namely, the idea of territorial and secular leadership in place of the immemorial institution of a ruler, who was the high priest of the clan god or goddess and dealt mainly in spiritual sanctions.[69]

This latter quality to Guan political legitimacy—that of spiritual sanctions—is crucial for understanding Basel missionaries' dealings with the Guan. The missionaries were interested in converting the ɔhene kings, and in seeing an end not only to *abosom* worship at the shrines, but also to ancestral

[67] Kwami Labi, "Akanization of the Hill Guan Arts," *Research Review of the Institute of African Studies* 18, no. 2 (2002), 4.

[68] A useful comparison might be made with the political structure of the Israelite tribes prior to the creation of the Saul-David-Solomon unified kingdom—the so-called Judges. The editors of the Jewish histories were clear that the Judges were the preferred political system, and that kingship was a dangerous import from surrounding polities in the region.

[69] Kwamena-Poh, *Government and Politics*, 20.

veneration—which was entirely distinct, and which distinction the missionaries took years to appreciate. The Basel missionaries expected debate, conversation, and fraternal relations with a heathen king, and they were prepared to submit to his authority when no religious tripwires were crossed, even when his orders had their origin in religious practice.

On the other hand, the missionaries had no framework for cooperation with traditional priests, regardless of who they were. The latter were simply to be opposed. In an Akan setting in which kings and priests played distinct political roles, indigenous Christian conflict with shrine priests sometimes, but not always, overlapped with political insubordination. However, among the Guans suppression of religion had social and economic marginalization as a consequence. Since the best sources for Guan oral traditions were to be found in religious songs and incantations, the silencing of these songs amounted to the death of oral traditions.[70] Throughout Akuapem's history, structural barriers to state formation have manifested on a spectrum between simmering resentments and open rebellion. At the heart of the problem was the gap between the ideological foundations of the matrilineal kingship and the king's patrilineal subjects. The kings drew their understandings of successful articulation of authority from the homogeneous kingdoms to their west, including not only Akyem Abuakwa, whence the Akuapem kings descended, but also Asante, the ideal-typical Akan kingdom, of which McCaskie said:

> In any society where hierarchies of differentiation and control are presided over by the state, a fundamental object of that state must be to impose ideological definition on knowledge and belief, to regulate the boundaries between the two, and to exercise an absolute discretion in shaping both of them.[71]

In Akyem Abuakwa on the eve of the 1730 war with Akwamu, political-military organization was subject to ongoing reorganization, with villages reallocated among divisional chiefs on an ongoing basis; the point was to keep the major divisions roughly equal in numbers and strength through constant reshuffling.[72] Reshuffling the constituent villages and districts may have helped unify the state in a religiously homogenous state like Akyem Abuakwa, but that option was not simply not available to the royal house of Akuapem, constituted of matrilineal and patrilineal peoples speaking different languages,

---

[70] Bagyire VI, "The Guans," 24.
[71] McCaskie, *State and Society*, 21.
[72] Roland R. Atkinson, "Old Akyem and the Origins of Akyems Abuakwa and Kotoku 1675–1775," in *West African Culture Dynamics: Archaeological and Historical Perspectives*, ed. B. K. Swartz and Raymond E. Dumett (The Hague: Mouton, 1980), 358–59.

some of who were ruled by shrine priests. Akuapem then and now struggled for unity, even before the tumultuous years of violent midcentury social-economic change: were were the people Kwasi Cornelius encountered in a secluded ravine in 1875 refugees, invaders, or settlers of a new village subject to the Akuapem king? How long would they be there, and with whom would their loyalties and responsibilities lie?

### THE COSMOLOGICAL BACKGROUND OF RELIGIOUS INNOVATION

In late August 1835, as part of their ongoing defiance of the king, residents of Adukrom (a Guan town located only a few miles from the royal palace in Akropong) reneged on their obligations to the "fetish," probably an *ɔbosom* spirit named Otutu, who had an important shrine in that town.[73] In response, the offended god withheld the needed rains. To judge by King Addo Dankwa's response (which he later narrated to Andreas Riis), this religious provocation, coming so near to harvest, amounted to an act of sabotage that could endanger the entire community: he felt compelled to hurry back and forth among his restive subjects along the mountain ridge, enforcing their observation of ritual responsibilities.[74] Under normal circumstances, the king was expected to remain in ritual seclusion in his palace at this time of the year, a period set aside for respect for the dead. Riis would experience this three years later in another nearby kingdom, when he was denied an audience with that state's *ɔmanhene* during festivities for a recently-deceased chief.[75] Addo Dankwa's emergency excursion to Adukrom—he was in such haste that he went without first sending his messengers—hints at the severity of the threat. The rebels were effectively pulling a powerful god into their dispute with the king. The timing was terrible: the harvest was at risk because of these disturbances in the spiritual realm. In this instance, Addo Dankwa was successful. After he had managed to enforce sacrificial compliance in Adukrom, a large snake had appeared in the street—a clear sign of Otutu's approval. Sure enough, while the king was on his way back to Akropong, the clouds had burst, and the delayed rains returned. With political and spiritual order thus restored, the yams would ripen, societal relations could be renewed, and the state purified.[76]

---

[73] Kwamena-Poh, *Government and Politics*, 134.

[74] Andreas Riis, "Einige Mittheilungen aus dem Tagebuche des Missionars Andreas Riis," *EMM* 1836, 553–54. Riis, who had only been in Akuapem for six months, was having everything explained to him through an interpreter. Unfortunately, in this chain of explanations, the details about the specific ritual responsibilities, fell missing.

[75] Andreas Riis, "Die Reise des Missionars in Akropong nach dem Aschantee-Lande im Winter 1839–40," *EMM* 1840, 208.

[76] McCaskie, *State and Society*, 162.

Not all was restored, however; the underlying conflict remained. By 1835, Akuapem had struggled for unity for a full century. Kings and priests agreed on the problem, but those rivals did not see the missionaries, or the Christian message, in the same way. As leaders in the ɔman, the former saw possibilities where the priests saw a threat to their status. This was partly because the missionaries had come seeking the goodwill of the former and announcing their rivalry to the latter. However, there was also something older going on—the missionaries were not the original authors of tension between Akuapem's chiefs and priests.

The kingdom's mid-nineteenth-century politics was inextricable from its religious ecosystem. Akuapem was a theater of rival spiritual economies—a stage upon which a matrilineal project of royal statecraft, anchored in ancestor veneration, contended with an older, and patrilineal, priestly tradition of sacrifice. While the contrast is not to be exaggerated, as both groups practiced ancestor veneration, and both groups sacrificed to territorial spirits, the conflict was life-defining to participants in the early nineteenth century. For this reason, the introduction of a new message—a message purporting to come from God on high—was fuel to the long-smoldering fire in the Akuapem kingdom.

Taken together, all these tensions—profound social turmoil and mass migrations, driven by global economic change, combined with longstanding political-religious disunity within a small kingdom in which very different visions of family structure contended with one another—had this as a consequence: in early- and mid-nineteenth-century Akuapem (along with neighboring districts to the east and west), men and women, high and low, felt a need for stronger social integrity. This felt need was not analogous to twenty-first-century sociological questions in Europe and North America of loneliness and isolation: it ran deeper. Within the confines of the moral imagination shared by nearly all its residents—the indigenous Guan, the Akyem migrants, the foreign slaves, and refugees—the kingdom's very prosperity and power depended on social cohesion, including harmony with the departed.

The Basel Mission arrived in a state of darkness about the Gold Coast, especially in their understanding of indigenous religion. They could not speak the languages, could not distinguish between various groups, and they misread indigenous motivations accordingly. Their messages made little sense, and they had little on offer that directly corresponded with indigenous felt needs. Rather, first the king and, incrementally, other men and women cultivated relationships with the missionaries in an attitude of investment: eventually, they might find some use for these foreigners. However, even when subsequently arriving missionaries had obtained fluency in Twi, and when Twi-speaking churches were thriving, indigenous expectations nevertheless rarely conformed to those of the missionaries. Former Basel Mission archivist Paul Jenkins has called, in the title of his article on the subject, this state of darkness a "scandal of enduring intercultural blindness."[77]

It was only in the third quarter of the century, with the Bible's publication in Twi (in stages between 1859 and 1871), that indigenous Christians began to connect their story with that of ancient Palestine—an intellectual move that allowed them to bypass German church history altogether.[78] At the center of their emergent Christian moral imaginary lay a preexisting vision of communal cohesion and for the incorporation of outsiders and strangers. This communal agenda predated the arrival of missionaries in Akuapem by many years; it reflected a strongly felt need for kinship at times of social fragmentation and endemic warfare. Indigenous reception, rejection, and reconfiguration of the Christian message, then, unfolded against the dual backdrop of dangerous times and a powerful desire for communal stability.

German missionary attitudes also evolved during these years, which were anything but intellectually uneventful back home. Between 1830 and 1930, the missionaries retreated from an early mindset of receptivity to African intelligence and leadership into a late-century lapse into paternalism. This process will be the subject of subsequent chapters, but a more basic argument forms the core of the present chapter: while missionary motivations changed radically over the century, indigenous Ghanaian priorities barely budged, even as kingdoms and empires came and went, and families were reconstituted in ways that would be scarcely recognizable to the ancestors.[79]

---

[77] Paul Jenkins, "Der Skandal fortwährender interkultureller Blindheit," *Zeitschrift für Mission* 23, no. 4 (1997): 224–36.

[78] Ghanaian theologians make this point forcefully in the present day, but in this matter, Ghana is not unique. It is no accident, however, that Akropong in Akuapem remains one of the intellectual centers of African Christianity in the twenty-first century, because it was there that the West Africa's earliest vernacular theological seminary was established. See Kwame Bediako, *Christianity in Africa: The Renewal of a Non-Western Religion* (Maryknoll, N.Y.: Orbis, 1996), esp. 164–69.

[79] Bediako, *Christianity in Africa*, 120. This unwavering African imposition upon the missionary message is one of the most impressive qualities to sub-Saharan church history, at least in consideration of the magnitude of the social disruption presented by Christianity's arrival, in many places hand-in-hand with colonialism. It certainly extends beyond Ghana: see Jesse Mugambe, "A Different World Right Here: The Church within African Theological Imagination," in *A Future for Africa: Critical Essays in Christian Social Imagination*, ed. Emmanuel Katongole (Scranton, Pa.: University of Scranton Press, 2005), 153–84.

Conclusion

The history of religious change in the Gold Coast kingdom of Akuapem cannot be isolated from the West African historical context, which has always been characterized by tremendous human diversity and a correspondingly high cultural value placed on social unity. Although most missionaries understood little about what was happening around them, their hosts were struggling to keep up with sweeping social, economic, political, cultural, and religious changes bearing down on their lives—they were living through a whirlwind. Akuapem had no history of ethnic homogeneity, and much of the political-religious agenda focused on creating social cohesion among a very diverse population. Cultural values favoring unity probably predated much of the indigenous religious apparatus that the missionaries were able to observe: what they saw as timeless heathenism was often a new practice, imported from elsewhere or improvised on the spot. The reason for these innovations was because the social order was under tremendous strain, and the spiritual toolkit for public healing was beginning to fail in the face of so much rapid change.

Trying times alone are insufficient as explanations for religious conversion, and the Gold Coast was not alone in West Africa in experiencing breakneck social change. In his posthumously published masterpiece, J. D. Y. Peel observed that late in the nineteenth century, the Yoruba of Nigeria and the Akan of the Gold Coast (of which the Twi speakers of Akuapem were one group) displayed very different patterns of religious response to the changing times. While Christianity had made minimal inroads in Akuapem before around 1870—only to grow very quickly within a few short years—the religion enjoyed an earlier response in southwestern Nigeria.

A century later in 1960, Peel wrote, "just over 60 percent of the Akan were . . . adherents of world religions, the great majority of them Christians." By contrast, a far greater portion of the Yoruba were Christian (although significant local and regional discrepancies abounded).[80] The two peoples had had very different religious responses to the foregoing century, he continued, "the strains of high colonialism had produced a Christian-prophet movement known as Aladura among the Yoruba, whereas the main Akan response had been to turn to pagan anti-witchcraft shrines." Shortly after 1960, Peel continued, the Akan caught up with their Yoruba neighbors. After a century of resistance to a Christianity associated with colonial impositions, the Akan embraced Christianity in great numbers in the early postcolonial period.

[80] J. D. Y. Peel, *Christianity, Islam, and Orişa Religion: Three Traditions in Comparison and Interaction* (Berkeley: University of California Press, 2016), 18.

Given similar social, economic, and colonial histories, Peel wondered, why did the two groups respond to Christianity in such different ways?

One important qualification is that Peel was treating the Asante kingdom as the type for all the Akan peoples, a conflation that does not work for Akuapem: the Asante royal house enjoyed a far greater control over its subjects' religious lives than Akuapem's kings, ruling over a heterogenous populace, could ever hope to attain. Nevertheless, Peel's observation that the Yoruba were "precocious" and the Akan "tardy" in conversion indicates that something more than politics and economics was involved.[81] Peel eventually concluded that worldview, or at least culture, needed to be part of the answer. Developing an argument from McCaskie, which held that all Asante social activities were rooted in a cosmic pattern reflected in complex calendrical observations, Peel concluded:

> Even after the British had dismantled the structures of Asante state control, the Asante long retained a lively sense that the integrity of their society depended on the sanctions of the traditional religion.[82]

The people of Akuapem were not identical with the Asante, of course. As I will argue in the second half of this book, not only were the former not "tardy" in conversion, but Akuapem's inhabitants—its Christians and non-Christians alike—had been experimenting with Christianity from the very beginning of missionary presence in their state. A full half century before the early-Pentecostal Aladura movement in Nigeria of the 1920s (or the contemporaneous mass conversions in Ghana under William Wadé Harris), Christians in Akuapem and its neighboring kingdoms had already spent years experimenting with the religion for its potential to meet their needs of healing, power, prosperity, and reconciliation. Nevertheless, Peel was correct that any explanation for mass conversion in West Africa must address cultural as well as geopolitical and economic factors. The restoration of social order was one of the highest priorities.

However, it is important to note the role innovation played all along: long before the first missionaries showed up in Akuapem, that kingdom's military and religious authorities were willing to experiment with sacrificial and ancestral protocols. In that way, the so-called indigenous religions were not calcified. They were subject to constant improvisation, and contemporary European observations do not so much record an ancient and timeless tradition as much as change underway. Nevertheless, while West African traditional religions

[81] Peel, *Christianity, Islam, and Orișa Religion*, 5.
[82] Peel, *Christianity, Islam, and Orișa Religion*, 33.

have always been subject to innovation, four concluding observations must precede the next chapter's discussion of nineteenth-century religious change.

First, the cultural values established over the last five or six centuries in West Africa's forest belt have proven utterly resilient in the face of some of the cruelest phases of human history. If most Ghanaians would eventually become Christians, they largely did so without rejecting an inherited sense of the possibilities of human life and the moral structures—transmitted in stories, proverbs, and songs—defining good and bad, important and unimportant, or desirable and repulsive ways of being human.

Second, religious practice proceeded from culturally grounded priorities and ethical foundations, rather than the other way around. I have called this foundation the "moral imagination," and it is perhaps Ghana's greatest contribution to twenty-first-century global Christianity. It is the capacity to dream into existence a way of being in the world in which we may live with people unlike ourselves. Missionary Johann Christaller—perhaps the most celebrated of the Germans in contemporary Ghana for his ethnographic work—understood this as he listened to his neighbors express their values to him. It was in pedestrian proverbs, more than in soaring philosophical castles, Christaller realized, that the tradition's greatness was expressed. Consequently, it was not always clear that the missionaries and the converts worshiped the same god; it was certainly the case that the locals accepted the message on very different terms than the missionaries had articulated.

Third, Ghanaian religious practice, as it emerged over long centuries spanning constant rupture, developed an irrepressible empirical and pragmatic strain. Many visitors from overseas (whether slave traders, missionaries, or imperialists) assumed that when locals expressed doubts about the efficacy of their religious praxes, they were expressing a willingness to convert. This was rarely the case, and even when they did convert, many did so—initially—on an experimental basis. This is not to say that truth was an irrelevant consideration, but that locals subjected Christianity to empirical tests. I develop this argument more fully in the next chapter, but for the present, the bottom line is that Ghanaians, for centuries, have asked of newly arriving religious messengers whether the message works relative to their felt needs.

Fourth, the entire system was ethnically ambivalent. Unlike much of Europe, Asia, and parts of eastern Africa, daily life experience rendered questions of ethnic and cultural purity meaningless or absurd. Cultural authenticity was nowhere close to as important as it was in nineteenth-century Germany, which was then undergoing an especially convulsive period of nationalism. In the Gold Coast, a high tolerance for cultural pluralism, combined with a penchant for experimentation, meant that there was nothing inauthentic or self-loathing about borrowing or importing from abroad. If, by the third quarter of the nineteenth century, a reformulated Christianity became part of the solution to the social crisis, this option only emerged after other religious tools had been found incommensurate with the task of healing social harms. The next chapter focuses on those tools.

# 2

# The Existing Ritual Toolkit

## INTRODUCTION

King Addo Dankwa was suffering from swollen feet in September 1835, making it painful to walk. The timing was more than unfortunate for this kind of ailment, because his office required him to move about Akropong and the nearby villages for much of the month. The annual *Odwira* festival was underway, and Addo Dankwa needed to supervise beautification projects and other preparations and perform the requisite rituals for the purification and renewal of his kingdom. *Odwira* was, and remains to the present day, the focal point of the year—the calendrical point at which the sacredness of the king pushed him into the place of responsibility before the ancestors. Unless he, and he alone, performed certain ritual components to the cycle, the royal stool risked losing its legitimacy and therefore its authority. Nothing less than the kingship itself was thus at stake as he sought treatment for his feet. On the evening of September 19 (a Saturday), a few days before the climax of the ritual cycle, missionary Andreas Riis was at the palace, and the ensuing discussion is utterly fascinating as a window into the religious misunderstandings at the beginning of the Christian presence in Akuapem.

The king told Riis that the cause of his ailment was "evil people, who have afflicted me by means of fetishes."[1] He added a word of frustration that any of his subjects would do this to him, when he had been so good to them. Determined to proceed with the approaching festival, Addo Dankwa had called in "one fetish priest after another" for treatment; Riis added in his journal that the entire courtyard was filled with power objects of various shapes and sizes.

---

[1] Andreas Riis, "Einige Mittheilungen aus dem Tagebuche des Missionars Andreas Riis," *EMM* 1836, 556. The King (or his spokesman) would have been speaking in Twi, and Riis was using an interpreter (probably from Twi into Danish, Riis' native language). Riis was writing in German. The English translation is mine.

"Each of these fetishes," the king continued, "have cost me dearly, but none have worked." The king was clearly asking Riis to attempt a healing, and the missionary seems to have understood the request. Relating "several examples of healing from the most difficult diseases" pursuant to "faith and trust in the healer of all sickness," Riis nevertheless offered nothing tangible: "You have tried everything else, so call upon Jesus, the crucified one."

Addo Dankwa demurred, but one of the priests spoke up. "We are fully aware that fetish priests have very little power. If God is calling someone, all the priests with all of their fetishes cannot save his life." At this point, the king interjected, "What about in Europe? Is there peace there, or do they not wage war with one another?"[2]

Riis misconstrued the king's comment on foreign politics as an attempt at changing the topic. He was wrong. A week earlier, several sudden and suspicious deaths had forced Addo Dankwa to initiate an investigation, to find out if sorcery was involved, and to make an exemplary punishment of any offenders.[3] It was obvious to everyone, including Riis (in notable contrast with the medical missionaries who would follow him late in the century), that there was no real distinction between spiritual and physical sickness. The significance of Addo Dankwa's rejoinder about war in Europe lay in his understanding that war itself was an expression of evil. If Europeans (understood to be Christians) were at war with one another, it followed that they were suffering from a sickness. Therefore, Riis' suggested remedy—calling upon Jesus—was obviously ineffectual, because Jesus was incompetent to heal disunity between his followers.

Like most people of the Gold Coast and West Africa during the nineteenth century, Akuapem's king and priests were agreed that physical ailments, political conflicts, and spiritual forces were kindred in nature. The question was not one of theory but of praxis: what were the most efficacious means of restoring wellness? In this chapter I inventory ritual tools available to the people of mid-nineteenth-century Akuapem. Although I focus on the social and the political to the exclusion of the biomedical, I recognize that this is an artificial division. As suggested by the priests' concession of their powerlessness in the face of divine will, few of the people querying the utility of the Christian religion did so in an attitude of epistemological doubt. Rather, they wanted to know if it worked. Converts, who often expected physical healings, did not greatly care if they needed to believe, because to them belief was a subset of deference to authority. The following is anything but comprehensive,

2   Riis, "Einige Mittheilungen," *EMM*, 556.
3   Riis, "Einige Mittheilungen," *EMM*, 555.

but will suffice, I hope, to explain indigenous patterns of experimentation with Christianity—which, in turn, I will discuss in greater detail in later chapters.

## Living Traditions

Nineteenth-century European sources on indigenous religion vary wildly in quality. Inventorying them in Ghana's first postcolonial decade, Philip Curtin realized that most explorer and missionary accounts were more useful as a mirror to Europe than as ethnography: they tell us about Europe's intellectual history.[4] More recently, Peel made a complementary observation. Missionary sources might not always accurately represent indigenous religions, but if used carefully and comparatively—and in conversation with other historical ethnographic scholarship—they might uncover something of which very few missionaries understood: living traditions, changing in real time.[5]

Both approaches are correct. To make adequate use of missionary sources anywhere, including in late precolonial Ghana, scholars must apply great sensitivity to the times and places, not only of the authors, but also of the subjects: everyone involved was changing, and often were doing so in conversation with one another. With respect to their history of the cult surrounding the god Tongnaab, which migrated south from what is now northern Ghana during the colonial period, Jean Allman and John Parker offer a word of caution applicable to late precolonial indigenous religion in Akuapem:

> African religious belief and practice is profoundly historical. Too often scholars have privileged the processes of conversion to Islam and Christianity as the central historical dynamic of African religion, thereby consigning indigenous belief to the realm of unchanging tradition.[6]

Basel missionary sources are among the best available in any language for the nineteenth-century Gold Coast, because the Basel Mission's emphasis on language learning required its staff to engage in a deep encounter with local ways. The quality of Basel missionary sources is thus directly related to the writer's knowledge of the language and length of stay. Many missionaries learned a great deal (and changed their minds accordingly) during the Mission's first few decades in the Gold Coast. In the 1830s, Andreas Riis conflated ancestor veneration with *abosom* worship, but by around 1850, Johann Widmann was able

---

[4]   Philip D. Curtin, *The Image of Africa: British Ideas and Action, 1780–1850* (Madison: University of Wisconsin Press, 1964), 318–42.

[5]   J. D. Y. Peel, *Christianity, Islam, and Orị̀ṣà Religion: Three Traditions in Comparison and Interaction* (Berkeley: University of California Press, 2016), 52–70.

[6]   Jean Marie Allman and John Parker, *Tongnaab: The History of a West African God* (Bloomington: Indiana University Press: 2005), 6.

to distinguish between various classes of spirits.[7] Nevertheless, Basel missionaries in the Gold Coast (who were in conversation with counterparts in India engaged in fairly sophisticated study of Indian religious texts),[8] consistently sought for, and accordingly found, abstract doctrines in Gold Coast religiosity. The presumption that religious praxis necessarily proceeded from religious belief led the missionaries into bewilderment; only Johann Widmann realized that the key to understanding indigenous religious thought was praxis, not theory.[9] They were hardly the only ones. Relative to "belief," McCaskie has argued, part of the issue is the Twi language: "belief terms open into a multiple universe of indistinct transitive objects; accepting, taking, asking, demanding, serving, and the rest." The great danger in cramming these kinds of dynamic exchanges into "second order categories" comes when the resulting representation reduces Twi belief to an "unexceptional or mundane ethics of existence." At its "widespread worst," McCaskie warns,

> This formulation is expressed in a bathetic series of circular tautologies and self-fulfilling pseudo-profundities, of which the following might be taken as a representative instance: "It may be said without fear of exaggeration that life in the Akan world is religion and religion is life." . . . This is profoundly ahistorical, and adds rather than subtracts mystification.[10]

At the same time, it is important to recognize that if the missionaries were growing in their understanding of indigenous religion, they were also living through anything but stable years in the Gold Coast, and that indigenous religious thinking was also evolving. Thus, contradictory missionary reports are not necessarily a reflection of inadequate missionary understanding of the conditions on the ground—they might also testify to changes afoot in indigenous religion. Some innovations might have their origins in missionary messaging, such as around the turn of the twentieth century when locals of Akyem related their dreams about God and heaven to a missionary—dreams that would have been unlikely eighty years earlier, when the dreamers' great-grandparents did not believe that God was remotely concerned with individual lives.[11]

---

[7] BMA D-10.4,3. J. G. Widmann, ca. 1850, "Cultus der Goldküste."

[8] Reinhard Wendt, *An Indian to the Indians? On the Initial Failure and the Posthumous Success of the Missionary Ferdinand Kittel (1832—1903)* (Wiesbaden: Harrassowitz, 2006).

[9] BMA D-10.4,3. J. G. Widmann, ca. 1850, "Cultus der Goldküste."

[10] T. C. McCaskie, *State and Society in Pre-Colonial Asante*, African Studies Series (Cambridge: Cambridge University Press, 1995), 102.

[11] BMA 2–10.2.7, unknown author, *Träume der Goldküsteneger* (eleven typed pages composed by a missionary in Abetifi sometime between 1902—the date of the youngest event cited—and the First World War).

A methodological word of caution: it is important to remember that neither the kings nor the priests in the Gold Coast were greatly concerned about whatever personal doubts an adherent might have entertained: dutiful participation was what mattered. The word "ethics," accordingly, has sometimes been used as a substitute for West African religions.[12] There is something to commend this approach, because ethics is both more and less than metaphysical doctrine: it is concrete and wrapped up in communal reciprocity. That is, the ritual toolkit centered on sustaining and repairing the social order and, in the Ghanaian case, expressed the overarching priority of the incorporation of outsiders. Johann Christaller's early identification of indigenous proverbs as the raw material for the Twi spiritual and moral imaginary has been taken up by African Christian intellectuals elsewhere.[13] However, the word *ethics*, originating as it does in a Greek discourse at least as old as the word *religion*, equally fails to account for the elaborate underlying ritual framework behind spiritual ethics, including the omnipresence of sacrificial blood: more than mere ethics was involved in Ghanaian ritual, even when its purpose was practical rather than liturgical.

## EXPERIMENTATION

The men and women of Akuapem, both those born in the kingdom and those who sought refuge there during one or the other of the mid-century wars, experimented with Christianity in an attitude of pragmatic problem-solving. Most were not, at least initially, greatly concerned with Christian doctrine, and certainly not in the missionary message of forgiveness of sin. Rather, they recognized that there was some kind of spiritual power resident within Christianity, potentially efficacious toward the pressing needs of the day.

Not infrequently they did this because they found their existing spiritual options ineffective or inadequate. In other words, in their quest for power, protection, healing, blessing, fertility, wealth, or shelter, some locals asked themselves whether Christianity might work as a possible solution when more obvious ones had proven ineffective. They were not only asking these questions of the Europeans' religion: the people of Akuapem were experimenting with multiple new religions at the same time in the middle of the nineteenth century. Akonnedi, for example, who would later become the most important deity of Larteh, had been imported from the north in the early nineteenth

---

[12]   C. A. Ackah, *Akan Ethics: A Study of the Moral Ideas and the Moral Behaviour of the Akan Tribes of Ghana* (Accra: Ghana Universities Press, 1988).

[13]   In the Igbo case, see Emefie Ikenga Metuh, *African Religions in Western Conceptual Schemes: The Problem of Interpretation*, Studies in Igbo Religion (Ibadan, Nigeria: Pastoral Institute, Bodija, 1985).

century.[14] Thus, careful attention to chronology and context is of the essence: the preferred religious foci of one generation might not be the same as for another. Akonnedi arrived around 1800, Odwira in 1811, and Christianity in the 1830s, but they were each appropriated by different kinds of people for different purposes.

Early- and mid-twentieth-century Christian scholars of indigenous religions—especially independent African churchmen—tended to see doctrine where there was none, at least in the sense of doctrine derived from the interpretation of sacred texts, themselves understood as revealed and unchanging.[15] Two main motivations seem to underlie this twentieth-century search for doctrine. One was to elevate African religions in the eyes of Europeans, who were otherwise disinclined to concede rationality in African ritual as a third religion alongside Islam and Christianity.[16] As African intellectuals within Christian denominations headquartered overseas, these theologians often had their European and American peers as their primary audiences. For example, Kenyan reformed theologian John Mbiti, who spent many years as a pastor in Switzerland, went to great lengths to argue that many African deities had their origins in derivative acclamations of one supreme god. Mbiti concluded that the meaning of time itself was central toward resolving any ontological differences in this matter.[17] Conspicuous in this literature was the use of scientific and economic jargon to describe the gods. In 1973, for example, Nigerian Methodist Basoji Idowu (who in 1976 became patriarch of his church) spoke of Yoruba "theology," with each god having his (always the male pronoun) own "sphere" of responsibility, like that of an "administrative head of a department."[18] "Theology" is certainly a misleading word to describe what was essentially an agnostic and pragmatic cluster of practices, extending from herbal medicine to political philosophy.

Likewise, in the Gold Coast (and a generation earlier than Idowu), J. B. Danquah, the Akropong-schooled independence leader and nemesis of Kwame

[14] M. A. Kwamena-Poh, *Government and Politics in the Akuapem State, 1730–1850*, Legon History Series (Evanston, Ill.: Northwestern University Press, 1973), 134.

[15] Jacob K. Olupona, *African Religions: A Very Short Introduction* (New York: Oxford University Press, 2014), xxi.

[16] Olupona, *African Religions*, xxi.

[17] John S. Mbiti, *African Religions & Philosophy* (New York: Praeger, 1969). For a theological analysis of Mbiti's thought on African gods, see Werner Friedrich Bonin, *Die Götter Schwarzafrikas* (Graz: Sammler, 1979).

[18] E. Bolaji Idowu, *African Traditional Religion: A Definition* (Maryknoll, N.Y.: Orbis, 1973), 169–70.

Nkrumah, cooked up a similar doctrinal synthesis for the Akan world.[19] As with Idowu's, Danquah's synthesis was inadequate as an ethnographic account. Danquah tended to "reproduce Akan thought," Ackah said, "in the dress of English philosophy of the 1920s and 1930s. . . . It is difficult at times to see how far what Danquah writes is truly Akan, and how far it is merely the genius of Danquah."[20] However, if Danquah was in fact inventing "tradition," his authority to do so originated in the regional cosmological superstructure, which for centuries has prioritized (and in contemporary Pentecostalism, continues to do so) concrete evidence over metaphysical precision.[21]

More recently with respect to Yoruba religion, Olufemi Taiwo rejected such attempts as Idowu's as grounded in an African need to rebut European supremacy:

> At the base of much of the discourse about African empirical analogues of concepts such as religion, philosophy and literature is what I call the cult of difference, under which for a phenomenon to be properly "African" it must be so radically different from other species of the same genus that our ability to identify it as an instance of the genus is impaired, perhaps lost.[22]

The reality, Taiwo continues, is that every distinguishing element of African Traditional Religion (and thus Taiwo's basis for rejecting the term) is shared with some other religious culture elsewhere, be it ancestral veneration, spirit possession, saints, or sacrifice. This argument is very helpful for clarifying the religious encounter in late precolonial Akuapem. Locals (not only indigenous residents, but also newly arrived refugees, slaves, and others) were unconcerned with national purity when seeking for a solution to pressing personal and intimate problems.

Neither the missionaries nor the endlessly bewildered European officers on the coast were successful at describing indigenous religious doctrine, because doctrine was rarely the point. Rather, practices and cults came and went against the fixed backdrop of social priorities, the guiding principle being a pragmatic openness to what worked. Early in the postcolonial years, anthropologist Meyer Fortes correctly insisted that doctrine was the wrong criterion for understanding the primal vision of West Africa:

[19] J. B. Danquah, *The Akan Doctrine of God: A Fragment of Gold Coast Ethics and Religion* (London: Lutterworth, 1944).

[20] Ackah, *Akan Ethics*, 3.

[21] Paul Gifford, *Ghana's New Christianity: Pentecostalism in a Globalizing African Economy* (Bloomington: Indiana University Press, 2004), esp. 85–90.

[22] Olufemi Taiwo, "Òrìṣà: A Prolegomenon to a Philosophy of Yorùbá Religion," in Jacob K. Olupona and Terry Rey, eds., *Òrìṣà Devotion as World Religion: The Globalization of Yorùbá Religious Culture* (Madison: University of Wisconsin Press, 2008), 86.

By comparison, for example, with the Greeks or Hindus their mythologies of the "spirit world" are thin and unimpressive. Worship in rituals of prayer and sacrifice . . . may be validated by reference to what we describe as spiritual beings, be they gods or ancestors or nature deities. But none of this, it is evident, necessitates a circumstantial cosmography of a "spirit world." *Religious beliefs and practices can be carried on perfectly well without a doctrine or lore of the nature and mode of existence of the "beings" to whom they are ostensibly directed.*[23]

Well into the twentieth century, for instance, the Gã practiced at least four different religions, two of which were of Akan origin, most likely dating to Akwamu occupation late in the seventeenth century. A third, *kple*, may have originated among the Kyerepong who had lived in the coastal plain before being displaced by the Gã.[24] That is: first, as invaders, Gã had appropriated an existing cult and indigenized it. Later, as conquered people, they absorbed two of their Akwamu overlords' gods. Eventually, most of the Gã people became Christians (of more than one European Christian tradition), and still later—in the late twentieth century—large numbers of Gã Christians abandoned the mission-derived churches of their childhoods, switching to the particularly potent variation of Pentecostalism originating in Nigeria.[25] The point has never been truth abstracted from quotidian concerns, but, as Kwame Bediako put it in 1992, the "stuff of the sacred in their human existence."[26]

---

[23] Meyer Fortes, "Some Reflections on Ancestor Worship in Africa," in *African Systems of Thought; Studies Presented and Discussed at the Third International African Seminar in Salisbury, December, 1960*, ed. Meyer Fortes and G. Dieterlen (London: Published for the International African Institute by the Oxford University Press, 1965), 128 (emphasis mine).

[24] J. H. Kwabena Nketia, "Historical Evidence in Ga Religious Music," in *The Historian in Tropical Africa; Studies Presented and Discussed at the Fourth International African Seminar*, ed. Jan Vansina, R. Mauny, and L. V. Thomas (London: Published for the International African Institute by the Oxford University Press, 1964), 267.

[25] Gifford, *Ghana's New Christianity*, 87.

[26] Kwame Bediako, "The Unique Christ in the Plurality of Religions," in *The Unique Christ in Our Pluralist World*, ed. Bruce J. Nicholls (Grand Rapids: Baker, 1994), 51. This article was first given as a 1992 speech at the "world evangelical forum" in Manila, Philippines, as part of a panel discussion involving four theologians from different corners of the world: Korea, England, and Papua New Guinea. Bediako's argument was made in close conversation with the latter, Joshua Daimoi, whose focus was on the uniqueness of the Christian Christ within the "animistic" setting, as Daimoi called it, in which biblical affirmations were evaluated and received. Bediako's paper, then, doubled as a discussion of the early generations of converts in the Gold Coast, and in comparative context with a primal religious context at the other end of the world.

## SACRIFICE

The growth of Christianity in nineteenth-century West Africa cannot be understood apart from a discussion of sacrifice. Like most peoples across the ages and around the world, the people of precolonial West Africa have always practiced variations of sacrifice and have done so toward distinctive ends. Early converts and non-converts alike took acute interest in ancient Hebrew ritual practices they discovered in Christian Scriptures. From precolonial times down to the present, African scholars working to devise indigenous theologies have often accentuated the sacrificial qualities to their Christology. While various ritual tools were available within indigenous Ghanaian religion—from prayers and sacred dances, from oracles and spirit possession to protective amulets—sacrifice was and remains foremost in importance. Sacrifice was the supreme tool by which supplicant humans could approach both gods and ancestors. In their classic comparative definition, originally published in French in 1898, Hubert and Mauss wrote:

> Sacrifice is a religious act which, through the consecration of a victim, modifies the condition of the moral person who accomplishes it or that of certain objects of which he is concerned.[27]

Sacrifice is a special form of a gift. In contrast to commercial transactions, gifts involve a measure of dissembling: the gifts exchanged are never equal in value, so that all gifts leave one of the parties in some kind of debt to the other.[28] Reciprocated gifts do not settle accounts, but set in motion successions of exchanges that do not merely represent, but in a sense constitute the relationship. More importantly, gifts are not negotiated. Instead the giver must guess what the recipient will regard as appropriate.[29] As a special kind of a gift, a sacrifice is given within a hierarchical context in which the normal cycle of reciprocity does not hold. Rather, the recipient (the ancestor or deity) retains the authority to reject the proffered gift. The heart of sacrifice—its emotional power—lies in the gap between the form of the offering—a gift—and the asymmetrical nature of the parties: the unpredictable nature of the outcome.[30] The fundamental anxiety behind sacrifice is great, and all the more so when the supplicant has so much to lose: in ancestral sacrifice, it is nothing less than one's very being as a social creature.

[27] Henri Hubert and Marcel Mauss, *Sacrifice: Its Nature and Function*, trans. W. D. Halls (1898; Chicago: University of Chicago Press, 1964), 13.

[28] Mary Douglas, "No Free Gifts," foreword to *The Gift: The Form and Reason for Exchange in Archaic Societies*, by Marcel Mauss (London; New York: Routledge, 1990), ix.

[29] William R. Jordan, *The Sunflower Forest: Ecological Restoration and the New Communion with Nature* (Berkeley: University of California Press, 2003), 67.

[30] Moshe Halbertal, *On Sacrifice* (Princeton: Princeton University Press, 2011), 3.

In southeastern Ghana, the particulars of sacrifice have varied quite a bit over time: the nature of the victim (which animals, for instance, including which kinds of humans might be eligible), who or what is being sacrificed to (gods, ancestors, or minor spirits), and how the sacrifice is made. Fundamentally, Hubert and Mauss summarized—and their definition seems broad enough to encompass Ghanaian modes over time—beneath superficial variations in form,

> [Sacrifice] always consists in one same procedure, which may be used for the most widely differing purposes. *This procedure consists in establishing a means of communication between the sacred and the profane worlds through the mediation of a victim, that is, of a thing that in the course of the ceremony is destroyed.*[31]

In accordance with the empiricist outlook behind much West African religion, these forms have been subject to constant innovation and change. It is therefore risky to extrapolate sacrificial patterns from present—or even colonial-era—practice. For example, Gã modes of sacrifice did not ordinarily fit within the religious framework of the Akan, but in 1688 the (Akan) Akwamu king, facing a grave military threat, did not greatly care about philosophical consistency: he was interested in whatever ritual tools might aid him in his war. In July of that year Danish Governor Fensman wrote in his journal that the Akwamu were mobilizing in response to an alliance between the ancient enemy of Akyem in the west and the Agona, heretofore subject to Akwamu. If much of the preparations involved raising armies from the empire's eastern districts, and building stockades and other defensive structures along the Akyem border, the king also ordered a child sacrifice:

> [The King] ordered his people to *panyar,*[32] here at Acra, Orsoe, Laberde, Test, and Qonga, a little child who according to the custom of the country has not yet been circumcised, which the negroes understood and had all their children and slaves' children circumcised, as the King gave the impression that these were to go to his fetish, sanctum or idol to be sacrificed, to give him better fortune in the coming battle.[33]

---

[31] Hubert and Mauss, *Sacrifice,* 97. Italics original.

[32] That is, to "arrest." Fensman, writing in Danish, is using a local Gã loan word from the homegrown Gold Coast dialect of Portuguese. "panyar" = Pt. *penhorar.* Ole Justesen, ed., *Danish Sources for the History of Ghana, 1657–1754,* 2 vols. (Copenhagen: Det Kongelige Danske Videnskabernes Selskab, 2005), 1007.

[33] Justesen, *Danish Sources.*

Writing twenty-five years later, Johannes Rask observed that the "Akras circumcise all their male children when they are about six or seven years old."[34] This meant that the king's 1688 directive applied to boys younger than six. The point is that, faced with a dangerous war, the Akwamu king was prepared to demand an extreme form of sacrifice, because cosmological accuracy was less important than the possibility of achieving a desired outcome: he was interested in whatever would work.

The Akan have historically sacrificed to two categorically distinct entities—to shrine spirits (*abosom*) and to ancestors (*asaman*), and especially (at least in the eighteenth and nineteenth centuries) to the deceased kings and queen mothers. The specifics had some grounding in the nature of blood: sheep's blood was understood as having a cooling effect and was thus useful for calming angered ancestors.[35] On the other hand, upon the death of a king, a human sacrifice might add to the retinue of a king or queen mother in their next stage of life.[36] Its purpose was to persuade these exalted persons to continue to intervene, from beyond the grave, on behalf of the living, and above all among those with whom they were bound by ties of blood (*mogya*). Sacrifice, as a ritual intended to create and restore communal belonging, was an answer to the most deeply felt need in the region, and as such was fundamental to the reception and reconfiguration of Christianity in Akuapem.

## PROFESSIONAL DIVISION OF LABOR

Alongside an empiricist outlook, another defining element to precolonial Ghanaian religion was its insistence on retaining the individuality—at least to a certain degree—of the supplicant. There was little to no anonymity before shrine spirits and late ancestors; this relational priority tended to limit supplicants' capacity to controlling the outcomes. In Halbertal's words, ritual "introduces a causal dimension that closes the gap between giving and receiving, thereby ensuring acceptance of the gift and leaving nothing voluntary to the recipient."[37] Read in this way, ritual is an attempt to reduce the giving cycle of sacrifice to a formulaic commercial transaction. However, especially in a sacrificial setting between deceased ancestors and their living descendants, real relationships are involved. Consequently, the comfort of anonymity, a feature

[34] Johannes Rask, *A Brief and Truthful Description of a Journey to and from Guinea*, in *Two Views from Christiansborg Castle*, ed. Selena Axelrod Winsnes (Accra: Sub-Saharan Publishers, 2009), 134.

[35] McCaskie, *State and Society*, 160.

[36] Eva Meyerowitz, *At the Court of an African King* (London: Faber and Faber, 1962), 107.

[37] Halbertal, *On Sacrifice*, 18.

of ritual thinking in much of the world, is not present: real relationships are understood to be involved, so there is no hiding behind the forms of gift.

The typical solution in the Gold Coast was a division of ritual labor: to the kings and heads of clans fell the task of making sacrifices to the *asaman* ancestors, and to priests the responsibility of tending to *abosom* spirits (although this division of labor is not to be overstated). That is, they distributed amongst themselves the dangerous task of standing before powerful and unpredictable beings, and did so according to fields of expertise. To the extent that the king, *ex officio*, was assigned duties toward the ancestors, the kingship may be described as sacred. A small detail in McCaskie's discussion of the Odwira of precolonial Asante speaks volumes. In the early nineteenth century, visiting chiefs sacrificed slaves at the crossroads leading into Kumasi, but by 1844 this practice had been proscribed—possibly to monopolize execution authority under the Asantehene.[38] The king's responsibility was great, and any change to the division of labor put him at risk.

In 1949, Meyerowitz had a remarkable conversation with a ritual executioner, who demonstrated the sacrificial process on his assistant, stopping just short of killing the young man:

> Then the old man sat down again and was sad because he had spoken to me about these things. All the executioners would now need to fast for a day to atone for this fault. I was sorry to hear that and expressed my sympathy, but he assured me that I need not be concerned because, after all, seeing that times had changed, it was a good thing to preserve the custom at least in a book so that future generations should know the truth.[39]

Embedded within this conversation was a conviction that the rituals of sacrifice were sacred and unmentionable upon penalty of lost efficacy, and that atonement (expressed as corporate fasting) was necessary to restore the sanctity of the ritual. It was, in other words, an attempt at securing guarantees from capricious beings. Halbertal points out the importance of formula: the supreme risk in sacrifice is the possibility that the offering might be rejected. The fatal possibility of rejection gives rise to an important function of ritual. In the context of sacrifice, ritual attempts to eliminate the free-choice factor: it turns a god or ancestor into a force of nature, as it were, thus ensuring the gift's efficacy or at least acceptance.[40] As people standing before the gods, priests and their assistants faced a different—if more predictable, because anonymous—kind of

---

[38] McCaskie, *State and Society*, 201.
[39] Meyerowitz, *Court of an African King*, 109. Although published in 1962, Meyerowitz dated this conversation in November 1949.
[40] Halbertal, *On Sacrifice*, 15.

danger. Accordingly, they were expected to undergo long periods of training, during which time strict taboos were to be kept. If a taboo was broken, punishment was required.[41]

## GODS AND SPIRITS

It is generally agreed that the cosmology of the Gold Coast region's peoples affirmed a high God of roughly analogous hierarchical standing (relative to humanity) as the God of Moses.[42] An immediate and all-important qualification, however, was that while the latter had a pattern of self-revelation (that is, personal contact with Abraham, self-disclosure as "I AM" to Moses, law-giving to the same, oracles in song to several prophets, and, in Christianity, God's incarnation as a human, and disbursal of the Holy Spirit), the Akan high God did not. The supreme God existed, but was not involved in daily life, and this made all the difference. *Onyame*, also called *Onyankopɔn*, did not behave entirely unlike the Platonic *demiurge*: he made the world, and subsequently removed himself. The only deities who mattered were those with whom one needed to interact, and to whom one had to answer for one's choices. Only one scholar has ever argued otherwise: Alfred Burdon Ellis, who insisted that *Onyame* could only be a European import. "Within the last twenty or thirty years," Ellis wrote in 1887,

> The German missionaries, sent out from time to time by the mission societies Basel and Bremen, have made Nyankupon known to European ethnologists and students of the science of religion; but, being unaware of the real origin of this god, they have generally spoken and written of him as a conception of the native mind, whereas he is really a god borrowed from Europeans and only thinly disguised.[43]

Ellis' claim did not sustain scrutiny, and he later changed his mind. Andrew Lang observed retrospectively that Ellis had appeared to be motivated by false presuppositions deriving from an evolutionary perspective on the history of

---

[41] T. N. O. Quarcoopome, *West African Traditional Religion* (Ibadan, Nigeria: African Universities Press, 1987), 76.

[42] Mbiti, *African Religions*, 30–31; Idowu, *African Traditional Religion*, 169–70; Charles Sarpong Aye-Addo, *Akan Christology: An Analysis of the Christologies of John Samuel Pobee and Kwame Bediako in Conversation with the Theology of Karl Barth* (Eugene, Ore.: Pickwick, 2013), 5–21.

[43] Alfred Burdon Ellis, *The Tshi-Speaking Peoples of the Gold Coast of West Africa: Their Religion, Manners, Customs, Laws, Languages, Etc.* (London: Chapman and Hall, 1887), 28.

religion, according to which the Akan could not believe in a high god because they were, *a priori*, primitives.[44]

Prior to his appropriation by Christians as the creator God of the Hebrew Bible—and thus his redefinition as a god who entered into genuine interactions and even pacts with humans—*Onyame* could not have been considered a communal asset, at least to the extent that he could not be called upon in times of trouble, and could not be manipulated by prayers or sacrifices. I retain him in this inventory, because over time *Onyame* would rejoin the world as an active participant in human affairs—a shift which might have several causes, but which at least in part must be attributed to indigenous engagement with Christianity.

However remote the high God may have been in the middle of the nineteenth century, one tier down were the *abosom*—several classes of spirits who were actively involved in human affairs. Around 1850, Johann Widmann (who by then had been in Akropong for around eight years) called them "under-gods" [*Untergötter*] because their existence derived from the creator—they were created along with the world. They were immortal, omniscient, and omnipresent, but they preferred to live in certain places such as under large trees in the forest, or in caves.[45] This description seems not to have changed much over time, and therefore suggests that Widmann had it right, at least in the general contours. In 1923 R. S. Rattray published the *Fofie* (sacred Friday) song-prayer of a priest of the god Tano—the highest of the children of Onyame—in the north-central region of Brong. This prayer, which was accompanied with obeisance to a statue representing the god, and the breaking of chicken eggs as offerings, combined praise with assertions that Tano certainly heard his supplicants, who wished him to come and hear them:

> You whose odawuru [gong] sounds even to Mecca.
> If you have gone elsewhere, come (hither).
> Kwampiri [a title], upon whom, when the waters are in flood, we call.
> Shooting stars, that abide with the Supreme Being,
> You weave [as it were] a thread [in a loom] across a path stretching afar.
> Today is sacred Friday and we wish to behold your face,
> So come and listen to what we have to tell you.[46]

What was likely to change over time were the details of how one or the other of these spirits might be assuaged or placated. And this is where the empirical logic came to play: if and when an *ɔbosom* (singular of *abosom*)

---

44  Andrew Lang, *The Making of Religion* (1898; New York: AMS Press, 1968), 243ff.
45  BMA D-10.4,3. J. G. Widmann, ca. 1850, "Cultus der Goldküste," folio 1.
46  R. S. Rattray, *Ashanti* (Oxford: Clarendon, 1923), 179.

ceased responding favorably to proffered sacrifices and prayers, a frustrated priest might try alternate means of reaching the spirit, but ultimately could not force it to act—it was the spirit's free decision. *Abosom* gods came and went in Akan practice, in something of an open market of devotion. Jack Goody, writing in 1957, put it this way: "Shrines are always waxing and waning in importance. That they do so is an indication of how loosely they are tied up with the system of social groups."[47] In combination with a general sense that *Onyame* was not present, the underlying conviction of active ancestral involvement in the world had as a consequence that pragmatic religious experimentation, within certain bounds, was likely to reveal best practices. Goody continued:

> One shrine becomes successful, another fades out. The inhabitants are very pragmatic about such things, as well as eclectic. If one shrine appears to be effective, they take it up. If it fails them, they drop it.[48]

The story grows more complicated when one considers the ways deities can fundamentally change as religious praxis demands. Akonnedi of Larteh, for example, is probably the most globally prominent of Ghana's indigenous spirits, with daughter shrines in the United States. Since the 1960s, through the outreach of her chief priest, Akonnedi became an important ancestral spirit for African Americans assumed to be descendants of enslaved Ghanaians.[49] Since many contemporary diasporic religious seekers desire a sense of autochthony and knowledge and spirituality untainted by racism, Akonnedi has come to represent for some the restoration of lost connections with ancestors.

Akonnedi was originally brought to Larteh in the late eighteenth century from the distant north (it is unclear exactly where).[50] Despite her global reach, Akonnedi only speaks (through human vehicles) in the archaic form of the Larteh-Guan dialect.[51] As Boakyewa demonstrates, however, one of the original reasons for the Akonnedi cult's rise to prominence in Larteh was because of its social mission: restoring social harmony in Akuapem's multiethnic context.[52] In other words, at a time of regional turmoil related to major disruptions to a violent global economic system, the people of Larteh supplanted (or at

---

[47] Jack Goody, "Anomie in Ashanti?" *Africa: Journal of the International African Institute* 27, no. 4 (1957), 359.

[48] Goody, "Anomie," 359.

[49] Kwasi Konadu, *The Akan Diaspora in the Americas* (Oxford: Oxford University Press, 2010), 215.

[50] Kwamena-Poh, *Government and Politics*, 19.

[51] Okomfo Ama Boakyewa, "Nana Oparebea and the Akonnedi Shrine: Cultural, Religious and Global Agents" (PhD diss., Indiana University, 2014), 2–3.

[52] Boakyewa, "Nana Oparebea," 17–26.

least supplemented) their shrine to Otutu with a new shrine to a god imported from the north.[53]

In the 1860s, indigenous people in southeastern Ghana applied this pragmatic logic to Basel missionaries. In the middle of the nineteenth century, Akuapem conversion had almost nothing to do with cold intellectual assent to missionary preaching and had very little to do with a felt need for forgiveness from sin. To a degree that very few missionaries understood at the time, the story was rather one of the renegotiations of the ties that could bind a community together. These ties included the dead ancestors, to which I now turn.

ANCESTORS

Akan religious systems had both "pantheons of gods and nature deities as well as ancestor cults."[54] This is an important distinction, and one which many of the missionaries failed to make, as did, indeed, most other nineteenth-century European observers. While the *abosom* gods were to be dealt with at arm's length and as carefully and meticulously as possible, ancestors stood at the very center of the spiritual economy. Fortes summarized this vision of ancestral involvement in the affairs of the living:

> An ancestor is a named, dead forebear who has living descendants of a designated genealogical class representing his continued structural relevance. In ancestor worship such an ancestor receives ritual service and tendance directed specifically to him by the proper class of his descendants. Being identified by name means that he is invested with attributes distinctive of a kind of person.[55]

In the precolonial Akan conception, a person is composed of four parts. Summarizing from McCaskie:

1. *Kra*, which is something of a divine spark derived from *Onyame*. It was the person's essence, and their birth day-name ascribes *kra*-meanings to the character of the child; *kra* thus functioned somewhat like fate or fortune. In academic literature it is usually spelled *Okra*.

2. *Sunsum*, which is roughly equivalent to conscience or soul. A *sunsum* can be trained and disciplined, and can leave the body at night and in dreams. Groups, such as nations, may possess a collective *sunsum*.

3. *Mogya*, or blood: the matrilineal element. Blood relations form the basis of society.

4. *Ntɔrɔ*, or semen: the patrilineal element.[56]

---

[53] Kwamena-Poh, *Government and Politics*, 134.
[54] Fortes, "Some Reflections on Ancestor Worship," 127–28.
[55] Fortes, "Some Reflections on Ancestor Worship," 124.
[56] McCaskie, *State and Society*, 168–70.

Ritual purifications involved both the female and male side of a person. The ancestors—*asaman* in Twi—were then and remain in the present day intimate members of the community. The death of a king or queen mother opens a dangerous rift in the fabric of the spiritual world, because the living king in his very body protects the people and answers for them before the gods and ancestors alike. When he or she dies, and thus passes to the other side of this dynamic, that protection is momentarily removed and must be filled as powerfully and as quickly as possible. The dead rulers travel to live with the gods, but it remains their duty to continue to give life to the people of their state. This they do by making the crops grow, and by acting as intermediaries between people and the deities.[57]

The essential personhood of an ancestor distinguishes him or her from a god or spirit. An ancestor's continued presence in the human community operates on a very different plane than that of a deity.[58] It is always important to bear in mind the underlying pragmatism to this primal vision. The distinction between ancestor and deity is less one of philosophical precision and more of practical outcomes: ancestors and gods impose their will upon communities in different ways, sometimes contradicting one another and sometimes complementing one another. It is rather a matter of emotion (including grief for the recently deceased and fear of one's own death), combined with pragmatic resource management: as a named member of the community, an ancestor has the authority and power to bless or curse or simply to go away. The ancestors, accordingly, are assets to be stewarded. Then and now, a clan richly endowed with ancestors was infinitely wealthier than a clan with few or none. But exactly how this took place in the middle of the nineteenth century was not set in stone. McCaskie put it thus:

> It seems evident that very widespread concern with the prolongation of corporeal existence was directly linked to the lack of rigorous theological intent and structuration that characterized all speculative belief concerning futurity.[59]

Most of the early missionaries failed to see the relevance of ancestor veneration to the acute social tensions within the kingdom. During the eighteenth century, as endemic warfare, functioning symbiotically with the coastal arms and slave trades, engulfed the region, waves of refugees had arrived in the hills. Under customary practices, these strangers might expect, and be expected, to

---

[57] Meyerowitz, *Court of an African King*, 107.
[58] Ajume Wingo, "Akan Philosophy of the Person," in The Stanford Encyclopedia of Philosophy (summer 2017 edition), ed. Edward N. Zalta, https://plato.stanford.edu/archives/sum2017/entries/akan-person/.
[59] McCaskie, *State and Society*, 123.

attain formal and ritual incorporation into an ancestral lineage. For the Guan as well as for the Akan, newcomers were to be ritually incorporated into the community. For the Guan, this was accomplished both by initiating the newcomer into one or the other of the autochthonous cults—whereby the newcomer is assigned a deity and a shrine at which to worship—and by assigning that person a membership in a local patrilineage. Gilbert notes that the Guan festival of ancestral veneration (which, as of her writing in 1989, was performed in only one remaining town) was called *Eba* in the Kyerepong-Guan language, meaning "to sew" and implies knitting the lineage together.[60]

## Clans

One of the obstacles to social harmony in eighteenth- and nineteenth-century Akuapem was the dual nature of human belonging in the land: matrilineal and patrilineal clans with distinct ways of making claims upon the loyalty of their members. Lineage and ancestry lie at the heart of several different sacrificial economies of the Gold Coast, and indeed much of West Africa, and more than one writer has come to focus on sacrifice while studying family life.[61] This is not surprising: comparative studies of social structures of gender and religious ritual have shown a stubborn consistency across very different times and places. In much of the world and throughout the ages, sacrifice has aided in paternal succession, be it in property, in family relations, or in the inheritance of family gods.[62] Put simply, sacrifice can alter a person's moral standing relative to the community, to the degree that an outsider may be fully incorporated into a clan by means of blood sacrifice, with all the rights, ritual responsibilities, and taboos involved. Blood sacrifice thus symbolically overcomes actual blood continuity with an individual's mother.[63] For that reason, blood sacrifice for ritual incorporation has not tended to appear in matrilineal societies, such as the Akan societies. Nancy Jay observes that rigidly patrilineal societies immediately to the east

[60] Michelle Gilbert, "The Cracked Pot and the Missing Sheep," *American Ethnologist* 16, no. 2 (1989), 216.

[61] Meyer Fortes, "Kinship and Marriage among the Ashanti," in *African Systems of Kinship and Marriage*, ed. A. R. Radcliffe-Brown and Daryll Forde (London: Published for the International African Institute by the Oxford University Press, 1950), 252–84. On changes to kinship and marriage with the cocoa economy, see Takyiwaa Manuh, "Changes in Marriage and Funeral Exchanges among the Asante: A Case Study from Kona, Afigya-Kwabre," in *Money Matters: Instability, Values and Social Payments in the Modern History of West African Communities*, ed. Jane I. Guyer, Social History of Africa (Portsmouth, N.H.: Heinemann, 1995), 189.

[62] Samson Adetunji Fatukun, "The Concept of Expiatory Sacrifice in the Early Church and in African Indigenous Religious Traditions," in *African Traditions in the Study of Religion, Diaspora and Gendered Societies*, ed. Ezra Chitando, Afe Adogame, and Bolaji Bateye (New York: Routledge, 2016), 71–81.

[63] Fortes, "Kinship and Marriage," 257.

of the Akan world (and the crest of the Akuapem ridge is the dividing line) have always practiced sacrifice for ritual incorporation, even though the Asante (Jay's case study) long practiced sacrifice, including human sacrifice, for myriad other reasons, including as appeasement within ancestral cults.[64]

Social cohesion in eighteenth- and nineteenth-century Akuapem involved both patrilineages and matrilineages, and the incorporation of strangers was accomplished by the newcomer's ritual adaptation into an existing lineage. By controlling membership in the matriclans (the *abusua*) the Akan states could effectively define newcomers' belonging to the society and thus to the very soil, which was owned by the ancestors. McCaskie writes—again, by reference to the Asante state, which was far more successful than Akuapem at imposing its totalizing social vision:

> By the clear and relentless demarcation of the boundaries of non-being or non-existence, the state ensured that membership in the one sanctioned form of jural corporateness remained the indispensable and mandatory condition of citizenship for a free Asante subject. In effect, it was also the only possible channel of aspiration for a non-Asante slave. An enslaved Asante retained minimal rights in law, including the possibility of redemption from bonded status. *But a non-Asante had no lever on jural corporateness, and thus did not exist—fully and legally—as a person.*[65]

It is important to note, because the social preeminence of clans constituted such a strong difference between Ghanaians and Germans (who long insisted on understanding Akuapem's divisions as *ethnic* in nature), that the "non-Asante" of which McCaskie spoke were not necessarily those of another ethnicity, but nonmembers of Asante matriclans. The longer individual Basel missionaries remained in the Gold Coast, the greater they came to appreciate this powerful drive to incorporate outsiders. Where newcomers tended to see disorder, veteran missionaries came to recognize the flexibility needed to adapt. In 1859, after ten years in three different districts, each speaking its own language, Johannes Zimmermann could write:

> Even in the most desperate African community every person is or soon will be enveloped into family or social life. There is no proletariat, there are no beggars, no orphans, nearly no widows, and no slaves, serfs, or lost children in the European sense.[66]

---

[64] Nancy B. Jay, *Throughout Your Generations Forever: Sacrifice, Religion, and Paternity* (Chicago: University of Chicago Press, 1992), 61–65.

[65] McCaskie, *State and Society*, 89. Emphasis mine.

[66] Zimmermann quoted in Albert Ostertag, "Die Goldküste und die Basler Mission daselbst," *EMM* 1859, 49.

The complication in the Akan world, including the ruling Akyem communities in Akuapem, centered on gender: "enveloped into family life," as Zimmermann wrote, meant incorporation into a clan. In much of the world, including in the ancient Near Eastern societies represented in the Bible, the point of ritual incorporation is to grow the community beyond natural reproduction—that is, to trump (maternal) blood relations. Since most of these cultures are patrilineal or patriarchal, a basic biological problem arises: these societies "meet a fundamental obstacle in their necessary dependence on women's reproductive powers . . . sacrificing produces and reproduces forms of intergenerational continuity generated by males, transmitted by males, and transcending continuity through women."[67] One of West Africa's major cultural frontiers—between male and female modes of denominating succession—runs right through Akuapem. Patrilineal Guan and matrilineal Akan have long lived alongside one another, while both simultaneously ascribing tremendous value to ancestral clans. A few words on the function of gender in Akan sacrifice are thus necessary.

An Asante saying on clans holds that *abusua baako mogya baako* (one clan/lineage is one blood).[68] This statement expresses the corporate unity of the clan and is intended to legitimate the rule of lineage exogamy: marriage within an *abusua* is interdicted with the same level of forcefulness as incest. Since Akan clans have long practiced ritual forms of assimilating slaves, immigrants, and other outsiders into existing maternal lineages, the saying indicates the depth to which an outsider, in joining a clan, has become a new person. Regardless of who someone's actual parents were, by joining an *abusua*, they submitted to the blood rules.

The *abusua*, membership of which is anchored in the blood—the *mogya*—of female descent, is the source and destination of an ancestral spirit.[69] As a result, a man's children were not his own, but belonged to his wife's clan, at least if she herself belonged to one. Indeed, wealthy men among the precolonial Akan often preferred to marry slave women, in the knowledge that their children would belong to them, rather than to the mother: the slave woman had no clan.[70] Such male aspiration against the dominance of the matriclans was in effect a man's wager on his own long-term prosperity, because in the event that the direct lineage faced extinction (or fell on hard times), the descendants of the slave woman had nowhere to turn. Excluded from the safety net of the matriclans, descendants of slaves effectively constituted a special class within a societal ideology in which there were to be no outsiders.

[67] Jay, *Throughout Your Generations Forever*, 31–32.
[68] Fortes, "Kinship and Marriage," 257.
[69] R. S. Rattray, *Religion & Art in Ashanti* (Oxford: Clarendon, 1927), 319.
[70] Rattray, *Religion & Art*, 43–44.

Parallel to and standing in tension with matrilineal clans, patrilineal inheritance—*ntͻrͻ*—was organized in various family groups (nine, in precolonial Asante), each with its own means of ritual purification.[71] There was no real concept of bastardy, but in cases where the father was not known or claimed, and a person thus not properly part of a *ntͻrͻ* group, such a person, especially a slave, was understood to "lack a whole body."[72] This would disqualify someone from any office requiring sacrifice. A person without a known father, who was thus excluded from a patrilineal group, could not purify his *ntͻrͻ*, and so could not undertake purification on behalf of others. Taken together, multiple vehicles for social belonging, corresponding with ancestral inheritance (both male and female), religious affiliation, and military service were meant to ensure that everyone was included. And yet, certain limits to the system—above all the necessity of sacrifice to achieve ritual incorporation—left growing numbers of people deprived and excluded, and times were growing very difficult, especially for those needing to take flight.

### The Sacred State

The implications of this sacrificial dynamic for the nascent translation of Christianity are considerable, because indigenous Christians have long sought—and continue to do so in the present—ways to navigate political and economic changes that have thrown people together without respect for their cultural particularities. It is a constant thread of West African moral thought from the earliest times to the present. The slave trade, the palm oil industry, colonial conquest, the cocoa economy, and, eventually, independence, painful military dictatorships, and present-day capitalism have all torn families apart and pushed others together.

Much of the literature on the Akan sacred state focuses on Asante, which was (by some distance) the most successful ͻman at realizing its aspirations—and the one most able to resist Britain. Asante differed in several crucial areas from the polyglot and diverse Akuapem. Foremost among these were the efforts the state took at monopolizing belief and horizons of aspiration. Within a total worldview, agriculture, economics, family life, social standing "were all locked together in an ideological grid of comprehensive definition, validation and mnemonic."[73]

Kinship, including royal descent, was "embedded in the structure of matriliny, but political power was articulated as male."[74] This tension was very important and has generated much confusion. The foundation for society were

[71] McCaskie, *State and Society*, 170.
[72] McCaskie, *State and Society*, 172.
[73] McCaskie, *State and Society*, 100–101.
[74] McCaskie, *State and Society*, 166–67.

the matrilineal clans, so the male occupant of the stool was the bridge between the clans and the military, and the heart of his ritual responsibility was the reconciliation between the two—an act performed, most prominently, at Odwira, which I take up below. This was done, Meyerowitz argued, "to maintain union with the dead and to keep the departed kings interested in their people so that they . . . may act as the supreme life-givers of the state."[75]

The felt need for a mechanism for turning strangers into neighbors, so fundamental to Ghanaian Christian history, predates the arrival of missionaries. For many years, the various Akan political-military-religious states accomplished that task by means of a system for appointing leaders, designated as occupants of various "stools" at local and regional levels without (much) respect for the clan memberships of the stools' occupants. Although the meritocratic quality of the system was never absolute, such that some stools were associated with certain families, the system was very effective at unifying people across all range of social divides. More significantly for present purposes, as something of a bureaucratic institution, the ɔman, then and now, was open for the incorporation of outsiders—typically as slaves whose children could become members.

The system was open in theory, but not always in practice. Once incorporated into clans, slaves often remained in involuntary sexual or patronage relationships with powerful men, and their children often remained poor with limited options for accessing communal farmland. Indeed, this contradiction—that the system was theoretically open for newcomers, but not always in practice—meant that many people fell through the cracks, especially at times, such as wars, in which large numbers of refugees pushed the system to its limits. It was from among these people that the first significant push came for reformulating the European missionaries' religion as a ritual tool for resolving a glaring social injury.

The Akan kings of Akuapem have always struggled to extend their authority, especially to the patrilineal parts of their kingdom, where the kings' chief claim to legitimacy—their ritual tendance to the (matrilineal) ancestors—is met with a shrug. For nearly a century after the formation of the kingdom, Akropong's legitimacy was tenuous at best and relied on shrewd politics and force of personality. The turning point at which the kings were able to win that argument—to turn aspiration into reality—came with the 1826 battle of Katamanso, at which the Akuapem army under King Addo Dankwa (together with several coastal communities and English and Danish forces from the Accra area), defeated the far greater Asante forces. Far more than serving as a fond

[75] Meyerowitz, *The Sacred State*, 62.

memory of glories past, that battle had an outsized religious outcome: When the Asante were defeated, Addo Dankwa's booty included the *Odwira Apa-fram*, that is, the Asante stool paraphernalia connected with the Odwira festival.[76] These materials were of supreme ritual significance to Asante, and its loss was a greater moral blow than the battle itself. Akuapem enjoyed supernatural assistance on the battlefield: in 1835, one priest told Andreas Riis that the Odwira had abandoned the Asante.[77] Either way, Addo Dankwa immediately understood what he had won. Together with his leading men, he set about instituting an Odwira ritual cycle in Akuapem.

### Odwira

Odwira was the annual node at which intercourse between the living and the dead was transacted and renewed, and communal ruptures healed.[78] It was the ornate and spectacular manifestation of Akuapem power and belief; it is thus the only way to approach the question of the indigenous evaluation of Christianity—Odwira encapsulated the criteria against which the men and women of Akuapem would seek to incorporate their foreigners. The heart of Akuapem's Odwira festival is (and always has been) the renewing of interpersonal bonds—both between the living and the dead—with the royal stool at the center of focus. Extending over several days, along with weeks of preparatory activities, it is the calendrical climax to the ritual year, adroitly combining elaborate royal protocol, the renewal of family ties, and harvest celebration. The word *odwira* speaks of *dwira*, or purification.[79] Used as the name for a ritual cycle centered on social ties, the word expresses a vision of purity centered on healthy relationships. Relational offenses (above all against the ancestors) are atoned for—with a mixture of libations, sacrificial blood, and prayers articulated with drums, dance, and words—in the explicit understanding that well-being in the world is inextricable from social harmony, and that social disharmony is impurity.

As a living festival, Odwira is subject to innovation, as some elements come and go. For example, ceremonial gunfire has recently been sidelined after an accidental death in the palace early in this century.[80] Historical reconstruction of the festival in the early and mid-nineteenth century is thus a delicate task: it is not clear that today's festival looks and feels the same, especially in light

---

[76] Kwamena-Poh, *Government and Politics*, 140.
[77] Riis, "Einige Mittheilungen," 559.
[78] Gilbert, "The Cracked Pot," 213–29.
[79] McCaskie, *State and Society*, 144.
[80] Interview, Ernest Nyarko, Akropong-Akuapem, October 23, 2015.

of so much change. Multiple political regimes have come and gone, several wars have swept over the kingdom, and the majority of Akuapem's population has eventually joined one or the other Christian congregation. More recently, Accra's suburban sprawl has begun to encroach upon the state, with mansions dotting the hillsides. In the following, I describe the general contours of the festival, relying on a mixture of secondary sources. These, in turn, often rely on foreign—that is, European—sources, but authors have needed to check European accounts carefully against oral traditions and other sources, because the former often did not understand what was going on. It is a complex cycle, each day having its dedicated ritual focus. The following summary derives from Kwamena-Poh and McCaskie's historical reconstructions (the former on Akuapem after 1826 and the latter on the Asante kingdom before then, but far more detailed, running to nearly one hundred pages).[81]

The period of preparation began forty days earlier. During those weeks drumming was interdicted, no funerals, weddings, or other social gatherings were to be held, and no new-season yam crops are to be eaten. In Asante, halfway through this period of preparation, the king would visit the royal mausoleum and sacrifice a sheep—a symbol of peace, innocence, and spiritual coolness (*dwo*, "a metaphysical and physical property of the space of culture; implying harmony, peace, order, and protection").[82] The King was in seclusion during most of this time. In 1839, Basel missionary Andreas Riis traveled to Kumasi during this period and was denied an audience.[83]

During the days immediately preceding the height of the cycle, the king ventured out again throughout his royal city, enforcing ritual compliance and ensuring that annually prescribed beautification projects were being done according to schedule. On the principal day, the king and his entourage took the royal stool and the skulls of fallen foes to a spring in a sacred grove for ritual cleaning. The precise moment seems to have shifted, perhaps when the talisman moved from Asante to Akuapem: whereas in Asante it took place on a Sunday, the nineteenth day of the cycle (called *Odwira Nwonakwasie*), it took place on September 24—a Thursday—in Akuapem in 1835.[84] Riis attended this ritual that day, but was required to remain behind a curtain at the spring itself (but said that his inquisitive interpreter slipped around the curtain to watch).

---

[81] Kwamena-Poh, *Government and Politics*, 149–50; McCaskie, *State and Society*, 144–242.

[82] McCaskie, *State and Society*, 160.

[83] Andreas Riis, "Die Reise des Missionars in Akropong nach dem Aschantee-Lande im Winter 1839–40," *EMM* 1840, 174–236 (216–35).

[84] On Asante: McCaskie, *State and Society*, 212; on Akuapem: Riis, "Einige Mittheilungen," 561.

This was a spiritually liminal moment—approximating what Walter Benjamin called the state of exception. It constituted the renewal of the state, with all the risk for violence and chaos entailed when the dead are summoned. In precolonial Asante, the moment was characterized by "transgressions, pollutions and orgiastic inversions . . . enacted as representational and highly dramatic antitheses, out of which were created the transcendental theses of purity and wholeness."[85]

The king then returned to the palace, where he was presented with the Odwira talisman itself, which would aid in the ritual that would follow. After weeks of diplomatic, military, and cultic preparation, after various rituals of purification and incantation of ancestors and spirits, everything was to be put to the test when the ancestors were fed by the hand of the king himself, their living representative, courtesy of food being placed in front of their stools in the royal mausoleum.[86] This ritual lay at the very heart of the legitimacy of the king. Kinship, including royal descent, was "embedded in the structure of matriliny, but political power was articulated as male." This tension was very important and has generated much confusion. The "fundamental social structuration," McCaskie says, was anchored in matriliny, and the male occupancy of the stool needed to be reconciled to that structure.[87] This was done, Meyerowitz said, "to maintain union with the dead and to keep the departed kings interested in their people so that they . . . may act as the supreme life-givers of the state."[88] Having performed libations and fed the ancestors, the king renewed the oaths of his office—and the state was renewed.

At this point, and not a moment before, the state of exception was concluded and festivities could begin—both Kumasi in Asante and Akropong in Akuapem transitioned into riotous eating, drinking, and celebration, accompanied by gift-giving. Riis wrote that he had received enough firewood, yam, and meat to last for several weeks.[89] This part of the cycle typically overwhelmed European observers, including Riis, who saw chaos where the locals saw the performance of the state's capacity to provide for and protect its subjects. "One cannot describe the strange and shifting feelings which impose themselves under such a press of crowds and exhausting visitations."[90] What Riis was experiencing was partly the point. The intensity

---

[85] McCaskie, *State and Society*, 212.
[86] Meyerowitz, *The Sacred State*, 62.
[87] McCaskie, *State and Society*, 166–67.
[88] Meyerowitz, *The Sacred State*, 62.
[89] Riis, "Einige Mittheilungen," 560–61.
[90] Riis, "Einige Mittheilungen," 562.

of the crowds, the sheer noise of the music-making, the drumming and dancing, the gunfire, the loud socializing, the smells of food and humanity, and—for a foreigner, as an object of curiosity who was recognized as being under the king's protection—the constant need to respond to strangers wishing to touch him, amounted to a cumulative articulation of the crown's capacity to secure ancestral blessings for his subjects. McCaskie has called the moment a *Gesamtkunstwerk*: a "participatory and communal catharsis on terms defined and orchestrated by the state."[91]

> The very calculated heightening of emotional involvement, and the incremental and systematic overloading of the sensory responses of all the Asante participants, were intentional or directed strategies that were integral to the performative enactment of the day's events.[92]

Odwira was thus far more than a mere harvest festival. It was the linchpin, the intersection at which the political and the religious overlapped in totality. As a ritual cycle imported to Akuapem from Asante with the capture of the talisman, it may well have saved the Akuapem state—ever prone to fragmentation, and especially at times of war and mass migration—from disintegration. The Odwira cycle was not so much celebrated as (to use McCaskie's term) *transacted*.[93] That is, it made intergenerational continuity possible, even during the bitter years of transatlantic slavery and the nearly untrammeled warfare that followed abolition. Odwira preserved and renewed relationships within and between clans and cemented and reenacted the king's supreme responsibility as protector and sustainer of his people.

It never ended, or diminished in importance, even after the majority of the population became Christians. Indeed, to a very real extent, it long surpassed, as spiritual source, whatever the Christian missionaries might have had on offer. It is for that reason that most of the early adapters, the people who did the most to give shape to an emergent indigenous Christianity, came from the ranks of the socially marginalized—the slaves, the ritually impure, and the refugees, who had no access to ancestral protection. In any case, Odwira constituted a perennial point of tension between the missionaries and the local Christians. "While it may be true," Afriyie notes, "that Christians were never categorically told not to participate in traditional

---

91 McCaskie, *State and Society*, 204.
92 McCaskie, *State and Society*, 204.
93 McCaskie, *State and Society*, 158.

observances, the nature of the teaching led people to the conclusion that they were not to participate in them."[94]

SANCTUARY SHRINES

There were always those who fell through the cracks. At the height of the slave trade, Akuapem's king was unable to prevent a multinational cast of foreign raiders and bandits from roaming the hills (Kwamena-Poh called them "guerillas"[95]). In 1747, for example, a Danish attempt at compensating the chieftain of Larteh for the murder of his brother at the hands of a Danish merchant was complicated by a Dutch raid on the same town. "The same negroes were robbed," the Secret Council recorded on August 11, "of most of their women and children."[96] Too many displaced peoples were seeking refuge, and too many irregular gangs were roaming the hills. As the existing social infrastructure reached its breaking point, an alternative solution arose: the shrine sanctuary.

Although these institutions were not unknown in the Twi-speaking countries, the system was mainly an import from the patrilineal peoples to the east, whence many of the refugees had come.[97] Sandra Barnes describes a slave sanctuary at Krachi, where the Volta slices through the range, which centered on the Dente shrine. This sanctuary managed to retain a measure of autonomy despite two centuries under the nominal suzerainty of Asante.[98] Krachi's political freedom was partly a function of geography—it was something of a frontier outpost at the periphery of a centralized state—but not entirely. The priests of Dente had earned a reputation of fortune telling, and the Asantehene's messengers sought guidance from them during the 1873–1874 war with Britain.[99]

[94] Ernestina Afriyie, "The Theology of the Okuapehene's Odwira: an Illustration of the Engagement of the Gospel among the Akan of Akropong-Akuapem" (PhD thesis, Akrofi-Christaller Institute, Akropong, Ghana, 2010), 9.

[95] Kwamena-Poh, *Government and Politics*, 81–82.

[96] V.-g.K.; 883 (Sekretprotokoller fra Christiansborg), in Justesen, *Danish Sources*, vol. 2, 701.

[97] James Sweet describes this system, as it operated in 18th-century Dahomey: James H. Sweet, *Domingos Álvares, African Healing, and the Intellectual History of the Atlantic World* (Chapel Hill: University of North Carolina Press, 2011), 25–26.

[98] Sandra Barnes, "Shrine Sanctuary and Mission Sanctuary in West Africa," in *Christianity and Social Change in Africa: Essays in Honor of J. D. Y. Peel*, ed. Toyin Falola (Durham, N.C.: Carolina Academic Press, 2005), 165–83.

[99] Donna Maier Weaver, "Kete-Krachi in the Nineteenth Century: Religious and Commercial Center of the Eastern Asante Borderlands" (PhD diss., Northwestern University, 1975), 56 (citing John Glover to Colonial Office, "Intelligence," dd. 2 Oct. 1873, Encl. 6 in No. 156, Further Correspondence, 1874, C. 892.)

Most sanctuaries had a very tenuous existence anchored in shared belief. Their legitimating force, Barnes observed, "was derived from and inextricably tied to supernaturally imbued power—power that was widely seen as inviable."[100] Which is to say: the shrine priests could guarantee protection to the extent that they convinced neighboring kings to respect their power to punish.

Precisely because this power originated in religious belief, the sanctuaries could, and did, become vulnerable in situations of religious change, as when Muslims migrating to and through Krachi in the 1870s simply disregarded the Dente cult.[101] However, expectations could change: what mattered was the ability of the host to guarantee protection. It did not matter whether that patron was a shrine priest or a missionary. All that mattered was that it worked.

There was at least one sanctuary shrine on the top of the Akuapem range: at Tutu near Aburi, about a four-hour hike from Akropong. Danish official Paul Isert (himself a German) visited the shrine in 1786, observing that the priest had amassed a considerable following of runaway slaves.[102] The shrine sanctuary was a place of rescue—a refuge of last resort for endangered people—and thus occupied a somewhat irregular status within Akuapem society. I will return to this theme later, when I will argue that as locals interacted with Basel missionaries in mid-nineteenth-century Akuapem and Akyem Abuakwa, and identified the missionaries as priests, they were in effect imposing upon them the existing category of sanctuary priests. This innovation will constitute the point at which Christianity began to become an indigenous religion.

### Conclusion: The Possibility and Impossibility of Christianity in Ghana

One of the emotional highpoints of today's Odwira week is a procession along the main road from Akropong's main square to the royal mausoleum, a few hundred meters away. Each leading clan participates in this "feeding of the ancestors," carrying food offerings (usually the first yams of the new season) to be laid before ancestral shrines located inside the closed mausoleum compound. As the food is being prepared and placed in containers to be carried into the street, a member of the family—male or female, but mostly female—will become possessed by an ancestral spirit. Accompanied by a retinue of the family, that person will carry the offering to the mausoleum. Along the way, the ancestor will speak out against moral blots in the family

---

[100] Barnes, "Shrine Sanctuary and Mission Sanctuary," 178.
[101] Barnes, "Shrine Sanctuary and Mission Sanctuary," 178.
[102] Paul Erdmann Isert, *Reise nach Guinea und den caribäischen Inseln in Columbien, in Briefen an seine Freunde Beschrieben* (Copenhagen: J. F. Morthorst, 1788), 277.

that would give the deceased occasion to reject the offering. These offenses include conflict between people, youthful disrespect of the elderly, and so on, and they must immediately be resolved, upon the traumatic threat of public vituperation and worse.

In October 2015, I stood on the side of the road in Akropong with Ernest Nyarko, then a theology student doing work on Akan family ethics. As the various clans passed by, more than one possessed porter stopped in his or her tracks, unable to advance closer to the mausoleum because of conflict within the family. Despite gentle prodding by the retinue, they would resist—a few even turning around and hurrying in the opposite direction, so repulsed was the possessing spirit by the moral circumstances of the family. One member of the retinue, prepared for this eventuality, would bend down on the street, pouring libations from a bottle and beseeching the ancestors to accept the splashed offering as a token of the family's repentance. In the end, all of the offerings were accepted, and the nightmare prospect of angered ancestors averted: conflict and disharmony purged from the clans. Meditating on the prophetic tradition in ancient Israel, Halbertal wrote:

> When the protocol is endowed with causal power, all personal elements are erased from the approach. We can imagine how shattering the prophetic corrective to such an urge was, when the prophets proclaimed that the whole structure of ritual could turn abhorrent to the recipient.[103]

This same logic is involved in ancestral sacrifice. As living members of a real community, tied to one another by maternal blood, ancestors and their supplicants were not going to convert the gift-giving into an anonymous ritual. The interpersonal relationship was what counted. Since one of the goals of ritual is to ensure the acceptance of the gift, in the absence of a high form of ritual, something else must take its place. Typically, that something is violence—sacrificial bloodshed, the sheer force of which compensates for the absence of a guarantee.[104]

This matters historically, because the people of mid-nineteenth-century Akuapem, facing nearly constant waves of warfare, along with the surges of refugees that inevitably followed, felt the need to incorporate newcomers into ancestral clans—but the sheer scale of the crisis was overwhelming the clans. The challenges to the ancestral ritual economy drove hundreds of desperate people to seek sanctuary at one or the other of the shrines in the Gold Coast.

---

[103] Halbertal, *On Sacrifice*, 18.
[104] Halbertal, *On Sacrifice*, 3.

The Basel Mission brought to the Gold Coast a very different religious outlook than that of the state Christianity of the forts. To adequately establish the full force of this encounter, I turn to the religious landscape of Akuapem and the region. When the missionaries came, announcing forgiveness of sin, no one was impressed, and for twelve years not a single person converted. Over time, as the locals heard more of what the missionaries had to say (especially after the latter gained fluency in Twi, and above all, after they had translated the Bible into that language), they singled out elements to the missionaries' message which were of use to indigenous concerns. Jacob Olupona has correctly pointed out the problematic nature of the word *religion* applied to West African devotion and belief.[105] However, this has also always been the case for Christianity anywhere: as a Latin word describing dutiful adherence to Roman gods and political cults, *religion* reflects uneasy tensions and compromises made in an entirely different setting. Christianity entered the Roman world as a repulsive alien practice, characterized in the main, in the eyes of authorities, by adherents' refusal to support the imperial cult.[106] On the other hand, by the eighteenth and nineteenth centuries, the word *religion* could not be articulated in English (or in German) except by reference to Christianity. The word itself had traveled a long distance by the year 1800, altering its meaning over time. In the process, a great diversity of African cultic, medical, political, economic, and liturgical practices and beliefs have been subjected to alien categories. Britain-educated Ugandan poet Okot p'Bitek was not inclined to engage in a defense of African religion along lines marked out by Europeans. Writing in 1970, he said that some African theologians, "burdened by European denigration of indigenous religions, dress up African deities with Hellenic robes and parade them before the western world to show that Africans were as civilized as Europeans."[107] Nevertheless, there was some value to a comparison of the gods, especially in the West African setting, because indigenous peoples in the region, including in the Gold Coast, did not simply choose to "step over" (to translate the Basel Mission's term for conversion, *übertreten*) from one static religion to

---

[105] Olupona, *African Religions*, 1.

[106] The missionary Paul was the focus of a riot in Ephesus when the silversmiths of that city, whose livelihood was at risk, accused him of denigrating their gods: Acts 19. It might further be noted that Olupona has recently used the word "World Religion" to describe contemporary Orișa worship in the diaspora: Jacob K. Olupona and Terry Rey, eds., *Òrìṣà Devotion as World Religion: The Globalization of Yorùbá Religious Culture* (Madison: University of Wisconsin Press, 2008).

[107] Okot p'Bitek, *African Religions in Western Scholarship* (Kampala: East African Literature Bureau, 1970), 88.

another. Rather, they actively plumbed Christianity for answers to immediately pressing needs, and often imported Christian notions back into their non-Christian practices. Peel argued that Yoruba Christianity, Islam, and Oriṣa religion were all created in conversation, and not always according to missionary control.[108] At the same time that the Basel missionaries came to identify *Onyankopɔn* (an alternate form of Onyame, emphasizing creation) with *Yahweh*, they also categorized Onyankopɔn's children Tano and Asase (water and earth, respectively) as idols. During the same years, indigenous Christians had begun making their own comparisons, designating the missionaries as shrine priests (*asɔfoɔ*, sing. *ɔsɔfoɔ*), and imposing corresponding demands on them.[109]

Locals of Akuapem initially tried to absorb the Christian God into this pluralistic paradigm. In 1866, for instance, David Asante (then pastoring the Guan congregation at Larteh) wrote that "many people cling to faith in amulets," and gave an example of a young couple who tied several to their baby for protection.[110] Eventually the husband cut them off, but Asante was clear that the act was one of faith, despite fear. "People are slowly coming to recognize," Asante continued, "that Christianity is not as bad as they feared."

> A priestess in Akropong has recently said: "The word of God is not at all as bad as some people think: it is the best means for the rearing and disciplining of the youth. Now—as long as they continue to present offerings at the festival, everything will be fine."[111]

If by 1866, Christianity was not as bad as people had feared, this was because, after thirty years of hard cross-cultural work, the locals had reached a point of understanding. They had gradually identified preexisting social and religious categories in which the missionaries might be assigned a sensible place, and, more importantly, had found ways to put the missionaries and their message to work toward nagging social and spiritual problems. The waves of conversion in the decade following 1866 must thus be understood as an artifact of African intellectual history. The missionaries, on their part, had learned the language; that alone set them apart from the Europeans who had been on the coast for centuries.

---

[108] Peel, *Christianity, Islam, and* Oriṣa *Religion*, esp. 150–71.

[109] More on this in chapter 5. Ulrike Sill, *Encounters in Quest of Christian Womanhood: The Basel Mission in Pre- and Early Colonial Ghana* (Boston: Brill, 2010), 198, citing BMA, D-1,2 Akropong 1844, Hermann Halleur 07.06.1844.

[110] David Asante, "Von der Außengemeinde Date," *HB* 1866, 99.

[111] David Asante, "Von der Außengemeinde Date," *HB* 1866, 98.

In the following chapter, I turn to the preexisting religion of the coastal forts. European Christians had been present along the coast for over three hundred fifty years by the time the first Basel missionaries appeared. That is to say: even today, in the third decade of the twenty-first century, as West Africa is developing into one of the centers of world Christianity, more than half of Christianity's history in Ghana has been as an ethnically syncretized, slave-trading religion. If most Ghanaians would ultimately become Christians, many would do so in an understanding of the irony and contradictions entailed by history.

# 3

# Three Hundred Years of Irrelevance

Christianity did not arrive in the Gold Coast with missionaries. In one form or another, the religion had been present in the broader region for nearly three and a half centuries before the first Basel missionaries appeared.[1] Throughout most of that time, a few important exceptions notwithstanding, Christianity remained nearly exclusively the religion of European merchants and their staff. Over time, and owing largely to European men's liaisons with local women, a small community of African Christians developed in the immediate neighborhoods of various European outposts. For people living in close proximity to some of the most dangerous nodes of the transatlantic slave trade, baptism and possession of a Christian name functioned as protection from enslavement. There was little else to commend the religion. With abolition came a gradual end to the threat (still present, albeit at a lower level, in the 1830s), and with it the practical usefulness of conversion.

For three centuries, most people of the southeast Gold Coast who were aware of Christianity felt no need for it. Some had moral or intellectual objections to Christianity, but the more common response was ambivalence: Christianity was irrelevant at best, and often malign. The sheer scale of time is worth bearing in mind: Christianity is both a young religion and an old one in Ghana. The focus of this chapter is the latter: although most histories of West African Christianity gloss over three or four centuries in a few sentences, consistent indigenous aversion to Christianity from the fifteenth to the nineteenth centuries merits some discussion. Why did so many Ghanaians find Christianity irrelevant for so long? I approach the question in the present chapter in a few ways.

---

[1] David Owusu-Ansah, *Historical Dictionary of Ghana* (Lanham, Md.: Scarecrow, 2005), 115.

After some preliminary words of comparison with Islam, which had also had its representatives in the southeastern Gold Coast, I turn to the religious history of the European trading companies. An important change took place two hundred years after the arrival of the first Portuguese ships: the mid-seventeenth-century transfer of Portuguese possessions to various trading companies representing Protestant kingdoms in northwestern Europe. I discuss these by means of a case study of the Dutch fort in Elmina. While important religious differences obtained between the Lutheran Danes, the Anglican British, and the Reformed Dutch, who all had forts located within an hour's walk from another around a broad cove in what is now Accra, the finer points of religious contrast do not appear to have impressed indigenous observers who were nevertheless well aware of political differences among their guests.

I will conclude with some remarks on the threat Christianity presented to indigenous social integrity. If the majority of Ghanaians would eventually become Christians, they did so after having made a measure of peace with the existing order, and not before. To an indigenous system that tended to prioritize social harmony, Christian reluctance to participate in socially-renewing rituals—such as Odwira—was emblematic of the antisocial nature of the European religion. To return to the priestess's comment with which I concluded the previous chapter: as long as Christians were prepared to continue to present offerings to the ancestors, everything could be tolerated. Aye-Addo has put it more broadly: "one of the greatest contributions that African cultures can bring into the Christian faith is the profound understanding of community. . . . The church is not only a sociological grouping but is also the body of Christ."[2]

For much of the last half millennium, Christianity was generally irrelevant to the lives of most Ghanaians and was not infrequently the cause of offense. Although Andreas Riis was the first European to build a house in Akropong, he was not the first to pass through the town. Other Europeans and Euro-Africans—so-called mulattos—had preceded him, by at least a half century, usually as Danish envoys or merchants. The road to the coast, which ran the length of the ridge, was wide and well-maintained in the 1830s, and contacts with the coast were increasing. In an 1837 report, Danish officer Wulff mentioned in particular the trade in palm oil, which was growing despite the "Duke" [Hertug] of Akuapem's interferences.[3] Riis' arrival in January 1835

---

[2]  Charles Sarpong Aye-Addo, *Akan Christology: An Analysis of the Christologies of John Samuel Pobee and Kwame Bediako in Conversation with the Theology of Karl Barth* (Eugene, Ore.: Pickwick, 2013), 173.

[3]  Wulff Joseph Wulff, *Breve og Dagbogsoptegnelser fra Guldkysten, 1836–1842*, ed. Carl Behrens (København: Nyt Nordisk Forlag, 1917), 128–46.

cannot be understood apart from the growth of global commerce, whatever romantic notions the missionary himself might have entertained.

Kwamena-Poh has related an oral tradition to the effect that Addo Dankwa told Andreas Riis that Christianity was the white man's religion and asked him to produce a black Christian.[4] This tradition is dubious as historical artifact, but nevertheless remains in broad circulation, with varied wordings; it has been told to the present author at multiple occasions. Nkansa-Kyeremateng put Addo Dankwa's instructions thus:

> When God created the world, he made the book for the white man and juju for the black man, but if you could show us some black man who could read the white man's book, then we would surely follow you.[5]

Some variation of this conversation may well have taken place, because there was certainly precedent: the Danes at Fort Christiansborg in Osu directed their religious work exclusively toward themselves and to the Afro-Danish (also called mulatto) community, the legacy of two centuries of Danish presence on the coast. There was little reason for Addo Dankwa to seriously contemplate Christianity as relevant toward his concerns.

Nevertheless, Addo Dankwa, whose personal cook had spent years in Denmark, and who was not a Christian, knew enough about Danish religion to doubt its capacity to be translated and applied to his kingdom's context and needs. He was not the only person to reach this conclusion. Not only Africans, but many Europeans also felt that Christianity was inappropriate for Africa. They arrived at this conclusion for many different reasons, including home-grown European ones—theological and political—which have nothing to do with Africa.

The basic irony is that while Africa, including Ghana, is emerging as a center in global Christianity, most of this change has come in the last hundred years—especially since independence. However, Christianity has had a concrete presence in Ghana for well over five centuries. During that lengthy history, several opportunities arose at which an African Christianity might have evolved or taken root, as it did elsewhere in the Iberian world (on either side of the Atlantic, not to mention analogous creations in the Iberian Indies, the Philippines, in Mesoamerica and elsewhere).[6] Yet while the Portuguese

---

[4]  M. A. Kwamena-Poh, *Government and Politics in the Akuapem State, 1730–1850*, Legon History Series (Evanston, Ill.: Northwestern University Press, 1973), 115, n. 2.

[5]  K. Nkansa-Kyeremateng, *History, Mission & Achievements: Presbyterian Church, Ghana* (Accra: Sebewie, 1996), 12.

[6]  Pablo Gómez, *The Experiential Caribbean: Creating Knowledge and Healing in the Early Modern Atlantic* (Chapel Hill: University of North Carolina Press, 2017).

language lived on in some coastal communities for centuries after the Portuguese themselves had been supplanted by other European rivals, the Catholic church did not.[7]

When the Dutch emerged as the leading European power in the Gold Coast, growing numbers of Africans traveled to the Netherlands or elsewhere in the Dutch world, beyond the dead end of enslavement. Some of these people were baptized, and a few would ultimately return to their homes, where they made nearly no impact toward the development of an indigenous Ghanaian Christianity. Although two merit mention here, there were many more for whom mere survival was accomplishment enough. As a young child in the year 1707, Amo of Axim (in the far west, near today's Ivorian border) was sent to the Netherlands under unclear circumstances. Baptized as Anton Wilhelm Amo, he would stay in Europe for thirty years, gaining a doctorate and becoming a professor of philosophy in Germany.[8] Suffering a number of career setbacks, probably originating in German racism, he resigned and returned home, where he died in obscurity. Twenty years after Amo's arrival in the Netherlands, he was followed by a young man who would become the first Ghanaian ordained in a Protestant Church. Jacobus Capitein, whose indigenous name is unknown, was missional in outlook and sought ordination in the reformed church in the explicit wish to preach to his countrymen.[9] I discuss Capitein below; Amo's story—perhaps more fascinating because he lived longer—must be shelved for a future time.[10] There were others, including in the Danish Gold Coast, such as Christian Protten, who spent several years in the Moravian community in Saxony. Protten made two attempts at initiating a mission in the Accra region.[11]

Aside from these world-traveling special cases, the more typical converts were African women who had married or entered into marriage-like relations

[7] M. E. Kropp Dakubu, "The Portuguese Language on the Gold Coast, 1471–1807," *Ghana Journal of Linguistics* 1, no. 1 (2012), 15–33.

[8] William Abraham, "The Life and Times of Anton Wilhelm Amo," *Transactions of the Historical Society of Ghana* 7 (1964), 60–81.

[9] David Nii Anum Kpobi, *Mission in Chains: The Life, Theology, and Ministry of the Ex-Slave Jacobus E.J. Capitein (1717–1747)* (Zoetermeer, Netherlands: Uitgeverij Boekencentrum, 1993); Albert Eekhof, *De Negerpredikant Jacobus Elisa Joannes Capitein, 1717–1747* (The Hague: M. Nijhoff, 1917).

[10] Amo has recently been rediscovered in philosophy for his rebuttal of Descartes' dualistic notion of the mind, but I am aware of no attempts at situating his life and work within world Christianity.

[11] Jon Sensbach, *Rebecca's Revival: Creating Black Christianity in the Atlantic World* (Cambridge, Mass.: Harvard University Press, 2005).

with European men stationed at coastal forts.[12] Many of these women were baptized and sought a Christian education for their children; when the Basel mission first arrived in the early nineteenth century, several members of this community joined the mission churches. A few of the early indigenous clergy of the Basel Mission, such as Carl Christian Reindorf, traced at least some parentage to the Afro-Danish community.

By the time that Capitein embarked on his short-lived evangelistic project in the 1740s, the Christian religion had sunk deep roots in other parts of the African Atlantic, including in Angola and Brazil. Why did so little growth take place despite so much intimate contact? It is hard to shake the conclusion that the slave trade must figure as a key part of the answer, because the trade brought so little of value to the existing societies. In contrast to Islam, which was also a slave-trading religion, Christians did not enter into sustained relationships with locals, did not contribute to local knowledge, and did not offer much of value beyond trade. To return to Addo Dankwa's charge to Andreas Riis: although the king was not opposed to Christianity in itself, he found it irrelevant.

Viewed over the long run, the basic pattern to Christian history in Ghana is that of punctuated equilibrium: periods of rapid growth separated by long years of stasis or slow growth. Most of this book focuses on one such period of growth—a few decades in the late precolonial period—which would be followed by another period, during the early colonial years, of incremental growth, infighting, and stagnation. What has happened since independence is of another category altogether: a change so great as to defy simplistic historical categorization. Those years are beyond the scope of this study, but the question remains: why did the Christian breakthrough of the 1860s and 1870s come after so many lifetimes of Christian presence in the Gold Coast?

Throughout the Atlantic period, at least two supra-regional religions were available to people of the southeastern Gold Coast—Islam and Christianity. Each had considerable potential, both as religions of spiritual power and as trade religions, participation in which made transnational and cross-cultural commerce easier. Both, in their own ways, were partially adaptable to local conditions and responsive to local demands. I briefly consider the former before moving to the latter. My ultimate argument will be that during the middle of the nineteenth century, when the people of Akuapem began to take control of Christianity, neither religion was much of an asset to the kingdom, and neither had much to offer toward resolving the kingdom's enduring problems.

---

[12] Pernille Ipsen, *Daughters of the Trade: Atlantic Slavers and Interracial Marriage on the Gold Coast* (Philadelphia: University of Pennsylvania Press, 2015).

## Islam

Islam, then and now in southern Ghana, was oriented toward the north—to the ancient empires of the Sudan—and to the global trade and pilgrimage networks beyond. Early in the colonial period, British officials in the Gold Coast recognized ancient and sustained connections with the Muslim interior, which they credited with the development and distribution of amulets and charms among all ranks of Akan men and women.[13] This was not an original idea. As early as the first decade of the eighteenth century, the Danish chaplain at Christiansborg speculated that the Accra custom of male circumcision had Muslim origins.[14]

Medieval and early modern Muslim history in West Africa represents a growing field of research and is beyond the scope of the present study, but two key themes in recent scholarship merit mention.[15] The first of these is the dismissal as Eurocentric of an earlier question, which preoccupied generations of missionaries and colonial agents: exactly how committed were West African Muslims to their faith? This was a question that many missionaries asked both before and after the colonial period. Over time, British and French colonial officials alike came to recognize the depth of Islam's roots in the region, although few missionaries were convinced until the twentieth century.[16] Usually unstated in the question, and the reason it was only asked by Europeans, was an assumption that Africans were children and therefore incapable of the kind of thoughtful, literate devotion that Europeans from the eighteenth century to the present have been willing to concede in West Asian Islam.

More recently, scholars of precolonial West Africa have taken pains to situate the regional story of Islam within the context of world history. This approach shows a good deal of promise toward undermining an enduring European conceit that West Africa had been isolated from the world before European arrival. Thus, Lovejoy's placement of Usman Dan Fodio's early-nineteenth-century rebellion in northern Nigeria within the broader framework of the age of revolution is valuable as global history, although Lovejoy's approach

[13] Alfred Burdon Ellis, *The Tshi-Speaking Peoples of the Gold Coast of West Africa: Their Religion, Manners, Customs, Laws, Languages, Etc.* (London: Chapman and Hall, 1887), 200.

[14] Johannes Rask, *A Brief and Truthful Description of a Journey to and from Guinea*, in *Two Views from Christiansborg Castle*, trans. and ed. Selena Axelrod Winsnes (Accra: Sub-Saharan Publishers, 2009), 134.

[15] A recent overview of the field may be found in François-Xavier Fauvelle-Aymar, *The Golden Rhinoceros: Histories of the African Middle Ages* (Princeton: Princeton University Press, 2018).

[16] Andrew E. Barnes, "The Cross versus the Crescent: Karl Kumm's Missiology," *Islam and Christian–Muslim Relations* 30, no. 4 (2019), 483–503.

cannot be uniformly applied to local situations such as Akuapem's.[17] At the same time, however, Islam must always be treated as a world religion, and not merely as a political position. At least by the early 1920s and likely beginning much earlier, the city Mecca was given the name *Nyame-fre-bere*, or the "place where God is called," and Akan people gave gifts to Muslim pilgrims to request prayers on their behalf.[18] Perhaps not all men and women converting to Islam in early-nineteenth-century Ghana were sincere in their beliefs, but many were, and to subordinate these people's conversions to calculating cynicism is no more convincing than when Europeans have dismissed Christian conversion as inauthentic: only God knows the convert's heart.

The second theme in recent scholarship on precolonial Islam in southern Ghana is that of wealth and power. According to this line of thought, West Africans, both Muslim and non-Muslim, have worked out mutually advantageous, although never fully resolved, ways of living with one another.[19] Muslims could offer valuable services to non-Muslim kings, ranging from the economic (trade negotiations, bookkeeping, calendar production) to the protective (above all in the production of amulets of power).[20] Muslims also understood and accepted that Islam would be confined to a "narrowly constrained spectrum of sanctioned practices" that fit within the preexisting bounds of state control.[21] In practice this meant no (or very limited) proselytizing. In turn, they would be accorded a measure of royal tolerance, ranging from residence permission to authorization to trade. As early as the eighteenth century, the Asante, ever sensitive to the "fragility of their achievement," took pains to quarantine Muslim political influence.[22] By the early twentieth century throughout Ghana, Muslim residences would evolve into segregated residential quarters called *zongos*, but there were too few Muslims in Akuapem to warrant such an arrangement, especially in the early nineteenth century.[23]

---

[17] Paul Lovejoy, *Jihād in West Africa During the Age of Revolutions* (Athens: Ohio University Press, 2016).

[18] R. S. Rattray, *Ashanti* (Oxford: Clarendon, 1923), 179, 227.

[19] Lamin Sanneh, *The Crown and the Turban: Muslims and West African Pluralism* (Boulder, Colo.: Westview, 1996).

[20] David Owusu-Ansah, *Islamic Talismanic Tradition in Nineteenth-Century Asante* (Lewiston, N.Y.: Edwin Mellen, 1991).

[21] T. C. McCaskie, *State and Society in Precolonial Asante*, African Studies Series (Cambridge: Cambridge University Press, 1995), 136.

[22] J. D. Y. Peel, *Christianity, Islam, and Orişa Religion: Three Traditions in Comparison and Interaction* (Berkeley: University of California Press, 2016), 35–36.

[23] Holger Weiss, *Between Accommodation and Revivalism: Muslims, the State, and Society in Ghana from the Precolonial to the Postcolonial Era*, Studia Orientalia 105 (Helsinki, Finnish Oriental Society, 2008), 248–49.

The Muslim presence in Akuapem during the period of this study was largely limited to small numbers of employees at various municipal courts—men of letters whose value was inversely proportional to European commercial power along the coast. To the extent that they offered their chiefs access to the ancient imperial and commercial world of the Sudan, Sahel and beyond, they were relics of an earlier age.

Finally, there were also Muslim slaves throughout the region. In 1835, Riis met one such "Dunkuneger," an interesting neologism probably combining the Twi word *donkor* (slave) with the Portuguese word *negro*. Riis, who was fairly new in the Gold Coast and was dependent on the services of an interpreter, probably misunderstood the man's social rank as an ethnic identity. This man was a laborer on a Danish plantation, and told Riis that he was a "Moor" who in his childhood had learned to read, write, and pray to Allah. Asked about the latter, the man told Riis that he prayed twice daily that God would someday allow him to return to his family.[24]

## CHRISTIANITY

Early Christian history in Ghana presents a striking contrast with that of Islam. While both religions offered connections with the broader world, complete with scripts and accounting, and adherents of both religions were ambivalent in their relationships to indigenous shrines, Muslims usually arrived in small groups (as opposed to ships) and needed to learn to speak local languages. By contrast, and with very few exceptions, locals understood Christianity as a set of rival European ethnic religions—the people of the Gold Coast being fully aware of the national distinctives between the various Europeans at the coast—with specifically national purposes. Christianity was above all the religion of the trading forts and slave castles. Its purpose was to serve the spiritual lives of the European residents, and especially to regulate the behavior of the European soldiers stationed within. While both Islam and Christianity were trade religions, in which common faith and practice potentially established the kind of trust needed to seal and lubricate trade beyond local networks, neither religion made many inroads in southern Ghana before the nineteenth century. Christianity was even less relevant: beyond the immediate neighborhoods of the European forts it was little more than a curiosity, recognized as the religion of the Europeans.

At present, there is little reason to believe that Ghanaian Christianity predates European arrival. Although it is possible that some African Christians

---

[24] Andreas Riis, "Goldküste in Westafrika," *HB* 1835, 62.

had previously passed through, traveling along the trade routes of the Sudan, or having crossed the Sahara, for all practical purposes, Christianity arrived in the Gold Coast five centuries ago with Europeans—primarily Portuguese merchants. Elsewhere in sub-Saharan Africa, Portuguese Catholicism sank deep roots. In Angola, the royal house of Kongo adopted Catholicism as something of a state church, complete with Kongolese language materials and the oldest cathedral south of the equator.[25] This was not the case in the Gold Coast. Precolonial Catholicism, largely represented by the Portuguese, had little enduring impact on the southeast Gold Coast, especially in the Accra region, where Danish, Dutch, and English Protestants had established themselves beginning in the mid-seventeenth century. In short, Catholicism did not factor in precolonial Akuapem's history.

Although Protestants had been present as merchants in the Gold Coast for centuries by the time the first missionaries traveled to Akuapem, relatively few indigenous people became Christian leaders equipped to express the message in indigenous terms. A few exceptions are worth noting, but not because of any enduring legacy. Rather, these premature efforts testify to the obstacles standing in the way of any African attempt at appropriating and reconfiguring Christianity for indigenous usage.

The first of these was in mid-eighteenth-century Dutch Elmina, when a native man named Jacobus Capitein returned after years in the Netherlands to serve as a missionary.[26] Ordained in the Dutch Reformed church and in possession of a doctorate from the University of Leiden, Capitein died in 1747 after only a few years in ministry and would not be replaced. Although he had viewed his work as evangelistic in nature, and although his translations of portions of Scripture into Fanti are among the oldest remaining expressions of indigenous Christian thought, Capitein was unable to transcend the Dutch foundations to his faith. In the end, and especially because of his short life, his legacy is little more than a curiosity. The other notable exception to the rule of European monopolization of Christianity in early-modern Ghana was Accra-born Christian Protten, a son of a Danish soldier and Gã mother. Protten spent several years in Europe, including at the home of the Moravian Brethren in Saxony, and married Rebecca, a former slave from the Danish West Indies. Over a twenty-year period, Protten made multiple attempts at establishing a

[25] Cécile Fromont, *The Art of Conversion: Christian Visual Culture in the Kingdom of Kongo* (Chapel Hill: University of North Carolina Press, 2014).

[26] David Nii Anum Kpobi, *Saga of a Slave: Jacobus Capitein of Holland and Elmina* (Accra: Sub-Saharan Publishers, 2001).

Christian foundation in the Gã country around Accra and is credited with publishing the first grammar of the Gã language.[27]

Neither Capitein nor Protten nor any other African of the Gold Coast left a Christian legacy that would inform the people of Akuapem during the formative years of their experimentation with Christianity. This basic reality does not mean that these people accomplished nothing. Rather, their struggles to transcend the European monopoly on the Christian religion during these years at the height of the transatlantic slave trade attest to the difficulty of their project. From the seventeenth to the nineteenth centuries, the predominant expression of European agency in the Gold Coast was trade—above all the slave trade. Any African understanding of, and experimentation with, Christianity during those years was unlikely to be anything more than an alternative expression. While a few Protestants took interest in the religious lives of their hosts and neighbors, there was nearly no meaningful indigenous Christian population in the region until the middle of the eighteenth century. Even then, Protestant activities were largely restricted to the neighborhoods immediately adjacent to European forts and settlements and were developed in response to the emergence of a mixed—so-called *mulatto*—population of the offspring of local Gã women and European employees of the forts. Church services open to locals were held in the forts.

In the Danish Fort Christiansborg at Osu, which would pass to the British in the 1850s, children learned to read and write in a schoolroom that doubled as a chapel (located two stories above the slave dungeon). Liturgical and sacramental services and elementary education were the entirety of the official program, and whatever Christian ideas and experiments the locals wished to develop were beyond the fort's concern or interest. When the Danish governor allowed the first Basel missionaries to come to Christiansborg, he was aware that these Pietist enthusiasts desired to evangelize among the locals—as, indeed, other Germans had done a century earlier in another Danish trading post near Madras in India.[28] Managers of the fort were ambivalent: they neither endorsed the missionary project, nor forbade it outright. Rather, they tolerated Basel Mission activities in exchange for the same educational services to the soldiers and mulattos. The overarching concern was stability for Danish

---

[27] Noel Smith, "Protten, Christian (B)," in *Dictionary of African Christian Biography*, https://dacb.org/stories/ghana/protten-cj/, accessed October 25, 2019.

[28] In 1859, Albert Ostertag clarified that the Basel Mission's standing depended on political favor: one governor treated the missionaries well, the next did not, and the next did again. Ostertag, "Die Goldküste und die Basler Mission Daselbst," *EMM* 1859, 33–40.

trading priorities. Christianity was a trade religion to the extent that it was little more than the ethnic religion of the European traders in the southeast Gold Coast.

## MONKEY GAMES

European visitors in the region mocked indigenous religion from the very beginning—long before they asked any systematic questions about underlying cosmology. In 1602, for example, Pieter de Marees saw a man performing a ritual and asked for the reason behind these "monkey games" [*Apenspel*].[29] It was a simple matter: Africans were *a priori* inferior to Europeans. In the eighteenth century, Ludvig Rømer struggled to learn much about religious praxis on the coast: trust was already broken by his day. Eventually he seems to have gained the confidence of Putti, a priest of the god Lakpa at Labadi (properly called La), a coastal community not far from Accra. "We have to be a long time on the coast," he wrote in 1760, "before a black will give any answer to our questions about his religion."[30] What seems to have been going on was less indigenous priests' desire for mystifying the foreigners than the foreigners' bad attitudes. "Furthermore," Rømer continued, "we must, in fact, have been there for several years without anyone seeing us laugh at their ceremonies" before a local would as much as entertain questions about his religious praxis. Freshly arrived in the hills in 1835, Andreas Riis, the first Basel missionary in Akuapem, did something different: he held his tongue and listened.

> Perhaps many people, hearing these tales, would question them and object, and perhaps justly so. But I said nothing at all and listened. Questions about fetish practices are not going to be answered, and talkback only makes people bitter. I am convinced that only the word of Christ, the died-and-risen, can convince the rebellious human heart.[31]

Riis was no ethnographer representing Africans to a scholarly audience at home. He was there to announce his God. But in an attitude of open listening, he and like-minded others had little trouble learning the underlying logic

---

[29] Pieter de Marees, *Beschryvinghe ende historische Verhael van het Gout Koninckrijck van Gunea anders de Gout-Custe de Mina Genaemt Liggende in het deel van Africa*, ed. S. P. L'Honoré Naber (1602; The Hague: M. Nijhoff, 1912), 76 (orig. 38b).

[30] Ludvig Ferdinand Rømer, *A Reliable Account of the Coast of Guinea (1760)*, trans. Selena Axelrod Winsnes (Oxford: Published for the British Academy by the Oxford University Press, 2000), 79 (orig. 50).

[31] Andreas Riis, "Einige Mittheilungen aus dem Tagebuche des Missionars Andreas Riis," *EMM* 1836, 554 (August 30 journal entry).

to indigenous religiosity. And, as Johannes Zimmermann observed in 1859, it was not devil worship. To say otherwise was rather "the verdict of those who will not listen to the people's innermost life," and was accordingly more a reflection of the fears with which Europeans approached Africans throughout the entire region, and not merely in the Gold Coast.[32] To those who cared to listen, this "innermost life" was articulated less in theological precision than in stories and proverbs, which collectively hinted at a comprehensive ideology. Introducing a translated and annotated collection of proverbs in 1882, Johann Christaller said that "an entire negro-theology might be derived from these proverbs, which would not bear the slightest resemblance to what is commonly called fetishism."[33]

In the late nineteenth century, European explorers and colonial ethnographers, committed to social-evolutionary notions of the savage and primitive, were effectively dressing up, in scientific language for the respectability of academic common sense, the same basic notion of monkey games De Marees had articulated centuries earlier. Even West African intellectual history was held out as evidence of inferiority. In 1879, Johann Christaller had, for example, published the Twi proverbs, untranslated.[34] However, in 1916 Robert Sutherland Rattray, a government anthropologist then stationed in the Ashanti Protectorate, translated Christaller's collection, adding the subtitle of "The Primitive Ethics of a Savage People."[35] It is as if, despite three centuries separating Pieter de Marees and R. S. Rattray, "monkey games" remained the default European approach to Africa.

For this reason, the Basel Mission's (inconsistently) inquisitive attitude to indigenous culture and priorities stands out. At a broader level, Basel missionaries did more listening than their published letters suggest. While the *Heidenbote* and the annual reports focus either on missionaries going places and doing things, like street preaching and building new chapels, or on being sick and dying, the mission's archives contain several unpublished manuscripts on indigenous religions and spiritual ideas.[36] Some of these were com-

---

[32] Zimmermann excerpted in Albert Ostertag, "Die Goldküste und die Basler Mission daselbst," *EMM* 1859, 49.

[33] J. G. Christaller, "Einige Sprichwörter der Tschi-Neger," *EMM* 1882, 316.

[34] J. G. Christaller, *Twi Mmebusem, Mpensā-Ahansīa Mmoaano* (Basel: Evangelisches Missions-Gesellschaft, 1879).

[35] R. S. Rattray, *Ashanti Proverbs (the Primitive Ethics of a Savage People)* (Oxford: Clarendon, 1916).

[36] See, for instance, BMA D-10.4,1, "Entstehungsgeschichten in Akuapem" (Akuapem creation stories); BMA D-10.1,4 Johannes Zimmermann, "Ethnographic Monograph"; BMA D-10.1,6, Miss. Kölle, "Gã Riddles and Proverbs"; BMA D-10.4,8 "African Folk Tales"

piled by the missionaries, and others were school essay assignments, which the teachers seem to have used for data collection. Two of the latter are worth noting. Sometime in the early 1870s, a Christiansborg teacher had his students write essays, in English, with this prompt: "Name and describe the Gods of the Accra people." Ten of the essays were sent to Basel, and all but one of them modified the question from one of ethnicity to one of territory, specifying towns. Nathanael Adsei, for example, wrote about the town of Teshi, Samuel Patrick about Osu, Theodor Flindt about Shai, Samuel Aserifi about Labadi, and so on. Each young man named and described an autochthonous village deity, and none of them indicated that its worship extended beyond definite territorial bounds. Samuel Patrick's answer is characteristic. Speaking of the god Krotey, he said in part:

> The reason why they worship him is that it form their limit in order to protect them from any injure which will come upon them & also suplied them with fishes. When the time to worship him is yet, the people collect some cowries to buy for him (or their idol). This is brought before the high priest so he placed his hands upon it and declare peace to his people. After this the people cry with a loud voice "Take away our sins, and go with it" so the eldest of Osu collect themselves in the house of the priest and they kill the ox his blood was put in a large African plate. (Kā) [sic].[37]

In a separate assignment, the students had to describe the Accra festival of *Homowo*, a yam-harvest festival unrelated to Odwira, of which seven responses were sent home.[38] Some of these essays reveal that the pupils of the mission schools were not always fluent in their religious traditions: several said that they had never visited the shrines. In this regard the missionaries were not always learning from insiders (with the exception of William Azu of Krobo, who had been trained as a priest before being sent to school), but from youthful translators. Writing about late nineteenth-century Equatorial Africa, Johannes Fabian has noted the importance of children employed in the European caravans, working as personal attendants and similar. "Children served as invaluable conduits of information about the often-brutal reality

---

(school essays in Christiansborg, 1875); and several others. A marginal note on the first of these, dated 1937, indicates that the document, of uncertain authorship, but in handwriting not unlike Widmann's, had been originally mailed, not to the Basel Mission, but the Calwer Vereinsbuchhandlung, an unrelated but closely associated printing press, one that would late in the century be incorporated into the Basel Mission, under the retired India missionary Hermann Gundert.

[37] BMA D-10.4,6 "School Essays on the Accra Gods," n/d, 1870s.
[38] BMA D-10.4,7 "School Essays on Homowo," 1875.

travelers faced in carrying out the intrusive work of scientific exploration and at the same time offered a psychological buffer against this reality."[39] The Basel Mission's earliest successes came among children—above all those enrolled in mission schools.

Nevertheless, the early Basel missionaries—those active in the Gold Coast before the 1870s—presented a singular exception to European dismissal and non-comprehension of indigenous religion as foolishness. They took local religions quite seriously, because these religions represented the lens through which locals engaged with the missionaries' message: could the missionaries guarantee protection from disease and from evil? If not, there was little to commend their teachings. Indeed, a close look at the chronology of conversion in Akuapem, taken up in chapters 5 and 6, reveals that locals only began converting in numbers after they had successfully found answers to these needs in the missionaries' message, and begun to impose their own categories upon the foreigners. The Basel Mission's definitive arrival of European missionaries in the 1820s was thus a turning point in Ghanaian religious history.[40]

### Outposts of Christendom

It was not only a function of accident that Christianity in the Gold Coast remained irreducibly European throughout this time and well into the colonial period. Rather, the Christianities arriving from overseas were historical artifacts, bearing the traces of centuries of intra-European conflicts, contradictions, and compromises. For present purposes, one of these points of conflict gave disproportionate shape to the cross-cultural process in the Gold Coast: the notion of Christianity as religion of territorial expanse and political legitimacy. While the Danish, Swedish, Dutch, Prussian, and British trading installations each had their own respective religious histories, corresponding with deep divisions in Protestant Europe, the finer points of doctrine are less important than the broadly held Protestant notions of Christendom, or Christianity understood as its territorial expanse. The forts were simply extraterritorial European enclaves. Christendom, defined in this way, has been the subject of missiological research for several decades. The conversation is quite broad and multifaceted, but for present purposes, three observations might be made.

First, as is often the case, some of the best and most important critical contributions about Europe's own syncretized Christianity has come from insiders, including Kraemer, Newbigin and Bosch, who had learned to hear the Christian message articulated through non-Western voices, but who were

[39] Johannes Fabian, *Out of Our Minds: Reason and Madness in the Exploration of Central Africa* (Berkeley: University of California Press, 2000), 31.

[40] Kwamena-Poh, *Government and Politics* 111.

also able to understand the system from within.[41] Second, because the logic of Christendom, which has never gone uncontested, proved so useful as an intellectual tool for European colonialism and civilizing missions (such that the French imperial government continued to sponsor Catholic missions in Africa long after establishing state secularism at home in the first decade of the twentieth century), it should come as no surprise that some of Europe's pioneering postcolonial theological scholarship originated among the first Europeans undergoing that painful transition: the Germans.[42]

Third, these and other twentieth-century critiques of colonial Christianity regularly drew upon anti-Christendom writings of Denmark's Søren Kierkegaard, whose sustained attack on the state church overlapped with the Basel Mission's first two decades in Akropong.[43] Kierkegaard himself gave little thought to missions, and often indulged in crass language for the purpose of provoking Danish Christians. He routinely called Lutheran clergy "cannibals," the state church "pagan," and likely had no interest in actual African or Asian religions.[44] In 1855, Kierkegaard wrote that "'Christendom' is the betrayal of Christianity; a 'Christian world' is apostasy from Christianity."[45] On the other hand, he thought that Pietism was "the one and only consequence of Christianity." The missiological quality to Kierkegaard's thought has rarely been teased out, even as generations of Protestant missionaries have expressed strong opposition to Christendom and state Protestantism, perhaps in part because Kierkegaard's project is mostly destructive and focused on individual faith.[46]

The Basel Mission was inconsistent in their language, despite having strong feelings about unsaved Europeans. Basel Mission writings sometimes distinguished and sometimes conflated two different terms, *Christentum* (Christendom) and *Christenheit* (Christianity). Nevertheless, although agents

---

[41] In the interwar era: Hendrik Kraemer, *The Christian Message in a Non-Christian World* (London: Published for the International Missionary Council by the Edinburgh House Press, 1938); In the postcolonial era: Lesslie Newbigin, *Foolishness to the Greeks: The Gospel and Western Culture* (Grand Rapids: Eerdmans, 1986); David Jacobus Bosch, *Transforming Mission: Paradigm Shifts in Theology of Mission* (Maryknoll, N.Y.: Orbis, 1991).

[42] John G. Flett, *The Witness of God: The Trinity, Missio Dei, Karl Barth, and the Nature of Christian Community* (Grand Rapids: Eerdmans, 2010), 12, 125–26.

[43] Søren Kierkegaard, *Kierkegaard's Attack Upon "Christendom," 1854–1855*, trans. and ed. Walter Lowrie (Princeton: Princeton University Press, 1946).

[44] Kierkegaard, "Christendom," 268, 290, respectively.

[45] Kierkegaard, "Christendom," 33–34. See also Stephen Crites, *In the Twilight of Christendom: Hegel vs. Kierkegaard on Faith and History* (Chambersburg, Pa.: American Academy of Religion, 1972), 58–63.

[46] Mark A. Tietjen, *Kierkegaard: A Christian Missionary to Christians* (Downers Grove, Ill.: IVP Academic, 2016).

of the Basel Mission imagined themselves to be politically neutral, few of their African interlocutors were deceived. When missionaries of various sending organizations began moving inland, local kings consistently pondered whether receiving or rejecting missionaries would destabilize political and trade relations with their European counterparts. Speaking of the Asante kingdom, in which Christianity was first expounded in a systematic manner in 1839 by the Wesleyans, McCaskie has observed: "first, and not at all always mistakenly, the Asante state believed [the Wesleyans] to be sanctioned representatives and/ or agents under the direct protection and patronage of the steadily increasing British presence."[47]

Protestant Christianity, in the eyes of its European representatives, was a religion of commerce backed by extraterritorial political claims: the state cult of the trading companies. Regulating themselves in part by their syncretized variants of what had once been a West Asian religion, Protestant Europeans traded slaves in the Accra area for more than a hundred and fifty years. Beginning in the middle of the seventeenth century, the Danes, the Dutch, and the English each established their own trading posts within about four kilometers of one another along the coast, incrementally developing them into forts against assault from inland. Each trading company brought its own chaplains and performed Christian rituals and worship services according to national mandates: Lutheran, Reformed, and Anglican, respectively. Before the end of the slave trade, most of the European residents of these outposts were members of Protestant state churches, aside from a few Jews and nonconformists.[48]

When the Basel missionaries arrived in the early nineteenth century, they bore a strikingly different approach to their religious habitus than that of the governors of the various forts, introducing a politically chaotic religion into the societies of the coasts, already destabilized by the recent abolition of the slave trade.[49] And yet they struggled to transcend cultural and ideological templates long in existence both at the forts and at home: sometimes they succeeded, and sometimes they failed.[50] To the extent that the locals, after the 1850s and especially after the promulgation of the Bible in translation, were able to reformulate the message to suit their purposes, they were diverging from the

---

[47] McCaskie, State and Society, 136.

[48] This would change in the nineteenth century, above all with the arrival of the British Wesleyans.

[49] Peter Haenger, Sklaverei und Sklavenemanzipation an der Goldküste: ein Beitrag zum Verständnis von sozialen Abhängigkeitsbeziehungen in Westafrika (Basel: Helbing & Lichtenhahn, 1997).

[50] Paul Jenkins, "Der Skandal fortwährender interkultureller Blindheit," Zeitschrift für Mission 23, no. 4 (1997), 224–36.

Christianity of the forts. The story of Ghanaian innovations in Christianity thus requires a discussion of the variants present that they encountered in the forts and slave ships. I do not argue, as the Basel missionaries did, that the latter was inauthentic. Rather, I make a genealogical claim: that the religious life of the forts bore the traces of tensions and conflicts within Western forms of Christianity. The specific lines connecting slave castles with, for example, the investiture conflict or the Thirty Years' War are beyond the scope of this study and certainly warrant further research. Again, however: large scales of time are involved, and the Danish Christianity of the 1640s was not the same thing as its counterpart two centuries later.

With only a few exceptions over the span of several human lives, the managers of European slave forts held nearly no expectation that the Christianity of the fort had the remotest relevance to the Africans with whom they had their dealings. There were, of course, exceptions. Aside from a few sporadic evangelistic attempts, mainly initiated by individuals, and which did not continue after that person's death or return to Europe (a few such examples are discussed below), a broader category of people falling under the purview of the fort chaplaincy was the Euro-African mulatto community, which in the main consisted of the descendants of the unions of European soldiers and local women. In the case of Christiansborg, management affirmed some kind of religious responsibility for these people, but—and this is crucial—because Christianity was Danish, and because these people were partly Danish.[51] This non-interest in missionary activity was a general feature of the Protestantism that operated in the Gold Coast—it was an expression of a conflation, back home, of church and state.

Moreover, because this conflation of Christianity with Europe was mainly an expression of the limits to the Protestant imagination, it inevitably referred to distinctions within European religious history, which, in themselves, were irrelevant to West Africa. Catholics, present in the region from the fifteenth century, had always given at least lip service to evangelism. Many of the Protestants, on the other hand, felt that religious work among the Africans was misplaced. However, these ideas were not static: they evolved over centuries. By the time the Basel Mission first arrived in 1828, most forts, which were essentially garrisoned trading posts, were in states of decline for a variety of reasons, including difficulties in remaining solvent once slave trading was officially proscribed. Nevertheless, for generations, fabulous amounts of wealth flowed both ways through the gates of these European outposts. Every one of the forts is as close to the sea as possible, because that was where their interests

---

[51] Ipsen, *Daughters of the Trade*, 114–40.

lay: the affairs and mindsets of the natives were of interest only up to the point of commercial intelligence and venal drives.

This is not to say the Europeans did not interact with the locals, raise children, or sometimes even learn local languages. However, most Europeans came and went within a few years, and it was the locals on the coasts, the Fanti in Elmina and Cape Coast and the Gã in Accra, and not the Europeans, who learned the most about their strange interlocutors. In Elmina, for example, the Portuguese language remained an indigenous institution well into the middle of the nineteenth century, at least two hundred years after the Portuguese fort had become Dutch.[52] The few European sources for Gold Coast politics before the late eighteenth century tend to be the journals of fort administrators reporting on one or another war of succession or multilateral war, leaving historians of that period with the task of reading ill-informed and contradictory Dutch, English, French, or Danish sources against one another.[53]

The Basel missionaries were aware that much Christian history had transpired on the Gold Coast—and that much of it was implicated in the slave trade. They were furthermore convinced that their mission included the moral and spiritual inversion of much of this legacy, which they understood as horrific and inextricable from the slave trade. This was a fair assessment, but it also reveals the protesting quality to the early Basel Mission's outlook, not only in West Africa, but in general. However, the slave trade had ended decades before the Basel Mission's arrival. The mission was not merely interested in restoration or reparations—although that was certainly part of the mission's vision. Well over a half century after the overseas slave trade's abolition, Basel missionaries continued to find the variant of Christianity they encountered in the forts to be morally reprehensible or inauthentic.

At one time or another, the long string of coastal commercial outposts in the Gold and Slave Coasts represented most seafaring European countries, and most of these forts' European employees were Christians to varying degrees of commitment.[54] The Portuguese had always maintained chaplains, mostly for the benefit of their European employees, but always with at least a theoretical interest in the propagation of the Catholic faith.[55] Elsewhere, Portuguese Catholicism made lasting inroads. For many generations,

[52] Kropp Dakubu, "The Portuguese Language on the Gold Coast, 1471–1807," 16.

[53] Albert Van Dantzig, "The Furley Collection: Its Value and Limitations for the Study of Ghana's History," *Paideuma* 33 (1987), 423–32.

[54] Danish Christiansborg had at least one Jew as an officer: Wulff Joseph Wulff, whose diaries have been published, and contain nearly no religious meditations: Wulff, *Breve og Dagbogsoptegnelser*.

[55] Ralph M. Wiltgen, *Gold Coast Mission History, 1471–1880* (Techny, Ill. : Divine Word, 1956). Also see, among many others, Lamin O. Sanneh, *West African Christianity: The*

Catholicism in Angola lived alongside indigenous religions, but remained largely in European priestly control, as the Church failed to establish a single theological seminary during three centuries of royal patronage. The short-lived early eighteenth-century Antonian movement, led by a Kongolese woman claiming to be the reincarnation of St. Anthony of Padua (a favorite saint in Kongo), who prophesied against the king, was the most prominent example of indigenous reformulation of European Christianity in the early modern era, and neatly prefigures the form and pattern taken in the twentieth century by so-called African Initiated Churches.[56]

## THE CHAPEL AND THE COUNTING HOUSE

The Dutch and Danes, on the other hand, entering West Africa during the seventeenth century, were less committed to providing religious services, and when they did, these were often done with an eye to the decent behavior of the fort's soldiers—young men far from home. In 1835 Andreas Riis could identify "no trace" of Christianity among the natives of Osu—the neighborhood in which the Danes had operated for nearly two centuries.[57] Riis' ascetic pietism no doubt figures in this equation and, as Ipsen pointed out, there were several mulatto families who considered themselves to be Christians, but Riis might not have been too far off. The key to safe African and Afro-European access to a slave-trading fort was their christening as Lutherans, without which they were at risk of enslavement overseas. Since baptism functioned more or less like a ritual passport, depth of Christian commitment was an entirely irrelevant question. In any case, the christened African women attached to the fort (and those who were under their protection) had a strong interest in avoiding the appearance of troublemaking: those who did not know (or did not respect) their place in a violent society could find themselves transported overseas. In such a world, the primary utility of Christianity was protection from enslavement, and anything beyond a rudimentary knowledge of Lutheran practice (including the wearing of European clothes and Sunday church attendance) was secondary.[58] With abolition, this delicate system came to an end, and the mulatto women were no longer needed as intermediaries. It was a generation later that Andreas Riis found no trace of Christianity in Osu.

---

*Religious Impact* (London: C. Hurst, 1983), 20–35.; and C. P. Groves, *The Planting of Christianity in Africa* (London: Lutterworth, 1948), 123–27.

[56] John Thornton, *The Kongolese Saint Anthony: Dona Beatriz Kimpa Vita and the Antonian Movement, 1684–1706* (Cambridge: Cambridge University Press, 1998).

[57] Andreas Riis, "Goldküste in Afrika," *HB* 1835, 61.

[58] Ipsen, *Daughters of the Trade*, 122.

Fort Elmina: Portuguese chapel, converted into a counting house. Photo by author, 2014.

When the Dutch trading company took over the Portuguese fort at Elmina in 1637, they more or less ceased all missionary activity, although "compared with other Europeans, the Dutch may well have been the least interested in efforts to educate and Christianize the African population."[59] Shortly after taking over Elmina, the Dutch converted the Catholic chapel into an accounting house, holding worship services elsewhere in the fort. The symbolism is rich; Max Weber would have felt validated in his unprovable notion that modern capitalism was the unintended economic expression of Dutch Calvinism. Especially appropriate would be Weber's concluding essay, in which he meditated on capitalism bereft of its soul—the "iron cage," in his terms, only too close in spirit to the actual iron cages, containing enslaved men and women, in the basement dungeons of Elmina.[60]

Services for the Dutch sailors and employees, however, remained on the agenda. These people tended to be drawn from the dregs of Dutch society, beggars and convicts, and more than half of them died within eight months of arrival.[61] At some point, the fort's managers converted a room above the male slave dungeon into a permanent chapel.[62] Captives waiting for transportation across the ocean were thus treated to whatever occasional liturgical activities penetrated the

[59] Johannes Postma, *The Dutch in the Atlantic Slave Trade, 1600–1815* (Cambridge: Cambridge University Press, 1990), 70. On the Dutch forts in the eighteenth century more generally, see P. C. Emmer, *De Nederlandse Slavenhandel, 1500–1850*, 2nd, expanded ed. (Amsterdam: Arbeiderspers, 2003).

[60] Max Weber, *The Protestant Ethic and the Spirit of Capitalism* (London: Routledge, 1992), 181.

[61] Kpobi, *Mission in Chains*; Postma, *The Dutch in the Atlantic Slave Trade*, 65–66.

[62] Niall Finneran, *The Archaeology of Christianity in Africa* (Stroud, Gloucestershire: Tempus, 2002), 153.

wooden platform above their heads, and got glimpses of the sanctuary whenever their jailers opened the trap door in the center of the chapel floor, the means by which food was dropped down into the fetid dungeon. The women's dungeon also had a trap door, but this one could be accessed by a staircase reaching the dungeon floor. This trap door was not used to deliver food, but rather opened directly into the Governor's private bedroom. Which of these two trap doors offered a more accurate description of Christianity is open for discussion.

The trap door opening to the men's dungeon is exactly in the middle of the sanctuary, which meant that, had one of the prisoners stood at the west end of the dungeon when the trap door was opened and looked up at an angle, he might have seen the following biblical inscription, painted high on the east wall of the room above:

ZION IS DES HEEREN RUSTE DIT IS

SYN WOONPLAETSE IN EEUWIGHEY

PSALM : 132

Translated directly, the inscription reads: "Zion is the Lord's repose.
This is his dwelling-place in eternity. Psalm 132."

This inscription offers a rich window into the history of Dutch Christianity in the Gold Coast. To my best reckoning, this inscription predates 1797, and is probably much older. Because of major changes in Protestant biblical hermeneutics during the nineteenth century, establishing a date for this inscription helps to define its meaning to those who put it on the chapel wall. The inscription is not a direct quote from Psalm 132, but an abbreviated excerpt from two verses in a broader passage. It is clearly drawn from the official state translation, the *Statenvertaling*, which went through several revisions, including spelling changes, between 1637 and the twentieth century.[63] This means that one might be able to match the spelling with a corresponding edition of the

---

[63] Nicoline van der Sijs, "De invloed van de Statenvertaling op de vorming van de Nederlandse standaardtal," in *Leeg en ijdel : De invloed van de bijbel op het Nederlands*, ed. Nicoline van der Sijs (The Hague: Sdu Uitgevers, 2005), 39–58.

*Statenvertaling.* During the period between the Dutch takeover of Elmina and its transfer to the British, twelve editions were published. Between 1688 and 1843, only two words changed in the *Statenvertaling* version of Psalm 132: *Eeuwigheyd* (eternity) became *Eeuwigheid,* and *Woonplaetse* (living-place) became *Woonplaats;* both of these changes were made between the 1789 and the 1797 editions.

The particular spelling in the Dutch inscription at Elmina thus appears to reflect a version of the *Statenvertaling* published before 1797; in light of the high turnover and mortality rates of officers at the fort, it is a safe guess that the verse was not penned much later than that date. Most likely it was written much earlier in the century. The inscription, in other words, was written in the chapel wall during the highest years of the slave trade at Elmina.

Given an origination date of no later than 1797, what did the inscription mean to its creators? It is an abbreviated excerpt from verses 13 and 14 of Psalm 132. This was a worship song, attributed in the Hebrew text to King David, and part of a block of songs collectively called the "Songs of Ascent." In the history of Christian hermeneutics, these songs have played a few distinct roles over the centuries. From the Reformation until the 1830s (that is, during the slave period at Elmina), the "ascent" in these songs was understood in Protestant commentary as that of a personal, devotional act—the soul's separation from the sinful world. This Christian interpretation was at odds with that of contemporary Jewish commentators in Europe, who tended to view the ascents as songs of pilgrimage or of return from exile. After the 1830s, most Protestant scholars incorporated variations of this latter viewpoint into their interpretations, but such a view would not have informed the eighteenth-century Trading Company officials at Dutch Elmina.[64] For them, the Lord's Dwelling-Place (that is, in Psalm 132, *Zion*) was neither cultic nor historical in nature, but strictly representative of personal devotion. And the content of this devotion was, in the main, focused on sober and dutiful attention to duty.[65]

According to this logic, Christianity overlapped extensively with duty. As duty mainly meant keeping the forts' soldiers and sailors from getting themselves in trouble, would-be evangelists—people who might meddle with native affairs—presented the governors with unwanted trouble. In 1990 Johannes Postma discovered a string of correspondence, written during the middle

---

[64]  Loren D. Crow, *The Songs of Ascents (Psalms 120–134): Their Place in Israelite History and Religion* (Atlanta: Scholars Press, 1996).

[65]  David Kpobi has connected the themes of Dutch thought on slavery with that of duty, observing that the question of slavery's ethics was only one of actual practice; there was nothing theologically problematic with the practice. Kpobi, *Mission in Chains,* 98.

decades of the eighteenth century, between Company officials in the Netherlands and in Elmina, on the question of converting the natives. In 1745, the director-general had written to his superiors, confessing the limits to his cross-cultural imagination:

> The more time I spend here and the more I penetrate the nature of the natives, the more difficult, if not impossible, it appears to me that—unless a miracle occurred—the natives could be converted to Christianity.[66]

A quarter century later, Company officials in Holland asked Elmina to initiate some missionary activity, to which the response came: the "natives are not inclined to accept Christianity," and "their heathen lives would bring shame to Christianity."[67] And in this latter opinion, one may see the real meaning of state Protestantism in the Gold Coast, even when sectarian and national variations are taken into account. To the managers of the coastal forts, Christianity was about stability and order, and this order was above all understood in cultural terms imported from Europe. Cross-cultural translation of the Christian message could only mean Europeanization, or of the territorial expansion of European rule. Christianity was thus not the opposite of heathenism, as the missionaries would later understand these terms, but of African culture. One result of this European conflation of Africa with non-Christianity, and thus with non-civilization, was that European responses to African religion varied little over a period otherwise marked by radical intellectual change in Europe. Before and after the Enlightenment and throughout the nineteenth century, Europeans in the Gold Coast persisted in viewing African religions as so much foolishness and chicanery. Thus Johannes Rask, the Lutheran chaplain of the (Danish) Christiansborg castle from 1708 to 1713, seems not only to have never engaged in evangelizing among Africans, but "never contemplated the idea."[68] Rask used the word *Christian* as a synonym for *European*. Indeed, the Danes employed religious workers exclusively for the pastoral care of the residents of the fort, and sometimes did not replace those who died (a number that included at least seventeen of thirty-six chaplains sent out between 1660 and 1850). On occasion decades passed with no cleric on site, as between 1809 and 1829.

Such prolonged absences between chaplains might have been for the best, considering the moral character of several of the men who came to Christiansborg as chaplains: inexperienced pastors who could not get a position at

---

[66] Postma, *The Dutch in the Atlantic Slave Trade*, 71.

[67] Postma, *The Dutch in the Atlantic Slave Trade*.

[68] M. E. Kropp Dakubu, "Foreword," in *Two Views from Christiansborg Castle*, ed. Selena Axelrod Winsnes (Accra: Sub-Saharan Publishers, 2009), 10.

home, students who had failed their exams, and worse. Without citing specific details, Debrunner mentions:

> [P]eople deeply in debt (Jacob Grundtvig), mentally unbalanced men (Kop), lazy fellows (Niels Grundtvig), drunkards (Meyer), rowdies (Jenssen), people more interested in trade (Klein), and even a crook (Porth).[69]

Debrunner failed to include, in this list of less than ideal Danish chaplains, missionary-minded chaplains. There were a few: a Danish major by the name of Wrisberg seems to have translated Jesus' Sermon on the Mount into 'Accraisk' (presumably Gã), while stationed at the fort.[70] Another was Elias Svane, stationed at Christiansborg for several years in the 1720s. Over three decades later, Rømer reported that Svane's name remained in high esteem among the locals: "I have never met him, but I cannot adequately describe the degree of veneration the Blacks have for him, even to this day."[71] But whatever missionizing the seventeenth- and eighteenth-century chaplains did was done on their own time, and without the governor's blessing. Which is to say: regardless of the sincerity of their devotion, relative to the governors' intentions of using the chaplaincy to maintain order in the fort, missionaries and like-minded chaplains were yet another class of troublemakers. The Roman Catholics, in contrast, never distinguished between chaplaincy and proselytism. In 1760 Ludvig Rømer recalled "a certain French Father . . . who zealously scolds us Protestants for not converting the Negroes to Christianity."[72]

One boy named Akuma, born in Akropong in 1772, was sold to a Danish merchant in Christiansborg as a personal attendant. This man—Wrisberg by name—took Akuma with him on his return to Copenhagen, where the youth learned to be a cook. Eventually he was freed and returned to Akropong, where he was to serve as the personal cook for the king. During his time in Denmark, Akuma arrived at the conclusion that it was impossible for an African to live as a Christian.[73] Most of the Danish governors at Christiansborg shared Akuma's outlook. To them, Christianity was in the first instance a disciplinary device for controlling the impulses of the young European men serving as fort soldiers. In challenging ethnic definitions to Christianity, missionaries

---

[69] Hans W. Debrunner, "Pioneers of Church and Education in Ghana: Danish Chaplains to Guinea, 1661–1850," *Kirkehistoriske Samlinger* 7th series, vol. 4, no. 3 (1962), 375.

[70] Georg Nørregaard, ed., *Guldkysten: de danske etablissementer i Guinea*, 2nd ed., Vore gamle tropekolonier, ed. Johannes Brøndsted, vol. 8 (Copenhagen: Fremad, 1968), 308.

[71] Rømer, *A Reliable Account*, 108 (orig. 105).

[72] Rømer, *A Reliable Account*, 16.

[73] Unnamed editor, "Nachrichten aus West-Afrika," *HB* 1857, 37.

potentially troubled the governors' ever-fragile hold on law and order in the fort. In the same way, and for the same reason, that interracial unions and the corresponding emergence of so-called mulatto communities adjacent to the forts presented a source of unending trouble for Company officials, cross-cultural conversion was neither desirable nor useful. In both cases, sexual and religious miscegenation both tended to undermine tidy mythologies indispensable to Atlantic commerce.

## DANGEROUS ECCENTRICS

In October 1835, King Addo Dankwa was already faced with the most dangerous revolt his brittle kingdom had faced in the century of its existence. And this was before someone in his own neighborhood had broken a taboo: the man had eaten a yam out of turn, before the ancestors had been fed.[74] As a punishment, the offended ancestors had intervened to stop the rains from falling, putting the yam crop at risk in the final weeks before harvest. Disaster might be averted with rainfall, but only if Addo Dankwa could secure strict ritual obedience from his subjects. If the late rains turned into a drought, and drought into hunger, the revolt could easily devolve into a civil war. And precisely for that reason, the king felt the need to stop in with his foreign guest and remind him to abstain from yams.[75] Addo Dankwa could not risk angering his ancestors any farther by allowing a foreigner to eat out of turn. Only if the season's first fruits were laid before the blackened royal stools (that is, monuments to their former occupants) in the Akropong mausoleum could the ancestors be expected to continue to intervene on behalf of the king, and without their help his kingdom could hardly expect to overcome the latest political threat to its existence.[76]

As he presided over his kingdom's ninth Odwira, Addo Dankwa thus had broader concerns than the personal opinions of his Danish guest. Riis, on the other hand, was as oblivious to the broader context of Addo Dankwa's admonishment as he was to nearly everything else around him. He had even misunderstood the name of the kingdom, Akua-Apem ("the thousand armies") as "the thousand slaves."[77] For six months Riis had engaged in constant bickering with the laborers whom the king had assigned to him for help in building his house—quarrels that were certainly avoidable and owed at least in part to cross-cultural confusion. Addo Dankwa had taken a risk

[74]  McCaskie, *State and Society*, 159–64.
[75]  Riis, "Einige Mittheilungen", 554.
[76]  Michelle Gilbert, "The Sacralized Power of the Akwapim King," in *Religion and Power: Divine Kingship in the Ancient World and Beyond*, ed. Nicole Brisch, Oriental Institute Seminars (Chicago: University of Chicago Press, 2008), 172.
[77]  Riis, "Einige Mittheilungen," 511.

in sponsoring Riis, likely hoping that his Danish guest might be the key to quashing the ongoing rebellion. Paul Jenkins speculates that the mismanaged construction of Riis' house may have instigated several other acts of defiance against the king that year.[78]

King Addo Dankwa did not share in Riis' ignorance. As a man whose oldest son was fifty years old, as a king who had already been in office for two decades, he knew how to rule, and he already knew everything he needed to know about Europeans.[79] He had fought with and against the Danes, and he knew how they thought; one of his cooks (Akuma, mentioned above), had spent years in Denmark, and likely conferred with the king about Riis.[80]

The Basel Mission had arrived in the Gold Coast by invitation of the Danish governor several years earlier. However, all but one of the young men died within months, leaving the only Dane in the group, Andreas Riis, on his own. After a few ineffectual years at Fort Christiansborg, where he was expected to hold religious services for the soldiers, Riis found an excuse to move to Akuapem, which he did in March 1835, after an exploratory visit in January. King Addo Dankwa insisted he present some kind of Danish credentials: he was not interested in hosting a criminal or troublemaker whose presence might endanger his relations with Christiansborg. This request indicates that Addo Dankwa recognized some kind of Danish authority in his domain, however slight that might be.[81]

Riis may have more or less imposed himself on the king, but it was nevertheless true that he was in Akropong by Addo Dankwa's sufferance. The requirements that the king imposed upon Riis were not onerous and consisted exclusively of taboos to be respected: no bringing dogs into the village, no killing black monkeys, and no fieldwork on Fridays. The latter requirement indicates that Asaase Afua, the earth-fertility goddess and daughter of Onyame, was worshiped in Akuapem. Friday was her day, and Addo Dankwa needed to ensure that she was appropriately venerated by a weekly day of rest.[82] What then did the king feel he stood to gain from hosting a foreign guest? Especially at a time of political high stakes, a foreigner might be of some use, but he was also dangerous. As a nonmember of a local clan, who could not be relied upon to conform to purification taboos, Riis was a risk. "Osiadan," the builder,

---

[78]  Jenkins, "Der Skandal," 224–36.

[79]  Riis, "Einige Mittheilungen," 525.

[80]  On the intimate relationship between Akan kings and their personal cooks, who for ritual reasons were exclusively male, see Eva Meyerowitz, *The Sacred State of the Akan* (London: Faber and Faber, 1951), 54–55.

[81]  Kwamena-Poh, *Government and Politics*, 113, n. 7.

[82]  Meyerowitz, *The Sacred State*, 77.

as the locals had begun calling this strange man, was somehow connected to European wealth down on the coast, and as such might someday mature into an investment worth making, but after six months in town, he was only barely able to speak the language.[83] Andreas Riis might eventually prove worth the trouble of the hospitality extended him, but in the meanwhile Addo Dankwa needed to make absolutely certain that Riis complied with the rules. Having been personally admonished by King Addo Dankwa not to eat any yams until Odwira (which was then four weeks out), Riis had no problem giving his assent, as he felt its observation was not sinful: "I adhere to the blacks' customs insofar as I can do this without sinning."

> Christian prudence demands that I do nothing to awaken hatred in heathen hearts as long as it can avoided. Therefore, I abstain from yams, so that they cannot blame some misfortune on the white man, who ate yams before the designated day.[84]

However, Riis' response to the king evidenced confusion over the source of the restriction:

> I am not abstaining from eating yams because of the fetish, because I know only one god, who is high above all things, but out of respect to you, so that I cannot give people occasion to accuse me [if someone has a misfortune].[85]

Addo Dankwa had reminded Riis to respect a taboo, which related to the *asaman* ancestors, and Riis had responded in categories of the *abosom* spirits. While the mistake was not grave, Riis' attitude of compliance also described its limits.

### THE VIOLENCE OF CONSCIENCE

Late in the nineteenth century, a new generation of Basel missionaries, their Christian faith increasingly syncretized with European imperialism and more convinced of their right and responsibility to impose upon indigenous social life, retreated from this stance of open inquisitiveness. Many of these people

---

[83] Kofi Asare Opoku, "Riis the Builder" (unpublished manuscript: Akrofi-Christaller Institute library, Akropong-Akuapem, Ghana). Brokensha adds a note, from conversations with people in Larteh, that Riis "spent so much of his time on building" that some people may have thought Christianity was a house-building technique. See David Brokensha, *Social Change at Larteh, Ghana* (Oxford: Clarendon, 1966), 18.

[84] Riis, "Einige Mittheilungen," 554–55.

[85] Riis, "Einige Mittheilungen," 554–55. To state the obvious: Addo Dankwa and Riis were communicating through an interpreter, who most likely fully comprehended the context and meaning of the king's instructions. However, it was Riis and not the interpreter who preserved the account of the conversation.

assimilated to mainstream European missionary attitudes of paternalism. However, during their first few decades in the Gold Coast, they carried a very different mindset into their interactions with the locals. And why was this? In light of the broadly-held European and American missionary conviction in the middle of the nineteenth century—and this conviction was remarkably inert in the face of profound turbulence at home during those same years—that Christianity, culture, and civilization were impossible to isolate from one another, how did the men and women of the Basel Mission break out of these stultifying intellectual horizons?

There was no categorical indigenous intellectual reason for rejecting Christianity altogether. West African intellectual history, both in Muslim and non-Muslim regions, reveals a pervasive capacity to reimagine the foreign and reformulate it to suit local needs, and there was no reason in itself that locals could not do the same with Christianity. The struggle to conceive of an African Christianity was a European cognitive problem. However, it is important to be clear that ambivalence over doctrinal truth was not at all the same as openness to social and political disruption. Most precolonial states in the Akan cultural realm, while being theoretically open to innovations, nevertheless idealized a form of social harmony in which the state retained a monopoly on belief, on the narrative of the past, and on ritual. In this regard, Ghanaian religious history diverges in striking ways from that of other peoples (such as the Yoruba) to the east, despite having a broadly similar experience with the Atlantic economy and with Islam and Christianity.[86]

The heart of the matter is the relationship between political authority and belief. McCaskie's definitive intellectual history of the Asante state, which does not always translate to the fragmentary and comparatively poor Akuapem, meticulously argues that social-political-ideological harmony was always the goal of the various ɔman states, although only Asante came close to realizing its totalizing aspirations. The rulers of the ɔman states, while open to new ideas and ritual tools, were consistently jealous in policing idiosyncrasy within their domains. "In any society where hierarchies of differentiation and control are presided over by the state," he concludes,

> A fundamental object of that state must be to impose ideological definition on knowledge and belief, to regulate the boundaries between the two, and to exercise an absolute discretion in shaping both of them.[87]

[86]  Peel, *Christianity, Islam, and* Orisạ *Religion*, 18.
[87]  McCaskie, *State and Society*, 21.

Which is to say, while the arrival of a new religion was not theoretically problematic, it was nevertheless politically dangerous. Although he was no priest, the king was the central personage in a sacred state, and "the continuity of the state depended largely on the proper performance of their religious rituals by both king and subjects."[88] Therefore, any discussion of Ghanaian Christian history must consider the violence to the centralized political order represented by Christian insistence of individual conscience.

A British-led army sacked the Asante capital city of Kumasi in 1874, but the Asante forces, lurking in the forest, refused to engage, knowing that the approaching rains would force the invaders to retreat. The ensuing settlement was thus ambiguous, with both sides claiming a measure of victory. Soon thereafter, Methodist missionaries arrived in Kumasi, demanding "freedom of conscience" for individuals.[89] The Asante court, which had a long history with Muslims, and had worked out modes of coexistence with them, fully understood the political threat constituted by these demands and rejected them.

If nothing else, freedom of conscience constitutes an assertion that an individual's loyalty to the state has its limits. It therefore represents a profound threat to any state that derives its legitimacy and authority from compliance with ritual. Several centuries of bloodshed over Christian faith bear witness to the problem in Europe itself. Back home in the United Kingdom, even the Methodists used coins bearing the likeness of a queen whose attributes included defense of the faith. When they demanded freedom of conscience in Asante, these Methodists undoubtedly understood their petition through the lens of their own denominational memories of political struggle—remembering how precious freedom from state persecution was to their own fathers.

PUNCTUATED EQUILIBRIUM

From the early centuries down to the present and across many different branches of Christianity, nearly all missionaries have seen themselves as answering a biblical mandate they understood as inseparable from basic Christian worship. However, many other non-missionary Christians, over space and time, have looked at the exact same Scriptures without seeing what to the missionaries was obvious. Erdmann Neumeister (1671–1756), pastor and songwriter in Hamburg, was a lifelong antagonist of missionaries. He concluded an Ascension Day sermon (the day in which Jesus was said to have risen to heaven, and on which occasion he had left his followers with his most

---

[88]  John Middleton, "One Hundred and Fifty Years of Christianity in a Ghanaian Town," *Africa: Journal of the International African Institute* 53, no. 3 (1983), 5.

[89]  McCaskie, *State and Society*, 139.

explicit instructions for propagating their faith: "go into all the world . . .") with this couplet, in which Neumeister rejected Jesus' words:

Long ago, it was said, go into all the world
But now: remain where God has placed you.[90]

In 1906, two generations into an enormous expansion of European missionary activity in Asia, Africa, and the South Pacific, German theologian Adolf Harnack could articulate as obvious that "one can say that world missions necessarily proceeded from the religion and spirit of Jesus."[91] Harnack was wrong: vast stretches of Christian history have proceeded, during which periods only a few eccentrics have engaged in missions. The reality is that Christian proponents of mission have routinely felt the need to justify their activities to their fellow believers. The historical record seems to describe something of a punctuated equilibrium, by which missionary movements have troubled long-placid waters, before eventually burning themselves out, and the waters returning to their placid state. More than one African Christian historian has expressed frustration that Christianity arrived in much of the continent as a syncretized European folk religion, given that an African variation of the same had been present in Africa—in Ethiopia—for centuries.[92] If a very basic human desire, especially during wars and other periods of poverty and crisis, is to achieve predictability and sustainability, missionary activism has often frustrated progress toward that goal. The reverse was also the case: missionaries returning from the field to the city of Basel, then undergoing uncontrolled urban and industrial growth, had a knack for making themselves unwelcome.

If the history of Christian missions may be summarized as punctuated equilibrium, one of the biggest and deepest periods of equilibrium unfolded in German-speaking Protestant lands between the sixteenth and early eighteenth centuries. During a period of expansive Catholic missionary activity

---

[90] Gustav Warneck, *Die Mission in Bildern aus ihrer Geschichte* (Gütersloh: Bertelsmann, 1897), 3.

[91] Adolf von Harnack, *Die Mission und Ausbreitung des Christentums in den ersten drei Jahrhunderten*, 2nd ed. (Leipzig: J. C. Hinrich, 1906), I:32.

[92] Girma Bekele, *The In-Between People: A Reading of David Bosch through the Lens of Mission History and Contemporary Challenges in Ethiopia* (Eugene, Ore.: Pickwick, 2011). Mark McEntire tells of interacting with Ethiopian Lutheran and Presbyterian seminarians, who "typically understand their movement as a kind of Protestant Reformation, standing over against the Ethiopian Orthodox Church." Mark McEntire, "Cain and Abel in Africa: An Ethiopian Case Study," in *The Bible in Africa: Transactions, Trajectories, and Trends*, ed. Gerald O. West and Musa W. Dube (Leiden: Brill, 2000), 253.

throughout the world, from the Americas, to Africa, India, China, and Japan, the Protestants of Europe and North America were almost entirely focused on internal affairs.[93]

For the better part of a century and a half after the Reformation, almost no Protestant missions took place, aside from a smattering of individual and freelance efforts. Charles Groves put it simply: "Only slowly did the Protestant Churches come to recognize" missionary work as an obligation.[94] Relative to Lutheran and Calvinist Europe, late nineteenth-century missiologist Gustav Warneck attributed this delay to two causes: a lack of exposure to the outside world, and confessional theologies that actively discouraged all missionary ideas.[95] As a consequence, when Protestant Germans began engaging in missionary work, it was the nonconforming and transnational churches and networks that led the way—those who were the least bound by the existing political order. First came the German-Danish project in South India, instigated by August Hermann Francke and implemented by Bartholomew Ziegenbalg in 1706 (discussed in chapter 4). This was followed shortly by the Moravians under Francke's admirer Zinzendorf in the Danish West Indies in the 1730s. The timing of the latter had a consequence that some of the Protestant world's first missionaries, having little by way of systematic theory or ideology, only figured out what they were doing after they were already on the field. Moravians began work in Saint Thomas at exactly the time that several shiploads of Akwamu prisoners of war arrived in those islands. Warneck argues that this first Pietist foray withered under "rationalism" (he uses the

---

[93]  On the impressively transnational quality to sixteenth and seventeenth-century Catholic missionary work in southern India, see Julia Lederle, *Mission und Ökonomie der Jesuiten in Indien: intermediäres Handeln am Beispiel der Malabar-Provinz im 18. Jahrhundert* (Wiesbaden: Harrassowitz, 2009). In Atlantic Africa, Catholics had translated the catechism into KiKongo as early as 1557. On Catholicism in Kongo, see John Thornton, *The Kongolese Saint Anthony.*

[94]  Groves, *The Planting of Christianity*, 166.

[95]  Warneck called this a "choir of missionary opposition": Gustav Warneck, *Abriss einer Geschichte der protestantischen Missionen von der Reformation bis auf die Gegenwart* (Berlin: Warneck, 1898), 23–41. Published in English as *Outline of the History of Protestant Missions from the Reformation to the Present Time* (Edinburgh: James Gemmell, George Bridge, 1884), 25–26. Warneck's assessment met with nuanced pushback from within precisely those German missiological quarters that were the least committed to Lutheran orthodoxy. Missiologist Hans-Werner Gensichen, for example, while recognizing that Luther himself had "no distinct theology or methodology of heathen missions," also observed that all humans are heathens vis-à-vis God. Hans-Werner Gensichen, *Missionsgeschichte der neueren Zeit* (Göttingen: Vandenhoeck & Ruprecht, 1961), 5–8.

image of early flowers having been killed by a frost), and that the "present," that is, the late nineteenth-century German missionary undertaking, represented a mostly new ("re-awakened") project with little to do with that of the eighteenth century.[96] This is partly correct: Basel missionaries arriving in the Gold Coast in the nineteenth century were only vaguely aware of their Moravian predecessors in the region. But it was also an overstatement. Moravian influence was more devotional than practical. The young Basel Mission community leaned on the Moravian network for inspiration.[97] There are numerous anecdotes of daily devotional readings taken from that community's lot casting of Bible verses.[98]

European commercial interests in West Africa were not identical with those of Christian missionaries, of course. To conflate the two would be to tie "particular religious manifestations into a purely synchronic set of determinations."[99] Missionaries, especially evangelical ones, may have consistently attempted commerce, but then again they also consistently prayed and sang, ritually remembered the blood and broken body of Jesus, performed baptisms in his name, and so thoroughly immersed themselves in Bible reading that their letters home often read like devotional commentaries on ancient West Asian revelations. "Whatever else one may say about the social impact of Christian missions in Africa," Peel said, "the story will be radically incomplete if its effects are not adequately tied into the religious project which brought the missionaries in the first place." At a deeper level, Peel concluded, "the redemptive sacrifice of Christ—which stood at the very heart of evangelical preaching—does *not* imply double-entry bookkeeping or vice versa."[100] At the same time, not all the missionaries had an easy time making this distinction.

---

[96]  Warneck, *Abriss einer Geschichte*, 53.

[97]  The earliest editions of the *EMM* carry several stories of Moravian work in Newfoundland and Greenland. More importantly, the first Basel undertaking in Sierra Leone was made after a visit to Moravians in Pennsylvania.

[98]  Hermann Gundert spoke of "enduringly heart-felt support" for the Brethren and for the "declining Halle mission" from among the "awakened" (participants in early nineteenth-century revivals in southwest Germany, which number included Gundert himself). Hermann Gundert, *Die evangelische Mission: ihre Länder, Völker und Arbeiten* (Stuttgart: Verlag der Vereinsbuchhandlung, 1893), 24–25.

[99]  J. D. Y. Peel, *Religious Encounter and the Making of the Yoruba* (Bloomington: Indiana University Press, 2000), 5.

[100]  Peel, *Religious Encounter*, 5.

## CONCLUSION

Writing about the nearly-extinct Christian churches of the Middle East, Philip Jenkins once observed that many Christians, especially evangelicals based in the West, often cultivate a historical understanding of their faith as one of progress (often through struggle) toward an ultimate victory—a longed-for moment at which the global community of Christians will contain representatives of every people group around the world.[101] Not only is this story incomplete, Jenkins argued, but in bypassing the numerous historical examples of church extinction, especially in Muslim lands (a pattern that long preceded the series of crises in our own century), Christians risk unlearning the lessons of decline and loss. Jenkins was writing about parts of the world that were once Christian and are no longer.

Jenkins' warning against projecting teleological narratives of progress backward in time encapsulates the work of this chapter. For more than half of its long history in Ghana, Christianity has aroused little interest among Ghanaians, and there was little reason for contemporaries—either African or European—to imagine Christianity as African. Only when Ghanaians were able to impose their own agenda upon this religion did most people see any relevance to their lives in what was, for the first three centuries, a religion of the transatlantic slave trade. As of the year 1800, nearly all Christians in the Gold Coast were either European men, their African wives or concubines, or the issue of these relationships. Although the Atlantic slave trade was coming to an end, there was no real reason to believe that the state of Christianity in coastal West Africa would change in character at any time in the future. Unless these three hundred years of irrelevance are kept in full view, the story that follows—that of the punctuation of centuries of equilibrium in the third quarter of the nineteenth century—might easily be misunderstood as one of continual progress. And that would be to get the story wrong. If most Ghanaians would eventually become Christians, they did so not because of the European legacy, but despite it.

In the next three chapters, I turn to the moment of breakthrough. Nearly four centuries after the first Portuguese padre passed through the Gold Coast, a homegrown reformulation of the message appeared, articulated in the vernacular, which sufficient numbers of locals and displaced persons found

---

[101] Philip Jenkins, *The Lost History of Christianity: The Thousand-Year Golden Age of the Church in the Middle East, Africa, and Asia—and How it Died* (New York: HarperCollins, 2008), 2–3.

compelling. It is a delicious story—endlessly fascinating as a record of the ways people change as they live with and listen to one another. However, that story must be told with a measure of sobriety. Any reasonable response to the long history of Christianity in Ghana must include anger over so many years of rape, murder, and destruction in the name of Christ.

# 4

# Satan's Strongholds

## INTRODUCTION

On July 10, 1862, twelve years after its acquisition by the British, Fort Christiansborg was shaken by an earthquake and rendered uninhabitable, and British soldiers stationed there needed to stay in tents on the beach for several years. On the front page of the September 1866 edition of the Basel Mission's *Heidenbote*, accompanied by a drawing of the tent city, the newsletter's editor indulged in some ruminations on this image of destruction:

> Sooner or later it [the fort] will crumble. May the same mighty hand, which has destroyed the "Christian Castle" [*Burg*, the German equivalent to the Danish *Borg*] whose walls have seen so much anguish and cries of terror of shackled and tormented slaves, and many deeds of European lewdness and wickedness, continue to destroy Satan's defenses along this coast.

Colonial forts as satanic: even by the standards of a mission that had never endorsed European activities in the coast, this was an impressive rhetorical move. The editor concluded with a prayer:

> May He erect Christ's Castles, in which Ham's children, yearning for freedom from the slave shackles of the flesh and of idol worship, might find refuge.[1]

---

[1]   Joseph Josenhans, "Das Fort von Christiansborg," *HB* 1866, 117 (September). This is the latest reference I have found to Ham in a Basel Mission publication, but the cursed son of Noah made a reappearance, nearly two decades later, in an article written in the new *Deutsche Kolonialzeitung*, the German Colonial Newspaper, by Paul Steiner, since 1872 a missionary in Accra, and who, upon returning to Switzerland in 1890, was the editor of the *EMM* for another twenty-one years. P. Steiner, "Land und Leute von Akra," *Deutsche Kolonialzeitung* 2, no. 1–2 (1885), 10. Steiner's 1885 reference to Ham constitutes a strong suggestion that the notion remained in currency on the field despite its disappearance from

There are two astonishing inversions to this editorial. First, the author describes the colonial forts strung along the coast as satanic defenses, rather than, as was inscribed in the chapel at Elmina, "the Lord's repose." Second, the editor identifies "Ham's children" as worthy of divine protection, rather than as objects of punishment. Implied here was the very old hypothesis, originating in the sixth-century Babylonian Talmud, that Africans had descended from Noah's accursed son Ham.[2] Taken together, these poetic inversions hint that the missionaries establishing themselves in the Gold Coast during the decades between the end of the transatlantic slave trade and colonial conquest were of a decidedly different outlook than most of the Europeans who had preceded them over three and a half centuries along the West African shore.

These newcomers, who did not shy away from demonizing their own civilization, were strange people, alienated from their homelands but unwilling to assimilate to indigenous ways in their adopted ones. For all their dreams of converting the mighty Asante Empire, the missionaries found most of their success among sick, poor, disabled, enslaved, foreign, and otherwise marginalized peoples. Most of the early converts were those who were least likely to be reached by ritual efforts at communal incorporation, and accordingly most likely to fall through the cracks. The present chapter focuses on these foreigners. My argument is that, in contrast to late nineteenth-century missionary comrades of many nations who would follow them throughout Africa, these men and women were not representative Germans. This is no small point: it is imperative to everything else that follows, because as long as the missionaries are treated as "part and parcel of colonialism," it will be very difficult to understand indigenous Christians, and indigenous Christianity, as anything other than as the fruit of European ambition, however eccentric they might have been as individuals.[3]

More importantly, unless missionaries are carefully historicized, indigenous Ghanaian success at translating the message, at reinventing the Bible, and at subordinating the missionaries' agenda to an older and more pressing set of autochthonous priorities will appear as little more than false consciousness, doomed to failure. In other words, simplistic conflation of European missions,

---

Basel Mission publications. It is not insignificant, however, that Ham's return to print coincided with Germany's entrance into Europe's Scramble for Africa.

[2]    Edith R. Sanders, "The Hamitic Hypothesis; Its Origin and Functions in Time Perspective," *The Journal of African History* 10, no. 4 (1969); Philip S. Zachernuk, "Of Origins and Colonial Order: Southern Nigerian Historians and the 'Hamitic Hypothesis' c. 1870–1970," *The Journal of African History* 35, no. 3 (1994).

[3]    Birgit Meyer, *Translating the Devil: Religion and Modernity among the Ewe in Ghana* (Trenton, N.J.: Africa World Press, 1999), xxi.

along with their messengers, with Europe's simultaneous imperial and colonial ambitions is a Eurocentric mistake—an assertion of authority to define African converts' authenticity. For this reason, I fail to be intrigued, as if it were in itself an astonishing or paradoxical notion, by the title of Sonia Abun-Nasr's otherwise careful biography of the eminently intriguing David Asante: *African and Missionary.*[4] Western Christian missions in Africa are not the same thing as Western colonialism in Africa, but neither were they distinct—the problem is complicated by the unclear boundaries between the two.[5] Some missionaries and some colonial officials, as well as some African Christians and some African non-Christians, have indeed seen it this way, but many others have not.

This chapter makes two arguments. The first is that the missionaries were strange people. They were eccentrics at home and abroad alike, even among their like-minded sending communities. More than one historian has gone to great lengths to explain and historicize the Basel Mission, but in so doing has skirted around an obvious response to the German-speaking Pietist men and women who gave their lives in great numbers as they responded to God's calling in Ghana: these were not normal people. However, precisely because the missionaries' purchase on the world of their childhoods (or on the European social world of the coastal castles) was so weak—precisely because they were able to look at the European legacy in Africa and call it satanic—the Basel missionaries were uniquely open to African impositions and innovations.

The variant of Christianity that landed in the Gold Coast in the hearts and minds of the Basel missionaries was usually at odds, not only with three hundred years of precedent on the coast, but also with the state churches they had left behind at home. These missionaries were strange people at home even before they left, and they were strange people among the Europeans collected around the coastal forts. Even before they had settled in, they were misfits, and that was before local communities and local experiences had begun to shape and reshape them. Usually submerged into a category of German Protestantism called Pietism, the variant that arrived in Akropong is unique enough to demand some discussion. I place the creation of the Basel Mission in its local and historical context of Pietist missionary experience, as well as in the early nineteenth-century revivals in the German and Swiss borderlands. The argument here is that the development of Basel's missionary subculture cannot

---

[4]    Sonia Abun-Nasr, *Afrikaner und Missionar: die Lebensgeschichte von David Asante* (Basel: Schlettwein, 2003).

[5]    John Stuart develops this point in detail with respect to British Missionaries' inconsistent and ambivalent relationships with colonial authorities in the final decades of colonial rule: *British Missionaries and the End of Empire: East, Central, and Southern Africa, 1939–1964* (Grand Rapids: Eerdmans, 2011).

be adequately understood as sprouting from German or Swiss soil alone. It was rather the outcome of a dialectic process whereby missionary experience overseas fundamentally challenged the self-understanding of the sending communities.

The second argument develops one aspect of the strangeness of the missionaries: their understanding of Satan, whose defenses on the coast manifested, in Basel missionary eyes, as colonial forts. This eccentric Pietist rejection of European civilization as demonic did not so much reflect the imposition upon Africa of medieval Christianity, but represented rather a new reconfiguration of Christianity, arrived upon in global conversation. In the middle decades of the nineteenth century, rural German and Swiss Pietists began to integrate into their existing religious lives the stories they were reading in missionary magazines from around the world, from India to Tahiti. The Pietist missionary community cultivated a globalized imagination, such that they sometimes had an easier time relating to fellow believers in India or Persia or Ethiopia than to their non-Pietist next-door neighbors.

In 1850, for example, responding to commonplace European justifications for African subordination under the Curse of Ham, Johann Widmann dismissed the notion with little thought: Africa's broken condition reflected European malevolence, more than any ancient curse.[6] Ten years later, an unsigned editorial in the *EMM*, probably by Albert Ostertag, went further, identifying the slave traders themselves as Africa's curse. Thinking about the United States on the verge of its civil war, the editor spoke of "God's mysterious hand" or judgment:

> Since Christians [*die Christenheit*] refuse to be moved to love and compassion for Africa, God, whose thoughts about Ham are thoughts of peace, has sent terror and need, in order to force Christians to care about Africa.[7]

To the extent that the idea of the Curse of Ham represented a European Christian refusal to recognize Africans as humans, that curse had been lifted, however temporarily, in the Basel Mission's early thought. It was a unique moment in the history of world Christianity, and it would not last.

---

[6]  J. G. Widmann, "Station Akropong," *JB* 1850, 188.

[7]  Albert Ostertag, "Gottes Gedanken über Afrika," *EMM* 1860, 239. Incidentally, David Asante was living in Basel at this moment, and Ostertag, as one of the institute's core teachers, was in daily contact with him.

## PIETISTS BECOME MISSIONARIES

In order to approach these questions, I begin with the invention, or perhaps the emergence, of a new kind of Christian: Pietist missionaries. The two words must always be articulated together, because not all Pietists were interested in missionary activities, and even fewer missionaries in nineteenth-century Africa were Pietists. As both heirs of a religious movement that was a century and a half old and also as youthful activists inclined to feel that most of their fellow believers were insufficiently devoted, the missionary community of early nineteenth-century Basel, which gave birth to the Basel Mission, was both bookish and distrustful of received wisdom. In this respect the Pietists were acting like many others before them. Andrew Walls has argued that most missionary movements in Christian history, including the earliest centuries, originated as youth awakenings, and specifically as protest movements.[8] Pietist missions largely fit into this scheme; indeed, Walls probably had Pietists in mind when he first introduced it, and only retroactively mashed Franciscans and Moravians and others into his template. Pietism may be said to have originated as a Lutheran devotional network in the aftermath of the Thirty Years' War and at least partially in response to religiously motivated communal violence.[9] In contrast to the Methodists in England or the Pietists in Sweden, most German Lutheran Pietists did not leave the state churches. Rather, they formed a devout core within the churches, largely female in number (despite male dominance of Pietist organizations) and characterized by spiritual-emotional seeking and networking. Only in the second generation, around the beginning of the eighteenth century, did these people begin to build distinct institutions—schools, orphanages, printing presses, hospitals, and so on.[10]

---

[8] Andrew Walls, "The Eighteenth-Century Protestant Missionary Awakening in Its European Context," in *Christian Missions and the Enlightenment*, ed. Brian Stanley (Grand Rapids: Eerdmans, 2001), 22–44.

[9] This is not a straightforward question. Some scholars insist the term ought only to apply to Philip Jakob Spener (1635–1705) and his immediate associates. Others include as Pietism the broadly transnational (and multilingual) cluster of interrelated movements extending down to the present. "The issue," Carter Lindberg summarizes, "is whether Pietism is a concept of a particular period of history or an a-historical, typological concept." Carter Lindberg, "Introduction," in *The Pietist Theologians: An Introduction to Theology in the Seventeenth and Eighteenth Centuries*, ed. Carter Lindberg (Malden, Mass.: Blackwell, 2005), 3–4.

[10] Klaus Deppermann, *Der hallesche Pietismus und der preussische Staat unter Friedrich III. (I.)* (Göttingen: Vandenhoeck & Ruprecht, 1961). Rainer Lächele, ed., *Das Echo Halles: kulturelle Wirkungen des Pietismus* (Tübingen: Biliotheca Academica, 2001).

The missionaries themselves were avid consumers of church history, and especially of the early medieval conversion of the Germanic tribes. As in West Africa in the eighteenth and nineteenth centuries, Christianity had arrived in northern Europe in an unwieldy mixture of idealistic preachers—some of whom were monastics given to on-the-field innovations that later Catholic hierarchs suppressed—and conquering kings. Peel mentions Boniface, the eighth-century Anglo-Saxon missionary to the Friesians and Saxons, who, Peel observed, "shared many assumptions with the paganism [he] opposed."[11] Andrew Walls made this point in various ways over many years, and well before Peel. Walls' observation, in teaching church history in Sierra Leone in the 1960s, was that the indigenous Christians taking his classes had an intuitive understanding of the pre-Nicean (325 CE) dynamics of the Christian church.[12] This history mattered to the German Pietists, who were active students of their own heathen inheritance, and who tended to interpret both Africa and contemporary Germany through that historic lens. In the years of the Basel Mission's stillborn first attempt in the Gold Coast, the society's head (Inspector) Christian Gottlieb Blumhardt published a multivolume history of Christian missions, in which he nuanced the various German heathen responses to Christianity.

Blumhardt's was no contribution to German historiography: his volumes read like a thousand-page devotional, in which God's faithful messengers ("Sendlinge") prayed for, and were supernaturally filled with, compassion for the lost heathens, even to the point of death. Blumhardt continually spoke of a debt incurred by those heathen beneficiaries of missionary sacrifice, a debt that was owed to the lost elsewhere in the world. The preface to his third volume, on the Middle Ages, nicely captures the feel of Blumhardt's language:

> Our missions history now leads us to the terrible midnight hour of [the Church's] deepest humiliation, in which the wanderer, urgently scanning the skies, can scarcely capture a few flickering stars of hope on the horizon. Sunken into repulsive peonage to the reigning spirit of the world [*Weltgeist*], tragically fated to serve as means to passing ends, she appears to have entirely thrown away her early glory, in which in the days of the apostles she traveled great distances to the peoples of the world.[13]

[11] J. D. Y. Peel, *Religious Encounter and the Making of the Yoruba* (Bloomington: Indiana University Press, 2016), 6.

[12] Andrew Walls, "World Christianity and the Early Church," in *New Day: Essays on World Christianity in Honor of Lamin Sanneh*, ed. Akintunde E. Akinade (New York: Peter Lang, 2010).

[13] Christian Gottlieb Blumhardt, *Versuch einer allgemeinen Missionsgeschichte der Kirche Christi*, 5 vols. (Basel: J.G. Neukirch, 1828–1837), v.

Missions, in this logic, begin as discontent with calcified religion at home, more than as concern for the souls of the heathens: the latter only came with time. Indeed, Blumhardt's history of Christian missions served a contentious rhetorical purpose, which was to argue that his elders' noninterest in missions was a simple function of the deadness of their faith. In this way, Blumhardt's approach to history was decidedly contemporary.

Pietism had changed in fundamental ways since its first appearance in the seventeenth century. In 1717, the North Sea breached its protective dikes in Friesland, and over twelve thousand people drowned. The disaster repeated itself a century later, albeit on a smaller scale, and thousands more died. Comparing religious responses to these two events, Manfred Jakubowski-Tiessen has argued that Pietism had become a very different religion over the course of the eighteenth century. Pietist writers interpreted the 1717 disaster as the beginning of the end of the world, and they offered scriptural support for their view. In contrast, preachers and writers read the 1825 flood as God's judgment for the people's sin. Perhaps superficially similar in viewing God's hand in a terrifying event, these two interpretations diverge considerably in their social implications: if the end is approaching, retreat from the dangerous world becomes a rational and attractive answer, but if divine judgment is being meted out, repentance for sin—and calling upon one's neighbors to do the same—is the only reasonable response.[14] The former response had an ascetic, and the latter an activist quality.

During the eighteenth century, a quietist and isolationist faith had become a socially activist faith. This change is important for understanding the encounter in the Gold Coast. Christopher Clark has identified the eighteenth-century change from asceticism to activism with August Hermann Francke in Saxon Prussia, who channeled "the surplus spiritual energies of Lutheran nonconformism into a range of institutional projects." To Francke, social activism was inextricable from evangelism; his network of charities "gave bread to the poor, and simultaneously sought to win their ears and hearts for the good news."[15] "People are only willing to receive spiritual care," Kurt Aland quotes Francke as saying, "when

---

[14] Manfred Jakubowski-Tiessen, "Zeit- und Zukunftsdeutungen in Krisenzeiten in Pietismus und Erweckungsbewegung," in *Geschichtsbewusstsein und Zukunftserwartung in Pietismus und Erweckungsbewegung*, ed. Wolfgang Breul and Jan Carsten Schnurr (Göttingen: Vandenhoeck & Ruprecht, 2013), 175.

[15] Christopher M. Clark, *Iron Kingdom: The Rise and Downfall of Prussia, 1600–1947* (Cambridge, Mass.: Belknap Press of Harvard University Press, 2006), 135.

their bodily difficulties are first relieved."[16] It was under Francke that German Protestantism first ventured into overseas missionary work, in 1706 in the south Indian city of Tranquebar near Madras, then leased by the Danish crown. The Tranquebar mission's importance in India is a matter of some historiographical debate, but it was clearly successful at developing an indigenous clergy and vernacular traditions.[17] More importantly for present purposes, it was only after Pietist missionaries arrived in Tranquebar that the Pietists learned how to be missionaries. Having gone overseas with little or no cross-cultural experience, and no role models, they leaned heavily on their indigenous coworkers, many of whom were literate in Tamil and who wrote extensively to Halle on stationary made of palm leaves. Heike Liebau, who has studied these palm-leaf manuscripts in Danish archives, has made a bold and convincing argument that Pietist missionary ideology was initially composed in the Tamil language, before being received upstream into Pietist networks through newsletters and inspirational pamphlets.[18] Beyond this finer point concerning the degree to which indigenous South Indian converts directly shaped the form of transnational Pietism, the experiment in Tranquebar was certainly influential back home, in the eighteenth-century creation of a missionary variant of continental Pietism. From Tranquebar forward, Pietist missionaries were always committed not only to language learning, but also to vernacular publication, to offering educational services to local authorities, and to studying local cultures (something approaching ethnography, but not quite). Subsequent German ventures in Africa (and Asia) all prioritized vernacular language learning to a far greater extent than did English or American Protestant missionaries.

The Basel Mission understood itself to be building on previous Pietist (and Brethren) missionary experience, but the Mission's members and leadership, especially before 1850, changed their minds repeatedly as the network absorbed lessons and experiences from the field. Thus, young people applying for admission in the late 1840s, like Johann Christaller, had grown up reading missionary newsletters in their homes, while those of the 1820s, like Andreas

---

[16] Kurt Aland, "Der Pietismus und die soziale Frage," in *Pietismus und moderne Welt*, ed. Kurt Aland (Witten: Luther-Verlag, 1974), 133. Aland is citing Franke's unpublished "Grosser Aufsatz" of ca. 1716, p. 147.

[17] Daniel Jeyaraj, "Die Ordination des ersten protestantischen Pfarrers in Indien 1733," *Zeitschrift für Mission* 23, no. 2 (1997), 105–25.

[18] Heike Liebau, *Die indischen Mitarbeiter der Tranquebarmission (1706—1845): Katecheten, Schulmeister, Übersetzer* (Tübingen: Verl. der Franckeschen Stiftungen Halle im Max-Niemeyer-Verl., 2008).

Riis, had initially relied on their youthful energy to compensate for nearly total ignorance about what they were trying to do.[19]

## BETWEEN THE HEATHEN PAST AND THE COMING KINGDOM

Even as it evolved into a globally activist faith over the course of the eighteenth century, German Pietism was also developing regional particularities. The core of the Basel Mission drew on Pietist communities and networks in southwestern Germany, particularly in small Swabian cities near Stuttgart in the rolling hills of Württemberg, to the east of the Black Forest. Württemberg Pietism of the late eighteenth and early nineteenth centuries shared much of its aesthetic orientation with the broader evangelical world, but there are three other qualities to this subgrouping, which would become important factors in the religious encounter in Ghana. Taken together, these qualities made German Pietists more receptive to African input than nearly any other Europeans in West Africa.

The first of these was a taste for education. In his study of British missionary training programs before the Indian Mutiny of 1857, Stuart Piggin observes that prior to the creation of the Basel Mission training institute, British missionary societies offered only limited training to their staff.[20] Württemberg Pietism, by contrast, established a wide variety of educational institutions, including schools for the poor and disabled. The Basel Mission would take this approach to the Gold Coast, where missionaries often taught industrial trades, such as barrel-making, alongside reading and writing.

The second particularity of late eighteenth-century German Pietism was a strong but unique millenarian strand: a belief in Jesus' impending return (and the concomitant end of the world), which combined end-times calculations with institution building. This is a relatively uncommon combination. Christian history has seen many end-times movements, but few of these have simultaneously maintained a social-works orientation. The work of building

---

[19] Birgit Herppich argues that the organizational culture of the Basel Mission's training institute was very important in leading this change, including its inculcation of inflexibility on the field. *Pitfalls of Trained Incapacity: The Unintended Effects of Integral Missionary Training in the Basel Mission on Its Early Work in Ghana (1828–1840)* (Eugene, Ore.: Wipf and Stock, 2016).

[20] Stuart Piggin, *Making Evangelical Missionaries 1789–1858: The Social Background, Motives and Training of British Protestant Missionaries to India* (Abingdon: Sutton Courtenay Press, 1984), cited in Herppich, *Pitfalls of Trained Incapacity*.

institutions has not always come easy to people expecting the world to burn up in the near future.[21]

The third feature of early nineteenth-century Pietism of southwestern Germany was an intuitive understanding of ritual's role in communal renewal. Perhaps derived from the small-town and agrarian network's awareness of the rhythms of life, the Basel Mission network held annual festivals to generate interest, to renew friendships, to tell stories, and to sing. These so-called *Missionsfeste* (sing. *Missionsfest*) were emotional, entertaining, and appealed to the lower classes in a spirit of mild anticlerical defiance, should the cleric in question be a rationalist. I turn to these festivals below.

A further distinction must be stressed between Pietists in general and the missionary subset thereof, especially in their understanding of history. The missionaries were not normal Pietists, even within the community of people who attended missionary festivals and donated.[22] Those who actually went abroad were temperamental activists and risk-takers. Early nineteenth-century Pietists in southwest Germany and northwest Switzerland tended to have a pronounced otherworldly streak, which manifested as a desire to escape a world headed for destruction. This escape could mean simple abstinence from gambling, dancing, and the theater, but it could include spatial withdrawal into separatist communities such as Korntal (established 1819) and Wilhelmsdorf (1824).[23] To many Pietists, but not all, self-segregation was an effective way of protecting oneself from an increasingly dangerous and sinful world, while patiently waiting for (and sometimes dedicating much time to calculating) the end of the world.[24] But those who, having grown up constantly alert to signs that the end of the world is approaching, nevertheless ventured abroad as missionaries often combined this millenarian view with an activist logic, by which they could help hasten the second coming. Judith Becker observes that the missionary community posited a dualistic tension between the dark, bad, and threatening present and the bright future. Becker argues that overseas

---

[21] Thomas K. Kuhn, "Diakonie im Schatten des Chiliasmus. Christian Heinrich Zeller (1779–1860) in Beuggen," in *Das «Fromme Basel». Religion in einer Stadt des 19. Jahrhunderts*, ed. Thomas K. Kuhn and Martin Sallmann (Basel: Schwabe, 2002), 93–110.

[22] Michael Kannenberg, *Verschleierte Uhrtafeln: Endzeiterwartungen im württembergischen Pietismus zwischen 1818 und 1848* (Göttingen: Vandenhoeck & Ruprecht, 2007); Jan Carsten Schnurr, *Weltreiche und Wahrheitszeugen: Geschichtsbilder der protestantischen Erweckungsbewegung in Deutschland, 1815–1848* (Göttingen: Vandenhoeck & Ruprecht, 2011).

[23] Meyer, *Translating the Devil*, 30–38; Paul Jenkins, "Villagers as Missionaries: Wurttemberg Pietism as a 19th Century Missionary Movement," *Missiology* 8, no. 4 (1980), 425–32.

[24] Kannenberg, *Verschleierte Uhrtafeln*.

missions reconciled this tension by imagining fellowship with distant peoples within the "Reich Gottes," the unseen Kingdom of God. Mission helped bring the day closer at which what is unseen would be unveiled.[25]

Favorite biblical imagery included eschatological passages from Micah, Isaiah, and Revelation. One of these, Micah 4, contains the well-known prophecy that "in the last days" war would come to an end as the peoples of the world "beat their swords into plowshares" (Mic 4:3). That image, however, is immediately preceded by what the Pietist missionary community identified as the interrelationship between missions and the end of time:

Many nations will come and say,

> "Come, let us go up to the mountain of the Lord,
>    to the temple of the God of Jacob.
> He will teach us his ways,
>    so that we may walk in his paths." (Mic 4:2)

Before swords are beat into plowshares, in other words, "many nations will . . . go to the mountain of the Lord." World peace, in this interpretation, which was to be established by none other than the returned Jesus, would come about after the "nations" ("heathens" [Heiden] in Luther's German translation) came to the mountain of the Lord. Overseas missions, according to this line of thought, might include many means, such as education or translation, but the end goal was to help history move a little closer to its conclusion by adding to the number of peoples around the world coming to the mountain of the Lord. This kind of grand scheme does not necessarily proceed from an initial emotional commitment to the various peoples, such as the Akuapem, but rather from Bible study.

A favorite New Testament prophecy among the missionaries was Revelation 21:24–26. This story concludes a revelation about the end of time. After many wars and troubles of all sorts, a "new Jerusalem" is lowered down from heaven, and:

The nations will walk by its light, and the kings of the earth will bring their splendor into it. On no day will its gates ever be shut, for there will be no night there. The glory and honor of the nations will be brought into it.

---

[25] Judith Becker, "Zukunftserwartungen und Missionsimpetus bei Missionsgesellschaften in der ersten Hälfte des 19. Jahrhunderts," in *Geschichtsbewusstsein und Zukunftserwartung in Pietismus und Erweckungsbewegung*, ed. Wolfgang Breul and Jan Carsten Schnurr, *Arbeiten zur Geschichte des Pietismus* (Göttingen: Vandenhoeck & Ruprecht, 2013), 258.

As with the Micah 4 passage, the logic here is that only once the *nations*—again, *ethnoi* in Greek, and *Heiden* (heathens) in Luther's German—were prepared to thus enter into Jerusalem, only then will the vision become a reality. Mission among the heathens was thus active motion toward bringing healing to the suffering homeland.[26]

The first generation of Basel missionaries, including indigenous employees, were explicit in conversation with their African interlocutors that their project was oriented toward bringing about the end of time. One of these was Andrew Wilhelm, a "recaptive" (enslaved African liberated from a slave ship by the British Royal Navy) of the Egba people of southwestern Nigeria, who in the 1820s had trekked overland from Sierra Leone back to his homelands. Wilhelm, who had spent several years in a Basel Mission church in the Sierra Leone town of Hastings, expressed this notion in the 1830 *Church Missionary Record*. Referring to the nineteenth chapter of Revelation, in which Jesus' second coming is depicted as the Lamb of God's marriage to the church, he wrote: "At the Marriage-Supper of the Lamb, the tables will be furnished with guests: His Father's *house will be filled.*"[27] Since the unity of all peoples at the end of time also implied the overcoming of denominational walls between Christians, the Basel mission remained nondenominational in theory throughout its entire history, although mainly Lutheran and Reformed in practice. On the field, however, missionaries broke many denominational barriers. This tactic was a pragmatic move in a challenging field, but was also a matter of devotional praxis and, increasingly as the century wore on, fraternal identification with the other expatriate Europeans.[28] This ecumenical approach was a good deal more complicated in India, the Middle East, and East Africa, where interdenominational cooperation necessarily involved ancient Christian communities, than in the Gold Coast, where the missionaries could dismiss most other European Christians as denizens of Satan's Strongholds. For example, in an 1829 letter from Cairo, a certain Missionary Kugler, on his way to Abyssinia, wrote of several encounters with

---

[26]  Becker, "Zukunftserwartungen und Missionsimpetus," 258.

[27]  Andrew Wilhelm quoted in "West-Africa Mission," *Church Missionary Record* 1, no. 1 (January 1830), 5. Italics original. On the remarkable Wilhelm more generally: Kehinde Olabimtan, "Wilhelm, Andrew (C. 1802 to 1866)," in *Dictionary of African Christian Biography*, http://www.dacb.org/stories/nigeria/wilhelm_andrew.html, accessed October 11, 2019. On recaptives, from the perspective of the spread of Christianity in West Africa, see Lamin Sanneh, *Abolitionists Abroad: American Blacks and the Making of Modern West Africa* (Cambridge, Mass.: Harvard University Press, 1999), 110–12.

[28]  Relations with the Wesleyans were complicated in the Gold Coast: this missionary society was simultaneously a competitor and a friend. The Wesleyans usually maintained lower standards for behavior, with the result that they were able to absorb people whose misdeeds had gotten them kicked out of Basel congregations.

Amharic-speaking Orthodox Christians, who had undertaken a pilgrimage to Jerusalem. The pilgrims had taught Kugler a song of atonement in Amharic. The point of learning the song, Kugler said, was preparation for heaven, at which he hoped that he would be found a "faithful servant" of Christ.[29] Likewise during these early years, the Basel Mission cultivated a close relationship with the leadership of the Armenian Orthodox church, who supported the missionaries in their work among pagans in the Caucasus in exchange for the missionaries teaching biblical Greek to local priests.[30]

Although many of these men and women were farmers and villagers, they were also integrated into a globalized world. Poverty connected them with America, of course, but their religious lives took them even farther afield. Akropong-born Theodor Bohner, describing his father Heinrich's origins in the 1840s in Feil, a small village in the Palatinate, recognized in the heightened religiosity of his father's community a spiritual and intellectual [geistig] seeking:

> For seekers among the peasantry, the only pathway to a spiritual-intellectual life was religion. For that reason, in Feil as in so many villages across the Palatinate, whatever energies were left over from daily drudgeries and labor were directed into a life in the Bible, the hymnal, and the Church. Elsewhere in the fatherland, it might have been different, but that is how it was here.[31]

The younger Bohner seems to be suggesting ("elsewhere in the fatherland . . .") that the piety of the farmers was a function of their dearth of options.[32] He was speaking partially autobiographically about his own personal journey away from his father's faith, a journey which was neatly captured by his use of the word "fatherland" (*Vaterland*): later-century German nationalism, including Theodor Bohner's, was a form of religion.

This, then, is a brief sketch of the milieu and subset of Christianity whence came the Basel Mission. That organization would take on a life of its own, but in its early years was very much an expression of a very particular spiritual,

[29] "Aus einem Briefe von Missionar Kugler in Egypten," *Calwer Missions-Blatt* 3, no. 1 (1830), 3–4.

[30] August Heinrich Dittrich, Felician Zaremba, and Heinrich Benz, "Reise nach Tiflis und Georgien, und Aufenthalt daselbst, vom May 1823 bis Febr. 1824," *EMM* 1824, 460–93, esp. 478–82.

[31] Theodor Bohner, *Der Schuhmacher Gottes. ein deutsches Leben in Afrika* (Frankfurt: Rütten & Loening, 1935), 12.

[32] Birgit Meyer makes a similar argument, saying that, in contrast to the ideal type of the ascetic Calvinist capitalist in Max Weber's exploration about disenchantment, "most nineteenth-century Pietists were balancing on the edge of poverty." Meyer, *Translating the Devil*, 33.

organizational, and social subculture. Although they were diverse amongst themselves, and were mostly open, at least in theory, to collaboration with other Christians, Basel's missionaries were not Christians-in-general; they were unclear on whether they worshiped the same God as, for example, the governors at the colonial castles. Those were, after all, satanic outposts.

### BIRTH IN WAR AND HUNGER

This general description of activist Pietism, which emerged gradually in the eighteenth century, requires careful chronological nuance. Although the Basel Mission arose out of a well-established religious subculture, it specifically came out of an early-century revival. The Awakening, the *Erweckungsbewegung* or the *réveil*, as it was termed in francophone Protestant Switzerland, tends to resist historical definition, because the "Pietist and evangelical religion created a sense of common understanding and purpose between groups separated by geography, nationality, and confession."[33] As with other Christian revivals in history, the Awakening expressed a youthful discontent with a state church that had no answers for the revolutionary warfare and endemic poverty afflicting the region.

However, unlike most revivals originating as youth movements, this one had a relatively long life—well over thirty years. The secret to the Awakening's sustained endurance lay in part in the Pietist network's effective harnessing of youthful discontent with the church and with the world into a long-term deferral of gratification: in Jon Miller's phrasing, "missionary zeal and institutional control."[34] Moreover, because the Awakening's rural German heartland was faced with pervasive poverty throughout the period, the movement spread across the oceans along routes of German emigrant settlement.[35] In a study of three Protestant revivals (the first of which began in 1815), which he understood as reactions to secularization, Hartmut Lehmann argued that for many Pietists, the struggle against Napoleon overlapped considerably with that against secularism, because the connection between the French Enlightenment and Bonapartist aggression seemed so obvious to the devout Protestants of southwestern Germany.[36] The Basel Mission was only one of a cluster

[33] Walls, "The Eighteenth-Century Protestant Missionary Awakening," 40.

[34] Jon Miller, *Missionary Zeal and Institutional Control: Organizational Contradictions in the Basel Mission on the Gold Coast, 1828–1917* (Grand Rapids: Eerdmans, 2003).

[35] Ulrich Gäbler, "Erweckung in europäischen und im amerikanischen Protestantismus," *Pietismus und Neuzeit* 15 (1989), 24–39.

[36] Hartmut Lehmann, "Neupietismus und Säkularisierung. Beobachtungen zum sozialen Umfeld und politischen Hintergrund von Erweckungsbewegung und Gemeinschaftsbewegung," *Pietismus und Neuzeit* 15 (1989), 44–47.

of Pietist religious works in the city and region, and most of these arose during the years of occupation.

The German Evangelical Missionary Society, which would gradually come to be known as the Basel Mission, was founded in July 1815. It was the creation of a long-established network of like-minded Pietists, who had been gathering in homes—that is, beyond the official purview of the churches—for prayer meetings. A wartime experience with Eurasian paganism stirred them to think missionally. Throughout that spring, Basel was a minor stage in Napoleon's final Hundred Days campaign. The French commander of the border town of Huningue (Hüningen in German) began bombarding Basel in May, and continued to do so until well after Waterloo, when he was pacified by Russian imperial troops. The Basel Mission's fiery birth remained part of internal organizational lore for a generation. Nine years after the founding, Christian Blumhardt recalled at the annual meetings (held during the Missionsfest):

> How strange was the Lord's leadership! As strange armies, of peoples whose names we did not know, of Kalmyks, Bashkirs, Buryatians, and others, came to our city to save us from bombardment from Hüningen, He put in our hearts the thought to show them eternal salvation—and therefore the idea of a small missionary school.[37]

Having secured a charter from the city on July 27, the organizers, centered on a handful of men, including Nicolaus von Brunn (aged sixty-one), Christian Friedrich Spittler (aged thirty-three), and Christian Gottlieb Blumhardt (aged thirty-six), set about organizing a training institute.[38] They did not have a concrete idea of what this institute would look like. Nature intervened, however, in the form of the so-called "Year without Summer." Failed crops due to late frosts led to hunger and bread riots throughout Europe, with western Switzerland among the hardest-hit regions.[39] The Basel Mission was getting underway, in other words, at a moment of war and famine. It was exactly at this moment that the training institute opened its doors, on August 26. The biblical reading, by lot, fell that day to Zechariah 4:6, an end-times vision in

[37] W. Schlatter, *Geschichte der Basler Mission*, vol. 1, *Die Heimatgeschichte der Basler Mission* (Basel: Verlag der Missionsbuchhandlung, 1916), 17.

[38] W. Schlatter, *Geschichte der Basler Mission 1815–1915*, vol. 1, *Die Heimatgeschichte der Basler Mission*, 21.

[39] Gillen D'Arcy Wood, *Tambora: The Eruption that Changed the World* (Princeton: Princeton University Press, 2014).

which an angel speaks with the prophet. "How will this happen? Not by might (German: *Heer*, indicating an army) or by power, but by my spirit."[40]

The organizers actively sought, and expected, the miraculous in daily life, and used language strikingly familiar to observers of contemporary Pentecostalism. As a mid-century teacher at the institute recalled:

> The sainted Inspector [Christian] Blumhardt [co-founder of the Mission] used to say: "If only we trust in God's will and in his calling, then we need be afraid of nothing in this world. If necessary, even the resources we need would come flying through the window."[41]

For a variety of reasons, the training institute's importance is not to be understated in the Basel Mission's subsequent history in Ghana. First of all, it preceded, by several years, the sending of missionaries. Initially having no field of its own, the Basel Mission seconded its earliest graduates to existing societies (chiefly the Church Missionary Society, one of whose board members, Karl Friedrich Adolf Steinkopf of Stuttgart, was a product of the Awakening).[42] Consequently, much of the Basel Mission's organizational culture (and its dysfunction) was established *before* the society first ventured into the Gold Coast. Moreover, as others have noted, this sequence meant that theory came before practice and experience, leading to an organizational leadership datum that "in order to set mission policy, it was not necessary to know much about the field."[43]

This early attitude was often counterproductive. In a recent sociological study of the training institute's first dozen years, Birgit Herppich applied Robert Merton's concept of "trained incapacities" to explore the problem. Developing ideas from Thomas Veblen, Merton defined this kind of failure of training as "that state of affairs in which one's abilities function as inadequacies or blind spots." Actions based upon training and skills that have been successfully applied in the past may result in inappropriate responses under changed conditions. An inadequate flexibility in the application of skills, will, in a changing

---

[40]   Richard Haug, *Reich Gottes im Schwabenland: Linien im württembergischen Pietismus* (Metzingen: Franz, 1981), 219.

[41]   Ostertag, "Die Goldküste und die Basler Mission daselbst," 33.

[42]   W. Schlatter, *Geschichte der Basler Mission 1815–1915*, vol. 1, *Die Heimatgeschichte der Basler Mission*, 10.

[43]   Paul Jenkins, "The Basel Mission, the Presbyterian Church, and Ghana since 1918," in Jon Miller, *Missionary Zeal and Institutional Control: Organizational Contradictions in the Basel Mission on the Gold Coast, 1828–1917* (Grand Rapids: Eerdmans, 2003), 211.

milieu, result in more or less serious maladjustments.[44] Within the Basel Mission subculture, the priority given to education, and especially historical and cultural studies about peoples around the world, meant that early missionaries had a strong penchant for interpreting their experiences in comparison with others' experiences around the world and through time. They cultivated a strong sense of organizational memory, which included an acute awareness of their origins in fear and hunger.

## Festive Life

There was another key ingredient to the missionary subculture in Pietist southwest Germany and northwest Switzerland: festive life—the Missionsfest, to which I now turn. Heinrich Bohner was eight years old when his father announced that the boy was old enough to come along to a Missionsfest, probably in a nearby town in the rural Palatinate.[45] This was one of the Basel Mission's annual public celebrations of the mission work, where people assembled in one or another southwestern German, Alsatian, and northwestern Swiss small town squares, for singing, listening to speeches and stories from abroad, and prayer. During the early and middle years of the nineteenth century, these festivals were often the biggest annual event in town, drawing hundreds and even thousands of farmers and small-town supporters to slightly bigger towns. Collectively these Missionsfeste became the ritual climaxes to the Pietist calendar. In their very scope and bustle they cemented the sense of belonging and fellowship among often-isolated Pietist families. Even the missionaries in the Gold Coast held a Missionsfest, sharing the news from elsewhere in the world and encouraging the African congregants to view themselves as part of a global movement. Although the festivals served several organizational purposes at once, their emotional force cannot be understated: by the 1840s, Missionsfest assumed a ritual scope approximating Catholic pilgrimage.[46] While the organizational capacity of the Basel Mission proceeded from quiet living room prayer meetings and the modest and internally motivated pooling of halfpenny donations into hundreds of thousands of francs, the festivals were intensely emotional and at times overwhelming. In 1850, Philip Heinrich Bohner was proud to announce to his wife Barbara that "Henne darf mit," "Heinrich may come along." Eighty years later, Heinrich's son Theodor invented a conversation between the young boy and his mother in advance of

---

[44] Robert King Merton, *Social Theory and Social Structure* (Glencoe, Ill.: Free Press, 1957), 197–200, cited in Herppich, *Pitfalls of Trained Incapacity*, 8.

[45] Bohner, *Der Schuhmacher Gottes*, 15.

[46] Kannenberg, *Verschleierte Uhrtafeln*, 290.

the festival, worth quoting despite its late and fictional composition, for the childlike feel to these annual rituals. More than a few missionaries first heard about the outside world through these events, especially outside the official programming, in individual conversations with the visiting missionaries.

> "Mommy, what is a Missionsfest?"
> "At a Missionsfest people sing songs, and hear stories about missions, and then they pray."
> "For whom do they pray?"
> "For the heathens."
> "Why do they pray for the heathens?"
> "So that they become Christians."
> "Mommy, why should the heathens become Christians?"
> "Dumb child, we are Christians, and the heathens should be as well. That is why the Lord Jesus died on the cross. Don't you love the Lord Jesus?"
> "Yes, but Mommy, what do the heathens look like?"
> "Haven't I shown you pictures of them? They are black negroes or brown Hindus or yellow Chinese with braids."
> "Do the heathens come to the Missionsfest?"
> "What questions you ask! They live over the seas, and you need to take a ship to reach them. But a missionary, who has been among the heathens will come and tell stories. My! They tell wonderful stories. In the afternoon, you know, when we will be sitting at long tables under the trees in the churchyard, drinking coffee."[47]

In his marvelous treatment of the early nineteenth-century Missionsfest, Michael Kannenberg presents an impressive case that the festivals combined mobilization for missions (including fundraising) with the formation of an enthusiastic sub-community within the existing state churches. Kannenberg calls this dynamic "Missionsfest as ritual," which might not be an overstatement.[48] By the 1830s, many villages throughout southwestern Germany and northwestern Switzerland had their own Missionsfeste. If the official agenda for a given festival centered on organizational life for missionary societies, above all (but not exclusively) that of the Basel Mission, the main attraction for many of the attendees was the heightened emotionalism of revival and song. This was only one example of the infusion of transnational spiritual experience into rural faith, through the vehicle of the Missionsfeste, whereby the state church's skeptical gatekeepers could be triangulated.[49]

---

[47] Bohner, *Der Schuhmacher Gottes*, 15–16.

[48] Kannenberg, *Verschleierte Uhrtafeln*, 290.

[49] Kannenberg tells of "non-Pietist" clerics encountering pushback during the festival, while the enthusiastic peasants occupied the church grounds. *Verschleierte Uhrtafeln*, 291.

This popular movement took a turn for the supernatural in 1844, when former Basel Mission Training Institute teacher Johann Christian Blumhardt (nephew of the society's cofounder) began applying what he had been reading about in missionary reports and began healing diseases and exorcising demons in his own village. For several years, Blumhardt's presence as speaker on a local festival's lineup assured a large turnout among the rural population; in the "general opinion," his sermon was the "center point of the festival."[50] Blumhardt's wife Doris wrote of the 1844 Missionsfest in Calw (in which village the Basel Mission would later establish its printing press), which was "massively attended; the crowd was estimated at six thousand as a minimum; the festival was a blessing for everyone."[51] Adolf Christ-Sarasin, a Basel Mission board member and member of a prominent business family in that city, had traveled to the same Missionsfest in Calw:

> Everywhere, stacked on top of one another, stood Württemberger peasants [Landvolk]. No one could sit. Thousands were crowded into every alleyway; a falling stone could not have touched the ground. . . . The singing was more impressive than the speeches, rising from six thousand throats.[52]

### CALLING INTO MISSIONS

Immersed in this way in newsletters, prayer meetings, halfpenny collections, and festivals, all reiterating the same message, a young person might discern a calling into missions as obvious and organic, even if a massive and sustained campaign lay behind it. That was how Johannes Christaller experienced his calling. Christaller was born in the village of Winnenden in Württemberg in 1827 to a tailor and a baker's daughter from the nearby town of Grunbach. The two married when both were aged thirty-five years. The people of Winnenden denied the bride citizenship in their town on account of her advanced age, "because they feared they might need to support weakling children" and because she could only present a dowry of 132 guilders.[53] A few years later, when Johann Christaller was five, his father was

---

[50] Adolf Christ-Sarasin, quoted in Dieter Ising and Gerhard Schäfer, eds., *Johann Christoph Blumhardt. Möttlinger Briefe 1838–1852, Anmerkungen*, vol. 4 (Göttingen: Vandenhoeck & Ruprecht, 1997), 220.

[51] Dieter Ising and Gerhard Schäfer, eds., *Johann Christoph Blumhardt. Möttlinger Briefe 1838–1852, Texte*, vol. 3 (Göttingen: Vandenhoeck & Ruprecht, 1997), item no. 1217, "Doris Blumhardt an die Eltern, 14.5.1844," 227–31.

[52] Christ-Sarasin quoted in Ising and Schäfer, *Johann Christoph Blumhardt*, 4:220.

[53] Else Schubert-Christaller, *Missionar J.G. Christaller: Erinnerungen aus seinem Leben* (Stuttgart: Evang. Missionsverlag, 1929), 6.

found dead in a vineyard, frozen to death. Denied welfare assistance by the stroke of a municipal pen, the fatherless Christaller had no money for fees and thus could not attend school. However, he taught himself to read and write in German and Latin. One night, at the end of a prayer meeting for the missionaries, Joseph Josenhans (then serving as pastor at Winnenden, later head of the Basel Mission) concluded with a "free" (that is, unscripted) prayer that "God might select someone from this congregation, who might be sent out as a messenger to the heathens [Heidenbote]." Young Christaller was in attendance and felt that the prayer was for him. He responded a few weeks later, when his sister, reading the *Heidenbote* one evening, announced to the room that her brother should go to become a missionary.[54] A few years later, Christaller sought and gained admittance to the Basel Mission seminary despite his lack of a formal education. Everyone who worked with Christaller recognized the youth's exceptional intelligence. Josenhans' letter of recommendation mentioned the young man had "all the advantages and deficits of an autodidact."[55]

Christaller's story stands in for several others. The Pietist missionaries were villagers, but they were also daydreamers and eccentrics among their co-religionists.[56] Jon Miller has nuanced this portrait by exploring the actual professions of the first twenty-five young men sent to the Gold Coast: three shoemakers, five weavers, four carpenters, a sail maker, a glazier, two pot makers, two farmers, a servant, a lathe operator, a student, two teachers, and a scribe. Miller moreover identifies a gendered contrast: most of the women hailed from higher families—the daughters of teachers, pastors, and councilmen.[57] However, the fragile economic conditions of northwestern Switzerland and southwestern Germany in the mid-nineteenth century forced many of the artisanal families to emigrate to America.[58] Of the men and women buried at Akropong and Kyebi, most had grown up poor, a broken bone or an early frost away from destitution. Something else needs to be added: during these mid-nineteenth-century years of breakneck industrialization in the urban west of German-speaking countries, as the social fabric stretched beyond the breaking point, rural inhabitants were increasingly strangers in their own countries, let alone overseas.[59] Moreover, these missionaries, with their

[54]  Schubert-Christaller, *Missionar J.G. Christaller*, 8.

[55]  Schubert-Christaller, *Missionar J.G. Christaller*, 9.

[56]  One of Paul Jenkins' early epiphanies, as archivist for the Basel Mission in the 1970s, was the very modest social origins of most of the volunteers. Jenkins, "Villagers as Missionaries."

[57]  Miller, *Missionary Zeal and Institutional Control*, 53–56.

[58]  Bohner, *Der Schuhmacher Gottes*, 9.

[59]  Meyer, *Translating the Devil*, 30.

relatively homogeneous origins, had been incorporated into an organizational culture dominated, at least for the first few decades, by the training institute, which, owing in part to its lack of diversity, tended to hobble students' imaginations. Birgit Herppich:

> Especially when groups engaging in cross-cultural Christian ministry are essentially homogeneous in terms of their religious and socio-ethical emphases (like the Basel Mission and its participants) their training processes have a strong propensity to establish inflexible mental frameworks of theological assumptions and social ideals that are potentially detrimental to intercultural engagement.[60]

Among the distinctly German and Pietist notions of communal belonging that the Basel missionaries brought to Africa, two tended to make the missionaries susceptible to political maneuverings by local kings. The first was a sense of spiritual homelessness: relative to their preconceived definitions of calling and sending, the missionaries could not go native without ceasing to be missionaries. They were people without a home, however much they were changed by their experiences in Africa. This notion drew on many years of Pietist experience of viewing themselves as a faithful minority within their own villages. At times, they endured testy relationships with the state churches, under whose authority they lived. Missionary nonbelonging, both at home and abroad, was a highly unstable and emotionally fraught situation, and it rested on a two-tier conception of the Kingdom of God. The latter referred to an unseen but very real domain of human and spiritual well-being. The Kingdom of God was a community that was not at all to be confused with church membership, as the latter necessarily included many wolves disguised as sheep. Nevertheless, the Kingdom of God was partially to be seen in the church of the present. It was an eagerly awaited nowhere land. To be a missionary was to be a citizen of that nowhere: it was to be a forever foreigner.[61] Such utopian thinking recurs in Christian history, above all in expressions of youthful protests against calcified church hierarchies—in Barth, in Kierkegaard, and farther back, to any number of monastic movements. In this regard, missionary rootlessness was both longitudinally prophetic and immediately disruptive.

The second missionary notion, uncritically shared throughout German nationalist thinking of the time (and thus representing one area in which the Basel Mission had assimilated into the broader midcentury German cultural ecosystem), was equally unstable: the primacy the mission tended to ascribe to

---

[60] Herppich, *Pitfalls of Trained Incapacity*, 5.
[61] Kuhn, "Diakonie im Schatten des Chiliasmus," 93–110.

language as social denominator. German Pietist missionary understanding of ethnicity and race turned on the notion of language. Specifically, language was the "spiritual homeland" [*Heimat*] of a given people [*Volk*].[62] Within this line of reasoning, the missionaries had a difficult time imagining multiethnicity in any other way than that of a birth defect: it could only present a handicap for the spiritual well-being of the Kingdom. However, it is in exactly this area that the missionaries' expectations diverged from those of the converts in the Gold Coast, and for the basic reason that language had very little to do with social divides. On the ground, even common people spoke multiple languages, and social structures, some of which were quite rigid, typically transcended language. Moreover, the students of the Basel Mission's middle schools in the Gold Coast were a decidedly diverse lot. Sitting in classrooms together with people of several different languages—Krobo, Akyem, Guan, Gã, Fante, and Ewe youths—the students were undergoing a rigorous socialization that tended to separate them from their communities of origin. Relative to the staggeringly multilingual southeastern Gold Coast, the German presumption that language was the principal building block of race was a laughable notion.

Recent scholarship on cross-cultural encounters in the pre- and early colonial Gold Coast has tended to focus on Africans and Afro-Europeans who were able to navigate between worlds.[63] Such studies are a helpful corrective to Eurocentric obsession with foreign initiative against an African setting imagined as timeless and unchanging or unchangeable. The challenge, however, is to adequately demonstrate multiple dynamics at once: Europeans, especially those living deep in the Gold Coast's rural interior, were also becoming new people as they sought to integrate their experiences. A further challenge is the very notion of a "hybrid" culture as Ipsen refers to the mulatto women of Accra.[64] By writing about cultural mixing as if it were remarkable, Ipsen actually reaffirms twentieth-century European understandings of ethnicity as something concrete and definite. However, the West African reality, at least in

---

[62] Erika Eichholzer, "Missionary Linguistics on the Gold Coast," in *The Spiritual in the Secular: Missionaries and Knowledge about Africa*, ed. Patrick Harries and David Maxwell, (Grand Rapids: Eerdmans, 2012), 72. Eichholzer refers to a letter from J. G. Christaller: BMA D-10.5,17 f.

[63] For the British-colonial era: Carina E. Ray, *Crossing the Color Line: Race, Sex, and the Contested Politics of Colonialism in Ghana* (Athens: Ohio University Press, 2015). For the Danish era: Ipsen, *Daughters of the Trade: Atlantic Slavers and Interracial Marriage on the Gold Coast* (Philadelphia: University of Pennsylvania Press, 2015). For the Fante people to the west of Accra: Rebecca Shumway, *The Fante and the Transatlantic Slave Trade*, Rochester Studies in African History and the Diaspora (Rochester, N.Y.: University of Rochester Press, 2011).

[64] Ipsen, *Daughters of the Trade*, 11.

the coastal plains south of the forest, has always been one of linguistic, religious, and cultural pluralism—of constant interaction and negotiation with people unlike oneself. This ethnic mixing may have been especially pronounced in urban settings, and at major crossroads, but the historical record suggests that there was nothing exceptional about cross-cultural encounters in rural areas such as Akuapem, either. The tension between a missionary ideology predicated on distance from "the world" and an indigenous expectation of incorporating foreigners worked itself out in various ways. In chapter 7, I will look at one of the most important: the ways the pervasive experience of sickness, grief, weakness, poverty, and dependency on native compassion cumulatively remade the first few generations of missionaries. However, another related dynamic must first be considered: the ways missionary experience overseas flowed backwards, as it were, and came to bear on the religious life of Pietism in southwestern Germany.

### RETRANSLATING THE DEVIL

It would distort the record to insist that the people of Akuapem, or indeed of elsewhere in the region, were entirely uninterested in the missionaries' message of salvation, despite its articulation in the language and conceptual categories of the Europeans. However, they wanted deliverance and protection from evils external to themselves, and only rarely from their own evil natures. If a recent historiographical consensus maintains that the Christian Satan (versus the Muslim one) was a European import to the Gold Coast, this fact must not lead to the conclusion that the idea of Satan was an unwelcome one, or that it has not been useful.[65] Indeed, as Birgit Meyer, who more or less opened the conversation in the late 1990s, has observed regarding twentieth-century Pentecostal praxis among the Ewe, local Christians came to demonize traditional religions, but did so within preexisting religious frameworks for incorporating new gods and spirits.[66] Meyer's conclusions have not gone uncontested. In a study of contemporary Ghanaian Pentecostalism, Paul Gifford argues that the very idea of the devil has been much easier for people to swallow than the counterintuitive Christian concept of the cross.[67] It does

---

[65] Gifford cites numerous examples of Ghanaian Pentecostal authors putting biblical teachings on Satan to work at solving quotidian problems. Paul Gifford, *Ghana's New Christianity: Pentecostalism in a Globalizing African Economy* (Bloomington: Indiana University Press, 2004); Sandra E. Greene, *Sacred Sites and the Colonial Encounter: A History of Meaning and Memory in Ghana* (Bloomington: Indiana University Press, 2002); Meyer, *Translating the Devil*.

[66] Meyer, *Translating the Devil*.

[67] Gifford, *Ghana's New Christianity*, 45–46.

not follow that the devil that early Ghanaian Christians read about from their Bibles was the same devil that the German Pietists knew. Likewise, the German Pietist devil of 1900 was not the same malevolent spirit as that of 1750, let alone that of Martin Luther's time. European religion was undergoing constant and radical transformation throughout the period in which the German missionary societies were active in the Gold Coast.

In order to tease out the particular ways the "diabolization" of indigenous culture took place, Meyer has focused on what she calls "peasant popular religion" in southwestern Germany, with particular attention to 1844's outbreak of exorcisms and claimed miraculous healings associated with Johannes Christoph Blumhardt, a pastor and former employee in the Basel Mission's home office. A close look at the timeline of these events reveals a dialectic process between missionary experience overseas and village life in rural Germany, mediated by the transnational evangelical missionary network. Rather than whispers of the ancient Germanic pagan past coming back to life in mid-nineteenth-century Württemberg, these healings and exorcisms reflected missionary ideas on evil in the broader world, from the South Pacific to Germany. Blumhardt's healings and exorcisms, in other words, did not represent a revival of autochthonous German superstitions so much as the Pietist missionary subculture's demonization of the same, and in conversation with emergent intercultural missionary ideas. Moreover, since Blumhardt's healings reflected mediation made possible by global communication and transportation networks, the wave of claims of the miraculous could not have taken place any earlier than they did in the 1840s.[68]

What happened was straightforward: in early 1844 word spread throughout the region that a pastor—Blumhardt—in the town of Möttlingen (about twenty miles west of Stuttgart) had exorcised a demon from a parishioner, who had in the process also been healed of a bone disorder. Thousands of people came to Blumhardt, seeking their own physical healings and spiritual deliverance. A great deal of debate ensued. After two years, the state church of Württemberg, acting on the instructions of the government, forbade the healings: the guild of doctors had argued that healings, miraculous or otherwise, constituted an infringement upon their charter. At this point, the healings ceased, and much of the popular interest dissipated.[69] Blumhardt

[68] Peter Geschiere has made a similar observation for late-twentieth century postcolonial Africa: the occult has no trouble at all in adapting to the times: Peter Geschiere, *The Modernity of Witchcraft: Politics and the Occult in Postcolonial Africa* (Charlottesville: University Press of Virginia, 1997).

[69] This summary drawn from Dieter Ising, *Johann Christoph Blumhardt, Life and Work: A New Biography* (Eugene, Ore.: Cascade, 2009); Richard Haug, *Johann Christoph*

subsequently obtained a special vocation from the state church to open a spiritual-therapeutic retreat center at a shuttered sanitarium at nearby Bad Boll.[70] For the next seventy years, first Johann Christoph Blumhardt, and then his son Christoph Friedrich Blumhardt, evangelized and performed healings and exorcisms. The two men are commonly called the "elder" and the "younger" Blumhardt; they were distinct and idiosyncratic, but the younger's therapeutics, which extended into politics (he joined the Socialist Party and had his ordination stripped as a consequence), were a natural outgrowth of his emphasis on the Kingdom of God, which he took wholesale from his father.[71]

I have stressed the festive and networked quality to the Basel Mission's presence at home, especially after the organization began sending its own missionaries in the late 1820s. Through newsletters, festivals, traveling furloughed missionaries, and fundraising campaigns (which brought about broad purchase on the mission by small-time donors, including children), the mission was able to bring experiences attained abroad to bear on those remaining at home. Not only did the missionaries develop new understandings of their faith in cross-cultural encounter, but the sending community also received and reconfigured these reported experiences back into their congregations. In other words, the missionaries did not merely splash into West Africa and, once ensconced, begin imposing upon indigenous cultures a monolithically archaic German Christianity. Rather, the missionaries went through stirring and terrifying spiritual experiences, including some that they acquired secondhand by watching Africans or by reading newsletters. This appears to be the case with Blumhardt.

Born in 1805 to a baker, Johannes Christoph Blumhardt showed a sharp enough intellect to gain admittance to the Stuttgart gymnasium, despite needing tuition assistance. After gymnasium, he enrolled in the theological faculty at Tübingen University, graduating at the age of twenty-four. A few months

---

*Blumhardt: Gestalt und Botschaft* (Metzingen: E. Franz, 1984); Friedrich Zündel, *Pastor Johann Christoph Blumhardt: An Account of his Life* (1881; Eugene, Ore.: Cascade, 2010 [1881]).

[70] The family handed Bad Boll over to the Moravian Brethren after Christoph's death in 1919, who used the facility as their Western European headquarters.

[71] Gerhard Sauter, *Die Theologie des Reiches Gottes beim älteren und jüngeren Blumhardt* (Zürich: Zwingli Verlag, 1962); Karl Barth, *Protestant Theology in the Nineteenth Century: Its Background & History* (1952; London: SCM Press, 1972), 643–53. Barth emphasizes that Johannes Blumhardt was not a systematic thinker, but more of a practical man—"more a pastor than a preacher"—whose ideology must be extracted from his work; it is argued here that he tended to learn as he went along, and had no trouble rejecting ideas that were of little use to him.

later, his uncle Christian Gottlieb Blumhardt hired him as a teacher at the Basel Mission Training Institute. For the next seven years, he taught Hebrew, Greek, history, and geography to missionary candidates. One of Blumhardt's secondary assignments was corresponding with missionaries in the field, as well as reading reports from other mission agencies. His letters and journal entries make for a fascinating read—Blumhardt, perhaps more than most of the others in the home office, thought and wrote in a casually global fashion. Significantly, he did so not as an ideological cosmopolitan, but in personal relationship with correspondents all over the world. In a letter dated March 23, 1835, Blumhardt said:

> I derive great satisfaction from dear friends, visiting here from all regions of the world. They are a living witness to the bonds of love, by which the gospel envelops all peoples.[72]

He proceeded to specify visitors working in India and Persia, with whom he would have conversations about the Bible. Over and over again Blumhardt would say that the meaning of the Bible evolved for him as he spoke and corresponded with people working in Dagestan, Persia, India, Suriname, Malta, Sierra Leone, Accra, and elsewhere, in addition to all over Europe and North America. The youthfulness of the movement was on full display here, as Blumhardt and his interlocutors marveled over their experiences, as they went out to the various missions festivals to tell local villagers all the things that were happening.

During these years, as the exotic quality to this correspondence grew more natural to him, he began to recognize the quotidian quality of the work in which he was training people: they may have been located on the other end of the world, but these missionaries were still doing commonplace pastoral things, like weddings and funerals. Several of Blumhardt's missionary correspondents were also pastors in their respective mission fields, serving German expatriates alongside their evangelistic work among non-Christians. Blumhardt began to understand the overlap: pastoral work among the poor and needy in Germany was very much the same as pastoral work in Greenland. In 1832 Brunn told him, while discussing the Basel Mission's work in the Russian Caucasus (where a discouraged missionary wrote of wanting to

---

[72] Johann Christoph Blumhardt to Willem Groen van Prinsterer (March 23, 1843), item no. 287 in *Johann Christoph Blumhardt. Briefe*, vol. 1, *Frühe Briefe bis 1838. Texte*, ed. Dieter Ising (Göttingen: Vandenhoeck & Ruprecht, 1993), 307–8.

preach to heathens but rather found himself spending the bulk of his time pastoring the Christians):

> The church consists of three kinds of building stones: those which immediately fit in place; those which need to be hammered to size, and those which, no matter how much work goes into them, are not of use for the building.[73]

This conversation was an epiphany to Blumhardt, who suddenly came to view the daily work of pastoring a local congregation as a subset of world missions. This discovery eventually led him to accept an offer to take over the pastorate at Möttlingen, which he viewed as analogous to missionary work. At his installation sermon on September 29, 1838, he told his new parishioners:

> I cannot describe what I learned and experienced at that school [that is, the Basel Mission training institute]. It was an ongoing period of blessing for me. As a gathering place of so many believers from all regions of the world, I learned to view the entire world, insofar as Christ is not there, through eyes of compassion. Thus, I came to esteem the value of pastoral work.[74]

Blumhardt approached his pastorate as if he were a missionary anywhere. He continued his work of publishing and correspondence at the same clip, taking over editing duties of the *Calwer Missionsblatt*, a monthly newsletter summarizing stories from missionaries working in several evangelical associations. He also hosted missions festivals, helped other nearby towns in doing the same, and set about writing a universal history of Christian missions. In 1840, he invited Andreas Riis, then on furlough from Akropong, to address his congregation.[75] Blumhardt was far from the only pastor of such a mind, although he was certainly one of the most enthusiastic.

The work of taking care of his parishioners intervened, and he complained to his friends about meeting his publishing deadlines. A "nerve fever" epidemic broke out in Möttlingen in December 1839, lasting until June. This would preoccupy Blumhardt for months: cooking food for the sick and hungry, trying to find employment for youths who had lost their hearing, and visiting the sick in

---

[73] Nicolaus von Brunn to Johann Christoph Blumhardt, item no. 206 in *Johann Christoph Blumhardt. Briefe*, vol. 1, *Frühe Briefe bis 1838. Texte*, 262.

[74] Johann Christoph Blumhardt, Möttlingen (Germany), September 29, 1838, item no. 635 in *Johann Christoph Blumhardt. Briefe*, vol. 3, *Möttlinger Briefe 1838–1852. Texte*, ed. Dieter Ising (Göttingen: Vandenhoeck & Ruprecht, 1993), 21–23.

[75] Johann Christoph Blumhardt to Christoph Gottlob Barth, September 29, 1840, in *Johann Christoph Blumhardt. Briefe*, vol. 3, *Möttlinger Briefe. Texte*, item no. 813 (B1A, Kapsel I A 2/III), 69.

their homes. Throughout this epidemic, which broke out again in the autumn, he raised donations for missions from among the hungry.[76]

In January 1840, in the middle of a letter to a friend about the spread of the disease, he mentioned praying "for an outpouring of the Holy Spirit, from North America."[77] It is not immediately clear if he was thinking about a specific event, but the 1830s were indeed a time of spectacular revivals in the United States, which was characterized in part by speaking in tongues (this may have been the "outpouring" for which Blumhardt was praying).[78]

This aside of Blumhardt's—of reading about faraway events and attempting to replicate them in the immediate environment—helps explain what followed. It was a practice he had learned while in the Basel Mission's home office. In March 1832, for example, a letter had come in from a Basel missionary named Hübner working among the German settlers in Georgia and Armenia on the Russian-Persian frontier. A prayer meeting had evolved into an exorcism, as a local elder begged the congregation to take the devil out of his throat, which they did.[79]

At the time, Blumhardt found the episode "repulsive," but three years later von Brunn attempted to replicate it in the mission house. Whereas earlier Blumhardt knew of these things only by hearsay, now he was an eyewitness, as von Brunn attempted, and failed, at freeing two supposedly possessed children by persistent prayer and the laying on of hands:

> Today with v. Brunn; parents and children both present; the boy falls in a faint at the laying on of hands and from his belly a voice utters unintelligibly; von Brunn shows great power and liberty, commands in Jesus' name that the spirit must leave and never return. Songs, laying on of hands for the girl, von Brunn very weakened. The boy feels something yet in his belly; a further endeavor and struggles. Less in the belly and a further endeavor and pronouncement: we will not rest. Von Brunn is entirely exhausted and things did not go on.[80]

In context, it is clear that neither Blumhardt nor von Brunn knew what they were doing. Having had no training in dealing with spiritual

[76] Blumhardt, *Johann Christoph Blumhardt. Briefe*, vol. 3, *Möttlinger Briefe. Texte*, 38–53.

[77] Blumhardt to Christian Gottlob Barth, January 18, 1840, in *Johann Christoph Blumhardt. Briefe*, vol. 3, *Möttlinger Briefe. Texte*, item no. 685 (B1A, Kapsel I A 2/III), 49.

[78] Whitney R. Cross, *The Burned-over District; the Social and Intellectual History of Enthusiastic Religion in Western New York, 1800-1850* (Ithaca: Cornell University Press, 1950).

[79] Blumhardt, *Frühe Briefe bis 1838. Texte*, item 202, p. 262.

[80] Blumhardt, *Frühe Briefe bis 1838. Texte*, 325–26.

beings—Blumhardt's 1829 graduation examination had covered questions of doctrine and nothing of praxis—these men were experimenting and cooking up ideas in light of events they were reading about elsewhere. The conversation went the other way as well. In a letter dated November 11, 1836, to a missionary in India, Blumhardt wrote of his landlord beating his wife, and wondered if the devil was involved.

> The episode made me think about the work among the heathens and reminded me of the word that we are not fighting against flesh and blood, etc. And I think that praying against the devil is an important thing in the heathen world.[81]

This statement shows how Blumhardt thought: at multiple scales at once. "Flesh and blood" here refers to Paul's letter to the church at Ephesus:

> For our struggle is not against flesh and blood, but against the rulers, against the authorities, against the powers of this dark world and against the spiritual forces of evil in the heavenly realms (6:12).

Thus, in Möttlingen in 1842, when one of his parishioners, a young woman named Gottliebin Dittus, came to him with what would culminate, two years later, in a spectacular exorcism, he initially had no idea what to do. Instead, he interpreted his struggle through the lens, not of peasant popular religion, which he flatly dismissed as superstition, but of the South Pacific, where missionary newsletters reported on shamanism.[82] Dittus, who was renting a home in town with her sister, had seen a spirit in the house, and over the next few weeks began pulling up floorboards, where she had found coins (one of which was minted in 1828), wrapped in blackened paper, which she brought to the pastor. Clearly, this was an artifact of peasant popular magic, but Blumhardt was terrified, because, as in nearly everything else, he connected it to the mission field; at that moment was working on his history of missions: "Oh! How terrifying to encounter such things, especially while I am working on the Cook Islands."[83] In the published book, he wrote the following about those islands:

> [The first European visitors] thought they were seeing paradise, and accordingly insisted on viewing the natives as innocent, happy children of nature. But how they were disappointed! Because nearly everywhere, human

---

[81] Blumhardt, *Frühe Briefe bis 1838. Texte*, item 349, p. 339.

[82] Johann Christoph Blumhardt and E. Zuber, *Krankheitsgeschichte der Gottliebin Dittus. Ausführlicher Original-Bericht* (Basel: Brunnen-Verl., 1850), section 2.

[83] Johann Christoph Blumhardt to Christoph Gottlob Barth, item no. 1032 in *Johann Christoph Blumhardt. Briefe*, vol. 3, *Möttlinger Briefe. Texte* (May 6, 1842), 121.

sacrifice, and even cannibalism, infanticide, shameless bestiality, murderous wars, and unspeakable horrors at home. Their gods were of the rawest kind.[84]

Over the next two years, Blumhardt's encounters with this young woman escalated, culminating in the infamous exorcism in late December 1843. Throughout the ordeal, Blumhardt interpreted what was going on by reference to missionary activities around the world. Blumhardt seems to move seamlessly in his imagination from the Pacific to the West Indies to his local village. The practical logic was not only that Europe was a mission field, but that acquired missionary experience in the field was universally transferrable. For example, one day in February 1843, Dittus spent several hours in a trance, telling Blumhardt afterwards that she had been flying over the ocean, and had seen churches burning on small islands. Several weeks later, reading about an earthquake in the Caribbean, which had flattened the Moravian church in Antigua, Blumhardt retrospectively concluded that on the day of the trance the demons had been attempting to show Dittus their victory over the mission to the heathens.[85]

## CONCLUSION

In analyzing Blumhardt's story for the purpose of understanding Pietist missionaries in Ghana, Birgit Meyer made the simple mistake of assuming that Blumhardt's devil was an expression of "peasant popular religion."[86] Thus she repeatedly used the word "still" to describe what was in fact a new-old thing; a belief derived in transnational dialogue with missionaries of many different countries: "Spirits were still a reality to many people"; "the Pietists . . . still lived within this context," and so on.[87] Like Pieter De Marees in 1602, Meyer dismissed Christian belief in the world of spirit as monkey games. This was a small mistake, but one that opened the door to unsubstantiated conclusions. Alone on account of this kind of condescension, Meyer's research on the Pietist background behind the encounter among the Ewe (the main focus of her otherwise superior study in the cross-cultural process) should probably be treated with the same nose-holding skepticism as is appropriate for *Apenspel*.

Meyer's sources are rather thin. Two of the three were contemporary ethnographic studies from the first three decades of the twentieth century, and the third (Pfister) leans extensively on one of the other two (Bohnenberger) as

---

[84]  Johann Christoph Blumhardt, *Handbüchlein der Missionsgeschichte und Missionsgeographie* (Calw: Verlag der Vereinsbuchhandlung, 1844), 285–86.

[85]  Blumhardt and Zuber, *Krankheitsgeschichte der Gottliebin Dittus*, section 8.

[86]  Meyer, *Translating the Devil*, 49.

[87]  Meyer, *Translating the Devil*, 49.

a source. None of the three references any kind of historical research, and none so much as mentions demons.[88] In his 1904 edited compendium of folklore in Württemberg, Karl Bohnenberger identified a geography of superstition, in which the strength of the "old belief" had retreated to communities inaccessible by rail. This unsystematic body of lore included deities (Odin and his Wild Hunt), territorial spirits (such as those inhabiting wells, forests, and individual houses), formerly human spirits (tormented dead people, including "a baptized Jew"), and other mysterious manifestations, both sentient (dwarves) and not (amulets and clothing with powers; coins that return to their previous owners; leftover baptismal water, useful for curing bed-wetting, and so on). Significantly, Bohnenberger made no mention of demons, as found in the New Testament, or of exorcism, as if it were not part of the German religious past.[89]

With regard to the decline of witch trials in southwestern Germany, Brian Levack has argued that it was the Pietists, beginning in the late seventeenth century, who had led the way, and for a very specific religious reason, which had little to do with enlightenment: they believed that God, not the devil, caused misfortune.[90] Furthermore, Pietist focus on spiritual sobriety did not accommodate sorcery, even as Pietists recognized that some people attempted to control their worlds in that way.[91]

The Basel Mission had first encountered spirit possession in West Africa fifteen years earlier. At that time, they did not yet have a category by which to make sense of what they were seeing. Ministering among the Sierra Leone recaptives and among the black American settlers in Liberia, for example, the formative generation of Basel missionaries had encountered volatile and traumatized people, who received the missionaries' message with a nonchalant African presumption that the unseen spiritual world, filled with sentient creatures, interfaced with the world of the seen, and that possession and emotion

[88]   Karl Bohnenberger, "Aus Glauben und Sage," in *Volkstümliche Überlieferungen in Württemberg: Glaube, Brauch, Heilkunde*, ed. Karl Bohnenberger (1904; Stuttgart: Kommissionsverlag Müller & Gräff, 1980); Georg Buschan, *Das deutsche Volk in Sitte und Brauch: Geburt, Liebe, Hochzeit* (Stuttgart: Union Deutsche Verlagsgesellschaft, 1922); Friedrich Pfister, *Schwäbische Volksbräuche: Feste und Sagen* (Augsburg: B. Filser, 1924).

[89]   Bohnenberger, "Aus Glauben und Sage," 9.

[90]   Brian Levack, "The Decline and End of Witchcraft Prosecutions," in *Witchcraft and Magic in Europe. The Eighteenth and Nineteenth Centuries*, ed. Bengt Ankarloo and Stuart Clark (Philadelphia: University of Pennsylvania Press, 1999), 67. Levack adds that the witch trials declined *before* prosecutors ceased believing in witchcraft's power. This decline was, accordingly, more a function of legal process than of worldview change, also the decline of local justice vis-à-vis the state.

[91]   Andreas Gestrich, "Pietismus und Aberglaube," in *Das Ende der Hexenverfolgung*, ed. Sönke Lorenz and Dieter R. Bauer (Stuttgart: F. Steiner, 1995), 271–80.

were two ways of knowing about the former. German missionaries encountering these African religious experiments were initially terrified, but grew accustomed to the matter, and began to bring it home with them. Johannes Gerber, writing in August 1829 from Hastings in Sierra Leone, said:

> While their corporeal convulsions and violent emotions terrify and confuse me, I am beginning to see penetrating changes in their lives as a result. I have come to recognize that a divine work of grace has begun, even if combined with the negro's excitable nature and ignorance.[92]

In this and in similar missionary newsletters from Sierra Leone and Liberia, and from the first generation's experiences in the Gold Coast (that is, before Andreas Riis, the sole survivor, returned to Basel in 1839, disheartened and without a single convert to his credit), the devil does not appear. The missionaries were confused and troubled, but at this early point, they did not ascribe to the devil what they were seeing. In 1835 Riis had identified the Akuapem gods as empty idols, and their priests as charlatans. Indigenous religion was not Satan worship, but merely false.[93]

This is because, as of 1835, Satan was not yet part of Riis', or of the Basel Mission's, conceptual toolkit. Rather, Pietists understood the devil as an agent of an individual's struggle against sin, generally synonymous with "the flesh." Likewise, Blumhardt had initially tried to make sense of his encounter with possessions by reference to the lessons from the witch trials of the seventeenth and eighteenth centuries, which he considered ancient history: "even if some people have brought (possession) upon themselves, this is usually not the case, as we learned during the witch trials."[94] What was rather the case, to Blumhardt, was not some long-dead evil, but a contemporary one, which was religiously interconnected with the goings-on in rural Germany.

> I slowly came to recognize that in our days . . . a worm has been eating at evangelical Christianity, which is the sin of apostasy. . . . By apostasy I mean every reliance on an unseen power, rather than on God, . . . whether for health, or for profit.[95]

Many Christians, Blumhardt concluded, took a magical approach to their Bibles, citing verses as if they were formulas, "just like the negro with

---

[92] Gerber quoted in "West-Afrika. Colonie Sierra Leone," HB 1829, 90–91.
[93] Riis, "Goldküste in Afrika," HB 1835, 61–65.
[94] Blumhardt and Zuber, Krankheitsgeschichte der Gottliebin Dittus, section 10.
[95] Blumhardt and Zuber, Krankheitsgeschichte der Gottliebin Dittus, section 10.

his juju."[96] This line of thought gets to the heart of the dynamic. Beliefs about the devil, which the Basel missionaries carried to Ghana after the mid-1840s, developed in conversation with contemporary missionary activities around the world. Rather than digging up an ancient Satan from Germany's medieval and early modern past, the missionary community relearned to think in such terms from cross-cultural experience. And to the extent that the missionaries demonized indigenous spirits they had previously dismissed as delusions, they were building upon a previous demonization of the half-hearted Christianity of southwestern Germany, a verdict they applied equally to the state churches in the coastal forts. The German missionaries in the 1850s and 1860s could see the devil in the Gold Coast, then, because he was not an autochthonous German devil. He was himself a newly retranslated entity.

The missionaries were not normal people to start with, even at home. They grew increasingly abnormal as southwestern Germany and northwestern Switzerland urbanized and industrialized over the mid- and late-nineteenth century years they were living in Africa. The longer they lived in Africa, the more they thought like Africans.

---

[96] Blumhardt and Zuber, *Krankheitsgeschichte der Gottliebin Dittus*, section 10.

# 5

# How the Missionaries
# Became Shrine Priests

## INTRODUCTION

A few hours after King Kwaw Dade died in July 1866, a slave woman named Yaa came knocking on Johannes and Ernestina Mader's door in Akropong. With the King's death, the royal veil of protection over the town was temporarily removed, and "bad things" were going to happen that night, as the royal executioners later told David Asante at the entrance to the sacred grove, a little down the hill.[1] Yaa needed a place to hide. Nights like this were dangerous, above all, for the vulnerable. As a slave and a foreigner—a Krepi[2]—Yaa was certainly vulnerable, but there was something else: she had lately punched Kwaw Dade's senior wife in the face. Therefore, on a bad night, Yaa was going to be one of the first victims. She was not without options,

---

[1] The European missionaries' accounts, Widmann's and Mader's, were compiled and published that October: J. G. Widmann and Johannes Adam Mader, "Der Tod des Königs von Akropong," *HB* 1866, 129–31. The word "bad" here is *schlecht* in German, but was probably originally *bɔne*, which is much stronger and more weighted word than *schlecht* and refers more generally to evil and taboo. Kwasi Wiredu, "Papa nNe Bɔne," in *Listening to Ourselves: A Multilingual Anthology of African Philosophy*, ed. Chike Jeffers (Albany: State University of New York Press, 2013), 158–175; and Ernestina Afriyie, "Taboo," in *Africa Bible Commentary*, ed. Tokunboh Adeyemo (Grand Rapids: Zondervan, 2006).

[2] The Krepi were a small people living along the Volta to the north of the rapids where the river slices through the Akuapem ridge. Throughout the entire period of this study, they were subject to someone else's authority. At the time of Kwaw Dade's death, the Krepi were under the Asante, and after 1874 were the prize in a contest between Peki and Salaga. David Brown, "Anglo-German Rivalry and Krepi Politics 1886–1894," *Transactions of the Historical Society of Ghana* 15, no. 2 (1974), 201–16.

however: she knew where she might find sanctuary from the executioners. The Maders took her in:

> That night a slave woman came to us, who had punched the chief wife. We hid her for a day and a night, while they were looking for her. She was meant to be one of the first sacrificial victims.[3]

By 1866, the Basel Mission had already spent decades in the Gold Coast, trying to debate indigenous lords into Christianity and, failing that, had contented themselves with educating their children. At the same time, however, especially in Akuapem, hundreds of people like Yaa had sought refuge with the mission. Much of the growth of Christianity in Akuapem before around 1870 had its origins among these desperate people. As with displaced persons anywhere, few of them recorded their meditations on this matter, leaving the missionaries to guess their motives—and subsequent observers, accordingly, to interpret the missionaries' own mixed intentions.

The Basel missionaries were clearly unprepared for the momentous developments then convulsing the region. These had begun several years earlier, as the palm oil boom had enveloped the Krepi, Krobo, and Anlo lowlands to the east of the kingdom, triggering fights big and small (and likely lay behind Yaa's enslavement). For the most part, however, King Kwaw Dade had managed to keep his kingdom safe. His death, of old age and in the comfort of his own bed, thrust Akuapem into a state of insecurity, a terrifying prospect that likely contributed to the locals' drive, ritually enacted that night, to ensure the kingdom's future by sacrificial means. Yaa was high on the executioners' list for petty and personal reasons, but the overarching context was bigger—and more important—than palace intrigue. The night of Kwaw Dade's passage to the ranks of the ancestors was merely one of many, which would draw Akuapem into a broader geopolitical whirlwind. The region was already in a broader state of turmoil, which would culminate in Britain's wars with Asante and the subsequent imposition of indirect rule throughout the Gold Coast.

Before that point, however, the lowland conflicts indirectly weighed upon the mountain kingdom of Akuapem, as crowds of displaced persons sought refuge inside its frontiers. Some refugees, arriving in small groups, placed themselves under the protection and patronage of various wealthy or aristocratic families, and others set up informal camps in secluded ravines.

---

[3]  Widmann and Mader, "Der Tod des Königs von Akropong." Most Basel Missionary stories, written by and attributed to the husbands, are written in the first person singular. Mader's account here is written in the plural: Yaa came "to us"; "We hid her," etc. It is my assumption, from this language, that Ernestina helped hide Yaa.

Beginning with Kwaw Dade's death, and continuing with the wave of sacrificial killings that ensued, many of these displaced persons began sheltering in the shadow of Basel Mission chapels. These settlements marked the beginnings of Christian villages that the Basel Mission eventually came to call "Salems." Within a few years, many of these foreigners would form the majority of the Christian communities associated with the Basel Mission in Akuapem (and to a lesser extent, in adjacent kingdoms). The missionaries would eventually assert control over the settlements, dictating nearly every element of everyday life. Later generations of the Salem residents, from the 1880s down to the German and Swiss missionaries' deportation during the First World War, grew to resent the settlements as quasi-prisons. However, chronology is of the utmost for understanding these developments: the settlements came *first*, before the missionaries had any idea of what was happening or how to respond. The Salems were an indigenous creation.

Moreover, since the settlements were originally an indigenous initiative, their meaning must be sought within the contours of West African intellectual history: they were outgrowths of existing social practices. By erecting shelters in the immediate vicinity of Basel Mission chapels, refugees had pulled the Germans into a very old indigenous framework of spiritual patronage. The settlements, then, constituted an indigenous imposition upon the mission of homegrown categories of spiritual protection, and specifically those of priestly sanctuary. In this chapter, I argue that the system of mission sanctuary developed years before the foreign missionaries themselves knew what was happening. In effect, the Salems were an indigenous creation, built upon an extant toolkit of ideas, which the missionaries struggled to comprehend, only stepping in to regulate the community after hundreds of souls had gathered themselves.

Men and women of the Gold Coast, from kings on down to slaves, had long sought to make use of the Basel missionaries. They did this in several different ways. Some wanted to get rich from trade, hoping the missionaries would provide access to coastal merchants. Others wanted a European education (above all literacy and numeracy) for their children. Still others merely wanted them to survive after other children had died. Some wanted protection from evil spirits or from angry ancestors. Others, particularly those at the outer margins of society, simply wanted sanctuary. The unfortunate Yaa belonged to the latter class of people. Together with others like her—slaves, foreigners, the disabled, and the poor—a large number of the first generation of converts in Akuapem evaluated Christianity against a different scale than that of the missionaries. The latter were interested in saving souls, and in establishing ethnic-specific churches, each with its own class of leaders equipped to read and preach Scriptures in translation. Missionary accounts of new converts thus abound with asymmetry: on the one hand the missionaries celebrated as they imagined a new soul, kneeled before his or her savior in heaven, while on the other hand, the converts themselves expressed satisfaction at being enveloped into a new community—the church.

The foreign missionaries only added to the confusion in their presumption of political neutrality. In a context, such as in Akuapem, in which political legitimacy was rooted in the king's stewardship of the spiritual world for the good of the community, missionary insistence on converts' abstinence from traditional sacrificial and ritual protocols was anything but politically neutral. Rather, it was a way of fudging the problem of authority. Political neutrality, an artifact of German Pietists' bitter experiences with their own kings back home, made little sense in the Gold Coast. During the early 1860s, for example, the Krobo principalities in the Volta lowlands to the east of Akuapem, who had been early adopters of the palm oil boom—and had thus emerged as something of a cartel of small plantation states—grew increasingly restive under Kwaw Dade's insistence on exacting tribute. Early in the decade, Krobo King Odonkor Azu embarked on an elaborate scheme to use the Basel missionaries in his effort to assert Krobo sovereignty from Akuapem.[4] In that case, the missionaries, led by the dynamic Zimmerman couple—he a German, and she an Angolan survivor of kidnapping and transportation on a slave ship to Jamaica—had successfully evaded political entrapment, but the general pattern was for men and women of the region to experiment with the possible uses of a missionary. When the missionaries took on refugees, then, such as Yaa, they were inadvertently allowing themselves to be dragged into local conflicts, and without fully comprehending the consequences.

Johann Widmann was initially unaware that Yaa was sheltering with the Maders across the street.[5] As the senior missionary in town (by 1866 he had

---

[4]   Veit Arlt, "Christianity, Imperialism and Culture: The Expansion of the Two Krobo States in Ghana, c. 1830 to 1930" (PhD diss., University of Basel, 2005).

[5]   That is, if Widmann is telling the whole story. By 1866, he had developed a Ghanaian style to his narratives, speaking of the unspeakable only when necessary. But the present author finds it unlikely that Widmann was unaware that Yaa had sought sanctuary with Mader, unless the latter household had conspired to hide this matter from their senior. The Widmanns and the Maders lived across the street from each other, and the two wives, Rosine Widmann and Ernestina Mader, were sisters. Ulrike Sill, *Encounters in Quest of Christian Womanhood: The Basel Mission in Pre- and Early Colonial Ghana* (Boston: Brill, 2010), 86.

been living in Akropong for twenty-three years), he had other responsibilities. These included functioning as something of an elder in town:

> The king's brother Ata Patu came to me and told me that the king had died that morning. But I should say nothing. The death of an African Lord cannot be immediately announced. It is known and not known. ["Man weiss es und weiss es nicht."] . . . Later he returned, with an elder, to make the announcement official.[6]

As a semi-insider to court gossip, Widmann likely knew what Yaa had done to the king's senior wife. But as the ranking missionary, as the ɔsɔfoɔ-priest of a god not worshiped in the palace, and as the elder presiding over a settlement of indigenous adherents, it was also to Widmann that, on this night, several of the most endangered people turned:

> Our house became an asylum [Rettungsherberge] for several slaves. Two old women and a young woman with a child on her back came, lest they be captured and killed. Later came the grown daughter of a slave woman named Adobea, one of the king's wives. She was afraid they would make her go with the king.[7]

It was likewise to Widmann's house that two different groups of executioners came, looking for Yaa, apparently unaware of each other:

> Around eight or nine on Thursday night some drunk men came asking who was here, and why they had sheltered here, and told us not to let them out, but demanded a slave named Yaa, a Krepi, who had punched the king's senior wife in the face. We assured them that she was not here, and they left. The elders told David Asante that these men had not come from them, but later they came, also looking for Yaa.[8]

Indigenous missionary David Asante was working in Larteh at the time, a town situated atop a parallel ridge to Akropong and separated by a heavily forested ravine, and the grove is somewhere on the Akropong side of that slope. Part of 2015's Odwira involved calling the recently deceased king to service as an ancestral spirit, and many people—at least ten—warned me against so much as asking about the grove's location: it was entirely out of

---

[6] Widmann and Mader, "Der Tod des Königs von Akropong," 129.

[7] Widmann and Mader, "Der Tod des Königs von Akropong." Notable here is the tone: Widmann is not shrill in his revulsion at ritual killing, but merely steadfast in opposition. Nor does he spell out "Make her go with the King" for his home audience; he is not intent on dramatics.

[8] Widmann and Mader, "Der Tod des Königs von Akropong."

bounds to a foreigner. As a member of the royal house, however, David Asante was not at risk and made the hour's hike to the grove, where he was admitted. Although not allowed into the killing circle, David Asante's admittance to the sacred grove is an important reminder that ancestry trumped cultic rank, at least among Akuapem's royal matriclans. The implication is too important to miss: Christianity was a foreign religion, but foreignness itself was a factor of negligible importance in the kingdom. Like most of the peoples of the Gold Coast, the Akuapem were not greatly concerned with cultic purity, and had imported too many foreign rituals and gods to count. On the other hand, matriclan lineage was very important. Asante's admittance to the grove indicates that—in the eyes of the royal families, at least—Christianity was at least theoretically capable of incorporation into the existing spiritual-political economy. Although not allowed into the killing circle itself, Asante was included in the various runs of messages to and from the grove.

Yaa had made the good decision to hide with the Maders, and she was thus spared, although only for a night, after which something strange happened:

> The next night, as we were preparing to smuggle her out of town, she slipped out, and was captured by the miserable backslider William Irenkyi, and likely delivered to the executioners.[9]

Yaa's story was perhaps exceptional in its bloody outcome but exemplifies a broader pattern. During the Basel Mission's first few decades in the Gold Coast, many people sought to attach themselves to the missionaries as in a patronage or protective relationship.[10] Indeed, this indigenous initiative constituted the core of the Basel Mission's success in late precolonial Akuapem, especially in light of the mission's failures for more than the preceding three decades to attract much religious interest from the locals. Rapid Christian growth after 1866 cannot be understood apart from the failure of the existing social order to incorporate those consigned to the margins of society.

---

[9] Widmann and Mader, "Der Tod des Königs von Akropong." Mader gives no indication of why Yaa left his house. Was she surrendering? Was she possessed? Did she not agree with the Maders' arrangements?

[10] Paul Jenkins, "Slavery and Emancipation in the Reports (1868–1900) of a Ghanaian Pastor—Kofi Theophilus Opoku (B. 1842)" (paper presented at the Annual Meeting of the African Studies Association, San Diego, Calif., 2015).

## FROM THE MARGINS

For all the Basel Mission's dreams of converting kings and establishing a Christian bourgeoisie,[11] and despite the Mission's success at recruiting and training a handful of indigenous workers from aristocratic families (David Asante, Theophilus Opuku and a few others), it was by and large not the strong, the healthy, the intelligent, or the highborn who embraced the missionaries' message. Rather, it was mostly outsiders who entered the young church. For a poor person on the margins of society, inclusion in a separate Christian community could be a very attractive proposition, but for this person's children, a generation later, that same separate community was intolerable. The dynamic is furthermore very sensitive among Ghanaians, even a century and a half later, and accordingly merits close attention to situation and chronology.

At the time of these events, David Asante was responsible for the Guan-speaking congregation at Larteh. Asante was officially a "missionary," which office at this time ranked above pastor (*Pfarrer*) or catechist. He was the only African of that rank. His day-to-day activities overlapped considerably with those of the latter offices, and letters to the home office from Asante's contemporaries Alexander Clerk and Theophilus Opoku read very much like Asante's in the tone of address and the description of their practical activities. During the years of his pastorate in that town, the congregation grew to include two or three hundred souls. Sonia Abun-Nasr suggests that Asante was securing for himself a social rank comparable with a subchief in one of the town's quarters.[12] While he mostly reported to the home office about encounters that the Mission would have understood as religious in nature, from conflict with the priests of Dente to internal church issues, like questions of amulet usage, Asante also routinely commented on economic and social matters. Later in 1866 he wrote:

> In general, the Christians are very poor. Some keep their hungry children indoors, so that they might find food for them. Many of the children of the Christians go naked because their parents cannot afford clothes.[13]

[11]  In this very same issue of the *HB*, the Basel mission reported on sending a new commercial clerk to the Gold Coast, Johannes Binder (who would remain in the field for twenty-seven years). Basel Mission inspector (executive) Joseph Josenhans, speaking at Binder's deputation ceremony, "spoke from 1 Cor. 15:30–34 on the importance of the non-ordained workers. These help grab the heathens and lead them into a Christian 'Bürgertum.'" *HB* 1866, 98.

[12]  Sonia Abun-Nasr, *Afrikaner und Missionar: die Lebensgeschichte von David Asante* (Basel: Schlettwein, 2003), 131–73.

[13]  David Asante, "Von der Außengemeinde Date," *HB* 1866, 98.

This kind of poverty—where children go naked and hungry—speaks of no insignificant social marginalization: the people who placed themselves under David Asante's patronage were by and large those for whom the existing social-political-religious structure had failed to secure protection or even food security.

The situation in Larteh was unexceptional. Writing in the same year, David Eisenschmid reported nine new baptisms in the kingdom of Akyem Abuakwa, to the west of Akuapem. Three were from Kukurantumi, a town along the road from Accra to Kumasi, and six were from the Akyem capital city of Kyebi.[14] Eisenschmid's report came early in his work in Kyebi, and bears close inspection, because this small sampling of conversion exemplifies the low social standing of the first generation of converts. The three young converts in Kukurantumi were, along with summaries of Eisenschmid's comments:

- **Joshua Abisaw**. "He had been dedicated to the fetish from before his birth; his mother had previously suffered several miscarriages. His original name was 'Ask Death.' He owed his life to the fetish, and was pawned to a master who beat him."

- **Yaw Badu**, now Moses. "He had been pawned for 18 Thalers to pay for his father's funeral. One day he learned that the fetish meant to kill him. He tried to appease it with gifts, but came to believe that the priest was extorting him. He fled to Kukurantumi, where he met Brother Kromer."

- **Paul Jeasene**. Son of the chief by a slave woman, pawned by his mother's brother for US$36.[15] "By character he is fiery and fearless. Formerly he fought frequently. If this trait were to be sanctified [*geheiligt*] by grace, something might be made of him."

[14] Akyem Abuakwa was a forest kingdom, in which most of the population was concentrated in the west. In the east, close to the border of Akuapem, the forest was very dense and moist and, accordingly, barely habitable. Since it was from this side that the Basel Mission first entered into Akyem Abuakwa in 1853, and since, furthermore, a small but bloody war destroyed the entire city of Gyadam, where the mission had begun work, it was not until 1861 that the Basel Mission reached the royal city of Kyebi. W. Schlatter, *Geschichte der Basler Mission 1815–1915*, vol. 3, *Afrika* (Basel: Verlag der Missionsbuchhandlung 1916), 69–71.

[15] Late in the century and especially to the east in Dahomey, US dollars would become a prominent currency. This is an early mention this far to the west, before the cocoa economy has developed. See Robin Law, "Cowries, Gold, and Dollars: Exchange Rate Instability and Domestic Price Inflation in Dahomey in the Eighteenth and Nineteenth Centuries," in *Money Matters: Instability, Values and Social Payments in the Modern History of West African Communities*, ed. Jane I. Guyer (Portsmouth, N.H.: Heinemann, 1995). Regarding his pawning: in a matrilineal system, he belonged to his mother's clan, in this case to his uncle. For this reason, kings often preferred lowborn wives, knowing that they, the fathers, would have more authority over their children. However, here we see this was not always the case.

And regarding the six youths baptized in Kyebi, Eisenschmid continued:

- **Wilhelm David**, originally from Sarmang, aged eighteen. Eisenschmid has nothing but good to say of him: "He is internally motivated and determined to serve the Lord all the days of his life. . . . May the Holy Spirit's work in him continue, so that he may be a light for others in his hometown."

- **Joseph Kwaku Dako**. "He is not bright, has trouble learning. But he loves Bible stories and is not afraid of the fetish."

- **Noa Asante**, aged eighteen. Crippled. ["Knochenfuss"—PGG: club-footed?] "The Lord has compassion and wants at least to heal his soul. . . . Some day he will stand alongside his brothers before the Lord in praise."

- **Georg Otemeng**, aged twenty-three. "Even among the heathens he has had a reputation for trouble. But he wants to be done with the life of sin. . . . Would Paul or Jesus have refused him?"

- **Jonathan Asumeng**, aged twenty. He wanted to be baptized, "but he is a pawn, and his master would not allow it. Eventually he was allowed to convert, but the king demanded he give his master a sheep as penance."

- **Sophia Dede**, "a servant girl in the Christallers' household. She is originally from Aburi."

Nine youths were thus added to the Akyem congregations. Two were either physically (Noa) or perhaps mentally (Joseph) disabled. Several were in some form of debt or bondage, and two (Georg and Paul) were troublemakers unlikely to remain faithful to the missionaries' sober message, as Eisenschmid fully acknowledged. "But we serve a Lord," he concluded, "who loves them a thousand more times over than we ourselves do, and who will bring to completion the work he has begun in them, even if it must proceed by way of falling down and rising again."[16]

That the socially marginalized should have constituted the bedrock to the early Church in Akuapem should come as no surprise: similar patterns are to be found throughout Christian history, where the people with the least purchase on the existing order also have the least to lose in breaking ties.

---

[16] David Eisenschmid, "Täuflinge auf der Station Kjebi," *HB* 1866, 66. Eisenschmid is paraphrasing the apostle Paul's letter to the young church at Philippi: "I am confident of this, that he who began a good work in you will carry it on to completion until the day of Christ Jesus" (Phil 1:6).

A particular twist in West Africa during this period was that the converts included a disproportionate number of people who were not members of any living clan—that is, people who for one reason or another had no access to the departed ancestors. To any society that has chosen to anchor communal reproduction within a vision of ongoing interventions by the departed in the affairs of the living, patterns of family lineage matter a great deal. The implications of the ancestral cult extend beyond mere questions of inheritance to touch on the incorporation of strangers and their gods.[17]

However, social exclusion also extended to people from within the matriclans who were born with defects, from albinism to deformities. Such children evidenced in their bodies evil intervention in the womb and could bring misfortune upon the community. Some were abandoned or killed ("thrown into the bush"), and some ended up under missionary protection (which practice gave the missionaries compelling anecdotes for one of their favorite newsletter themes: the heartless heathen parent). Take young Friedrich, for example: a six-fingered child who had been given to the mission at Aburi in the 1860s. In 1872 when Johannes Dieterle, visiting Friedrich's hometown, asked the boy's father to visit his son, the man quoted back to him an indigenous proverb: do not turn around to look for something which has been thrown away.[18] To Dieterle (in the country since 1846 but having only one year earlier, in 1871, returned from a two-year furlough in Europe), such parental rejection was all the evidence he needed of the heartlessness of heathenism, never mind the packs of street children he would have encountered only months earlier in rapidly industrializing Basel. Either way, displaced people were not hard to find in Akuapem and elsewhere in the Gold Coast of the middle of the

---

[17] Parrinder contrasts the patrilineal Yoruba and the matrilineal Akan in his study of West African religion. Geoffrey Parrinder, *West African Religion: A Study of the Beliefs and Practices of Akan, Ewe, Yoruba, Ibo, and Kindred Peoples* (London: Epworth Press, 1969), 176–77; also see Anthony Ephirim-Donkor, *The Making of an African King: Patrilineal & Matrilineal Struggle among the Effutu of Ghana* (Trenton, N.J.: Africa World Press, 1998); Eva Meyerowitz, *The Sacred State of the Akan* (London: Faber and Faber, 1951); Meyer Fortes, "Kinship and Marriage among the Ashanti," in *African Systems of Kinship and Marriage*, ed. A. R. Radcliffe-Brown and Daryll Forde (London: Published for the International African Institute by the Oxford University Press, 1950); R. S. Rattray, *Ashanti* (Oxford: Clarendon, 1923). It is worth mentioning that while nearly all secondary sources, from the middle of the twentieth century to the present, draw extensively (and often critically) on Rattray's work in the 1920s, J. B. Danquah, who was more of a philosopher than an ethnographer, but who was nevertheless deeply acquainted with Akan traditions, was highly critical of Rattray. Danquah, *The Akan Doctrine of God: A Fragment of Gold Coast Ethics and Religion* (London: Lutterworth, 1944).

[18] Johannes Christian Dieterle, "Eine suchende Familie," *JB* 1872, 115.

nineteenth century. This chronological point is very important for the successful establishment of Christianity in the Gold Coast, because the Christians
entered into a crowded spiritual marketplace with an impressive-looking ritual
corpus, including baptism and Eucharist, which was theoretically capable of
incorporating people otherwise beyond reach, and without regard to ancestry.

Not a single man, woman, child, or slave converted to Christianity during
the Basel Mission's first dozen years in the Gold Coast. This was partly because
of a language issue—the missionaries were still learning to speak the native
tongue—but was mostly because they had nothing of value to offer. However,
once some locals found ways to categorize the missionaries within preexisting
categories, a trickle of conversions commenced. This was something that the
locals had been attempting from the start: to draw on spiritual powers they
ascribed to the missionaries. Sixteen years earlier in 1850, Johann Widmann
had recounted a ritual at which he was asked to add his god to an existing
inventory of shrine spirits:

> A priestess was inaugurating a new house and buried a talisman under the
> threshold and then poured libations and called upon the god for blessing.
> When I said . . . that we must turn to the only true God, the priestess handed
> me the bottle of rum and requested that I do just that.[19]

This early encounter had taken place eight years after Widmann's arrival
and a quarter century before his death. By 1850, he had already acquired a
solid fluency in Twi, but his understanding of Akuapem's pragmatic religious
logic was still a work in progress. By the time of King Kwaw Dade's death in
1866, however, Widmann was less inclined to dispute the epistemic foundations of indigenous claims. He was rather prepared to engage these claims on
their own terms.

If Basel missionaries operated in a given village in accordance with a
local lord's suffrage, their presence was not always easy to live with. A missionary could bring a number of benefits to a locality, but always at a cost. At
the most superficial level, missionaries—as guests—needed protection and
support. Noa Azu (1832–1917) was a young priest and historical song singer
in 1856 when Johannes and Katherine Zimmermann moved to his village of
Odumase in the Krobo district. He wrote down his memories in the Krobo
language, along with the received history of his people, and these were published posthumously and in English translation by his son Enoch Azu in
1929. According to the elder Azu, the Eastern Krobo king had supported the
missionaries to the end of his life in 1867, even though he refused baptism.

[19]   J. G. Widmann, "Station Akropong," *JB* 1850, 193.

He nevertheless donated to the mission every Sunday, "going to church with a boy carrying cowries in a basket behind him. His motto was 'my white strangers must not feel hungry.'"[20]

There was a risk in hosting a missionary, however. These were men and women single-mindedly focused on bringing religious change into a social situation in which nearly the entirety of political legitimacy rested on an ideological framework which encompassed (at least in theory) all knowledge and belief. Missionaries were dangerous, because of the way the spiritual and the political worlds were interdependent. Writing about the Asante state (which admittedly differed in important ways from the fissiparous Akuapem state), T. C. McCaskie has argued that the worldview was total: agriculture, economics, family life, and social rank "were all locked together in an ideological grid of comprehensive definition, validation and mnemonic."[21]

On the other hand, and within certain limits, even Asante's system was open for religious innovations, and Akuapem's even more so. The reality was that many of the kings and priests of the late precolonial Gold Coast were keen observers of the Europeans and were willing to experiment to find ways of preserving the order. The missionary interposition theoretically threatened not only the sacred kingship, both of Asante and of the other Akan kingdoms, but also—more fundamentally—the foundations of clan and family life, and unless the locals could make use of Christianity and of its foreign shrine priests, an entire social order was at risk.

If a missionary was a burden and a danger, what then was the payoff to the chiefs for the risk of hospitality? Motivations varied, of course, between the rich and powerful and the poor and insecure. An indigenous chief might profit for his trouble by three ways: education, commerce, and prestige. There were few opportunities for aspiring parents to obtain literacy for their children in the mid-nineteenth-century Gold Coast, and missionary schools presented an excellent opportunity for economic advancement. At this time, Akuapem was a relatively poor state; unlike in wealthy Asante, where the Kumasi court was able to hire literate Muslims as accountants, lawyers, and astrologers, there were few such people in Akuapem. In 1860 in Kyerepong-speaking Adukrom (a few miles north of Akropong), for example, the local chief/priest employed a man who claimed to read Arabic, but (according to Johann Auer) "he held his book [the Qur'an?] upside down and recited from memory."[22] Missionary

[20] Noa Akunor Aguae Azu, *Adangbe (Adangme) History*, translated by Enoch Azu (Accra: Govt. Print Office, 1929), 61.

[21] T. C. McCaskie, *State and Society in Pre-Colonial Asante*, African Studies Series (Cambridge: Cambridge University Press, 1995), 102.

[22] Johann Gottlob Auer, "Predigerseminar," *JB* 1861, 173.

schools gave the chiefs the opportunity to advance their own families' pros-
pects, and indeed many mission school alumni were later able to help the traditional authorities navigate the onset of colonial rule from the mid-1870s.

However, education also tended to reshuffle social relations, especially in
a setting like the mission's teacher academy at Akropong, where locals were
in the minority in 1860. The majority of the student body that year consisted
of Fanti, Akwamu, Kyerepong, Gã and Krobo men who had left home to
study under the missionaries.[23] These students were not only gaining experiences that set them apart from their communities of origin, but they were
also learning new ways of cross-cultural conflict and interaction. However, as
educated Christians, they also rarely encountered people like themselves. For
that reason, Auer undertook to introduce his young men to peers. Over the
August vacation in 1861 Auer hiked with the whole graduating class to visit
the English college at Cape Coast. After first marching south to Accra, they
then walked on the beach for a hundred miles.[24] Thus far, education's utility
to the community was dubious: what good was all this training if one had to
hike a hundred miles to find a peer? If, on the other hand, the missionaries and
the Christian religion could be incorporated into the existing order, there was
little reason not to do so.

Consider the following case, from Larteh sometime after December 1859.
Koko, the wife of Jonathan, the first convert in that town, began having a series
of extramarital affairs "because she believed that since he no longer adhered to
the fetish she had nothing to fear." However, "the Lord struck her with sickness
and she was not healed until she repented" and was baptized in 1861 as Sara
Koko.[25] This story, summarized by Johann Widmann, is worth closer inspection.
It takes the narrative form, as does much of the Pietist storytelling apparatus, of
a three-stage sequence of fall, punishment, and restoration, but it also shows the
degree to which Widmann, who by 1861 had lived in Akropong for eighteen
years, had attained a social rank not unlike that of one of Larteh's shrine priests.

The first stage constituted a void—that is, the breaking of two social bonds
in short order. First, by converting to Christianity, Jonathan had broken with
the "fetish" (in this case the Larteh cult of Akonnedi) that guaranteed social
order by means of the threat of spiritual sanctions. This initial rupture was
followed soon thereafter by Koko's breaking of the marital bond. In patrilineal

[23]  Johann Gottlob Auer, "Predigerseminar," *JB* 1861, 164.
[24]  Johann Auer, it might be added, likely understood the students quite well, being only a few
years older than them and something of an angry young man himself within his own agency.
He married an American woman without informing his superiors; he later switched over to the
American Episcopal mission in Liberia. See Joseph Josenhans, "Bericht," *JB* 1862, 36.
[25]  J. G. Widmann, untitled report in *JB* 1861, 174.

Larteh, a broken marriage was a problem owned by the entire extended family, including the ancestors, whose continued approval regulated the marriage, and who owned whatever children issued from the union.[26] A nineteenth-century marriage ceremony in Larteh, moreover, was enacted before the neighborhood shrine to Tsao, the god of procreation, who by the subsequent granting of children sealed the marriage.[27] In abandoning Akonnedi and Tsao, Jonathan had effectively abandoned his family, the living elders of which served as the guardians of morality and harmony in the household. Indeed, the severity of traditional punishments for female adultery indicates that the concept long predated Christian irruption.[28] Jonathan's unfaithfulness to the gods legitimated his wife's subsequent extramarital sexual relations.[29]

To this dual rupture, originating in Jonathan's conversion and completed in his broken marriage, came a second act in the form of punishment (Koko's sickness). However, according to Widmann, it was "the Lord," not Akonnedi, who was the actor: it was Widmann's God—and Jonathan's—who struck Koko with sickness.[30] Significantly, the Christian God's mode of punishment of the wayward wife corresponded precisely to preexisting sanctions and remedies. Looking at the same town a century later, David Brokensha observed that in Larteh,

> adultery is condemned as liable to lead to supernatural punishments, to the harm of all; . . . this view is generally endorsed both by the Christian churches and by the shrines, notably by Akonnedi.[31]

From the very beginning of a Christian presence in Larteh, then, and even before the first few converts were organized into a church, the new (Christian) god had begun guaranteeing social harmony by way of sanctions nearly identical to those of the indigenous religions. In the third act, Widmann's story diverged from the standard Pietist testimonial pattern: Koko's repentance did not follow inner conviction of sin. Rather, it came in response to corporeal sickness, which, it seems, could be cured in no other way than by appeasing the angered deity. Restoration came when Koko underwent baptism, a ritual that, in Widmann's eyes, healed her body, her marriage, and thus the entire community of which the couple was a part.

[26] Agnes Klingshirn, "The Changing Position of Women in Ghana: A Study Based on Empirical Research in Larteh, a Small Town in Southern Ghana" (PhD diss., Philipps-Universität Marburg, 1971), 91.
[27] David Brokensha, *Social Change at Larteh, Ghana* (Oxford: Clarendon, 1966), 222.
[28] Fortes, "Kinship and Marriage among the Ashanti," 276.
[29] Klingshirn, "The Changing Position of Women in Ghana," 104.
[30] Widmann, untitled report, *JB* 1861, 174.
[31] Brokensha, *Social Change*, 230.

## SHRINES BECOME SETTLEMENTS

During the late 1850s, the small congregation of converts was an overwhelmingly poor and sick group of people. Converts had already been treating the missionaries' chapels as a special type of shrine, attached to which they might find spiritual protection, so it was a simple next step to ascribe to the missionaries themselves cultic powers analogous to those of the shrine priests. This process of seeking sanctuary would become Christianity's breakthrough in cultural translation, and it was almost entirely the initiative of indigenous people. This process is utterly important toward an accounting of Christianity's rapid growth after Kwaw Dade's death—after decades of apparently fruitless incubation.

From the time they first arrived in Akuapem in 1835, the missionaries had set about drawing stark lines of contrast between themselves and the people they called "fetish priests," who in Twi are called the asɔfoɔ (singular ɔsɔfoɔ).[32] Asɔfoɔ were hereditary priests who "owned" the abosom, the shrine deities. But within nine years, locals—non-Christians every one of them, because the Basel Mission had no converts at all for a dozen years—began calling the missionaries asɔfoɔ as well.[33] By conflating missionaries and their rivals, the men and women of Akuapem were essentially insisting on incorporating these foreigners into an elastic spiritual ecosystem in which new cults could easily arrive and displace older ones.[34]

People in need of protection, not all of whom were Christians, had begun settling around the missionaries' chapels as early as the 1840s. However, it was not until the mid-1860s, when the settlement at the Akropong chapel exceeded five hundred souls, that the missionaries recognized that they had stumbled into some kind of responsibility for the welfare of the people living in these Christian villages. In the early 1980s, John Middleton observed that historical descriptions of the indigenous Christian settlement at Akropong sounded similar to that of cult groups surrounding an exponent of a new god—not

---

[32] Andreas Riis, "Goldküste in Westafrika," *HB* 1835, 61–65. On this office, for which there are at least two distinct words, see Eva Meyerowitz, *The Akan of Ghana, Their Ancient Beliefs* (London: Faber and Faber, 1958), 55–57.

[33] Sill, *Encounters in Quest of Christian Womanhood*, 198, citing BMA, D-1,2 Akropong 1844, Hermann Halleur 07.06.1844.

[34] From a historical perspective, see T. C. McCaskie, "Accumulation, Wealth and Belief in Asante History. I. To the Close of the Nineteenth Century," *Africa: Journal of the International African Institute* 53, no. 1 (1983), 23–79. Also Kofi Asare Opoku, "Communalism and Community in the African Heritage," *International Review of Mission* 79, no. 316 (1990), 487–92.

an unknown kind of movement in the region.[35] Beginning in the mid-1840s when several West Indian settlers arrived in Akropong, and accelerating in the 1850s, excluded Christian converts began relocating near the Basel Mission buildings.[36] At first, it was an individual or a family, and the process went by without much notice until an identifiable "Christian Quarter" had emerged.[37] Even then, the missionaries did not think much about what was happening until after King Kwaw Dade's death, when the settlement grew from dozens to hundreds of people in a few short years.[38]

Orange Tree Alley, Akropong. In 1866 Yaa hid from the royal executioners in one of these houses; a few years later informal shelters to the right of the lens (adjacent to the chapel and long since dismantled) would be organized into a separate community under missionary patronage. Photo by author, 2015.

These settlements, retroactively termed *Salems*, have been one of the sorest points in Ghanaian church historiography. To take but one example: European missionaries "came disregarding the traditions and culture of the people . . . because to become a Christian, to them, meant . . . being incorporated into a

---

[35]  John Middleton, "One Hundred and Fifty Years of Christianity in a Ghanaian Town," *Africa* 53 (1983), 246–57.

[36]  W. Schlatter, *Geschichte der Basler Mission 1815–1915*, vol. 3, *Afrika*, 66–67. See also Noel Smith, *The Presbyterian Church of Ghana, 1835–1960: A Younger Church in a Changing Society* (Accra: Ghana Universities Press; London: Oxford University Press, 1966) 49, 93, 115.

[37]  *JB* 1861, 161.

[38]  W. Schlatter, *Geschichte der Basler Mission 1815–1915*, vol. 3, *Afrika*, 72–73.

different community, by settling on mission land."[39] Paul Jenkins, later the Basel
Mission archivist, recalls from the 1960s: "In those heady nationalistic days . . .
the Basel Mission was the target of a particularly bitter critique. Its Salems . . .
had uprooted Ghanaians from their culture, it was argued, and separated them
from traditional loyalties."[40] Ulrike Sill's treatment of Christian domestic life in
Basel Mission communities in the Gold Coast went further. Recognizing the
regrets with which many Ghanaians in the present recall the ways Christianity
separated the converts from their families, Sill insisted that the tangible "icon"
of separation—the Salem—was not be confused with the spiritual separation
which usually, but not always, accompanied that settlement.

For modern Ghanaians, the icon of the Basel Mission policy in its relationship with the polities of the then Gold Coast was the "Salem" or the Christian
quarter. Nowadays it carries the image of strict separation or indeed opposition
between the newly emerging Christian community and the already existing
community and town.[41] However, this popular image is incomplete. "Historical
evidence on the nature of the Salem," Sill continued, "is by no means unequiv-
ocal [as to the] assertion that the missionaries were creating a totally separate
Christian community."[42] Paul Jenkins has observed, from Theophilus Opoku's
pastoral report from 1883 in Kukurantumi in Akyem Abuakwa, that not all
Christians lived in the Salem, and moreover: "this seems to have been typical
of all Basel Mission Church congregations, and is a point which is often forgot-
ten when criticisms are levelled at the Salem policy of the Basel Mission."[43] If
the missionaries instituted rules and orders (*Gemeindeordnung*), by which the
Salem was to be run, this imposition only came in 1869, *after* the fact of large-
scale African Christian settlement (hundreds of families, hailing from dozens
of towns across the ridge).[44] As careful attention to chronology makes clear,

[39]   K. Nkansa-Kyeremateng, *Kwawu Handbook* (Accra: Sebewie, 2000), 76. This indirect
way of expressing grief about the past is a Ghanaian cultural preference with which German
and Swiss tastes aligned closely, and which presented a striking contrast with the British. See
Michelle Gilbert, "Disguising the Pain of Remembering in Akwapim," *Africa* 80, no. 3 (2010).
Also see Kwasi Yirenkyi, "Transition and the Quest for Identity: A Socio-ethical Study on
the Problem of Identity and Political Role of the Ghanaian Clergy in a Modernizing Society"
(PhD diss., University of Pittsburgh, 1984), 83–84.
[40]   Paul Jenkins, "The Basel Mission, the Presbyterian Church, and Ghana since 1918," in
Jon Miller, *Missionary Zeal and Institutional Control: Organizational Contradictions in the
Basel Mission on the Gold Coast, 1828–1917* (Grand Rapids: Eerdmans, 2003), 215.
[41]   Sill, *Encounters in Quest of Christian Womanhood*, 195.
[42]   Sill, *Encounters in Quest of Christian Womanhood*, 195.
[43]   Paul Jenkins, "A Conflict of Faiths at Kukurantumi," *Transactions of the Historical
Society of Ghana* 13, no. 2 (1972), 246.
[44]   Anne Beuttler, "Church Discipline Chronicled—a New Source for Basel Mission Historiography," *History in Africa* 42 (2015).

these men and women came seeking shelter and asylum, years before the missionaries had an idea of what they were doing. Aside from Abokobi in the Gã district (built by Christian refugees of a British bombing of the mission station at Osu near Accra), there was no template for a separate Christian community. On the other hand, the indigenous social-religious toolbox contained a unique institution, which the Salems undoubtedly resembled: the shrine sanctuary.[45] Indeed, the particular history of the Salem looks very much like that of that kind of settlement. If the missionaries found themselves running a sanctuary, it was initially imposed on them by the demands of indigenous Christians. Before there was a Salem, there was a sanctuary.

An impossible dilemma confronted any would-be indigenous convert: the fundamental social ideology focused on incorporating all residents, foreigners and slaves included, into existing family networks, and rituals of ancestral veneration were the most efficacious means toward that end. On this point, however, the missionaries could see very little room for compromise, even after they had learned to differentiate ancestral veneration from worship of spirits. Consequently, the Basel Mission's call to conversion was simultaneously a call to abandon family, living and dead. Conversion was, accordingly, very costly, especially for those who were tightly embedded in the existing system.

The high social cost of conversion was part of the reason why conversion was far more attractive to the people at the margins of society—those whom the ideology of incorporation had bypassed. These were the poor, the chronically diseased, the crippled and mentally handicapped, and slaves. These people were also very vulnerable. When crops failed, they would be the last to be fed. When kings died, they would be most at risk of a ritual killing. Moreover, when misfortune struck, when a god or ancestor was expressing his or her displeasure, they would be the first and most obvious culprits, because of their abstinence in sacrifices. In short, many of the first converts were in need of protection.

Sandra Barnes has observed that missionaries in both the Gold and Slave Coasts "were caught in the dilemma of whether or not to provide refuge to escaped slaves and other vulnerable peoples."[46] Barnes cites the case of Samuel Annear of the Church Missionary Society. Annear arrived in 1844 in Badagry, a coastal town in what would become Nigeria, at the outset of a succession conflict in nearby Lagos, a conflict that blossomed into a war

---

[45] Middleton, "One Hundred and Fifty Years of Christianity," 246–57.

[46] Sandra Barnes, "Shrine Sanctuary and Mission Sanctuary in West Africa," in *Christianity and Social Change in Africa: Essays in Honor of J. D. Y. Peel*, ed. Toyin Falola (Durham, N.C.: Carolina Academic Press, 2005), 180.

culminating in an 1852 British bombardment.[47] He stumbled into providing sanctuary to indigent and runaway people, including homeless widows with hungry children. "The children were instructed," Annear wrote, "in the ways of the Christian deity who provided the very spiritual foundation on which the mission house existed."[48] However, the nature of that foundation was unclear. The entire region was in a state of turbulence, and the Basel missionary couple Gollmer (who had been seconded to the CMS), coworkers of Annear's in Badagry, found that starving people were not interested in appeals to the eternal fate of their souls. In the chilling 1853 words of CMS writer Sarah Tucker:

> The cry, "We are hungry, we are hungry!" at the close of some searching appeal to their consciences, or of some touching declaration of the love of Christ, would painfully discourage the messenger of glad tidings.[49]

Shrine sanctuaries, although mainly known among priest-states to the east of Akuapem, were also present in Akan country. Rattray visited a sacred grove in the Asante kingdom in the 1920s, and learned:

> [If] any person were sentenced to death for a crime or about to be killed at a funeral custom and managed to run away and catch hold of the fig tree [in that grove], the life of that person would, as a general rule, be spared, the person becoming a servant of the grove.[50]

Although the Basel Mission in the Gold Coast entertained grandiose dreams of converting the Asante Empire, locals increasingly had an immediate and politically subversive use for the mission facilities: as something of a sacred grove for the ritually unclean, the outcast, and people who were in danger. By the 1860s, furthermore, the number of indigenous Christians had reached a point at which newcomers were joining a ready-made community. The prospect of genuine inclusion made attachment an attractive proposition, especially for the socially marginalized, disabled, diseased, and the "bad-luck people," those with whom no one would associate because a spiritual being appeared to be after them.

The practical social reality was that nearly everyone was unfree in one way or another, and bound to someone above him or her, including jurally "free" people. As elsewhere, a very thin line separated domestic slavery and family

---

[47] J. F. Ade Ajayi, "Nineteenth Century Origins of Nigerian Nationalism," *Journal of the Historical Society of Nigeria* 2, no. 2 (1961).

[48] Annear quoted in Sandra Barnes, "Shrine Sanctuary and Mission Sanctuary," 181.

[49] Sarah Tucker, *Abbeokuta; or, Sunrise within the Tropics: An Outline of the Origin and Progress of the Yoruba Mission* (London: James Nisbet, 1853), 101.

[50] Rattray, *Ashanti*, 129–31.

duties on the one hand, and domestic violence and slave oppression on the other: it happened within the context of complicated personal relationships. During the half decade preceding formal organization of the Salem, a certain Heinrich Yaw Kwapong joined the settlement as a redeemed slave. In 1863, three Christians in Akropong, slaves all, were sold "abroad," that is, to other kingdoms. One of these, Yaw, was redeemed by David Asante, the funds (47 thalers) being raised from within the congregation.[51] In the eyes of everyone involved, Asante's intervention would have put Yaw under his patronage and protection, and thus his moral and legal authority, despite the Basel Mission's loathing for slavery. This is because European notions of individual auton-omy simply made no sense in a West African kingdom undergoing a disrup-tive recovery from centuries of international slave trading. In fact, the whole story illustrates the complexities of social bondage in post-transatlantic slave trade Ghana, most of which was crudely glossed as "slavery" by sanctimonious Europeans.

Yaw, his sister Akua, and their mother had recently entered some kind of unfree service to a wealthy nobleman named Kwaw Kotenku (who, according to Widmann, "mostly marries his slaves").[52] Having taken the mother as one of his wives, he subsequently decided to marry Akua as well. However, Akua had an affair with the mayor of Akropong, which led to a big brawl in the streets. The cuckolded Kwaw sold Akua abroad (probably down to Accra), but Yaw redeemed her from his side earnings as a woodcutter. Nevertheless, Kwaw sold her a second time when she came back to Akropong. Finally, when Yaw opposed the men transporting her to the coast, Kwaw sold him as well—until David Asante and the congregation at Larteh redeemed him.[53] In complex social and legal settings such as this, joining the Christian congregation meant entering the protective umbrella of the Christian *asɔfoɔ*—David Asante or the missionaries. The web of relationships activated in any communal conflict, such as that involving Yaw, could quickly grow complicated, thus illuminating the value people saw in a foreign patron who might be able to offer protection, whether from an angry spirit or from an angry aristocrat.

In 1864, Johann and Rosine Widmann took in an eight-year-old girl named Ofokua who had leprosy, placing her in an indigenous Christian home. This girl had previously been designated as a future wife for the king, but while her leprosy freed her from that burden, it also resulted in her exclusion from

[51] J. G. Widmann, "Mannigfacher Kampf und Sieg," *JB* 1863, 95–97. Widmann, writing in German, used the word *Sklave*, equivalent to the English *slave*.

[52] Widmann called her Akua, but the term was actually her rank—Akua indicated "sub-ject" in general and was used for "slave" and "free" subjects alike.

[53] Widmann, "Mannigfacher Kampf und Sieg," *JB* 1863, 95–97.

her family of origin. Ofokua was baptized as "Margaret" on the same day that Widmann's congregation buried another diseased girl, named Mansa, who had suffered from gout and who had sought refuge from her village after being driven out. Mansa had only lived a few more days.[54] In 1864, missionary Julie Mohr adopted the newborn daughter of a banished priest's assistant.[55] The stories go on and on, and far outnumber cases of confession and repentance: people came to the missionaries seeking a sacrificial apparatus sufficiently potent to engender protection, communal cohesion,[56] survival of children,[57] food security,[58] and more. Kwamena-Poh added an anecdote from Mampong, undated but from this same general period, of refugees from the Shai Hills to the southeast, escaping "tribulation" for breaking taboos related to *dipo* (female puberty) rites.[59]

Taken together, these anecdotes suggest a cross-culturally dialectic process by which Africans were actively imposing a social category upon the church. Irrespective of the missionaries' insistence on faith and teaching, these people were a community in which belonging outweighed orthodoxy of belief as a motivation for membership. Nearly all these people (overwhelmingly disabled, diseased, and displaced—and young) attached themselves to the missionaries—who had been widely understood as an order of *asɔfoɔ* priests for over twenty years—around whom an existing community of followers was gathering. Within this community, they did not hear a message about a new god, but rather about how to reach a god they already knew in their incantations. As Robin Horton summarized:

> Hence the African convert has not accepted an addition to the pantheon of lesser spirits. Rather, he has accepted change and development in his concept of the supreme being.[60]

Horton's point, however, is incomplete unless the social context in which this change and development took place is borne in mind: there was not one kind of "African convert."

[54]  J. G. Widmann, "Die Elenden suchen Hilfe," *HB* 1865, 35.
[55]  Julie Mohr, "Die Kinder des Fetischpriesters," *HB* 1865, 84–85, from a letter dated August 4, 1864.
[56]  David Asante, "Von der Außengemeinde Date," 97–99.
[57]  Johannes Christian Dieterle, "Eine suchende Familie," 114–15. Here a man asked missionary Dieterle to baptize his surviving children after an angry spirit had killed several.
[58]  David Asante, "Von der Außengemeinde Date," 97–99.
[59]  M. A. Kwamena-Poh, "Church and Change in Akwapem," in *Domestic Rights and Duties in Southern Ghana*, ed. Christine Oppong, Legon Family Research Papers (Legon: Institute of African Studies, University of Ghana, 1974), 65.
[60]  Robin Horton, "African Conversion," *Africa* 41, no. 2 (1971), 100.

The turning point in Akuapem came with Kwaw Dade's death in mid-1866. The ensuing months and years saw repeated human sacrifices, and more and more people fled to the Christian settlement at Akropong. "Hardly a month passes," Johannes Mader wrote in 1869, "without death-festivals; when a local elder named Bambu died, several slaves were butchered, including a woman who had been purchased in Abirew for that express purpose."[61] The missionaries' unending frustrations with what they felt was the shallowness of converts' beliefs indicates that the Akuapem converts were not, in general, responding to the missionaries' call to repentance from sin. Rather, indigenous non-Christians were aware of their Christian neighbors, and they had been watching and discussing for years. When hard times fell upon them, they understood attachment to the Christian community as a pragmatic option—although perhaps an option of last resort.

As early as 1850, Johann Widmann complained that "few are concerned with the salvation of their souls . . . they are rather interested in protection."[62] When this protection failed, people rarely hesitated to turn to whatever else might protect them. In the same year, Joseph Stanger wrote from Accra that his interpreter, a young man named James Okai, had died. He had lost both arms to a shark and, while still recovering, was poisoned to death by his family, likely to prevent contagious evil from spreading from him to strike the rest of his kindred.[63]

Personal statements by the newly baptized reveal a constant thread of looking for protection from evil beings, or from bad people, or from themselves, from an inability to stop getting in trouble. In 1869, Nathanael Aboate and his wife Maria Kobe, both in their early thirties, from the Guan town of Awukukwa, were receptive to David Asante's evangelistic message after their third child in succession had died, despite having paid the shrine priests handsomely for this child's protection. Likewise, and published in the same issue of the *Heidenbote*, David Aboagye spoke of turning to Christianity after his brother's wife died when struck by a falling tree branch, despite wearing a protective amulet that her husband had bought with "much money."[64] These people were not coming to the church at the conclusion of some kind of syllogistic process of metaphysical calculation, but out of grief and desperation.

Patronage, above all for protection, was the basis of political power in late precolonial Akuapem, as it was generally in West Africa. Protective

---

[61]  Johann Adam Mader, "Christenthum und Heidenthum in Akropong," *JB* 1868, 107–8.
[62]  Widmann, "Station Akropong," 194.
[63]  Joseph Stanger, "Usu/Accra," *JB* 1850, 206.
[64]  Johann Adam Mader, "Der helle Schein in zuvor dunklen Herzen," *HB* 1869, 6.

talismans (*suman*) were a lucrative industry throughout the Gold Coast and beyond. In Asante, Muslims monopolized this sector of the economy, constructing *suman* with excerpts of the Qur'an and Hadiths sewn into leather pouches. This industry is worth examining at least superficially, because the West African culture of talismans made from pieces of scripture contains some clues as to indigenous expectations of Christianity and Christian Scriptures, which some locals understood as analogous to Islam.[65] British visitor Bowdich was in the Asante royal city of Kumasi in 1817 and saw a coat covered in amulets "sold for the equivalent of thirty slaves."[66] A few years later in 1824, Joseph Dupuis recorded the following exchange between the Asantehene and two Muslims of his court:

> "What is your custom," said the king, addressing himself to Kantoma and Abou Becr, "when great men make friends?" "They swear upon the sacred book" (the Koran) was the reply. "That is good," said the king, "because then, if they keep evil in their hearts, the book must kill them."

When the two readily agreed with an orthodox Muslim description of the Qur'an as God's word, the king continued:

> "Ah," said the king, "I like that, it is strong sense, it is the fetishe of your country. Ashantee has no fetishe like this, but the Ashantee custom is good too. I know that book (the Koran) is strong, and I like it because it is the book of the great God; it does good for me and therefore I love all the people that read it."[67]

This tradition was still alive in 1869, when Basel missionaries Friedrich and Rosa-Luise Ramseyer, together with their infant son, were abducted from their home in Akyem Abuakwa and marched to Kumasi. Their captor, General Adu Bofo, Ramseyer wrote, wore a protective coat covered with many "grigris" [*sic*] or pouches containing scripture, meant to repel bullets.[68]

---

[65]   David Owusu-Ansah, *Islamic Talismanic Tradition in Nineteenth-Century Asante* (Lewiston: Edwin Mellen, 1991).

[66]   T. Edward Bowdich, *Mission from Cape Coast Castle to Ashantee: With a Statistical Account of That Kingdom, and Geographical Notices of Other Parts of the Interior of Africa* (London: John Murray, 1819), 272.

[67]   Joseph Dupuis, *Journal of a Residence in Ashantee* (London: Henry Colburn, 1824), 160–61.

[68]   Friedrich August Ramseyer and Johannes Kühne, *Vier Jahre in Asante. Tagebücher der Missionare Ramseyer und Kühne*, ed. H. Gundert, 2nd ed. (Basel: Missionskomptoir, 1875), 20. The English translation uses the word *charms*.

However, the locals and the missionaries understood protection quite differently. The indigenous corpus of spiritual-medical therapies focused on divination of symptoms, which reached the entirety of the body and beyond, extending to the broader community. An individual's physical ailment, for example, might well have its origins in a close relative's strained marriage. Sickness, understood in social categories quite distinct from the Western biomedical paradigm then making its appearance in medical missions in the Gold Coast, was a corporate affliction. In a 1980 study on the religious core to Akan medicine, Kofi Appiah-Kubi makes the revealing observation that in many circumstances, the kindred of a patient are instructed to participate in the regime of healing.[69] Treatment was improvised accordingly: herbal medicines in intricate conversation with amulets, appeals to the ancestors, sacrifices to the *abosom*, and dietary prescriptions. If one remedy failed, another might be tried, and if one *ɔbosom* failed, another might be embraced. This was the logic leading a certain Benjamin to baptism in Aburi in 1865. "Four years ago, he was a persecutor of the Christians," Dieterle wrote on November 5. He came down with a painful case of what must have been elephantiasis and could not walk. He saw "many fetish priests," but to no effect. A Christian named Noah visited him, but the ailing man had no interest in joining Noah's religion, until one day, when his wooden talisman (Dieterle: "fetish") fell apart when he was moving it: the wood had been eaten by worms. He rejected it, saying to himself: "If Christ can help me to walk again, then I will become a Christian." He began having friends carry him to church, and his leg began to heal. "Now he can walk," Dieterle concluded, "and hopes for a full recovery."[70]

The relationship between protection and conversion is best illustrated by another example from a generation later. In 1891 in the small town of Tutu[71] in southern Akuapem, indigenous pastor Nathanael Asare described one man who had sought out inclusion in the Christian settlement in nearby Aburi. This forty-year-old Christian, whom Asare did not name, was the brother of the "fetish-carrier" (probably an *ɔkɔmfo*) for a priest of the god Tano.[72] This office meant that at the prescribed time of a ritual or a sacrifice, he would become possessed by an *ɔbosom*: either by Tano himself or one of Tano's "sons,"

[69] Kofi Appiah-Kubi, *Man Cures, God Heals: Religion and Medical Practice among the Akans of Ghana* (Totowa, N.J.: Allanheld, Osmun, 1981), 15–17.

[70] Johannes Christian Dieterle, "Der wurmstichige Fetisch," *HB* 1866, 11. For the *Heidenbote*'s European readers, editor Joseph Josenhans appended a question: "Dear Reader, what is your fetish?"

[71] Misspelled as Fufu in the published report.

[72] Nathanael Asare, "Aus der Arbeit eines eingeborenen Missionsarbeiters," *JB* 1891, 46–47.

with which the priest's *suman*, his talisman, was associated.[73] Tano is one of the highest gods in the Akan pantheon, and the office of *ɔkɔmfo* to Tano was no small matter. In Rattray's discussion of the relationship between the *abosom* spirits, their *akɔmfo* (sing. *ɔkɔmfo*) ministers, and the associated apparatus of the *suman*, rendered in 1891 by the Basel Mission in German as "talisman" but by Rattray as "fetish," Rattray quotes an *ɔkɔmfo* in the Asante state as saying that "an *obosom* [sic] 'is carried' and has its own *ɔkɔmfo*."[74] Complicating matters is Rattray's usage of the imprecise word *fetish*, which European sources of the nineteenth and early twentieth centuries tended to apply both to the material objects (the *suman*) and to the spirits with which they were associated (the *abosom*), this despite the fact that Rattray knew better (he furthermore specified that the *abosom*'s power derived from an entirely different source [God, *nyame*] than did that of the *suman*, which came from the natural world, from plants, animals, forest monsters, and, sometimes, ghosts). Rattray also conflates *akɔmfo* oracles and *asɔfoɔ* priests. Meyerowitz has the former serving in a subordinate and assisting role to the latter.[75] Christaller's 1881 dictionary reads:

> "o̱-kòmfó = o̱bòsomfó, a fetish-man, possessed with or prophesying by a fetish; soothsayer, diviner. . . . The ko̱mfo pretends to be the interpreter and mouth-piece either of the guardian spirit of a nation, town or family, or of a soothsaying spirit resorted to in sickness or other calamities." [76]

Although not every *ɔkɔmfo* enters his or her office in hereditary fashion, some did: the choice did not belong to the individual. Rather, the individual was elected by the spirit (and according to Meyerowitz, some *asɔfoɔ* priests did double duties, serving as their own *akɔmfo*.)[77] In this particular instance, the election to *ɔkɔmfo* ran through male bloodlines in this family. As a result, the forty-year-old man was next in line to the office should his brother die.

There was little question to anyone present in Tutu (at least in Asare's account) that a Christian ought not to serve as assistant to a priest of Tano, and especially when spirit possession was involved. This man had angered Tano by converting to Christianity, but since the convert had a son, who was third

---

[73]  Rattray describes at length a visit, in the early 1920s to the principle temple of Tano in northwestern Ghana; this description extracted partly from there. R. S. Rattray, *Religion & Art in Ashanti* (Oxford: Clarendon, 1927), 172–200.

[74]  Rattray, *Religion & Art*, 23.

[75]  Meyerowitz, *The Akan of Ghana*, 55–57.

[76]  J. G. Christaller, *Dictionary of the Asante and Fante Language Called Tshi (Twi)* (Basel: Printed for the Basel Evangelical Missionary Society, 1881), 242.

[77]  Meyerowitz, *The Akan of Ghana*, 55–57.

in line for the office, nothing bad had happened: the line would be unbroken. But then the man sent his son to the Wesleyan school at nearby Aburi, with the obvious implication that conversion—and thus rejection of the boy's designation as future ɔkɔmfo—would break the blood lineage. Thus angered, Tano struck the boy gravely sick. The boy's parents were terrified, and behind the man's back his wife visited Tano's priest for advice. The latter informed her, and subsequently the entire community, in what Asare described as a high-tension public confrontation, that by converting, the Christian man had incurred Tano's anger, and that Tano intended to kill the boy with this sickness. The man refused to yield, however, announcing to the community that he did not intend to renounce his baptism, even if Tano killed his son. At this point, Asare wrote, the boy was suddenly healed and, accordingly, Tano and his priest publicly humiliated. However, that was not the end of the story: although the unnamed Christian (or perhaps Asare) had evidenced power to counteract Tano's punishment, the encounter had taken place in front of the entire community and was evidently quite terrifying. Retribution could be expected: either from hostile villagers who felt this man had endangered the entire community in his provocation of Tano, or from Tano himself. Consequently, Asare concluded, "since he wants to avoid the temptation of the heathens, he has decided to resettle into the Christian station [at Aburi]."[78]

Slave conversion, along with that of the poor and the disabled, was tolerable to a limited degree. However, the conversion of a forty-year-old man, the father of a child chosen for ritual spirit possession (that is, no normal child, but one of extraordinary value to the community) was not. To this man who had been publicly threatened by the priest of a powerful god, the Salem at Aburi constituted a sanctuary, where he might be protected by an even more powerful god. By refusing to participate in Tano's cult, and by removing his son from the line of succession, he had broken his standing with the community, the ancestors, and the god Tano. And therein lay the attraction of the sanctuary: its indigenous settlers were putting themselves under the protective powers of either a priest or a missionary—in this case, an indigenous pastor (Asare)—in exchange for protection. The man at the center of this story had exchanged one ɔsɔfoɔ-priest, along with his associated cult, for another. He was seeking protection from an angry god, but also from unwanted possession.

Late nineteenth- and twentieth-century European observers of spirit possession often inquired about the metaphysics or psychiatric machinery behind possession, while to the locals, the predominant problematic was the

[78] Nathanael Asare, "Aus der Arbeit," 46–47.

misfortune possession represented to an individual or a community. Mary Field, for example, tried to reduce spirit possession to a mental breakdown:

> The possessed person is in a state of dissociated personality. . . . It is the total banishment of all but one stream [of consciousness] which is the essential feature of dissociation. It is not true of the possessed person that, as Africans have it, "something has come to him;" rather it is that something has *gone* from him.[79]

Spirit possession accentuated differences between European and African outlooks on the nature of the self, but also constituted a clear gap between nineteenth-century European and New Testament ways of thinking: it was an accepted fact of life in ancient West Asia, but in Blumhardt's time was largely peripheral both to German theological discourse and Pietist subculture. Thus when Johannes Christoph Blumhardt brought exorcism to his parish in 1844, he was, like the Africans in Akuapem, meeting a pressing indigenous (rural Black Forest) need by means of an imported and reconfigured religious technique.

However, that episode did not last, and spirit possession and exorcism did not enter the German ecclesiastic mainstream.[80] Consequently, many West African readers of the Bible had an easier time reading their own situations into the text than many Europeans of the same period, churchmen and theologians included. For the former, possession was not a question of sanity, but of social emergency. Charles Taylor has made a similar point: treatment, not psychological speculation, may be the humane response to assertions of possession.

> The people of New Testament Palestine, when they saw someone possessed of an evil spirit, were too immediately at grips with the real suffering of this condition, in a neighbor, or a loved one, to be able to entertain the idea that this was an interesting explanation for a psychological condition . . . [81]

Unwanted possession represented a great personal misfortune, to which, in the case of the man who liberated himself from Tano, the answer was communal:

---

[79]  M. J. Field, "Spirit Possession in Ghana," in *Spirit Mediumship and Society in Africa*, ed. John Beattie and John Middleton (London: Routledge & K. Paul, 1969). Italics original.

[80]  Faith healing from ailments remained a constant thread within German Pietism, and by the emergence of Pentecostalism in the first decade of the twentieth century, at least some German Pietists, including Elias Schrenk, who had served with the Basel Mission in the Gold Coast, were able to deliberate on the new movement from a position of personal experience with faith healings. See Elias Schrenk, *Ein Leben im Kampf um Gott* (Basel: Verlag der Missionsbuchhandlung, 1905).

[81]  Charles Taylor, *A Secular Age* (Cambridge, Mass.: Belknap Press of Harvard University Press, 2007), 11.

joining the people gathered at the Christian village, the Salem. To its pioneers, the Salem thus represented protection from the consequences of a previous rupture, rather than the rupture itself. As long as there obtained some kind of obedience to the king, whereby the residents of the Salems obeyed the king—in, for example, time of war—the conflict was manageable.

In the 1920s, J. B. Danquah, then serving as legal counsel to the royal court of Akyem Abuakwa (the forest kingdom immediately to the west of Akua-pem), recalled the Salem of the capital city of Kyebi, where he had spent much of his childhood. The institution of the Salem created, in effect, two towns: a "heathen town" and an *"oburoni kurom,"* a "European town."[82] Commenting on Danquah's statement, Sydney Williamson suggests it meant that the con-verts appeared as Europeans to their fellow Akyem.[83]

Similar stories abound in twentieth-century historical literature, espe-cially after Ghana had achieved independence. The cumulative experience of the Salems was one of painful social segregation. In reference to Kwawu, an ethnically homogenous district to the north of Akyem Abuakwa, Kofi Nkansa-Kyeremateng has spoken of the irritation the Salems represented to a society committed, at an ideological level, to social equality within a given clan.[84] The practical reality was that rank and social disparities passed from one genera-tion to the other. This meant that an intrusive, or an alternate system (as repre-sented by the Salems)—in which rank and standing were reshuffled—effectively spoke to the states' failures at their guaranteeing the social order upon which their own legitimacy turned. This was especially the case in Asante, but to a lesser extent in Akuapem and Akyem Abuakwa. According to McCaskie:

> The entire weight of the ideological structuration of historical experience served to privilege aspiration to the most tenuous membership in jural corporateness over an individual 'freedom' that connoted the non-being of exclusion from Asante society.[85]

In other words, socially marginalized people in the Gold Coast viewed social exclusion as a form of death—of "non-being" in McCaskie's words. At least since the worst days of the Atlantic slaving period, ruling elites throughout the Akan states had anchored a delicate social order in the ritual capacity of ancestral clans (both matrilineal and patrilineal) to incorporate strangers, and

---

[82]  J. B. Danquah, *The Akim Abuakwa Handbook* (London: F. Groom, 1928), 90.

[83]  Sydney George Williamson, *Akan Religion and the Christian Faith: A Comparative Study of the Impact of Two Religions* (Accra: Ghana Universities Press, 1965), 56, n. 36.

[84]  Kofi Nkansa-Kyeremateng, *The Story of Kwawu* (Accra: Presbyterian Press, 1987), 8–11.

[85]  McCaskie, *State and Society*, 100–101.

in the efficacy of sacrifice to influence a dangerously capricious spiritual world. This social order was strongly shaped by Atlantic warfare and the political and economic insecurity with which it was associated. In such a setting, individual nonconformity, even by the socially excluded, was a threat to the general welfare. To an extent, the social order depended on the threat of exclusion—a threat which, in the middle of the nineteenth century, included enslavement abroad.

In 1868, Johann Mader mentioned several towns in Akuapem as having Christians who were isolated, adding that the congregants were so few in number that it was hard for the church leaders to arrange marriages between Christians.[86] As a result, "mixed" marriages were typical during these years. Nine years later, the *Heidenbote's* editors estimated 39 percent of adult Christians were part of such mixed marriages.[87] To understand the appeal of the Salem, when its distorting qualities were so apparent to subsequent generations, it is vital to understand its benefits. Why would someone voluntarily remove to the "European town"? To the destitute poor, the disabled, the refugees, the cursed, and the foreigners who initially sought sanctuary with the missionaries, Salems were less about broken relationships than about the possibility of protection and inclusion. Many, or even most, of the initial settlers were not Christians. They spoke several languages and came from near and far. To many of this first generation, the social life of the Salem represented an alternate form of inclusion and thus a new chance at life.

The question was furthermore complicated by fact that there was a Pietist template of sorts back in Germany: Korntal and Wilhelmsdorf, two rural settlements "privileged" by Württemberg's King Wilhelm I in 1819 for Pietist nonconformists to state Lutheranism, in a royal attempt at containing emigration.[88] While the missionaries thought of their Christian settlements in the Gold Coast as analogous to the two German villages, to the first generation of Ghanaians living around the mission chapel, the Salems meant inclusion for the excluded, protection for the exposed, and even the possibility of marriage.

What did this look like in practice? In general, and in accordance with the Basel Mission's recognition of what they saw as the legitimate temporal power of a king and military leader (in absolute contrast to the illegitimate power of a priest), the missionaries insisted the Salem community avoid provoking

---

[86]  Mader, "Christenthum und Heidenthum," 108.

[87]  *HB* 1877, 69.

[88]  Samuel Koehne, "Pietism as Societal Solution: The Foundation of the Korntal Brethren," in *Pietism and Community in Europe and North America: 1650–1850*, ed. Jonathan Strom (Leiden: Brill, 2010), 329.

the king, and send its fighting-age men to the latter's service in times of war.[89] However, this dichotomy describes missionary obliviousness to the inextricability of spiritual and political power. To the missionaries, the segregation of the indigenous Christians from the non-Christians, Adam Mohr argues, was the "spatial embodiment of a discourse of separation from . . . Akan religion."[90] This spatial separation (which in Akropong constituted only about 100 meters) was not great, but the message was clear enough. Especially relative to the priests of territorial spirits, the Salem was very much an assertion, not merely of sanctuary, but also of power—the protective power of the Christian God.

## CONCLUSION

To those on the outside, the Christian sanctuary was at times an intolerable social irritant. Since Christian conversion was most appealing to the socially marginalized, converts were often subject to harassment and fines.[91] In an 1869 letter from Tutu on the Akuapem ridge (undated but filed in the Basel Mission archives between other letters from early August of that year), indigenous pastor Alexander Clerk wrote of "the heavy penalty of 1,500 heads cowries, 12 sheep or 12 anchors rum" incurred over a dispute over the Salem community's use of land belonging to someone else.[92] Economic harassment and communal exclusion had a social result for the Basel Mission: the organization had acquired, in the moral sense of all participants, some kind of responsibility for the welfare of the Salem residents. To the missionaries, this responsibility could only mean working to organize the residents' economic independence. Since the mission was already invested in literacy and vocational education, the obvious answer was to direct the converts toward external markets, where their literacy might have economic value. In the main, this meant raising cash crops: coffee, initially, and rubber and oil palms from mid-century on, until both were sidelined by a genuinely homegrown industry, cocoa. In 1877, an unsigned editorial in the *Heidenbote* concluded thus:

> In the last decade, we have observed congregants' decreasing patriarchal dependency upon the missionaries and the mission for their material needs.

[89] Sill, *Encounters in Quest of Christian Womanhood*, 198.

[90] Adam Mohr, *Enchanted Calvinism: Labor Migration, Afflicting Spirits, and Christian Therapy in the Presbyterian Church of Ghana* (Rochester, N.Y.: University of Rochester Press, 2013), 39.

[91] The leveling of fines was both a key symbol of executive authority and the principal source of state revenue; indigenous Christians were continually subject to fines by local chiefs.

[92] BMA D-1 (Reel 21, 1869–1870, part 2), item 39, Clerk to Committee.

In the beginning, the mission was unavoidably drawn into the needs and difficulties of their everyday life, but this situation is increasingly being replaced by indigenous Christians' and congregations' economic independence. All energy is applied to accustoming them to providing for themselves, rather than being provided for.[93]

This "decreasing patriarchal dependency" points to the beginnings of a major generational change. The converts' children, coming of age with a measure of economic and social stability made possible by their parents' incorporation into the Salem, saw things differently than their parents. Sidney Williamson (a Methodist missionary from England, in the Gold Coast from 1933 to his death in 1959) framed the problem as missionaries ripping the delicate social fabric. "The convert, hitherto integrated into his community, must be at least spiritually prised loose from his traditional social setting and called to live as a man apart."[94] What arguments such as Williamson's fail to account for, however, is historical nuance—specifically, the already-existing social marginalization of most of the first converts. If later generations came to view the Salem as a form of exclusion, the first converts did not see it that way: they had been socially excluded before joining the Salem. For some of them, the reverse was true: having no security, having no family, the Salem actually created a new community. But for the second generation, those who were born and raised in the Salem, the felt reality was that of stifling and sometimes arbitrary communal pressures.

[93] "Die Station Akropong im letzten Jahrzehnt," *HB* 1877, p. 69.
[94] Williamson, *Akan Religion and the Christian Faith*, 56.

# 6

# Divergent Modes of Hermeneutics

## Introduction

The wave of sacrificial killings that followed King Kwaw Dade's death had begun to recede by October 1868, when the Basel Mission consecrated a new chapel at Tutu. Before a crowd of several hundred people, two Germans (Johannes Mader and Elias Schrenk) and two natives of Akuapem (Alexander Clerk and David Asante) preached, and the contrast is striking. The four men were reading from the same Bible but had chosen passages that could hardly stand in greater contrast: the Germans preached captivity and death, and the Ghanaians strength and blessing.[1] Having translated the Bible, the missionaries were no longer its hermeneutical gatekeepers.

Richard Werbner has described the spectacular mixture of verbal improvisation and memorized verse, by which Botswana's Tswapong diviners address clients' situational needs for specific moral guidance, as "acrobatic stylistics."[2] Something similar began to emerge with the arrival, in the Gold Coast, of the Bible in Twi translation. A message of divine self-disclosure, of power over evil, and of new possibilities for the incorporation of strangers, and translated into words which had never before been used in that way in Twi, amounted to acrobatics at the very least. But the missionaries had already been active in Akuapem for over three decades, and what little success they had seen had largely come as the result of indigenous creativity in devising uses for these foreign

---

[1]  Johannes Christian Dieterle, "Die Einweihung der neuen Kapelle in Tutu," *HB* 1869, 8.

[2]  Richard P. Werbner, *Divination's Grasp: African Encounters with the Almost Said* (Bloomington: Indiana University Press, 2015), 72.

*asɔfoɔ*—these shrine priests. Despite all the indigenous congregations' creativity, and especially as the missionaries found themselves in the unexpected position of running quasi-sanctuaries, the message remained in the hands of the foreigners, along with those among the locals who could read German, English, or, for a very small number, Greek and Hebrew.[3] The distribution of the vernacular Bible changed everything. This chapter looks at the threat presented by the vernacular Bible to indigenous foundations of political legitimacy (which was irreducibly religious), and the contrasting ways missionaries and indigenous Christians read the Bible (and the efforts the latter made at incorporating the former into their hermeneutical conclusions). My argument is twofold.

First, in translating the Bible into Twi, the Basel Mission introduced into indigenous discourse an assertion that the supreme God had self-revealed in history. This simple message had profound implications for a social order rooted in a sacred kingship defined by ancestral veneration. At issue was not so much the ancestral cult itself, but an understanding of the human past, according to which good and evil, truth and falsehood were inseparable from social responsibility. The biblical message was a powerful contradiction to the king's claim—justified by his tendance to the dead—on the loyalty of the living.

Second, as indigenous Christians collaborated and contended with the missionaries in developing a Christianity commensurate with local needs, they increasingly anchored their efforts in the Bible as that book became more available. Thus, to understand indigenous Christians' agendas in thinking about Christianity, one must look closely at their use of the Bible—especially with sensitivity to its arrival in print. The Bible likewise constituted the center of the missionaries' moral universe. In stark contrast with contemporaneous trends in biblical scholarship in the missionaries' homelands, to those in the field, the Bible remained a vehicle through which God could speak directly to the seeker. Accordingly, missionary receptivity to indigenous reconfigurations of Christianity was greatest when these were anchored in biblical teaching. For that reason, to fully appreciate the role reciprocity played in the cross-cultural encounter, it is of utmost importance to look at the process of translation, and the concomitant training of a cohort of indigenous specialists in hermeneutics and preaching.

### ROYAL OWNERSHIP OF THE PAST

At least since the invention of the Akan military state in the seventeenth century, and probably earlier yet, sacred kingship was rooted in the king's stewardship of the attentions of the deceased ancestors. Royal responsibility implied a

---

[3] The seminary's first cohort had graduated two years earlier in 1866: *HB* 1866, 132.

conflation of knowledge about the past with social duty: subjects were accountable to the king because the king was accountable to the ancestors on behalf of his subjects. Knowledge about the past—about the ancestors—was thus inextricable from multiple levels of protocol. Correspondingly, the introduction, via the vernacular Bible, of a line of existential truth that had no bearing on ancestral veneration amounted to a dangerous irruption into indigenous political standards of legitimacy. To get at this point, I turn to the nature of royal ownership of the past. Having outlined that mixture of argument and belief, I will be able to examine the Twi Bible's vocabulary on truth.

The office of the king—represented as stool—centered then and now on the king's responsibility for stewardship of the attentions of the late ancestors. The ancestors—delineated, among the Akan (including the Akyem ruling class in Akuapem), according to female descent—concerned themselves with communal customs and morality. They punished violators (often with otherwise unaccountable diseases) and blessed the dutiful (with well-being, prosperity, and full cradles) according to their—or their kindred's—deeds. Although the ancestors would not be expected to relent in their persecution of moral and ritual violators until wrongs were made right, angered ancestors might be appeased by appropriate sacrifices and libations as tokens of repentance.[4] As Kwasi Wiredu has noted, however, these ideas "are a natural outgrowth of a conception of personhood which is entertained among the peoples of West Africa with only variations of detail."[5] These sacrifices were made at multiple scales: within individual families, and on behalf of the entire kingdom by the king. The latter consisted, in the main, of the king's overtures to his predecessors on the royal stool.[6] The blackened stools of the royal lineage were housed in a special building, off-limits to commoners. The king's sacredness referred to his accountability to these spirits, as represented by the stools they had once occupied. A misfortune afflicting the entire domain, and which was understood to reflect the active agency of the royal ancestors, was therefore the king's responsibility. For this reason, meticulous attention to chronology of royal lineage was a matter of life and death: if the king got it wrong, the lives of the people could be at risk.

---

[4]   K. A. Busia, *The Position of the Chief in the Modern Political System of Ashanti* (London: Published for the International African Institute by the Oxford University Press, 1951), 24.

[5]   Kwasi Wiredu, "Death and the Afterlife in African Culture," in *Person and Community: Ghanaian Philosophical Studies, I*, ed. Kwasi Wiredu and Kwame Gyekye (Washington, D.C.: Council for Research in Values and Philosophy, 1992), 139.

[6]   The king also needed to indirectly tend to the gods, or rather, to support the priests in that office by enforcing protocol concerning the nonhuman spiritual world.

Given the Basel Mission's orientation toward language learning and cultural immersion, it should come as no surprise that several of the earlier missionaries took great interest in the histories of the various kingdoms among whom they were living, and they occasionally wrote down lengthy lists of deceased kings, delineated by royal spokesmen. Twentieth-century research revealed that some of these histories contained discrepancies: the claimed list of ancestors sometimes did not add up.[7] However, chronological discrepancies in regnal lists did not always reflect mistakes in oral tradition, because chronology was not the purpose. Rather, the official king lists represented something more akin to an inventory of assets—a possible source of insight and assistance, to be drawn upon in times of confusion and need. A missing king was a king who, as ancestor, had proven himself less than useful. Because of these kinds of omissions, mid-twentieth-century historians working from missionary sources came to reject the king lists as history, with Ivor Wilks going as far as to say that these so-called tribal histories had no historical content.[8] However, what if historical content was not the point at all? If the missionaries' royal interlocutors were explaining to their eager foreigners the basis upon which the king stood, the regnal lists could be understood as religious texts: the point was not chronological facticity, but moral honesty.

The problem was most apparent in a Basel missionary's report on the Akyem Abuakwa royal lineage. Sometime during the early 1860s, Karl Strömberg interviewed a senior official named Apietu on the kingdom's history. Apietu fed Strömberg a king list omitting several early kings. This omission implied that Ofori Panin (d. 1727) was the kingdom's founder, when the kingdom was in fact at least a century older.[9] In trying to make sense of this omission, Addo-Fening has pointed out that Strömberg's informant was no common elder. He was a relative of the current king and implicated in that family's fortunes. Moreover, Apietu held the office of *Apesemakahene*, the chief of the *apesemakafo* (the ritual officials), which put him in charge of ceremonial

---

   [7]   Ivor Wilks, "The Growth of the Akwapim State: A Study in the Control of Evidence," in *The Historian in Tropical Africa: Studies Presented and Discussed at the Fourth International African Seminar*, ed. Jan Vansina, R. Mauny, and L. V. Thomas (London: Published for the International African Institute by the Oxford University Press, 1964), 393.

   [8]   Ivor Wilks, "Tribal History and Myth," *Universitas* 2, no. 3–4 (1956), 84–86, 116–18; Jan Vansina, *De la tradition orale; essai de méthode historique* (Tervuren: Museé royal de l'Afrique centrale, 1961), 17, n. 47; David P. Henige, *The Chronology of Oral Tradition: Quest for a Chimera* (Oxford: Clarendon, 1974), 97ff.

   [9]   Robert Addo-Fening, *Akyem Abuakwa, 1700–1943: From Ofori Panin to Sir Ofori Atta* (Trondheim: Department of History, Norwegian University of Science and Technology, 1997), 5.

libations to the ancestors.[10] Wilks has explained that office, getting to the heart of the matter:

> In Akan society it is customary to create tangible memorials—the so-called "ancestral stools"—to the deserving dead. . . . A stool may have its own 'stool room,' or may share one. In either case it will have a custodian [the office held by Apietu], who should visit it at least once in every (forty-two day) month, calling the name of the ancestor, recounting in verse his or her great deeds, and providing (soul) food and drink.[11]

The key word here is *deserving*. Veneration in the afterlife generally corresponded with accrued merit during a lifetime, but not absolutely: it also depended on the ongoing relationship with said ancestor. If a deceased ruler proved uninterested in the affairs of his living descendants, intervening with neither instructions nor blessings nor sanctions, he may find himself alienated from the lineage. In a kingdom, such as Asante, enjoying long-term stability, little will have changed over the years, but if, as with Akwamu, the stool house needed to be relocated (the stools having been hidden in the forest until the 1730 war's conclusion), it may have been possible to leave behind stools whose occupants were no longer assets to the community. Wilks:

> Regnal lists in a sense "index" such stools. If the stools are devotedly served by their custodians, and are housed in an orderly manner, then it may be possible to compile from them a list of rulers arranged in the correct time sequence.[12]

As *Apesemakahene* to Akyem Abuakwa, Apietu certainly knew the chronology. He would have been making no mistake in his account of ancestors to his guest.[13] However, what he told Strömberg nevertheless omitted a few kings. Was he misrepresenting the past for strategic advantage? Was he only detailing the kings with whom the kingdom continued to hold a relational connection—an inventory of assets, as it were? These questions were beyond Strömberg's capacity to understand, and Apietu certainly knew that

---

[10]   Addo-Fening, *Akyem Abuakwa, 1700–1943*, 13.

[11]   Ivor Wilks, *Akwamu 1640–1750: A Study of the Rise and Fall of a West African Empire* (1958; Trondheim: Department of History, Norwegian University of Science and Technology, 2001), xxviii.

[12]   Wilks, *Akwamu 1640–1750*, xxviii.

[13]   Wilks later modified his opinion on the reliability of these sources. "In 1956 I was in a highly skeptical frame of mind," he wrote, adding that "I have long since abandoned such a severely functionalist approach. My subsequent work on Asante led to an appreciation of how accurately knowledge of the past might be transmitted over the generations by highly trained practitioners in, for example, the form of songs and poems." *Akwamu 1640–1750*, xxiii.

he was dealing with a simple man (Strömberg was a sailor from Sweden and no shrewd diplomat).[14] If Apietu's motivations, and those of other missionary informants across the region, remain opaque, the point is that representations of ancestral lineages spoke to the politics of the present, and missionaries could easily and unwittingly be used to change the past. Within the bounds of royal capacity to define the terms of social responsibility, knowledge about the past was knowledge of the living ancestors, and, more importantly, stewardship of an inherited relationship with the same. There was no history "out there," independent of duty within a tightly defined social order.

Kwasi Wiredu has argued that "truth" as a cognitive concept has multiple words in Twi, none of which approximates Enlightenment-era European notions of cognitive autonomy from church and state alike.[15] The basic issue was that while historical truth is not exactly a null category, nevertheless, in McCaskie's words, "its ethical rather than cognitive weighting meant that it was not equipped to develop the momentum or 'escape velocity' to break away from ideological structuration."[16] In the precolonial Akan states, in other words, truth was too wrapped up in duty (to the king and to the ancestors) for independent speculation. These related but distinct notions of truth correspond to two different phrases in the Twi language. On the one hand, there is the phrase *ete saa*, which gestures at basic facticity, something like the English phrase "it is so." The more morally salient word is *nokware*, "truthfulness."[17] These linguistic parameters presented a translation problem. Neither term carries the same weight as the biblical (especially New Testament Greek) vocabulary for truth, which encompassed not only honesty, but also the identification of God's word with Jesus.

Ultimately, the Basel Mission chose the latter term. I will expand upon the specifics of vocabulary below, but at a more general level, the contrast between these two visions of the past roughly describes the challenge the biblical message presented to indigenous modes of political legitimacy. The king's responsibility lay in his stewardship of the ancestors, which meant that he—at the risk of his own head—defined the moral truth (*nokware*) about the kingdom's past, regardless of chronological facticity (*ete saa*). But the introduction of the Twi Bible in stages during the late 1860s provided an alternative moral

---

[14] Strömberg was a Swedish sailor by vocation and was only in the Gold Coast from 1859 to 1865, after which time he returned to Sweden.

[15] Kwasi Wiredu, "Truth and the Akan Language," in *Readings in African Philosophy: An Akan Collection*, ed. Kwame Safro (Lanham, Md.: University Press of America, 1995), 188.

[16] T. C. McCaskie, *State and Society in Pre-Colonial Asante*, African Studies Series (Cambridge: Cambridge University Press, 1995), 252.

[17] Wiredu, "Truth and the Akan Language," 188.

foundation for the indigenous Christian community's relationship to truth, duty, and loyalty. The underlying proposition of the (Hebrew/Greek) Bible was that the supreme deity had self-disclosed—that the Bible was God's word. Superficially in that regard, this argument about the Bible was little different from that made by Muslims, who had long been present in the region, about the Qur'an. The decisive difference lay in translation into the vernacular: in this new text, God spoke in identical words as the ancestors, even to the point of redefining old notions.

## Yahweh as Onyame

Before the translation project began in the late 1850s, Basel missionaries had needed to acquire a robust facility, not only with the language, but also with the entirety of the cultural context. They did this in two ways: cultural immersion for the missionaries, and inclusion in the translation team of well-connected native speakers. In the preface to his 1875 grammar, Christaller described his methodology for language learning:

> The pupils of the Catechist Institution, and assistants that had come forth from among them, were made to translate, orally and on paper, from Bible History, from the Bible itself and other English books, and to write down old stories, fables of the natives or historical facts, and essays on various subjects; public assemblies were attended, and the speeches delivered in them were dictated from memory by the native assistant and penned down by the missionary. . . . In these and other ways, also by intercourse with other natives, young and old, the knowledge of the language was increased.[18]

This strategy emerged from team leader Christaller's conviction that God was already known in part. Years later, introducing a collection of Twi sayings in 1882, Christaller said, "an entire negro-theology might be derived from these proverbs, which would not bear the slightest resemblance to what is commonly called fetishism."[19] Christaller was following Basel Mission ideology in this regard. Language learning lay at the center of the mission's agenda, because it was there that "the people's innermost life" resided, in the 1859 words of missionary Johannes Zimmerman (who was then working among the Krobo people to the east of Akuapem).[20]

[18] J. G. Christaller, *A Grammar of the Asante and Fante Language Called Tshi [Chwee, Twi] Based on the Akuapem Dialect with Reference to the Other (Akan and Fante) Dialects* (Basel: Printed for the Basel Evangelical Missionary Society, 1875), ii.

[19] J. G. Christaller, "Einige Sprichwörter der Tschi-Neger," *EMM* 1882, 316.

[20] Zimmermann excerpted in Albert Ostertag, "Die Goldküste und die Basler Mission daselbst," *EMM* 1859, 49.

The translation team consisted of Johann Christaller, David Asante, and Theophilus Opoku (the latter two both of the royal household), along with a revolving cast of assistants. Over a dozen years, they produced and published stand-alone sections of the Bible, beginning with the gospels, in order of publication as follows (which sequence hints at the missionaries' homiletic priorities):

1859: Matthew, Mark, Luke, John (the four together in one volume), Acts

1861: Genesis, Romans, John's epistles, Revelation

1862: 1 and 2 Corinthians, Galatians, Ephesians, Philippians, Colossians, 1 and 2 Thessalonians

1863: 1 and 2 Timothy, Titus, Philemon, 1 and 2 Peter, James, and Jude

1864: New Testament entire

1866: Psalms, Proverbs

1871: Old and New Testament combined[21]

Early on—and probably building on a consensus established before the translation project began—the team identified the supreme deity of the Bible, euphemistically approached in Hebrew as the Tetragrammaton (YHWH), with the markedly similar Akan high god *Onyame* (also called *Onyankopɔn,* creator god), who was already known to the Akan. But this god was withdrawn and only indirectly concerned with human affairs (the lesser deities, the *abosom,* becoming in *Onyankopɔn's* absence the focus in sacrifice and incantation). In 1705, "long before," to quote Geoffrey Parrinder, "any missionaries, except travelling padres, began settled work in West Africa,"[22] Willem Bosman had noticed that, despite West Africans' belief in a supreme god, in practice he was absent from daily life and ritual:

> It is certain that his Country-Men have a faint Idea of the True God, and ascribe to him the Attributes of Almighty and Omnipresent; they believe he created the Universe, and therefore vastly preferr [sic] him before their Idol-Gods: But yet they do not pray to him, or offer any Sacrifices to him.

The reason was simple: *Onyame/Onyankopɔn* was too high to be troubled with pedestrian human problems, and the lesser deities filled the void.

---

[21]   Dennis M. Warren, *Bibliography and Vocabulary of the Akan (Twi-Fante) Language of Ghana* (Bloomington: Indiana University, 1976), 85–89.

[22]   Geoffrey Parrinder, *West African Religion: A Study of the Beliefs and Practices of Akan, Ewe, Yoruba, Ibo, and Kindred Peoples* (London: Epworth Press, 1969), 14.

God, say they, is too high exalted above us, and too great to condescend so much as to trouble himself or think of Mankind : Wherefor he commits the Government of the world to their Idols ; to whom, as the second, third and fourth Persons distant in degree from God, and our appointed lawful Governours, we are abliged [sic] to apply our selves.[23]

When the Basel Mission's translation team came to identify *Onyankopɔn* with Yahweh, they were thus not claiming to be introducing a new god, as Paul had done in preaching to the Athenians about an unknown god (Acts 17:23: *agnosto theo*), but to be redefining a god already recognized. The principle difference was that while the old god had not self-disclosed, the new one had: the title the translators gave to the Bible was *Anyamesɛm*, or *"Onyame's* word."[24] The new teaching alone was not a tremendous problem: Muslims taught the same thing. But translated into the same vernacular—Twi—in which the lesser deities were worshiped, and the ancestors attended, this redefinition of *Onyame* amounted to a threat to royal capacity and authority to define moral truth. In McCaskie's words:

> The capacity to dictate the fundamental conditions of epistemological discourse legitimates control over the social expressions of power, and is part of the same imperative that seeks to transform representations from arguments to statements.[25]

The rupture with the old gods was nearly absolute, even to the point of redefining them. Ulrike Sill makes the astute observation that the otherwise impeccably detailed Johann Christaller conveniently omitted the goddess Asase Yaa—or earth—from his "systematic overview of deities and beings associated with the spirit world." [26] Asase was the consort of the high God. This matters because Christaller was on his way to identifying the latter with the biblical Yahweh. Sill concludes: "this absence makes one wonder: Was Asase Yaa seen as potentially contesting the (supposedly) singular position of *Onyankopɔn/Onyame*? Or had the verbal vicinity in invocations resonated,

[23] Willem Bosman, *A New and Accurate Description of the Coast of Guinea, Divided into the Gold, the Slave, and the Ivory Coasts* (London: Printed for James Knapton and Dan. Midwinter, 1705), 369.

[24] Warren, *Bibliography and Vocabulary*, 85. Generally on the identification of *Onyame* with *YHWH*, see Charles Sarpong Aye-Addo, *Akan Christology: An Analysis of the Christologies of John Samuel Pobee and Kwame Bediako in Conversation with the Theology of Karl Barth* (Eugene, Ore.: Pickwick, 2013), 9.

[25] McCaskie, *State and Society*, 21.

[26] Ulrike Sill, *Encounters in Quest of Christian Womanhood: The Basel Mission in Pre- and Early Colonial Ghana* (Boston: Brill, 2010), 331–32.

for the missionaries, with overtones of the infamous divine couple, Baal and Astarte, only too well known from the Hebrew Bible?"[27] The translated Bible thus presented a categorical contradiction to royal authority over the narrative of the past.[28] This point has incredible weight for the ensuing struggle, because the missionaries, David Asante included, were not, in fact, announcing an abstract truth divorced from duty. Christian *nokware*, at least its Pietist variation, was not Hegel's or Kant's, and whatever freedom of con-science it contained, autonomy—literally, in its Greek roots, "self-law"—was not part of the logic. At the very time at which the Twi translation work was being done, Christian "truth" was subject to a great deal of contentious redefinition back in Europe, and especially in German-speaking universities.

The Twi translators of the Bible were not bringing the European Enlight-enment to the Gold Coast, imposing upon the Twi-speaking world some kind of epistemic autonomy for indigenous religious skeptics.[29] They were rather announcing an alternative foundation for social order, a reshuffling of religious—and therefore political—hierarchy. This foundation was a deity, whom in the process of vernacularization they had identified with an extant god (*Onyankopɔn*). By appropriating this god for the Twi Bible, Sanneh says, the translators assimilated "the God of the ancestors . . . into the Yahweh of ancient Israel," who had self-revealed and self-identified as truth itself.[30] Indig-enous messengers, more than foreign missionaries, could impress upon their neighbors that "the idea of Sacrifice and Redemption, the idea of a Supreme God, the God of the Sky," was a "natural corollary of their original beliefs about the spiritual government of the world."[31]

The translation team had furthermore rendered *aletheia* (ἀλήθεια— "truth") as *nokware*, which is a problematic translation. While *nokware* indicates truthfulness, honesty, and justice, the Greek *aletheia* is a negative for-mation: literally "un-forgetting" or "un-concealing," suggesting clarity within

---

[27]  Sill, *Encounters in Quest of Christian Womanhood*, 331–32.

[28]  Wiredu, "Truth and the Akan Language," 187–89.

[29]  Martin Gierl, *Pietismus und Aufklärung: theologische Polemik und die Kommunikation-sreform der Wissenschaft am Ende des 17. Jahrhunderts* (Göttingen: Vandenhoeck & Ruprecht, 1997). At least some of the indigenous clergy were aware of the dynamic. In one of the most fascinating artifacts of the religious encounter between Africa and Europe, David Asante wrote Twi-language history of Christianity in Germany, including a discussion of the accom-modations medieval German Christians had made with their own pagan inheritance; Asante singled out day-names of Germanic deities (Thursday/Friday) as an example of the possibili-ties: *Germane Asase so Kristosom terew* (Basel: Verlag der Missionsbuchhandlung, 1875).

[30]  Lamin Sanneh, *Translating the Message: The Missionary Impact on Culture*, 2nd ed. (Maryknoll, N.Y.: Orbis, 2008), 159–60.

[31]  J. B. Danquah, *The Akim Abuakwa Handbook* (London: F. Groom, 1928), 90–91.

a world of deception; *nokware* meant something a little less than that. Making things more complicated was *aletheia*'s incorporation into Christian Scripture as identical with Jesus himself, used to most important effect in John 14:9:

> Jesus answered, "I am the way and the <u>truth</u> and the life. No one comes to the Father except through me."

> Yesu se no se, "Mene kwan nè <u>nokware</u> nè nkwa; obi mma agya no nkyɛn gye sɛ ɔnam me so."

> λεγει αυτω ο ιησους εγω ειμι η οδος και η <u>ἀλήθεια</u> και η ζωη ουδεις ερχεται προς τον πατερα ει μη δι εμου.

In this particular passage, one of six in the book of John in which the author identified Jesus with "I am" (εγω ειμι), the self-disclosure of the divinity to Moses, truth/*nokware* is made inseparable from God's claim upon the moral lives of humanity. As rendered in Twi, the implication was an assertion of the categorical primacy of Jesus over other authorities (king, ancestors, but also the missionaries themselves) in the moral lives of congregants. But there was a twist: biblical truth, in this line of thinking, subjected the missionaries every bit as much as it did the kings. According to Lamin Sanneh:

> Vernacular agency became the preponderant medium for the assimilation of Christianity, and although missionaries did not consciously intend to occupy a secondary position, their commitment to translation made that necessary and inevitable. The preexisting vernacular came to exert a preemptive power over the proprietary claims of mission over the gospel.[32]

Very few people in Akuapem converted to Christianity for the reasons the missionaries initially had on offer. The missionaries preached forgiveness of sins (*bɔnefafiri*) and assurance of a future in heaven. But the locals wanted something different: protection from evil. Such spiritual demands made sense within the local religious ecosystem, in which the king and the priests, vis-à-vis the ancestors and shrine spirits, respectively, stood in the place of danger to make intercession. Indigenous Christian demands on the missionaries included requests for physical healings, inclusion for disabled, disfigured, or otherwise repulsive people, and protection from bad spirits—all of which the converts could read out of their Bibles, but which, from mid-century on, were not on the Mission's home office agenda.

---

[32] Sanneh, *Translating the Message*, 161–62.

## THE POLITICS OF EUCHARIST

To the extent that Bible translation in West Africa constituted the introduction into indigenous religious discourse of a new assertion of divine intervention into the world, which could not be credited to local kings or priests, the process was irreducibly political. Between 1861 and 1877, the Bremen Missionary society, working a few days' hike to the east of Akuapem, produced a Bible translation in the Ewe language. In a recent assessment of that translation, Solomon Avotri turned to a particular miracle story—Jesus' casting out of demons (Mark 5). "The vernacularization of scripture," Avotri concluded, "gives space to the basic concerns of the Ewe about the life-destroying powers of the unseen world."[33]

Unless the missionaries could articulate their message against these basic concerns, they did not have much to offer. In fact, some of the missionaries (but not all) were drawn into that exchange. On the fourth of August 1869, for example, Johann Widmann wrote to the home office, reporting that the Asante army had abducted three missionaries from Anum north of the Volta. This was a terrifying event, which within a few years would lead directly to profound changes within the mission and its relationship to colonial politics, as the Basel Mission would later welcome Britain's 1873 invasion of Asante. It would be a few more years before the mission would make its peace with British indirect rule. Before that point, however, Widmann returned to his prior experience, from a decade earlier, of Akuapem's protection from Asante—a development the kingdom's people had interpreted as protection from heaven. The Asante would not be able to attack Akuapem, Widmann wrote, because "Lord Sabaoth" (that is, Tsebaoth—צְבָאוֹת, God the head of the armies of heaven) "will fight for us and I believe that the Asante will not be allowed to come here."[34]

Significantly, this assertion of Widmann's, handwritten in a letter home, was redacted from the subsequently published version of this letter.[35] Such editorial discomfort with the miraculous was not out of the ordinary; there is a disparity between handwritten (and nearly impossible to read) missionary correspondence and the edited versions of the same, published in the Basel Mission's three different periodicals. The former contained all kinds of miraculous and charismatic claims, while the latter have omitted them almost entirely. In 1865, Julie

---

[33] Solomon K. Avotri, "The Vernacularization of Scripture and African Beliefs: The Story of the Gerasene Demoniac among the Ewe of West Africa," in *The Bible in Africa: Transactions, Trajectories, and Trends*, ed. Gerald O. West and Musa W. Dube (Leiden: Brill, 2000), 324.

[34] BMA D-1.22 (August 4, 1869), J. G. Widmann to Basel.

[35] J. G. Widmann, "Anum und die gefangenen Missionsgeschwister in Westafrika," *HB* 1869, 129–31.

Mohr offered to lay hands on a dying infant, an ambiguous enough statement to slip past the editors, but context suggests that Mohr and her interlocutors agreed that a faith healing was what was being offered.[36] Home office deletion of accounts of the supernatural is part of a broader pattern: miracles, dreams and visions handwritten by the missionaries do not appear in published sources. For that reason, a history of Ghanaian Christianity will remain distorted as long as the published missionary sources are used to the exclusion of the handwritten correspondence, upon which the former were based.[37] However, demonstrations of spiritual authority over evil, such as Lord Sabaoth's fighting the Asante army, were simply expected by the local Christians: that was the currency of the religious landscape. In any case, direct intrusions of the supernatural played a prominent role in the Bible, and to the extent that the missionaries did not emphasize the supernatural, their control over the church was hobbled. The vernacular Bible thus became "an independent yardstick by which to test, and sometimes to reject, what . . . missionaries taught and practiced."[38]

Furthermore, native Christians' constant, unbending demands for protection from evil (Greek *kakos*, translated in Christaller/Asante/Opoku's Bible as *bɔne*), paired with (to the missionaries) a near total absence of anguish over sin (*hamartia*, rendered by the same word, *bɔne*, in that Bible), are not to be taken lightly.[39] Indeed, their insistence on reading and hearing the Bible in accordance with their own felt needs stood at the very center of the dynamic of translation. Protection from *bɔne* was only half the equation, and the negative half. Converts also took great interest in identifying a biblical solution to the pressing need of communal cohesion and the incorporation of others. Indigenous meditation on the church—understood as a new form of community—and, correspondingly,

[36] Julie Mohr, "Die Kinder des Fetischpriesters," *HB* 1865, 84–85, from a letter dated August 4, 1864. This is also a subtle indication that the laying on of hands (which Elias Schrenk, who had previously been treated by a Swiss faith healer, had brought to the Gold Coast in 1859) predated Pentecostalism in Christian practice in the Gold Coast.

[37] This disparity of the supernatural between the field and the home office seems to have escaped Jon Miller's notice, in his otherwise path-breaking organizational study, written from the perspective of a professor of sociology, on field-office contradictions. Miller subsumes most in-field innovations under the category of "deviance." *Missionary Zeal and Institutional Control: Organizational Contradictions in the Basel Mission on the Gold Coast, 1828–1917* (Grand Rapids: Eerdmans, 2003), esp. 124–55.

[38] Kwame Bediako quoted in Eric Anum, "Collaborative and Interactive Hermeneutics," in *African and European Readers of the Bible in Dialogue: In Quest of a Shared Meaning*, ed. Hans de Wit and Gerald O. West (Leiden: Brill, 2008), 148–49.

[39] Kwame Wiredu, "Papa ne Bɔne," in *Listening to Ourselves: A Multilingual Anthology of African Philosophy*, ed. Chike Jeffers (Albany: State University of New York Press, 2013), 158–75.

the sacrament of the Eucharist, was the most politically charged of these reread-ings of scripture. At least since the days of the Swiss Reformation, the Eucharist had carried multiple meanings of both community formation and worship—or, to put it in the missionary context, of a church being created and an individu-al's sins being forgiven.[40] But Basel missionary preaching in the Gold Coast had overwhelmingly emphasized the latter: forgiveness of sin, and to little effect, as the message did not correspond to a broadly felt need.

Indeed, there was little else that the missionaries had on offer that was attrac-tive: divine forgiveness of sins, as understood by the Germans, required a felt need for forgiveness, which was by and large not forthcoming from the locals, at least not in the highly contextual self-critical language expected by the Pietists. It must be made clear, as this topic has generated an enormous breadth of theolog-ical and philosophical speculation, from Ghanaians and foreigners—Christians and non-Christians alike—that sin and guilt are easily mistranslated notions, even within a single language and culture (for example, in nineteenth-century German Christianity), let alone in cross-cultural translation. I do not argue that sin was a concept imported by the missionaries, but rather that the missionaries were rarely impressed by the degree of an indigenous convert's internal convic-tion of sin. Some discussion has focused on the not entirely analogous question of taboo.[41] The question of guilt's external existence is no innocent question in a political setting such as the precolonial Asante state, in which the stool—that is, the office of the king, regardless of its passing occupant—asserted exclusive authority to define guilt.[42]

In 2013, Peter Sarpong, then the Catholic Archbishop of Kumasi, related a point of cross-cultural dissonance in the mass: in his priestly training, Sarpong learned to lead the congregants, at the point of the *mea culpa*, the common con-fession of sin and guilt, to strike their chests in a gesture of humiliation inher-ited from ancient Mediterranean communication. However, to the Asante, Sarpong, striking one's chest is a menacing gesture between men intending to fight. "With our mouths we were confessing our humility," Sarpong said, "while with our hands we were telling God that we were men, and were not afraid of him." Sarpong subsequently instituted all range of liturgical changes,

[40] Lee Palmer Wandel, *The Eucharist in the Reformation: Incarnation and Liturgy* (New York: Cambridge University Press, 2006).

[41] See nearly contradictory arguments on whether taboo existed, to the Akan, inde-pendently of human institutions: Afriyie, "Taboo," in *Africa Bible Commentary*, ed. Tokun-boh Adeyemo (Grand Rapids: Zondervan, 2006) as a Christian theologian in Akuapem, and Wiredu, "Papa ne Bɔne," as an Akan philosopher in the United States.

[42] McCaskie, *State and Society*, 252–59.

including, at this particular instance, the waving of white cloths.[43] Addressing the corollary question of atonement, Catholic theologian Pashington Obeng presents a case that atonement "is to be understood as the means by which the eternal and perfect ancestor [by which Obeng meant Jesus] reinvigorates and consolidates the community of the living."[44]

However, if assurance of divine forgiveness from sin was not a pressing need for most residents of the Gold Coast, there were certainly other things that might attract people. These were quite diverse in nature, however, and changed over time. Indigenous men and women had always been improvising their relationships with the missionaries by recourse to the moral tools of their tradition. They classified the missionaries as priests, and they established sanctuary settlements adjacent to the chapels. They were determining for themselves, well before the missionaries understood what was happening, the parameters of their ongoing relationship with tradition.[45] As Peel said in his rebuttal to a reductionist line of thought simplistically conflating the religious encounter with the colonial one:

> Whatever else one may say about the social impact of Christian missions in Africa, the story will be radically incomplete if its effects are not adequately tied into the religious project which brought the missionaries in the first place.[46]

Peel was right, but he did not go far enough: the story of African Christianity will be radically incomplete unless adequately tied into the preexisting religious priorities, against which locals initially evaluated, and began putting to work, the missionaries' project. The publication and dissemination of the Bible in the Twi vernacular changed the relationship. Because the missionaries, who in many ways remained committed to paternalistic control over their converts, were consistently receptive to teaching, as long as it was grounded in biblical exegesis, indigenous hermeneutics is politically significant in Ghana's Christian history. The interpretive discrepancy between the indigenous and foreign Christians lies at the center of my inquiry, because it belongs to the particular realm of translation so central to the history of world Christianity.

---

[43] *African Christianity Rising*, directed by James Ault (Northampton, Mass: James Ault Productions, 2013), DVD.

[44] J. Pashington Obeng, *Asante Catholicism: Religious and Cultural Reproduction among the Akan of Ghana* (Leiden: Brill, 1996), 203.

[45] Kwame Gyekye, *Tradition and Modernity: Philosophical Reflections on the African Experience* (New York: Oxford University Press, 1997).

[46] J. D. Y. Peel, *Religious Encounter and the Making of the Yoruba* (Bloomington, Indiana University Press, 2000), 5.

Derek Peterson has spoken of "creative writing," in the context of colonial Kenya, to describe indigenous Christians' success at imposing radically different meanings on Christian narratives that Western missionaries thought uncontested.[47] Indigenous success at subordinating missionaries to indigenous Christian priorities hinged on their use of the Bible. For all their paternalistic tendencies, the Pietists had this going for them: a willingness and capacity to change their minds when convinced from Scripture. Long before that moment was reached, however—long before the missionaries were prepared to recognize indigenous authority within the church—indigenous non-Christians had already shown great creativity in various attempts at subjecting the missionaries and their religion to preexisting social, religious, and personal priorities.

From an early date, the ritual of the Eucharist attracted quite a bit of indigenous attention, both from the Christians and the non-Christians of Akuapem. As men and women grounded in a sacrificial economy, they understood the power of ritual bloodshed, such as Jesus' instituted ceremony of remembrance, for establishing and re-enacting community. In 1865, Johann Mader, the generally ham-fisted principal of Akropong's seminary, was floored by seminarian Thomas Adade's sermon on John 2:18–22. This was a passage in which Jesus identified his own body with the temple, which he would rebuild in three days if destroyed. Drawing on Hebrew understandings of the Mosaic Law, Adade proceeded to argue that Jesus was including the communities of the Christian believers in his use of the word "temple" (asɔredan or house of prayer in Christaller/Asante/Opoku's Bible). Adade's application point that there was no such thing as a private sin—that all sin was against the community.[48]

Mader recognized Adade as speaking a truth, but the implication of Adade's exegetical innovation constituted a fresh interpretation—although not an entirely new one in Christian history—of the sacrament of the Eucharist. According to Adade's reading, since Jesus was implicating congregations of believers, rather than individuals, the meaning of the Eucharist shifted from personal atonement to one of communal purification. This theme has not gone away. Since the middle of the twentieth century, much Ghanaian theological meditation focused on the question of the nature of the messiah, often relative to Akan cosmology.[49] And here the profoundly political quality to the Eucharist begins to become clear: the ritual creation of a new people is potentially destructive of the very systems of belonging Africans had worked hard to build. The Eucharist redefines the foundation of communal belonging—and

---

[47]   Derek R. Peterson, *Creative Writing: Translation, Bookkeeping, and the Work of Imagination in Colonial Kenya* (Portsmouth, N.H.: Heinemann, 2004).

[48]   Johann Adam Mader, "Das Predigerseminar in Akropong," *JB* 1865, 95.

[49]   As an overview of the literature, see the first chapter in Aye-Addo, *Akan Christology*.

thus loyalty—away from blood ancestry and toward ritual kinship by means of the blood of God's son. For the same reason, the blood-sacrificial politics of the Eucharist tended to contradict the logic of clanship and genetic purity, according to which lineage defined belonging and social rank. Christian converts of different clans had more in common with one another than either did with their non-Christian clanspeople. Put simply, the tension at the heart of the Pietist missionary message was that while God accepted Africans (and Germans) where they were, and in their own language, he was simultaneously calling them into a new, transnational community, within which the German believer had more in common with the African believer than either had with his unbelieving next-door neighbors.

Adade was perhaps a special case: as a seminarian, he was reading Hebrew and Greek, something few of his future parishioners could be expected to do. However, printed New Testaments were already in circulation, and the whole Bible was in indigenous hands within a few more years. Subsequent missionary correspondence reveals a great deal of indigenous interaction with that text. As early as 1866 (the year after Adade's sermon), David Asante (at that time stationed in Larteh) mentioned being constantly asked by church members, reading their Bibles in their homes, to explain confusing passages.[50] (They would not have been reading the New Testament in Larteh Guan but in Twi, published in 1864, or sections thereof, published earlier.)[51] This aside is intriguing, as in the same letter Asante had mentioned that the congregation was poor to the point of malnutrition—but at least some of them were able to read.

Within a few short years, indigenous pastors' letters to the mission home office show near-constant quoting and referencing. Nathanael Asare, for example, concluded his 1891 story of the man whose son was healed in the course of a showdown with the Priest of Tano, but who was terrified for the future, with a prayer: "May the Lord strengthen him to stand firm to the end." This appears to be a paraphrased reference to Matthew 10:22–23. In this passage, Jesus had sent out his messengers and, having told them that they were going to be "sheep among wolves," told them "You will be hated by everyone because of me, but the one who stands firm to the end will be saved. When you are persecuted in one place, flee to another." This passage has attracted no small attention by African Bible commentators. Joe Kapolyo, for example, has written that Jesus was instructing his disciples to stand firm in the face of despair from public humiliation and opposition. Christians, Kapolyo concluded, "will

---

[50] David Asante, "Von der Außengemeinde Date," *HB* 1865, 97–99.
[51] Warren, *Bibliography and Vocabulary*, 85–89.

not be spared persecution but will be saved from God's wrath when he punishes their persecutors."[52] This was Asare's prayer for the man of Tutu.

For the converts, the attraction of Christianity was inclusion in a new community, especially one in which they could live in proximity to spiritual power for protection from unwanted possession by a lesser spirit. Atonement for sin was rarely on the agenda, although baptismal candidates occasionally express to the missionaries an interest in changing their lives. In the cases where the missionary recorded an explanation, however, it was because such people were tired of their bad reputations as louts or criminals, or were tired of paying fines for crimes committed. Not one expressed an interest in his or her sins being forgiven. Indigenous clergy had little more success than the missionaries at convincing locals of the need to care for their eternal salvation, as people evaluated the Christian message almost exclusively against preexisting concerns, regardless of the nationality of the messenger. Furthermore, in the indigenous spiritual economy, the missionaries' assurance of an afterlife in heaven "[made] little impression on the Ghanaian," said Peter Sarpong, then the Catholic bishop of Kumasi, in 1974: "His ancestors come back to life every day."[53] What was decidedly more attractive to the people was ritual inclusion, administered by the sacrament of the Eucharist, and sustenance in the here and now. Asare further noted in his 1891 report:

> Before every observation of the Lord's Supper, we hold a preparatory service, and not only the communicants, but everyone, not only Christians, but also the heathens, attends. Another festive gathering is our year-end service, which many heathens attend; what attracts them is that the Lord has preserved them year after year and has not punished them.[54]

### DIVINATION AND INTERPRETATION

Two distinct Basel missionary devotional practices overlapped with indigenous techniques of divination. Together they show a missionary openness to God's direct intervention, especially when it came through the Bible.[55] One of

---

[52] Joe Kapolyo, "Matthew," in *Africa Bible Commentary*, ed. Tokunboh Adeyemo (Grand Rapids: Zondervan, 2006), 1132.

[53] Peter Sarpong, *Ghana in Retrospect: Some Aspects of Ghanaian Culture* (Tema: Ghana Pub. Corp., 1974), 22.

[54] Nathanael Asare, "Aus der Arbeit eines eingeborenen Missionsarbeiters," *JB* 1891, 46–47.

[55] And in this regard the German Pietists were especially non-representative of their homelands. German universities were the very center of the emergent application of the historical-critical method of textual analysis to the Bible; David Strauss' *Life of Jesus* was

these practices was called "däumeln" or "thumbing," whereby a text was identified, at random, with the point of a finger, the logic being that God leads the seeker's finger to His words for that moment. The second practice, a little more formalized, was the casting of lots [Losen] for daily readings. In this practice, hundreds of biblical references were written on scraps of paper and drawn at random. Sometimes this was done at a local level, but more often in a central location (such as the Brethren headquarters in Herrnhut in Saxony), with the results published against a calendar. A seeker could see what the daily lot was, and correspondingly apply the message to his or her immediate and personal circumstances.[56] Basel missionary letters home routinely reference the daily lot along with the writer's description of a particularly terrifying or devastating experience, whereby the Bible verse was understood not only as God's word in general, but as God's word, specifically revealed for this particular reader at this particular moment. The lot, in this sense, simultaneously represented timeless wisdom and a miraculous intervention by God on high, and which the preacher or missionary was tasked with interpreting in the moment.

One of the most stirring examples of biblical interpretation as social change came in August 1860. Johann Gottlieb Auer, a teacher at Akropong's new seminary for pastoral training, took his students on a multiday field trip to the Guan-speaking villages in the northern parts of the kingdom. In contrast to the Twi villages (including Akropong, in which the political hierarchy was designed to replicate military formations), the priests of the local gods were also the chiefs in the Guan villages. As a result, conversion in these villages presented a far more profound assault on the extant order than in their neighboring Akan villages. In Adukrom, exclusion of converts operated at a more visceral level. During their first night on the road, Auer and his students had been denied shelter in Adukrom and had been refused use of anyone's fire for cooking. Nevertheless—and this is very revealing—several local people with physical deformities joined the students for the night: if Christianity was a threat to the religious and political order, it represented a chance for inclusion and companionship for the disabled and deformed.

The next morning, someone in Auer's group cast lots for the daily Bible readings and was led to the following prophecy of Isaiah, concerning the restoration of Zion: "The least of you will become a thousand, the smallest a mighty nation. I am

---

published in Tübingen in 1836, a full nine miles away from Johann Widmann's hometown, and in the same year of the latter's entry into the Basel Mission training institute.

[56] Heinz Renkewitz, *Die Losungen. Entstehung und Geschichte Eines Andachtsbuches*, 2nd ed. (Hamburg: Wittig, 1967).

the LORD; I will do this swiftly in its time" (Isa 60:22).[57] Auer then set about interpreting it, determining that it applied to the heathens in attendance. It is unclear who these people were, but the context of Auer's report suggests it was the sick and needy who had joined the seminarians overnight. Although Adukrom was a village ruled by a priest who tolerated no religious innovation, Auer was declaring, on the basis of his reading of a lot—which in turn was a decontextualized prophecy by an ancient Hebrew prophet—that the poor people of Adukrom would one day become a mighty nation.

One of these people was a young man facing some unspecified trouble. In his letter home, Auer used the loaded word *Gnadenzeit*, a "time of grace," a euphemism meaning the opposite: an intersection of judgment and opportunity—a time of hardship, understood as a tribulation, in which God slightly withdraws his protection in order to break a hardened will—with the corresponding invitation to repentance. Despite this trouble, the young man was unwilling to convert. Were he to do so, Auer reported him saying, "there would be no one to bury [his] father," which Auer then explained as "making costume."[58] It was clearly understood here, by both parties, that conversion implied a willful neglect of customary veneration of ancestors. But there is another possibility: Auer might have been altering the young man's words. To Auer's readers at home, the immediate reference would have been to Luke 9:59–60:

> [Jesus] said to another man, "Follow me." But he replied, "Lord, first let me go and bury my father." Jesus said to him, "Let the dead bury their own dead, but you go and proclaim the kingdom of God."

However, if Auer was addressing the Guan-speaking locals, he was most certainly speaking through an interpreter—probably one of his seminarians. He admitted elsewhere in the same letter that even his Twi was incommensurate with the task of preaching, not to mention his Guan. He handed these duties over to the students, mentioning a certain Isaac Addo as rescuing him when locals could not penetrate his thick accent ("His mouth is not yet clean," they said). Auer was not in Akuapem to evangelize, at least directly, but to train preachers at the new seminary, where he taught Hebrew, Greek, exegesis, and homiletics. He was thus part of a project putting hermeneutical power over these texts into the hands of native Christians like Addo, and which would see the latter strongly attracted to the Hebrew texts, texts that represented a sacrificial world the Ghanaians found immediately intelligible. Elsewhere Auer warned

---

[57] Johann G. Auer, "Predigerseminar," *JB* 1861, 172. It is unclear in which language this lot was cast; Isaiah was not translated at this time: Warren, *Bibliography and Vocabulary*, 85–89.

[58] Auer, "Predigerseminar," 172.

missionaries against making any mistakes in Hebrew grammar: the students had quickly surpassed the missionaries in their command of that language.[59]

### CONSECRATING A COUNTER-SHRINE

One of the consistent themes of the missionaries' devotional reading of the Bible was sober attention to duty, even at the expense of life, reputation, and family. This vision derived from their religious roots in Germany, and it successfully transferred to the need for moral, emotional, and spiritual fortification in the mission field. The call to submission to God's will had served them well, to the extent that the Basel missionaries—those who escaped tropical disease—proved capable of lengthy terms of service, and it was a message that they preached to their indigenous congregations. However, from the earliest recorded moments of indigenous preaching, alternate hermeneutical themes emerged. Looking at the same source text as the missionaries—at times even the same verses—through the lens both of the preexisting religious agenda in Akuapem, and the pressing needs of the present, native clergy and laypeople identified strength, healing, protection, and victory over enemy gods and men alike. These contrasting religious outlooks are consistent over the entire period of precolonial encounter and beyond and constitute a clear thread of indigenous intellectual history connecting Ghana's Christian foundations with the present day. As early as the middle of the nineteenth century—well before the formal birth of global Pentecostalism in the early twentieth—indigenous preachers were expounding a message, which more than one scholar has mistaken for a foreign (especially American) import.[60]

This divergence is not to be overstated, because the missionaries were no more static in their religious vision than were the Ghanaians. The biblical thread of strength and victory, especially in conflict with enemies, did not escape the missionaries' attention. From the mid-1860s, this theme, which had been nearly entirely absent in their writings of the 1840s and 1850s, appeared in missionary preaching with increased frequency. The most plausible explanation for this hermeneutical change is missionary assimilation into the indigenous ontological vision: the missionaries had finally begun, however tentatively, to provide the religious services that the locals had been

---

[59]  Auer, "Predigerseminar," 172.

[60]  Elorm-Donkor summarizes the literature: Lord Elorm-Donkor, *Christian Morality in Ghanaian Pentecostalism: A Theological Analysis of Virtue Theory as a Framework for Integrating Christian and Akan Moral Schemes* (Eugene, Ore.: Wipf and Stock, 2017), 17, mentioning a more recent paradigm of multiple centers and origins, developed most effectively by Ogbu Kalu and Allan Anderson.

demanding for decades. Nevertheless, the missionaries' default mode would remain introspection, and it would fall to the indigenous preachers to speak the words the congregants wanted to hear. To appreciate the autochthonous nature of this message of strength and victory, which I further develop in the following chapter, it is essential to compare foreign and indigenous preaching. The divergent modes of hermeneutics are most clearly delineated at moments, such as at church festivities, at which multiple sermons took place. One such celebration was the consecration of the new chapel in the town of Tutu in October 1868, with which I began this chapter.

Seven or eight hundred people came to watch as the Basel Mission consecrated a new ritual site (what the Germans called a chapel) not far from Tutu's existing shrine to the god Tano. The very act of establishing and consecrating a rival religious site—functionally a counter-shrine—could not fail to provoke, and onlookers hoping for drama were not disappointed. In line with indigenous custom and expectations, the ceremonies began by calling upon the deity expected to take up residence in the new edifice. A chorus of seminarians—indigenous preachers in training—opened in song, invoking, by name, to the only deity recognized in Akuapem as higher than Tano: Onyame. The song was "Jehovah, your name," a Twi hymn probably composed by Johannes Mader.[61] Missionary Johannes Dieterle then stepped forward and addressed God directly in a spoken prayer (of which no record was made), and read Psalm 84.

As with the opening song, this Psalm—published in Twi translation only two years earlier—was unmistakable as an assertion that the new chapel could access the supreme deity, heretofore inaccessible to humans. The first verse asserts that the supreme God (published in the 1866 Twi version of the book of Psalms as "Yehowa") resides in a temple, accessible to humans. As the missionaries, working from the Septuagint, had generated a different phrasing (and verse numbering) than in the German Bibles they were using (Luther's version), the following retranslates the German version:

> Verse 4: "Blessed are those who live in your house...."
> Verse 5: "Blessed are those who recognize your power...."
> Verse 7: "They attain victory upon victory, so that people can see that the true God lives in Zion."

Verse 7 corresponds to verse 8 in the Basel Mission's Twi; I underline the name for God:

---

[61] Johannes Christian Dieterle, "Die Einweihung der neuen Kapelle in Tutu," *HB* 1869, 8.

"Wɔnantew fi ahɔɔdeng mu kɔ ahɔɔdeng mu bepue <u>Onyankopɔn</u> anim wɔ Sion."

Placed into the 1868 context, this two-part overture announced a bold intention. First, the supreme deity, never before accessible at a shrine, was being called to take up residence in a manufactured structure. Second, there will be evidence that this god has done so: those who live in his house will attain victory upon victory. This formal opening was a clear assertion of divine power over and against the town's esteemed shrine.

Johannes Mader preached first, from Paul's appeal for unity in Ephesians 4:1–6, justified by his being a prisoner for the Lord.

> [1]I therefore, the prisoner in the Lord, beg you to lead a life worthy of the calling to which you have been called, [2]with all humility and gentleness, with patience, bearing with one another in love, [3]making every effort to maintain the unity of the Spirit in the bond of peace. (NRSV)

David Asante spoke next, taking as his text Ephesians 6:10–13:

> [10]Finally, be strong in the Lord and in the strength of his power. [11]Put on the whole armor of God, so that you may be able to stand against the wiles of the devil. [12]For our[b] struggle is not against enemies of blood and flesh, but against the rulers, against the authorities, against the cosmic powers of this present darkness, against the spiritual forces of evil in the heavenly places. [13]Therefore take up the whole armor of God, so that you may be able to withstand on that evil day, and having done everything, to stand firm. (NRSV)

Dieterle summarized Asante's message thus:

> Christians . . . should rather grow strong in the Holy Spirit and in the word of God, which they will soon have in their hands. That way, if the missionaries are taken from them, they will be able to stand on their own feet, remaining faithful, so that a new people will be born to the Lord, who will serve him willingly.[62]

The complete Twi translation was in its final editing stages before going to print, and Asante encouraged his hearers to use this coming book, together with the Holy Spirit, to grow strong. However, there was a very practical reason they should grow strong. Asante was telling his audience than they could and should become a "new people," not subordinated to a shrine priest or

---

[62] Dieterle, "Die Einweihung der neuen Kapelle in Tutu," 8.

missionary. Asante was asserting a connection between the impending arrival of the Bible and a rearrangement of existing loyalties.

Following Asante, Elias Schrenk preached from Romans 12:1–2 about becoming living sacrifices. This was a remarkable passage with which to inaugurate a chapel, at which a community of converts—some of whom, at least in nearby Akropong—had recently sought sanctuary from being made into sacrifices. The first verse reads, in English and in Twi (the latter being already in print):

> I appeal to you therefore, brothers and sisters, by the mercies of God, to present your bodies as a living sacrifice, holy and acceptable to God, which is your spiritual worship.

> Enti, anua nom, migyina Onyankopɔŋ mmɔborohunu so mitumo fo sɛ, momfa mo nipadua nsi hɔ sɛ afɔre a ɛte ase a ɛyɛ kroŋkroŋ a ɛsɔ Onyankopɔŋ ani a ɛne mo nyamesom a emu wo adwene no . . .

In their translation of this appeal, originally written by Paul to the Christian community in Rome, Christaller and Asante used the same word—*afɔre*—for sacrifice, as the vernacular term for sacrifice "to a God or to a fetish."[63] If the missionaries liked to speak of their "sacrifice" in going to Africa, there was not a single one of them who had ever been asked to become a human sacrifice, as had the people hiding in the Maders' and Widmann's homes two years earlier. If Schrenk, who had been in the country for nine years, had been trying to dissuade any casual seekers from considering joining the community, he could not have found a better passage.

Clerk, on the other hand, preaching from 1 Samuel 7:12, which was not yet in print in Twi: "Then Samuel took a stone and set it up between Mizpah and Jeshanah, and named it Ebenezer; for he said 'Thus far the LORD has helped us.'" Clerk's message was that "the Lord did not only want to bless his people in the spirit, but also in the flesh."[64] This was a remarkable use of the text, and it merits closer inspection, because Clerk clearly meant something more encouraging than the prospect of becoming a prisoner, as Mader suggested, or of becoming a human sacrifice, as would be the natural way of understanding Schrenk's message. The context was a miraculous conclusion to a battle: The prophet Samuel had called the Israelites to "[return] to the LORD with all [their] hearts," the main evidence of which would be that they would "put away the foreign gods and the Astartes from among [themselves]" and direct

---

[63] J. G. Christaller, *Dictionary of the Asante and Fante Language Called Tshi (Twi)* (Basel: Printed for the Basel Evangelical Missionary Society, 1881), 133–34.

[64] Dieterle, "Die Einweihung der neuen Kapelle in Tutu," 8.

their hearts to the LORD "and serve him only" (1 Sam 7:3). But while the Israelites were thus engaged, the Philistine army drew near, and the Israelites were terrified. But Samuel answered the approaching enemy army by sacrificing a lamb, "and the LORD answered him" (1 Sam 7:9). The next two verses read:

> [10]As Samuel was offering up the burnt offering, the Philistines drew near to attack Israel; but the Lord thundered with a mighty voice that day against the Philistines and threw them into confusion; and they were routed before Israel. [11]And the men of Israel went out of Mizpah and pursued the Philistines, and struck them down as far as beyond Beth-car.

It is at this point that Clerk's sermon text began. After the enemy army had been routed after having been thrown into panic by thunder from the Lord, "Samuel took a stone and set it up between Mizpah and Jeshanah, and named it Ebenezer; for he said 'Thus far the Lord has helped us'" (1 Sam 7:12). The context of this sermon, it must be remembered, was the inauguration of a sacred building in Tutu. This was very the town where, eighty years earlier, Paul Erdmann Isert had encountered a shrine sanctuary,[65] and where, twenty-three years later, indigenous preachers were still contending with Tano's priests.[66] Tutu was home to an important shrine in October 1868, when the twenty-five-year-old Clerk—who had been born in this very town—was preaching.

This setting, only minutes away from a regionally significant shrine, adds weight to Clerk's reference to an ancient people who were terrified when they were attacked while they were ritually abandoning their own gods. Clerk was clearly encouraging the converts to read themselves into the Old Testament passage, with the implication that God helps those who perform appropriate sacrifices in the close proximity of an enemy. Schrenk and Mader, preaching metaphorically about human sacrifice and imprisonment, likely saw the same significance in the chapel—as something of a counter-shrine. However, Clerk's application point makes clear that he expected this chapel to provide its adherents with power: "the Lord not only wanted to bless his people in the spirit, but also in the flesh." In contrast to Mader and Schrenk, Clerk did not seem to think that inner (spiritual) serenity to endure their being imprisoned or sacrificed was all that was on offer. Rather, like the Israelites in the story, Clerk expected power in the here and now.

---

[65]    Paul Erdmann Isert, *Reise nach Guinea und den caribäischen Inseln in Columbien, in Briefen an seine Freunde beschrieben* (Kopenhagen: J. F. Morthorst, 1788), 277.

[66]    Asare, "Aus der Arbeit eines eingeborenen Missionsarbeiters," 46–47.

This theme repeats itself many times over: missionaries and indigenous Christians read similar biblical passages, with the former focusing on suffering, and the latter on victory or healing. Three months after the inauguration of the chapel at Tutu, on the fourth Sunday in December 1868, this sequence repeated itself in Akropong at the inauguration of a new, bigger chapel, a celebration that extended over a two-week period.[67] Festivities included a dramatic opening of three doors: one for the Christian men, one for the Christian women, and one for heathens.

At the climactic service on December 20, first a German, and then a Ghanaian, each preached from the book of Isaiah. Both passages are poetic and grandiose, but while the German emphasized darkness, he was followed by a Ghanaian preaching healing: Theodor Breitenbach (a second-generation Basel missionary, who had been born in Bessarabia) took as his sermon text Isaiah 60:1–3:

> [1]Arise, shine; for your light has come,
>     and the glory of the LORD has risen upon you.
> [2]For darkness shall cover the earth,
>     and thick darkness the peoples;
> but the LORD will arise upon you,
>     and his glory will appear over you.
> [3]Nations shall come to your light,
>     and kings to the brightness of your dawn.

This text was a promise, articulated in the second person, that God's light would come to people who are still in the dark. For his sermon, however, Breitenbach chose to focus on darkness, however, concluding thus: "God alone has glory. Darkness is in human hearts and heads. We must turn to God, to Jesus, I invite you."

Theophilus Opoku followed Breitenbach with a message of miraculous healing from disease, which he extrapolated from the Isaiah 7:14 passage foretelling that a virgin would have a child whose name would be Immanuel:

> Immanuel means God is with us. Because I was ill, I could not witness the laying of this building's foundation. I never thought I would see this house of God. The Lord healed me miraculously. God is with me, and he gave me the honor to work at his spiritual temple in Mamfe. God is with us, and this building is proof. Even the heathens recognize this, as a priest in Mamfe recently told me.[68]

[67] Johann Adam Mader, "Die Einweihung der Jubiläumskirche zu Akropong," HB 1869, 42–43.

[68] Mader, "Die Einweihung der Jubiläumskirche," 42–43.

Table: Chapel Consecration Ceremonies, 1868, in Order of Sermons Preached

|  | Foreign Preacher | Indigenous Preacher |
|---|---|---|
| Tutu, October 1868 | 1. Johannes Mader<br>Text: Ephesians 4:1–6<br>About: As prisoners of the Lord, seek unity with one another.<br>Message: not summarized in report | 2. David Asante<br>Text: Ephesians 6:10–13<br>About: Grow strong in the Lord's power<br>Message: We must become a new people, who can stand if the missionaries are taken away. |
|  | 3. Emmanuel Schrenk<br>Text: Romans 12:1–2<br>About: Present your bodies as a living sacrifice.<br>Message: not summarized in report. | 4. Alexander Clerk<br>Text: 1 Samuel 7:12<br>About: Miraculous defeat of Philistine army following prophet's performance of animal sacrifice.<br>Message: The Lord not only wants to bless his people in the spirit, but also in the flesh. |
| Akropong, December 1868 | 1. Theodor Breitenbach<br>Text: Isaiah 60:1–3<br>About: God's light will come to people who are still in the dark.<br>Message: Darkness is in human hearts. | 2. Theophilus Opoku<br>Text: Isaiah 7:14<br>About: Virgin will have child whose name will be God-with-us.<br>Message: God is with us; God healed me miraculously. |

CONCLUSION

The Basel Mission had labored in the Gold Coast for nearly forty years by 1866, seeing little fruit while the missionary graveyards grew. Unbeknownst to the missionaries, the people of Akuapem and beyond had not dismissed Christianity, but had been actively deliberating amongst themselves, looking for some kind of use to which to put a promising but counterintuitive message. The breakthrough came in the 1860s, when the Christian congregation in Akuapem tripled in size in a half decade. This change was made possible by indigenous fluency with the vernacular Bible, including the sacrificial economy they found described there, which made sense in a way that the strange German missionaries did not. The growth of the indigenous church, then, came as believers acquired hermeneutical control over the vernacular biblical message.

Bible reading opened the door to further conflict when indigenous preachers identified latent politics to the message, which the Germans either did not see or interpreted through the lens of victory over disease or over enemies. Twenty years later in 1887, in the aftermath of a particularly violent round of repression in Kyebi, when a certain Stephen Ntiamoa was beaten to death, Christians returning from hiding found their chapel ritually defiled: the women of Kyebi had occupied and used the building as a menstrual house.[69] This seems to have been an attempt on the part of the women to drive away whatever spiritual power resided in the chapel, and thence to resolve the threat that building presented to the power structures within the community. Indigenous Christians could, and did, retaliate in symmetrical fashion. In the late 1880s, in a public provocation of the gods, Catechist Samuel Boateng ate fish from the sacred Pra River and defiled the same with taboo *Afasee* yams.[70] In the 1897 annual report, the unidentified Basel Mission correspondent told his European readers that in Abetifi, in Akyem Abuakwa, a "costumed fetish priest was unmasked." It is unclear who committed the scandal, although context suggests it had been a local Christian. The upshot was clear: "no priest dares to dance through the city anymore."[71]

Along with Alexander Clerk, Theophilus Opoku, David Asante, Nathanael Asare, and several others, Samuel Boateng was another indigenous pastor whose approach to Christianity focused on power over a spiritual world both seen and unseen—and in stark difference to the missionaries. Drawing on a vibrant West African moral imaginary with no tradition of speculative unbelief, these men read power encounters out of the Bible and understood them as formative of new communities. This vision presumed a near-total overlap between ethics and aesthetics and is the key to understanding indigenous Christian use of the Bible. These Christians read their Bibles, translated from ancient West Asian texts, in different ways than the missionaries did and, furthermore, did so in order to address spiritual and

---

[69] This incident took place in November 1887, according to oral memories collected by Thomas Yaw Kani in the 1950s in Twi, and translated into English in 1974. Thomas Yaw Kani and Fred M. Agyemang, *Persecution of Kyebi Christians: 1880–1887: An English Translation of "Kyebi Kristofo Taee,"* trans. Fred M. Agyemang (Accra, Ghana: Synod of the Presbyterian Church of Ghana, Literature Committee, 1975), 22. Stephen Ntiamoa, incidentally, had been baptized eleven years earlier by David Asante.

[70] M. P. Frempong, "A History of the Presbyterian Church at Bompata in Asante-Akyem," trans. E. A. Kyerematen, *Ghana Notes and Queries* 12 (June 1972), 22.

[71] *JB* 1897, 20. It goes without saying, of course, that Akyem Abuakwa in colonial 1897 was an entirely different situation than precolonial Guan communities in Akuapem, but missionary resistance to traditional priests was unbending, while missionary attitudes to indigenous kings were situational.

social problems the missionaries did not comprehend. Above all, they sought tools for community—for becoming "new people"—and for healing from diseases and for protection from angry spirits. The missionaries, focused above all on individual repentance from individual sin, had preached for decades with only very slow growth to show for their effort and sacrifices. But in the cracks, especially when and where the missionaries had no control over their own health and well-being, something of a genuine meeting was taking place, and at a much deeper level than within most other missionary societies in Africa at the turn of the century.

# 7

# States of Exception

## INTRODUCTION

Late in 1858 in the town of Larteh, indigenous evangelist Edward Samson Amaadi restored a dead child to life. The event went unpublished in Basel Mission sources, aside from a small remark buried 112 pages into the mission's annual report, following a discussion of the dimensions (15 feet by 40 feet) and building material (clay) of the new schoolhouse in that town, and it would never feature in an official history of the organization.[1] I discuss Kwame Akwatia's resurrection in the second half of this chapter. First, I ask why the Basel Mission neither celebrated the spectacular event nor gave much thought to signs of supernatural power, despite near-constant indigenous requests for the same. The asymmetry is very important for an understanding of the intellectual foundations of Ghanaian Christianity, because it represents such a strong ontological gulf between the foreign and the native Christians—one that predates global Pentecostalism by decades. From the earliest years that indigenous clergy, including Samson Amaadi (also known as Edward Samson), had entered the service of the Basel Mission, they left an impressive record of spiritual power confrontations, while the foreign missionaries did not.

Decades before the spectacular emergence of William Wadé Harris and Samson Oppong, independent evangelists whose early twentieth-century preaching campaigns involved similar demonstrations of power, indigenous pastors in Akuapem were proving more competent at inducing supernatural

---

[1]  J. G. Widmann, "Kirchenweihe in Late," *JB* 1859, 111–12.

power than the missionaries.[2] Moreover, they did this while employed by a European missionary society that was not in the habit, especially as the century wore on, of seeking the miraculous, or of seeing miracles in otherwise explainable events. More subtly, the most exceptional events in Christian Akuapem's early history all occurred beyond missionary control.

There were two reasons for this. First, the missionaries were unable to live up to indigenous expectations. This inability, in turn, had two factors. One was a high rate of death from disease—the missionaries were too weak to project majestic supremacy, leaving indigenous workers on their own, often for weeks at a time. The other was that the missionaries themselves, as the century wore on, were slowly losing faith in miracles as they assimilated to more standard modes of European Christianity in colonial Africa.[3] The second reason why the missionaries were not usually present for the signs and wonders that had the greatest religious consequences for native societies was because indigenous clergy were increasingly confident in the message of the supernatural, which they read from their Bibles. However, as the 1858 resurrection in Larteh indicates, it began before the Bible's final publication—but after the missionaries had been in Akuapem for nearly a quarter century.

### The Message of Death

The story of indigenous miracle-working cannot be told without a discussion of missionary death, disease, and suffering, which were constant, and which dominated missionary experience in the Gold Coast until late in the century. In 1897, German theologian Gustav Warneck quoted an unnamed new missionary who had arrived in the Gold Coast sometime earlier. Terrified by the "worn-down and wretched" faces of his brothers and sisters, this new arrival had written to his home office, "They look like corpses in a morgue."[4] In 1917, a visiting Scottish Wesleyan, A. W. Wilkie, had much the same response when he met some Basel missionaries: "We were much struck by the rapid aging of both men and women. We put down as over sixty, several who were really little over 40."[5]

[2]  T. C. McCaskie, "Social Rebellion and the Inchoate Rejection of History: Some Reflections on the Career of Opon Asibe Tutu," *Asante Seminar: The Asante Collective Biography Project Bulletin* 4 (February 1976), 34–38.

[3]  The Basel Mission had always collected beetles, studied plant pathologies, etc., but the real change in the miraculous came with the arrival of medical missionaries in the 1880s. See Adam Mohr, "Missionary Medicine and Akan Therapeutics: Illness, Health and Healing in Southern Ghana's Basel Mission, 1828–1918," *Journal of Religion in Africa* 39, no. 4 (2009), 429–61.

[4]  Gustav Warneck, *Die Mission in Bildern aus ihrer Geschichte*, 3rd ed. (Gütersloh: Bertelsmann, 1890), 77.

[5]  BMA D-10.2,16: Report of the Deputies to the Gold Coast (1917), 10.

Although the Basel missionaries had moved to West Africa in an idealistic project, something had intervened to detour their dreams. That something was profound and sustained hardship, and of a particular variety that was to strip from these men and women of their patronizing distance. More than simple culture shock: death, disease, and all range of encounters with a religious ecosystem foreign to their families and communities of origin separated them from home, and they became new people as a result. However, in the cracks of their program, in their grief, trauma, and sickness, in the failures and contradictions to their dreams and goals, they were able to meet their African hosts like few missionaries before or after.

Over the better part of a century, German and Swiss missionaries ailed in Ghana. Many died, but many others spent year after year in pain and in fever. In 1866, writing to the home office about Georg Schimanek, who had died shortly after his thirtieth birthday, after two and a half years in the Gold Coast, Johannes Dieterle said: "You are aware that Brother Schimanek was only healthy for a few weeks of his time in Africa."[6] A few months later, another missionary—Jakob Heck, who had spent nine years in Christiansborg—followed Schimanek to the grave. "Much of these nine years," Missionary Karl Schönfeld wrote, "was spent in severe and ongoing sickness, with lasting consequences. He was often bedridden rather than at work."[7] It was in these moments, however, that the missionaries most connected with their indigenous hosts. Bed-ridden, dying in childbirth, in fever for weeks on end, they were simply unable to project paternalistic mastery. Indeed, a reading of Basel Mission letters home can seem a lengthy list of death and disease, interspersed with occasional anecdotes of success. Former Basel Mission archivist Paul Jenkins made this discovery during a 1972 project of abstracting, in English, the inbound (that is, to Switzerland) Ghana correspondence:

> I made a strategic decision early on: not to attempt to write abstracts of accounts of missionary illness or death. I had real anxiety that at the end of 6–7 months' hard work I would hardly have covered 10 years, and that was the "economy measure" I adopted to try to get a broader chronological focus.[8]

Sickness and weakness occurred so often, lasted so long, and so dominated field experience that it cumulatively formed a major—perhaps the most important—driver of intellectual and spiritual change among the missionaries.

---

[6] Johannes Christian Dieterle, "G. H. Schimanek," *HB* 1866, 50 (reprint of letter originally written November 9, 1865).

[7] Karl Schönfeld, "Der Heimgang von Missionar Heck in Christiansborg," *HB* 1866, 118.

[8] Paul Jenkins, March 25, 2016, email correspondence with Paul Grant.

Some missionaries were sick as often as not. After years of preparation, some died almost immediately upon their arrival. Sickness and death were confusing and forced the missionaries to ask basic questions about what they were doing.

More importantly, death and disease became a spiritual lesson, one that was reflected in how the workers wrote and sang songs, how they read Scripture, and how they interacted with the locals. Locals' participation in the missionaries' grief constituted an important vehicle for the missionary reception of indigenous faith. In this regard the Basel missionary message presented a striking contrast with civilizing and colonial messages of uplift found not only in David Livingstone, but throughout Africa. Here, suffering *was* the message. Speaking at the 1866 deputation ceremony of a missionary named Johann Ulrich Lüthy, whose obituary would duly appear in the *Heidenbote* a mere three years later,[9] Inspector Joseph Josenhans said: "Missionaries in Africa must constantly be prepared, not only for labor, and not only for suffering, but also for labor in suffering."[10]

A few times a year, the *Heidenbote* published a detailed account of a funeral, most of which followed a similar routine. Dead missionaries were honored twice—in the church or chapel, with bells ringing, and then at the graveside. These practices were fairly noncontroversial, although unique, within the broader indigenous communities in which the missionaries found themselves, at least in regards to the burial of foreigners—that is, people without a clan and who are not going to be welcomed, as ancestors, to participate in the ongoing affairs of the community. To a reader of Basel missionary magazines, exotic and heroic stories of evangelization in Africa would not necessarily leap out as the most memorable, and for a simple reason: the sheer passion of the death stories. Disease and death overwhelm narratives of evangelization, in part because of the emotional heft of the grief, so dissonant with customary reserve, articulated in the passive voice. Success on the mission field was treated with Calvinist caution, with cool requests for continued prayer on the part of readers, while obituaries and death notices crackle with emotion, even in otherwise dreary annual reports. In his October 1876 report, for example, Johann Widmann (on the field since 1846, and who would die before the report's publication) wrote:

> Our African mission is under heavy attack ['ist schwer heimgesucht']; one worker after the other either sinks into the grave, or returns broken to his old homeland. It grows truly heavy around the heart. The passing of Brother Müh is especially painful. In this way the dear Lord strikes lines across our calculations and shows us, that he has other thoughts than ours.[11]

---

[9]  Joseph Josenhans, "Johann Ullrich Lüthy," *HB* 1869, 146–50.

[10]  Joseph Josenhans, "Monats-Chronik," *HB* 1866, 165.

[11]  J. G. Widmann, "Aus dem letzen Bericht des sel. Miss. Widmann in Akropong," *JB* 1877, 82.

The "Brother Müh" mentioned here had passed away on September 13, wrote Johann Mader, "in his thirty-first year of life, after he had laid a solid and hope-filled foundation for his missionary work, leaving behind a young, weeping widow," who happened to have been Mader's own daughter.[12]

For a Swiss-German organization for whom proper planning and calculating were expressions of devotion, when "the dear Lord strikes lines across our cal-culations," this constituted a profound spiritual challenge. Widmann resolved the contradiction by identifying death and suffering as an attack, but reason clearly did not satisfy. Many Basel missionaries were aware of these problems. By volunteer-ing as missionaries in the Gold Coast, they were committing themselves to count-less hours at the bedside of a diseased and dying colleague, and to a life lived in the expectation that it would end far from family and far from home. Not infrequently do these reports conclude with original poems and songs of grief and loss. In late 1857, for example, in intensely emotional language, drawn both from the Bible and from Goethe, Johannes Zimmermann bade farewell to August Steinhauser with a song, of which the first and third verses read:

> I grieve for you, beloved Brother August!
> Yes, you who were "Noble, Good":[13]
> What joy and pleasure I had with you!
> More wonderful than the love of a woman
> Was your loving friendship to me;[14]
> Not even in death will you depart from me.

> Farewell, because without many tears,
> Your deepest longing will be silenced:
> Blessed is the hero who dies in battle!
> The land of the Moors belongs to our Lord,
> And his warriors' corpses in the earth
> Are seeds, which never spoil.[15]

From the beginning, but especially after the first few deaths on the field, death became part of the Basel missionary calling to the Gold Coast. In an 1859 review of the thirty-three years of Basel Mission activity in the Gold

[12] Johann Adam Mader, "Aus dem Jahresbericht der Station Akropong vom Jahr 1876," JB 1877, 84.

[13] This is a quote from Goethe's *Faust II*, line 11917. The voice is that of a chorus of dead youths, in conversation with the Deep Father, simultaneously confronting love and death. Karl Alt, ed., *Goethes Faust: in sämtlichen Fassungen mit den Bruchstücken und Entwürfen des Nachlasses* (Berlin: Bong, 1909), 323.

[14] This is an altered reference to David's song, in 2 Samuel 1:19–27, lamenting his friend Jonathan, son of King Saul.

[15] Johannes Zimmermann, "Nachruf an den selig vollendeten Miss. Steinhauser," JB 1858, 102–3.

Coast, the *EMM's* editor (presumably Albert Ostertag) described the prayerful process of sending candidates to a field with a staggering death rate.

> When it came to the selection of assigned working areas, [the missionary society] was accustomed from the beginning to prayerfully and in sober calculation to seek clear signals [*klare Winke*] from the Lord. Only when the society believed they had heard the Lord himself calling, and had prepared the way for a messenger, did they step to the work. And then the steps were taken in the courage of faith, even when according to human appearances the way seemed impassible.[16]

Nevertheless, death came at a constant but unpredictable rate—some years were worse than others. It is important to understand the intensity of emotion in this process, because the inscrutability of God's will, together with the constant reminders, in an African society built around ancestral veneration, of one's foreignness, left the missionaries at a loss. In 1913, Immanuel Bellon had learned of the death by yellow fever of another missionary (Paul Weiss), immediately before his own and his wife's deputation ceremony in Basel. And since the young couple was leaving their child behind in the mission's boarding school, farewell was a weighty matter. "We pressed one last kiss on the lips of our child," Bellon wrote, "and then, in the midnight hour, we walked to the train station in boundless loneliness." After his arrival in the Gold Coast, he learned that yet another missionary had died, a certain Forster. When Bellon then concluded, "We stand in the land of death—pray for us," he was speaking neither metaphorically nor hyperbolically.[17]

One of the Basel Mission's characteristic responses to grief, confusion, and contradiction was song, rather than theological speculation. Precisely because the Gold Coast continued to be a graveyard well into the twentieth century, and because of the likelihood of death alongside the certainty of disease, the Basel missionaries clung tightly to their stories of divine calling. If that thread of calling were torn, much of their spiritual lives would quickly unravel. There needed to be some compelling reason to begin questioning these narratives. That reason was not in the first instance theological or rational, but emotional, and arose in grief and tragedy—above all in death. For the German mourners, then, the death of a colleague was thus an unwelcome window for confronting nagging questions about the purpose of all this grief.

The society's field songbook (published in 1879, so it is unclear what the missionaries in the Gold Coast were using before that date, aside from many songs from memory) contains a sizeable section organized topically, including songs titled "We are Afraid," "Early Death," "Back to Work" (after sickness), "Sustenance in Famine," and similar. Some of these songs crackle with emotion:

16 Albert Ostertag, "Die Goldküste und die Basler Mission daselbst," *EMM* 1859, 33.
17 Immanuel Bellon, "Des weißen Mannes Grab," *HB* 1913, 142.

grief is recognized not only as part of life, but as integral to the missionary experience. Among the more moving of these songs of grief was field song-book number 338, "At the Graveside of a Missionary Woman." These verses depicted the deceased missionary as the dove released from Noah's ark. At first, it found no place to land, and returned to Noah. Released a second time, it returned with an olive leaf—a message that the floodwaters were receding. Released a third time, it never returned: "But then the Lord called you away. And before we knew it, your hour had arrived." Grief was not denied, as if this was meant to be, but affirmed as the appropriate response to loss. Weeping was invited, and the mourners, gathered at the graveside, were directed backwards in their memories, to years of hardships, where they were encouraged to iden-tify God's solidarity in hardship: "He left home with you, he was always at your side, on the rolling seas he kept you from harm."[18]

Another song, published in the *EMM* in 1836, inverted the standard mis-sionary imagery of evangelism as the planting of seeds in natives' hearts: here it was the missionaries who needed, like seeds, to be buried:

> Far away on Tranquebar's shore[19]
> Under the burning sun,
> There is a garden, full of grace,
> In the midst of dry sand.
> Noble seeds and foreign names
> Lie deep in the garden's soil.

In much biblical and Christian imagery, God's word is often represented as a seed, but the reference is occasionally to a human death, as in John 12:24. This is the meaning that appears to be implied in this song: "Very truly, I tell you, unless a grain of wheat falls into the earth and dies, it remains just a single grain; but if it dies, it bears much fruit."

> Other seeds than they imagine
> They must sink into the deep soil, in bitter pain.
> Lamentation sweeps over them. From twin wells
> Pours water upon what they have sown.[20]

Here in the form of lament lies the very essence of the missionaries' experi-ence of death, and the survivors' strategy for giving biblical meaning to the

---

[18] Joseph F. Josenhans, *Missionsliederbuch für die Missionsgemeinde und die Arbeiter auf dem Missionsfelde* (Basel: Missions-Gesellschaft, 1879), no. 338.

[19] That is, Tranquebar in South India, where German Protestants first ventured into missionary service in 1706. The Basel Mission did not work there, but by the time of the mission's founding, Tranquebar had become a generic term for overseas mission fields.

[20] "Der Brüdergarten auf der malabarischen Küste," *EMM* 1836, 150–51.

loss. It was articulated repeatedly in letters home, read before groups of Pietist donors and supporters, gathered in homes and chapels scattered around Germany and Switzerland and beyond: death is a bitter and lonely contradiction. The only consolation is the dual assurance of God's presence in the suffering, combined with restoration at the end of time. In this and other similar songs, the Basel missionaries articulated a kind of homelessness, which kept them from over-identification with contemporary political developments in Germany and Switzerland.

However, the reverse is true as well: such sentiments could let the missionaries evade indigenous claims on their emotional loyalties. Throughout their tenure in the Gold Coast, Basel missionaries persisted in speaking of their work in Africa as sacrifice, done in lonely worship to their God. The cost of dying abroad was not so much the horror of dying young, it was the horror of dying away from home. There were exactly two solutions: to reimagine the Gold Coast as home, to melt into the community and, upon death, to continue to bless the survivors, or to sink into the soil in boundless loneliness, with the only consolation being resurrection at the end of the age. Increasingly as time went on, the missionaries chose the latter option, holding the indigenous congregations at arm's length. The missionaries were foreigners abroad and foreigners at home. When one of their own died in Ghana, their grief process frequently included framing the loss as sacrifice.

And this was unnecessary, because Ghanaian arms had been wide open all along, willing to reciprocate with loving embrace. In 1913, Gã pastor Jeremias Engmann, a seventy-five-year-old member of the 1866 graduating class (the first one) of the Akropong seminary, needed to bury a young man named Paul Weiss. Engmann's graveside sermon, abstracted in German translation in the *Heidenbote*, illustrates this dynamic. Weiss had died of yellow fever only shortly after his arrival in Abokobi; he had not yet acquired command over the language, and had, to all appearances, accomplished nothing at all. "Why did God call him to us," Engmann asked, "if [Weiss] would have to die so soon?" For Engmann, the message in Weiss' life was the fact of his love for "us":

> He left parents and siblings in Europe and came here out of love for us. Do you think he did not love his kindred? Who of us would leave his parents and siblings, in order to preach the gospel to his fellow humans? No one![21]

If even in death the missionaries remained foreigners, this was largely a reflection of their own insistence on remaining apart and determining the terms of their sacrifice. But at funerals, indigenous Christians increasingly

[21] Jeremias Engmann, "Sein Eifer in Sprachstudium war seine Predict," *HB* 1913, 120.

took the lead, choosing songs with a different emphasis than those selected by the missionaries. At Georg Schimanek's February 1866 graveside service in Aburi, for example, Christoph Bellon preached from 2 Samuel 1:19–20, where David, the future king of Israel, wept over his friend Jonathan's death: "A hero is fallen in Israel, who, while in Africa worked in constant sorrow, suffering in quiet, faithful obedience." However, the Twi-speaking congregation (which likely included the Akropong seminarians, including the young Engmann) answered the German preacher's sermon of grief with a song about resurrection: "the dead will arise."[22] This appears to be a hymn, originally composed in Twi: no. 828 in today's Presbyterian Hymnal: *Awufo nyinaa bɛsɔre*, probably composed by Oforikae (David Asante's brother), who had died in Basel in 1862.[23] In this song, Oforikae articulated expectations of the bodily resurrection of the dead upon the return of Christ—shared with the German Pietists—which were imported directly from the Bible.

When Sebastian Lindenmann died in 1866 of what appears to have been meningitis,[24] aged twenty-eight, after less than two years' service, his passage brought to a conclusion a heartbreaking mental breakdown that had begun months earlier. Jakob Heck related the story in what would, in turn, prove to be his own final letter home. Lindenmann was the merchant bookkeeper in the coastal stations. Having previously trained as an accountant for a Swiss firm, he was admitted to the mission on an abbreviated training program. He was sent to Christiansborg in 1864 as a secular clerk for the mission. When a small war broke out around the Volta delta, he hurried out to secure the mission's workshops. In the middle of the night the shop was raided by men covered in war-paint, and Lindenmann was frightened out of his mind. He climbed out the window, jumped the wall barefoot into a cactus hedge, ran semi-naked to the beach, and hiked twenty-two hours straight through back to Christiansborg, a hundred kilometers distant. He arrived, terrified, severely sunburnt, in a high fever, and suffering from dysentery. He would never be quite right again, Heck wrote. "God healed his body, but not his head." In his final sickness, he was delirious, sometimes speaking in English and Gã, passing quietly

---

[22] Dieterle, "Georg Schimanek," 50.

[23] Presbyterian Church of Ghana, *Presbyterian Hymns in Twi, Ga, Dangme and English* (Accra, Ghana: A-Riis Company, 2010), no. 828. This publication attributes the hymn to Johannes Mader, whom Oforikae assisted in the former's songwriting. When Oforikae died while a student in Basel in 1862, the Mission published a song that the youth had written: *HB* 1862; this song seems to be the same as no. 828 in the PCG hymnal.

[24] "Gehirnentzündung" (brain infection). "Most likely some type of protozoan or bacterial infection, possibly malaria, causing meningitis and encephalitis. Most often the vector is mosquito." (Personal Communication, Kay Grant, RN, March 26, 2016.)

around five o'clock. At the funeral, Heck preached in Gã from Revelation 2:7: "To the one who is victorious, I will give the right to eat from the tree of life." "The Lord sends us one grief after another," added the editors who published the obituary.[25]

If the poor young Lindenmann, suffering from what might be post-traumatic stress combined with meningitis, had actually lost his mind, he was not the only one. Much of the missionary work was done not in a state of cold sobriety, but rather in highly emotional, often delirious states, in which European condescension was breached. Writing about explorer narratives in Central Africa, Johannes Fabian has identified in European weakness—culture shock, intoxication, fever, and the side effects of drugs taken to combat fever—a "condition of possibility" for genuine, heart-to-heart meeting between Europeans and Africans. Drawing on the phrase "außer sich sein" in his native German, Fabian called this moment "ecstasy," arguing that many European accounts of encounter, especially those of ethnographers and explorers, misrepresented the narrator as being master of his environment.[26] In contrast to the cool and controlling language of much Basel Mission reportage—such as Widmann's burying the account of Kwame Akwatia's resurrection below construction dimensions of a schoolhouse—missionary obituaries dispense with the rational and embrace the ecstatic.

Exemplary was Johannes Zimmermann's report of the 1866 death of Georg Hetz. Hetz was a missionary of the North German society, working not far away in Wegbe in what is now Togo. Informed by his agency that the woman chosen for him as his bride was on her way, he traveled to Accra to meet her: Lydia Lüthin from rural northwestern Switzerland. Missionary Christian Locher married the young couple, who were meeting for the first time, immediately upon her April 3 arrival. However, war had broken out on both sides of the Volta, preventing them from returning to Wegbe. They went as far as Zimmermann's residence at Odumase to wait out the hostilities, but Georg died there, leaving Lydia widowed after two months of marriage. Hetz had been delirious, but Zimmermann inserted himself into the delirium, helping to make the incomprehensible at least human. His account of Hetz's death is strange indeed:

> He died of dysentery. It came on strong. We stood vigil for a week alongside Sister Hess. Once I found a snake in the bed of my sleeping sons. On the night of the 25th he sat upright, intending to depart. He was crossing the

---

[25] Jakob Heck, "Sebastian Lindenmann," *HB* 1866, 61–62.

[26] Johannes Fabian, *Out of Our Minds: Reason and Madness in the Exploration of Central Africa* (Berkeley: University of California Press, 2000), 8.

Volta. I asked him if he did not recognize me. That night my wife delivered a son. Early in the morning Brother Hetz died, aged 32, having spent 6 years in Africa, two months after his wedding. We buried him in the cemetery. . . . His burial was the hour of our preparation for the Eucharist. That evening was the Trinity-feast. He had wanted to celebrate it with us, but instead enjoyed it in heaven.[27]

What Zimmermann did in this dispatch was to use nonlinear narrative language to make the pain of Hetz's death greater and less intelligible, rather than manageable and rational. Indeed, if one reads behind updates on the progress of the cocoa and coffee groves, and the reports on schools and seminaries, this kind of experience appears as the context for much of the Basel Mission's work in the Gold Coast. Before the mid-1880s, most missionaries were nearly constantly sick, at least at a low level, and death was never far away.[28] Fevers came with great regularity, and the missionaries went about much of their religious work in a mental fog. On Sunday, May 6, 1866, the young Jakob Heck preached his final sermon, and he died later that week. In the subsequent obituary, Schönfeld added an amazing detail: "[Heck] stood at the pulpit in a fever, as happens so often among the brothers in Africa, who have to obey their calling with unsteady steps."[29] This small comment opens a world of perspective, and invites the reader to inquire, quite literally, of the sanity of missionary articulations: Is it possible that much of the time they were preaching while in a fever?

"We thought he might preach again next week," Schönfeld continued, suggesting that Heck's fevered preaching was not extraordinary, "but God's council—who can understand it?"[30] All that could be done was commit him to his maker, in partnership with indigenous Christians: "While catechists Reindorf and Ablo kneeled in prayer that the Lord receive his soul, I pronounced the blessing and he breathed his final breath."[31] And here is where indigenous hospitality came into play: the missionaries flattered themselves that they were

---

[27] Johannes Zimmermann, "Der Heimgang von Missionar Hetz," *HB* 1866, 133.

[28] In 1885 the Basel Mission's first doctor arrived, a moment which seems to have marked the end of missionaries' willingness (usually unspoken but obvious) to see indigenous healers.

[29] Schönfeld, "Der Heimgang von Missionar Heck in Christiansborg," 118.

[30] Schönfeld, "Der Heimgang von Missionar Heck in Christiansborg," 118. The word I have translated "council"—*Rath*—refers to God's actions grounded in God's own sovereign decisions. The word is used in several passages in the German Bible, the most important of which come in the book of Job, in which the problem of human suffering in the presence of a supposedly omnipotent God is articulated, without resolution. Job 15:8 reads in English: "Have you listened in the council of God? And do you limit wisdom to yourself?"

[31] Schönfeld, "Der Heimgang von Missionar Heck in Christiansborg," 119.

sacrificing for the Africans. Meanwhile, the latter understood the grieving process as a communal responsibility in which they were more than willing to reciprocate.

This proffered reciprocity in grief is the context, without which it is difficult to make sense of indigenous Christians' outlook on spiritual power, which extended to power over the grave. Throughout their entire tenure in the Gold Coast, the Germans had been subject to much indigenous deliberation and experimentation as locals requested healings. The missionaries were for the most part unable or unwilling to comply (Johann Widmann and a few others the notable exceptions). Especially after the 1885 arrival of missionary doctor Rudolf Fisch, whose strictly biomedical approach to healing played an important role in what Adam Mohr has termed "the disenchantment of Ghana's Basel Mission," missionary discussion of supernatural healing—already on the wane—disappeared nearly entirely.[32] However, the Mission's retreat into biomedicine exacerbated a gap in understanding with the indigenous Christians, for whom biomedicine did not address the evil spirits behind superficial symptoms.[33] Progressive missionary discomfort with the miraculous from mid-century on did not induce the men and women of Akuapem to follow suit. Instead, they instigated supernatural power encounters and performances in the absence of the missionaries or beyond their supervision.

Often bedridden for months on end, often bewildered and terrified, working hard not to doubt God, the sick missionaries received succor from their Christian and heathen neighbors. However, the indigenous communities were also suffering. They were also losing children, were confronting powerful and terrifying spirits, and were not satisfied to learn that the missionaries were as well. There was nothing exceptional about suffering: if there was going to be a rupture in the system, it would come through a state of exception. I develop this thought by returning to the case of Samson Amaadi and the dead boy.

### STATES OF EXCEPTION

Kwame Akwatia's resurrection from the dead was politically complicated, as these things tend to be. It has subsequently become something of a founding myth to Larteh's Christians. Several variations are in circulation, but all agree on the date. The only contemporary account I have found came in Johannes Widmann's annual report to his employers at the Basel Mission, written seven

---

[32] Adam Mohr, *Enchanted Calvinism: Labor Migration, Afflicting Spirits, and Christian Therapy in the Presbyterian Church of Ghana* (Rochester, N.Y.: University of Rochester Press, 2013), 48–52.

[33] Mohr, *Enchanted Calvinism*, 50.

months later.[34] Fifty years after the event, Samson recorded a two-page version as part of his autobiography.[35] In 1955 the Larteh congregation self-published another account, written by J. Kwesi Ansah.[36] David Brokensha and Noel Smith both published new versions in 1966, each citing Ansah's account while adding details not contained therein or in each other's: clearly they were drawing on uncited oral histories that they were supplementing with Ansah's.[37]

It took place on December 29, 1858. The boy's death the previous day had set the town to a boil, because one of the known gods had obviously struck the boy dead as punishment—not for an offense of his own, but for the Akuapem king's. Kwaw Dade should never have allowed a Christian evangelist to open a school in the town, never mind that the king had later tried to prevent the school from opening. The boy's death did not constitute the rupture, but merely reflected it—making manifest what was already broken in the unseen realm. The actual rupture had occurred several weeks earlier, when Samson Amaadi had arrived from the royal town of Akropong on the adjacent ridge.

Samson Amaadi, also called Edward Samson, was a Twi man from Aburi, a very different town in Akuapem. He was thus not really indigenous in Larteh: he spoke another language, he belonged to another (matrilineal) ancestral economy, and he worshiped another god. King Kwaw Dade had no interest in Christianity but saw in Samson a chance to impose a bit more control over a perennially rebellious town. He had informed, rather than asked, Larteh's priests that Samson Amaadi, in the employ of the foreign missionaries, would be allowed to open a school in their town. Shortly thereafter, the king changed his mind and forbade Larteh to finish building the school they had begun. According to Samson's own account, the king was responding to a priestess, who had prophesied that "unless the school was done away with, the fetish Konkom would destroy all the inhabitants of his town, both men and women."[38]

In late December, Kwame Akwatia died after a three-day illness (Samson later claimed that the boy had been poisoned by the fetish priest and priestess of the town). The body was laid out on the street for public display. The priests

[34] Widmann, "Kirchenweihe in Late," 111–12 (from a letter dated August 5, 1859).

[35] Edward Samson, *A Short History of Akuapim and Akropong Gold Coast and Autobiography of the Rev. Edward Samson of Aburi, Native Pastor* (Aburi [Ghana], 1908), 36–38.

[36] J. Kwesi Ansah, *The Centenary History of the Larteh Presbyterian Church, 1853–1953* (Larteh, Gold Coast: Larteh Presbyterian Church, 1955).

[37] David Brokensha, *Social Change at Larteh, Ghana* (Oxford: Clarendon, 1966), and Noel Smith, *The Presbyterian Church of Ghana, 1835–1960: A Younger Church in a Changing Society* (Accra, Ghana Universities Press; London: Oxford University Press, 1966).

[38] Edward Samson, *A Short History*, 37.

determined that the boy's funeral needed to be accompanied by ritual purification of the town and ordered the drumming to begin. The chief called Samson
forward to add his own prayers.

> On arrival I was empowered, by the aid of the Holy Spirit, to make fervent
> prayer; and during my earnest devotions, I heard some of the mourners, who
> were sitting near the body, saying in their own language (Kyerepon), "Ale
> Tink," which is to say "he is awake," and to the great surprise of all, the dead
> boy sat up on the bed.[39]

The sudden death of one of Amaadi's pupils was, in the eyes of the priests,
an avoidable tragedy—a message of warning from an offended god. However,
there was still a culprit to be blamed, and he was not the evangelist, nor was
it the missionaries. The focus of Larteh's priests' anger was rather the king
himself—King Kwaw Dade, who was anything but a friend of Christianity, but
who saw in the religion an opportunity for keeping Larteh's priests in check.
Therefore, when Samson Amaadi raised Kwame Akwatia from the dead, short-
circuiting the priests' ritual preparations for his funeral during their dancing
and drumming of purification and remonstration, everything was turned
upside down. Samson was clear:

> The fetish priests who had witnessed this undeniable miracle, which was
> wrought by our Lord and Saviour Jesus Christ, went home covered in grief
> and shame.[40]

Unsurprisingly, this upset shook the town, as a Twi man, an assistant to
the foreign Christians, had accomplished something none of the foreigners
had ever done (and likely had never attempted). The implications were clear
as day: the words of God were not only words of light in the darkness, but
were backed by real power, not merely over the grave, but over Akonnedi and
the other gods. Some began to treat Samson as a spiritual patron. The miracle made a "deep impression on the people," added Widmann. "The parents
now regard the catechist [Samson] as the protector of their child and they do
nothing without his permission."[41] Shortly thereafter, one of the priestesses,
together with her family, came to Samson seeking baptism, "and she gave me
all her fetishes, which I brought to the Rev. Widmann in Akropong."[42]

---

[39] Samson, *A Short History*, 38.
[40] Samson, *A Short History*, 38.
[41] Widmann, "Kirchenweihe in Late," 112.
[42] Samson, *A Short History*, 38.

A few months later, Widmann himself traveled to Larteh to bless the now complete church building and to baptize the first few converts. He included in his account brief notes on each person's motivations. Notable was how important power was to them: Christ's power to heal, and the power of God's word:

- **John Opaw**, who said: "The fetish is nothing, but by the blood of Christ we are delivered" [*erlöst*].

- **Immanuel Otenkorang.** "His mother had dedicated him to the fetish, but to no avail. Three times he has been sick to the edge of the grave. His mother . . . sent him to the school, where he has heard and eaten God's word."

- **Gabriel Atoklo**: "He had been sick and the fetish priests could not heal him, but for Christ's sake God had helped him."

- **Esau Asong Kwadjo**: "He saw how the fetish priests had deceived his parents and extorted money from them. He renounces the fetish and gives himself over to Christ."[43]

Edward Samson Amaadi was not the only one of his kind. Several other indigenous evangelists read messages of power and victory out of their Bibles. Their confidence led several of them (who were also ambitious young men) toward an attitude of confrontation with the existing lines of authority, be they human or otherwise. The complete Bible only appeared in Twi translation in 1871, well after the formation of a Twi-speaking Christian community. Before then, indigenous Christians had very little reason to distinguish between the messenger and the message. Both were foreign. Absent a deep engagement with what the translation team had titled *Anyamesεm*, or "God's words," locals and newcomers could only hope to incorporate the messengers themselves into preexisting religious and political categories. That is exactly what they did. Ghanaians were able to take the message in directions the missionaries could not anticipate for two main reasons. First, because the latter, often suffering for months on end from various tropical diseases, were unable to resist indigenous innovations, and second, because the missionaries successfully resisted incorporation into the indigenous communities—they remained categorically foreign. Missionary weakness, combined with the publication of a vernacular Bible, effectively stripped the missionaries of control over their own message.

In her study of twenty-first-century Nigerian Pentecostalism, Ruth Marshall paraphrased Carl Schmitt: "the miracle is to theology as the state

43 Widmann, "Kirchenweihe in Late," 112.

of exception is to the law."[44] However, Marshall was speaking about Nigeria's imperfect democracy. Akuapem in 1859, by contrast, was a sacred monarchy, and Larteh was an unhappy subject within that domain: a small theocratic city, centered on a regionally recognized—and feared—god and his shrine.[45] The stuff of the miraculous is politically dangerous enough within a natural law framework, such as Marshall's Nigeria, which is theoretically grounded on "the distinction between power and right" fundamental to the Western democratic tradition.[46] It constitutes a far more violent intrusion in a system, such as in nineteenth-century Akuapem, in which this distinction was neither affirmed nor desired: "Like the force behind the law that founds and guarantees the law," Marshall continued, "divine power is not means, but pure manifestation, pure violence."[47] Kwame Akwatia's resurrection was a devastating blow both to the priests of Larteh and, in a different way, to King Kwaw Dade. It established the Christian community in the imagination of the men and women of the kingdom, who until this time had mostly kept their distance from the missionaries and their indigenous associates.

As J. D. Y. Peel demonstrated for the case of the Yoruba, much of the initial African encounter with European Christianity unfolded far beyond the missionaries' limited purview.[48] Edward Samson Amaadi's activities in Larteh fit into this pattern: after more than two decades of ineffectual German missionary forays into that town from Akropong, the decisive change occurred within mere weeks of the first indigenous preacher's arrival. More broadly in Akuapem, throughout the early years of missionary efforts among the elites—the aristocratic families and the important matriclans—conversions were largely limited to the youths enrolled in missionary schools. However, to judge by consistent indigenous questions about Christianity's capacity for power and healing, many people—both Christians and non-Christians—were applying much thought and creativity to the possible uses of the message.

[44]  Ruth Marshall, *Political Spiritualities: The Pentecostal Revolution in Nigeria* (Chicago: University of Chicago Press, 2009), 213.

[45]  Kofi Asare Opoku, "Training the Priestess at the Akonnedi Shrine," *Research Review of the Institute of African Studies* 6, no. 2 (1970), 34–50. On the shrine: Okomfo Ama Boakyewa, "Nana Oparebea and the Akonnedi Shrine: Cultural, Religious and Global Agents" (PhD diss., Indiana University, 2014). On Larteh's politics: David Brokensha, *The Resilient Chieftaincy of Larteh, Ghana* (Ife, Nigeria: Institute of African Studies, University of Ife, 1968), Kwame Labi, "Akanization of the Hill Guan Arts," *Research Review of the Institute of African Studies* 18, no. 2 (2002).

[46]  Marshall, *Political Spiritualities,* 211.

[47]  Marshall, *Political Spiritualities,* 213.

[48]  J. D. Y. Peel, *Religious Encounter and the Making of the Yoruba* (Bloomington: Indiana University Press, 2000), especially chapters 8–9, 215–77.

The uniqueness of this particular dynamic suggests that something different was going on than in many other stages of African religious encounter, in which Europeans were able to maintain a controlling grasp on the message. In Akuapem, not only the Christians, but also the non-Christians, who were potentially interested in a new religion, as long as it was powerful, were the effective creators of the message. That something was sustained indigenous innovation and initiative. Partly because the Basel missionaries were consistently sick and weak, they were subject to autochthonous ontological imposition, from native workers and non-Christians alike.

By the 1860s, some of the missionaries had come to recognize that this indigenous innovation was more than an expression of confusion, but that the people, without altering their cosmology, were actively imposing a social standing upon the missionaries. In 1863, for example, Johann Widmann wrote of an aborted invasion of Akuapem by the Asante army, which resulted in local discussion of the missionaries' power. They had been very afraid [German: *bange*], and "at each of the stations a common prayer hour was held daily." The congregants turned in their fear to Psalm 50, a wartime song of David's: "Call on me in your need, and I will deliver you, and you will praise me."[49] The prayer worked: one day the Asante army retreated unannounced and went home. "The heathens had the impression," Widmann wrote, "that our help comes from the Lord, maker of heaven and earth."[50]

He was not exaggerating: coming, as it did, only five years after Kwame Akwatia's resurrection from the dead, this display of supernatural power moved another priestess in Larteh to abandon her shrine and convert. That conversion, Widmann said, provoked "no small fight."

> The whole city was in an uproar. On April 15 she was called before the (city) council, and they tried everything to intimidate her and silence her, but with the Lord's strength she survived the struggle and is now, with her family, a member of our congregation.[51]

In the eyes of many of the locals, Widmann had placed an endangered renegade—a priestess who, in abandoning the shrine, had put the entire city at risk of punishments from an angry god—under his protective patronage. The only way she could be expected to survive was because the leaders of Larteh

---

[49]  J. G. Widmann, "Mannigfacher Kampf und Sieg," *JB* 1863, 95–96 (dateline Akropong, August 6, 1863). Widmann referenced the verse without citation, suggesting that his audience at home would recognize the passage.

[50]  Here Widmann is quoting from Psalm 121.

[51]  Widmann, "Mannigfacher Kampf und Sieg," 95–96.

were prepared to credit the Christians with power from the "maker of heaven and earth." Conversion, in other words, brought common people into contact with previously unimaginable spiritual power. Robin Horton's 1971 famous definition of African conversion—that the convert "has accepted change and development in his concept of the supreme being"—is thus incomplete at best.[52] In the face of invasions repelled by heaven's hosts, in the face of resurrections, healings, and confrontations between rival spirits, change in one's concept of the supreme being alone cannot account for conversion: it was nothing less than a response to displays of power.

### CONFRONTING HUMAN AUTHORITY

Six years later, yet another conflict broke out in Larteh between an indigenous agent and the local authorities, when David Asante needed to defuse a machete-wielding mob of men in Larteh on July 24, 1869.[53] Despite his standing as a missionary with the Basel Mission, he most likely leaned on his birthright—his high rank in the royal aristocracy, together with his fluency in court language. Asante reported the incident in German.

Early that day, several men had forced their way into Asante's courtyard and cut down the church bell from its perch near the road. Asante had gone to the *Benkumhene* (Larteh-Ahenease's chief within Akuapem's ɔman political structure).[54] That man, he added, was "always friendly to us." Asante argued that the shrine priests (who were the real authorities in town, in contrast to the *Benkumhene*, appointed from Akropong) had allowed him to install his bell.[55] The *Benkumhene* ordered the bell returned, which the men did, while at the same time brandishing their machetes to warn Asante not to restore the bell to its place. After tempers cooled and the men departed, Asante had another problem on his hands: the small congregation of Christians was now determined to replace the bell, and to "defend it to the blood." Asante, together with the leaders of the congregation, was unable to dissuade the aggrieved Christians against forcefully, and probably foolishly, asserting themselves. The mob then returned, a fight broke out, and the bell was taken a second time.

---

[52]  Robin Horton, "African Conversion," *Africa* 41, no. 2 (1971), 100.

[53]  BMA D-1 (Reel 29) 1869, item #40: David Asante to Committee, August 4, 1869.

[54]  M. A. Kwamena-Poh, *Government and Politics in the Akuapem State, 1730–1850*, Legon History Series (Evanston, Ill.: Northwestern University Press, 1973), 159.

[55]  This incident indicates that the Akuapem king's long struggle with the Guan Priests of Larteh was not resolved by his success at imposing a sub-chief (an *-hene*) on the city, which had always been ruled by the priests. When the chief ordered the mob to do something they did not like, they obeyed as long as it suited them.

The underlying reason, Asante said, for local hostility to the bell was a belief that the bell could enchant the elderly.[56] And here was the key to the dynamic: the conversion of a member of the non-Christian community was far costlier when it involved an elder. A youth who converted could be shunned, but an elder could not. Ghanaian philosopher Kwasi Wiredu explains for the matrilineal Akan situation, but it is likely to have been mostly the same in patrilineal Larteh. The departed spirits of the ancestors (*nsamanfo*) stood as moral guardians over the community, punishing violators of certain classes of evil, and demanding ritual atonement via sacrificed sheep.[57] The well-being of the community—including both its cohesion and its prosperity—was thus contingent on the continued involvement in social life by the deceased, and the conversion of an elder effectively deprived the community of a future spiritual-moral guardian. Moral chaos would be certain to break out if living elders abdicated their involvement in the community. To a tenuous social system understood to be held together by the active intervention of the departed ancestors, the conversion of an elder amounted to a rupture in—and therefore an assault on—the town's continued existence. To the men of Larteh, the Christians could be tolerated as long as they contented themselves with remaining socially marginal, but if they were to try to make inroads among the clan elders—by enchanting them with the bell—they would become a threat. Furthermore, if the bell had genuine spiritual power, it might have been capable of destabilizing the town's politics. A mere decade after one of Asante's predecessors raised a child from the dead, the prospect of the conversion of the town's elders constituted an unpredictable threat. Asante did not mention any actual elderly converts in Larteh itself, but the mob's fear was likely grounded in the very prospect of the threat, compounded by hearsay of conversions elsewhere along the ridge.

Seven years later, David Asante pushed the limits of his authority. By this time, he had been transferred from Larteh to Akyem Abuakwa's royal city of Kyebi. In 1876, he baptized Yaw Boakye, who until then was a drummer for King Amoaka Atta I. With this act Asante announced that he was no longer satisfied to minister to the poor and the enslaved, as he had in his previous appointment in Larteh: whatever working agreement previous missionaries in Kyebi might have made with the king were annulled.[58] Along with the

---

[56] BMA D-1 (Reel 29) 1869, item #40: David Asante to Committee, August 4, 1869.

[57] Kwame Wiredu, "Papa ne Bone," in *Listening to Ourselves: A Multilingual Anthology of African Philosophy*, ed. Chike Jeffers (Albany: State University of New York Press, 2013), 168–69.

[58] Robert Addo-Fening, *Akyem Abuakwa, 1700–1943: From Ofori Panin to Sir Ofori Atta* (Trondheim: Department of History, Norwegian University of Science and Technology, 1997), 64–65.

other musicians, a drummer was part of the royal ceremonial group called the *werɛmpɛ* (also the name for the supreme ritual which was the group's responsibility), without whom the king could not perform the dangerous rituals his office demanded. Asante was thus striking at the heart of the kingship on two levels: first, the king needed ritual associates, and Asante was taking one away. Eva Meyerowitz (whose mentor in her ethnographic fieldwork was J. B. Danquah, none other than Yaw Boakye's son) noted that the *werɛmpɛ* group collectively represented a check on political disorder, as the sacredness of the Akan state was maintained less by the possession of sacred regalia than by the ritual performance of state offices by heralds, stool-carriers, gun-bearers, sword-bearers, horn-blowers, drummers, umbrella-carriers, and elephant-tail bearers.[59] Giorgio Agamben has described the *homo sacer*, his notion of the sacred man, who stands in the intolerable place of responsibility, in language of exposure: he stands alone, naked, at the threshold, where he must protect the community.[60] The king's *werɛmpɛ* group made that responsibility tolerable: it was a group of men together performing a sacred and dangerous office. If the ritual went wrong—if a taboo were violated, if, for example, a sheep cried out during its sacrifice—and a deity was angered, a member of that group could shoulder the blame, perhaps by becoming a sacrifice himself. However, by converting a member of the *werɛmpɛ*, Asante was effectively stripping a human shield from the twenty-three-year-old king. Robert Addo-Fening suggests Asante was setting himself up as a rival judicial authority to the king, who was his cousin.[61] But there might have been more to the story. At a deeper level, he might have been assembling a *werɛmpɛ* of his own.

Asante's fellow missionaries were concerned that the breach of decorum might bring trouble to the mission. David Eisenschmid, then stationed in Akropong, but who had spent several years in Kyebi, wrote to the home office that Asante was overstepping his authority. Indeed, the king eventually complained to Britain's new colonial authorities. After a court trial in Accra, the Basel Mission agreed to transfer Asante away, replacing him with the very young Karl Buck, who had arrived in the country only months earlier.[62] How-

---

[59] Eva Meyerowitz, *The Sacred State of the Akan* (London: Faber and Faber, 1951), 65.

[60] Giorgio Agamben, *Homo Sacer: Sovereign Power and Bare Life* (Stanford: Stanford University Press, 1998), esp. 63–66.

[61] Robert Addo-Fening in personal conversation with the present author, October 2015, Akropong.

[62] Addo-Fening, *Akyem Abuakwa, 1700–1943*, 66–67.

ever, Asante had crossed a line, and the Christian community at Kyebi experienced several waves of repression over the next two decades.[63]

On its face, these struggles were about political (especially encroaching colonial) power, and that is the level at which they have usually been treated.[64] The most sophisticated analysis of repression in Kyebi has come from Peter Haenger, as part of a study on slavery in the Gold Coast. Putting David Asante's conflict with the king in the context of the two men's shared royal lineage, along with the former's adroit navigation of court protocol in an effort to antagonize the latter, Haenger concludes that the disagreements "cannot be understood simply as the consequence of primarily religious differences."[65] This is correct, but the reverse is also true: the conflict cannot be understood simply in political terms—it was a religious power encounter in a political economy anchored by a sacred kingship. Asante's maneuvers amounted to the imposition of a European-like separation of church and state upon a kingship situated at the threshold between the two. Addo-Fening:

> The Basel Mission had entered Akyem with an ethnocentric purpose that included recasting Abuakwa society in the mould of a European society. They envisioned a purely secular Abuakwa state with freedom of worship and conscience for individual subjects regardless of their duties to the state.[66]

But this is too simple, even beyond Addo-Fening's ahistorical description of secular European societies.[67] The religious encounter, including Yaw Boakye's conversion, might have actually presented a greater rupture to Akyem politics than Britain's economic impositions (the most strongly felt of which, in Kyebi, was the colonial abolition of slavery).[68] David Asante had seen Switzerland and Germany with his own eyes and had been profoundly unimpressed. He had determined, on the basis of his personal experiences overseas, but also his

---

[63] BMA D-10.3.7c. Report by Pastor Esau Ofori, 1887, orig. in Twi, in German translation by J. G. Christaller.

[64] Sonia Abun-Nasr, *Afrikaner und Missionar: die Lebensgeschichte von David Asante* (Basel: Schlettwein, 2003); Hanns Walter Huppenbauer, *Königshaus und Missionshaus in Kyebi: Auseinandersetzungen der Basel Missionare mit den Königen von Akyem 1861–1890* (Affoltern am Albis: Eigenverlag, 2004); Addo-Fening, *Akyem Abuakwa, 1700–1943*.

[65] Haenger, *Sklaverei und Sklavenemanzipation an der Goldküste: ein Beitrag zum Verständnis von Sozialen Abhängigkeitsbeziehungen in Westafrika* (Basel: Helbing & Lichtenhahn, 1997), 132–40.

[66] Addo-Fening, *Akyem Abuakwa, 1700–1943*, 59.

[67] Abun-Nasr, *Afrikaner und Missionar*, 7.

[68] Haenger, *Sklaverei und Sklavenemanzipation*, 132–40.

detailed reading of the Bible, that all kings stood under divine judgment.[69] All local kings understood themselves to be accountable to their ancestral predecessors on the royal stool, in whose name they performed their ritual offices. But David Asante, along with the other indigenous pastors, argued otherwise: the kings were accountable to God, who had spoken words that could be read, and heard, in the Bible.

Addo-Fening may have been correct about the Basel Mission in general—including Eisenschmid and others who mistakenly assumed they could eschew politics. As the Mission's demotion of Asante after the court trial suggests, it was a conceit shared by the organization's home office. However, David Asante himself was under no such delusion. The foundation of Asante's line of thought was divine revelation—God's word, come from outside the system, revealed and not necessarily to be arrived at by reason alone. As a co-translator of the Bible from Hebrew and Greek into Twi, a project that had occupied much of his preceding fifteen years, Asante was clear about what he meant. Although the conflict at Kyebi was the most spectacular crisis of legitimacy provoked by Christian communities associated with the Basel Mission, it was not the only one.

Although indigenous Christians had been present throughout the kingdom for two decades, there was an important chronological pattern to these conflicts. Aside from the Akwatia episode of 1858, they mostly took place after the late 1860s and early 1870s, when two parallel developments were underway. The first, in chronological order, was the publication of the Bible in Twi, beginning with the New Testament from 1864, and the Old and New combined in 1871. The translation's potential to rupture was, if not the single most important factor in political-religious conflict in Akuapem and Akyem Abuakwa, at least a major element. It had to do with the relationship of time and truth on the one hand, and the ways the sacredness of the -*ohene* kingship focused comprehensive assertion of responsibility on the other, both of which were threatened by the vernacular Bible.

The second, following a few years later, was the progressive imposition of British indirect rule. The latter development would see missionaries drawn ever more into the mainstream of European ways of thinking in the colony. I return to this theme in the conclusion. The first few generations of missionaries brought with them from Switzerland and Germany a distrust of political entanglements, rooted in memories of state harassment of Pietist nonconformity. However, the Basel Mission's very notion of separate religious and

---

[69] David Asante, *Wiase Abasem mu Nsemma-Nsemma wo Twi kasa mu* (1874; Basel: Verlag der Missionsbuchhandlung, 1893).

political social spheres made no sense in the Gold Coast. Put more accurately, it was a violent doctrine: since the very foundations of Akan political legitimacy were grounded in cultic rituals, separation of church and state could only result in a hollowing-out of the foundation upon which indigenous politics was laid. Politics were even less avoidable in Akuapem, where the Akan king was locked in unending conflict with the Guan priests, who doubled as the temporal rulers of their respective towns, against which the king's -ohene appointees were often of little consequence. In 1844, during a seven-year interregnum following Addo Dankwa's 1839 suicide, the acting chief of Akuapem told Andreas Riis (recently returned after two years' furlough):

> Your missionaries are welcome to Akropong—even if a hundred more come, we would not mind. But the fetishes at Aburi, Larteh, and Adukrom are too powerful to allow you to open schools as you intend.[70]

This warning, by the highest official in the kingdom, corresponds with Guan assertions, made in the late twentieth century to Michelle Gilbert, that "the Akan [i.e. Akuapem's Twi speakers] fear them because of their gods . . . they say the [Akropong] people know how powerful the Guan gods are, as they came with nothing except a few minor family deities."[71] Such claims are certainly overstated, and tend to confuse bluster with cosmology: the open spiritual marketplace could not only see gods and spirits drifting in and out of authority, but could be wielded as political maneuver. Indeed, spiritual authority was less a piece to a political puzzle than the puzzle itself.

To the extent that they functioned as assets in a political rival's toolkit, sacred trees and rivers, and their associated spirits, could be dragged into pedestrian conflicts through ritual felling and defilement. One of these assets were the Odum trees, which the Germans called "African Oaks" for their size and social prominence. Odums cast shade over countless local marketplaces and town squares; the site for the town of Akropong was chosen in the 1730s next to one such tree (which as of 2019 was still healthy). An Odum tree—*chlorophora excelsa*—was held to house spirits whose graces could be cultivated for the benefit of the community; conversely, the tree could be cut down if the resident spirits were endangering people. Either way, appropriate protocols (such as offerings of eggs) needed to be first observed. The spirit of an Odum tree could reciprocate a chief's offerings by "chang[ing] into a

[70] Brokensha, *Social Change*, 10.
[71] Michelle Gilbert, "The Cracked Pot and the Missing Sheep," *American Ethnologist* 16, no. 2 (1989), 217.

human being at night and visit[ing] the Ohene (chief) of a village [to] inform him of the nefarious activities of criminals in his community."[72]

This broad recognition of the trees' spiritual power, not shared with the Germans, presented indigenous converts with openings for confrontation. In 1895, while building a chapel for his fledgling congregation in the small village of Bompata southeast of Kumasi in the Asante kingdom, indigenous catechist Samuel Boateng (mentioned in the previous chapter as having eaten fish from a sacred river) decided to make the roof out of the sacred Odum tree, which he and his people felled and split. "That tree," the ninety-five-year-old E. A. Frempong told his informant in 1972,

> was the shrine of Okomfo Amaning and at first the people resisted its destruction. Mr. Samuel Boateng over-ruled their objection and had his own way without much conflict. So also did he succeed in destroying a shrine of the fetish Dente belonging to one Kwame Dako.[73]

This story was not published in any Basel Mission publications, which in 1895 and 1896 focused on an abnormally high level of missionary disease and death. However, the incident suggests that Boateng was not simply looking for lumber for his chapel: he was attempting to demonstrate power over—or at least immunity from—a deity (Dente), the reverence of whom had long kept the Asante army from annexing the shrine sanctuary at Kete-Krachi (discussed in chapter 2). Nor was this kind of action a specifically Christian one: forty years earlier—that is, before there were any indigenous preachers in his kingdom—King Kwaw Dade had done the same thing. Having previously warned the missionaries not to touch Odum trees, lest they be killed by the *sasa* spirits living inside, the king had inconsistently (in Johann Widmann's opinion) ordered an Odum cut down for lumber.[74] Since it is unlikely that as paranoid and cynical a man as Kwaw Dade had cut down his own Odum, he was more likely cutting down the tree-informant of a rival, subordinate chief, or one belonging to a priest outside of the formal political order, per- haps in order to deprive that rival of potentially valuable information on the king himself. In a context of spiritual improvisation combined with political

---

[72] Samuel Awuah-Nyamekye, "Belief in Sasa: Its Implications for Flora and Fauna Con- servation in Ghana," *Nature and Culture* 7, no. 1 (2012), 6.

[73] M. P. Frempong, "A History of the Presbyterian Church at Bompata in Asante- Akyem," trans. E. A. Kyerematen, *Ghana Notes and Queries* 12 (June 1972), 21.

[74] J. G. Widmann, "Station Akropong," *JB* 1850, 192. Widmann added no other details, including the location of said tree. At this time of this writing, only six years after King Kwaw Dade's admonition to fear the autochthonous spirits, Widmann was on furlough in Württemberg.

turmoil, there was no difference between religious and spiritual power struggles. Boateng's demonstration of immunity was simultaneously an offer of protection, under the umbrella of his Christian religion, to would-be converts in need of sanctuary.

CONCLUSION

Indigenous Christians were not satisfied with promulgating their own understandings of community, but consistently attempted to incorporate the missionaries into the same. The volatility of missionary life in the Gold Coast—the constant presence of disease, death, grief, fear, and isolation—opened a window through which indigenous Christians were able to work on the missionaries, seeking to shape them, incorporate them, use them, and impose upon them homegrown spiritual and social agendas. In short, the Basel missionaries were most subject to indigenous moral imaginaries when they were at their weakest. In sickness and in fever, from infantilizing incompetence in language to terrifying encounters with spiritual entities and their priests, the missionaries heard their own words—the Bible (translated) and liturgical songs (some translated, some original)—spoken back to them.[75] When they were at their strongest, the missionaries could affect the distant coolness of an explorer or a scholar. This is the image they preferred to send home in their newsletters, as well as to scientific periodicals in ethnography, geography, and medicine, and above all in linguistics, to which the missionaries increasingly contributed late in the nineteenth century and early in the twentieth. In such settings, they spoke to a crowd that, throughout the nineteenth century, had roundly dismissed missionaries as ignorant at best.[76] However, this pretended scholarly

---

[75] The Presbyterian Church of Ghana—the successor body to the Basel Mission—includes useful annotations of authorship in their hymnal: which hymns were original in Twi, which were translated, and so on. Also see, as a biography of a prominent early twentieth-century indigenous hymn-writer (for whom Twi was a second language) that also addresses cross-cultural liturgical issues for the Twi church: Philip T. Laryea, *Ephraim Amu: Nationalist, Poet and Theologian (1899-1995)* (Akropong-Akuapem, Ghana: Regnum Africa, 2012).

[76] Erika Eichholzer, "Missionary Linguistics on the Gold Coast," in *The Spiritual in the Secular: Missionaries and Knowledge about Africa*, ed. Patrick Harries and David Maxwell, (Grand Rapids: Eerdmans, 2012); Sara Elizabeth Berg Pugach, *Africa in Translation: A History of Colonial Linguistics in Germany and Beyond, 1814-1945* (Ann Arbor: University of Michigan Press, 2012). On medicine, see Rudolf Fisch, *Tropische Krankheiten; Anleitung zu ihrer Verhütung und Behandlung für Missionare, Kaufleute, Pflanzer und Beamte.* (Basel: Verlag der Missionsbuchhandlung, 1913). Fisch had been sent to Akuapem in 1885, bringing the latest knowledge of bacteria and biomedicine with him; Adam Mohr identifies with Fisch's deputation a turning point in the Basel Mission's willingness to see indigenous doctors: Adam Mohr, "Missionary Medicine and Akan Therapeutics: Illness, Health and

sobriety obscured the quotidian grind of pastoral care and sickness. Much of the time, from indigenous demands for sanctuary to pleas for deliverance from possession and disease, the missionaries were responding to indigenous initiatives. Missionary receptivity to autochthonous impositions was at its greatest when the medium for encounter was the commonly agreed language of the Bible: indigenous talk-back was most likely to be received when it came saturated in biblical references.

Successful indigenization of the churches, including the translation of the Bible, has as one consequence that the missionaries were becoming less relevant to indigenous Christian communities, even as they were becoming more African in their basic spiritual outlooks on life. In Peel's words:

> The double irony of Christian missions since the early nineteenth century is that they have become progressively estranged from the dominant culture of the societies that sent them, while they have often succeeded in their target areas less for their own reasons than for the reasons of those they have evangelized.[77]

The Twi-speaking people of Akuapem had succeeded in enveloping the missionaries into most of their goals and categories. They demanded, and eventually received, sanctuary. Over time they went farther than the missionaries were able to go, identifying and beginning to replicate wonders of which they read in the Scriptures, which were now circulating in their own vernacular. As they interpreted "God's words" (Anyamesɛm), they applied them to their own world, including the miraculous parts. While many of the missionaries were dying, sick, and often out of their minds, the indigenous Christians took their performances of the miraculous on the road—to towns and remote locations where the missionaries were not there to supervise. Indigenous biblical hermeneutics thus did not end with theories about salvation. Rather, the Bible was a manual for how God's power was to be acquired. In this way, Ghanaian Christianity of the nineteenth century constituted an ontological bridge between the traditional religious ecosystem and the wonder-working Pentecostal ecosystems of the twenty-first century.

Years before the missionaries had gained stability in Akuapem, marginalized locals—slaves, disabled people, foreigners, and, especially in the Guan communities, converts excluded from community life—had imposed upon the missionaries preexisting social categories of sanctuaries. As time went on,

Healing in Southern Ghana's Basel Mission, 1828–1918," *Journal of Religion in Africa* 39, no. 4 (2009) 429–461.

[77] Peel, *Religious Encounter*, 5.

and the converts grew in health, wealth, and social standing, a new generation came to chafe under the restrictive bonds of the sanctuaries, bonds that their parents had cherished. Indigenous Christians came to focus their spiritual attention on victory and prosperity, and no longer merely on survival. The missionaries could only sit back and watch. Having translated what they believed to be God's word, they could not control its subsequent usage.

# Conclusion

## The Cross and the Machete

No casual visitor to southeastern Ghana in the present century can fail to recognize the religious drama unfolding. Ghana's place as a center in transnational Christianity is broadly recognized, Ghanaian Christian creative and intellectual ferment plays on a global stage, and the roots are deep. More than a few distressed Western observers have surveyed the bumper stickers, posters of evangelists, radio stations, and music videos, overwhelmingly but not exclusively expressed in English, seeing the malign fingerprints of American evangelicalism. Others have seen false consciousness in the humming energy, aesthetically dominated by Pentecostal assertiveness, as if vibrant confidence—indeed, joy—in faith is evidence of internalized self-loathing. The paternalism behind such contempt needs little discussion: there is a parasitic quality to Western need for indigenous peoples to remain untainted by globalization. V. S. Naipaul wrote a few years ago with respect to Uganda: "Foreign religion, to go by the competing ecclesiastical buildings on the hilltops, was like an applied and contagious illness, curing nothing, giving no final answers, keeping everyone in a state of nerves, fighting wrong battles, narrowing the mind."[1]

Naipaul was wrong, and in several ways. With all respect due to the late cosmopolitan, whose personal journey ran from an impoverished small town in the Caribbean to a global perch in England, Naipaul did not have the graciousness to concede in others the same global aspirations. He was not the only one to dismiss, in an attitude of disgust, Ghanaian assertions of healing

---

[1] V. S. Naipaul, *The Masque of Africa: Glimpses of African Belief* (New York: Alfred A. Knopf, 2010), 7.

and power as "foreign religion" and thus inauthentic. The *Economist* routinely reports on African Christianity as relevant mainly for migrants, hucksters, or corrupt politicians.[2] Often underlying the contempt is a two-tier fallacy.

The first mistake is a conflation of Christianity with the West. Although long outdated and always ahistorical, this mistake is understandable, in part because so many Western Christians, missionaries included, made the same mistake for so many years. The notion that Christianity is Western, and the West is Christian, was never uncontested. Long before there was talk of a "post-Christian" West, socialists, enlightenment rationalists, and more than a few evangelicals insisted that West was neither essentially nor practically Christian. Nevertheless, the conflation functioned as common sense for generations of Europeans, Americans (North and South alike), and South Africans, Catholic and Protestant alike. The second mistake derives from the first: a notion that African Christianity is irreducibly colonial. African novels of the independence generation—such as Ferdinand Oyono's *Houseboy*, Mongo Beti's *King Lazarus*, Chinua Achebe's *Things Fall Apart* and others—routinely expressed some version of this belief, and the critique has some validity. Especially where indigenous Christians enjoyed the protection and patronage of colonial governments, historians are not entirely wrong in seeing Christianity as a cultural legacy of foreign rule—a religious counterpart to the English or French languages—outliving its original utility.

Correlation does not imply causation, however. If Christianity was *a priori* European, one would expect it to fade (perhaps over a century or two) with independence. The opposite happened, of course. By the 1970s, African theologians and a few missionaries had recognized that a change of world-historical proportions was underway, as Africans embraced Christianity in ways nearly unexpected only a quarter century earlier. The trend showed no sign of abating in the 1980s, as the Pentecostal variant began to outpace other expressions of Christianity. By the beginning of our century, European and North American observers began to recognize the scale of what was happening. Having not shown much previous interest in African sociological or historical scholarship, the *Economist*, the *Atlantic*, and other Western journals began taking African Christianity seriously when African leaders within Western denominations asserted their disagreements with their North American and European brethren on matters of human sexuality. Tardy in taking notice of one of the major social developments in postcolonial Africa, these publications—as well as films like *God Loves Uganda* (2013)—explained what

[2]   See, for example, "Ecstasy and Exodus," *The Economist*, January 23, 2016, https://www .economist.com/international/2016/01/23/ecstasy-and-exodus, accessed May 20, 2020.

was happening in neocolonial terms. It was obvious that Africans were falling victim to Western, and especially U.S.-American cultural warriors. With respect to Ghana, such interpretations are the intellectual equivalents to the precolonial notion of fetishism: more evidence of African childishness—what Danish Governor Ludvig Rømer had called "monkey games." Implied is that since Pentecostal Christianity came from overseas, it is therefore foreign—and therefore impure, inauthentic, and malign. Beyond the sheer paternalism of such dismissals, the conflation of ethnic purity with strength has lain behind more than a little bloodshed in Europe's own history.

### THE PENTECOSTAL IMPULSE

Ghanaian Pentecostalism's institutional ancestry is clearly international—there seems little doubt that Pentecostalism was something originally brought to Ghana from abroad. Much of this conversation took place after independence, although a few (mainly American) denominations had been active in the Gold Coast since the early twentieth century.[3] A few astute observers have recognized that institutional genealogy is not the whole story. Among the most important of these thinkers is Kwabena Asamoah-Gyadu, who has regularly interjected corrections at academic conferences at Yale, Edinburgh, and Princeton, including gracious corrections of the present author. At the ontological level, Asamoah-Gyadu argues, and with convincing evidence, Ghanaian Pentecostalism looks a lot like early twentieth-century African-Initiated Churches—especially the movements begun by William Wadé Harris and Samson Oppong.[4] Asamoah-Gyadu's approach proceeds from the argument that the *spirit* of Ghanaian Pentecostalism is homegrown, even if the *vessel* came from overseas.

This line of thought, although infrequently cited in the foregoing pages, was of great conceptual importance for the argument therein. I have repeatedly stressed the historical consensus that so-called traditional Ghanaian religions have rarely had trouble crossing ethnic lines, because Ghanaian seekers have long approached foreign religions in an attitude of experimental pragmatism. If in Pentecostal Christianity, Ghanaians have imported and reconfigured a foreign religion, they are working from the same intellectual foundations as their

[3] Paul Gifford and Adam Mohr's work is especially convincing: Gifford, *Ghana's New Christianity: Pentecostalism in a Globalizing African Economy* (Bloomington: Indiana University Press, 2004); Adam Mohr, *Enchanted Calvinism: Labor Migration, Afflicting Spirits, and Christian Therapy in the Presbyterian Church of Ghana* (Rochester, N.Y.: University of Rochester Press, 2013).

[4] J. Kwabena Asamoah-Gyadu, *Contemporary Pentecostal Christianity: Interpretations from an African Context* (Oxford: Regnum, 2013).

ancestors: foreign parentage does not mean that the indigenized offspring are also foreign. In other words, to explain the effervescence of Ghanaian Pentecostalism in the twenty-first century, one must go even farther back in time than the AICs: one can see a spiritual impulse not unlike Pentecostalism in the miracle-working indigenous evangelists of the 1850s, the victory-teaching preachers of the 1860s, and the power-confronting converts of the 1870s. As a rule, these men and women did not view themselves as agents of British imperialism.

This book has made two broad claims about Christian history in precolonial Ghana. The first is that the initial three centuries of Christian history in the Gold Coast left only the thinnest Christian legacy: by the year 1800, Christianity was only slightly less European than when the Portuguese had first arrived. The second claim, made mainly in reference to the kingdom of Akuapem, was that widespread conversion did not come with the missionaries themselves but with what followed a few decades later: a satisfactory reformulation of the missionary message—largely the work of indigenous Christians. To the extent that today's Ghanaian Pentecostalism retains the experimental and empirical foundations that have nearly always characterized indigenous religion, it is Ghanaian. Even an exotic seed can thrive in good soil.

If that is the case—if the dominant expression of Christianity in twenty-first-century Ghana builds on ancient African intellectual roots—another question arises: why did the breakthrough take so long to manifest? Samson Amaadi had brought a dead child back to life nearly a full century before Ghana won its independence from colonial rule. A Pentecostal impulse had been manifesting itself for a century before the explosion of Pentecostal churches across the coastal region in the 1960s and 1970s. Why the long delay—the interlude?

The answer must lie, at least in part, in some kind of active resistance on the part of Christianity's institutional gatekeepers. In the late nineteenth century, these were, above all, colonial authorities and ecclesiastical authorities implicated in colonialism. By conspiring to throttle indigenous Christian initiatives, colonial officials and missionary societies were able to keep Christianity foreign for generations longer than indigenous pioneers like David Asante had hoped for. It was as if, at the very moment of cross-cultural breakthrough in the late 1860s and early 1870s, the authors of indigenous Christianity had their creative license revoked as the Basel Mission seized back control. After an early moment—a few intense years—of profound and genuine encounter, the Germans retreated.

This was a tragedy. Other missionary societies in Ghana, such as the Wesleyans, who in the 1870s required indigenous agents to be fluent in English, had struggled to resist imperialist modes of thought from the beginning. Supremacy as myopic ignorance is one thing, and supremacy as personal betrayal is far more upsetting. In the following pages, I look at the Basel Mission's embrace of colonialism. Close attention to the chronology—which corresponded closely with Britain's imposition of indirect rule—suggests that missionary colonialism was an obstacle to the growth of the church in Ghana, rather than its buttress. Separating Ghanaians' early experiments with Christianity's capacity for healing and power, and the markedly similar Pentecostal expressions of the present day, then, was a colonial interlude.

In 1872, fourteen years after Kwame Akwatia's resurrection, Edward Samson Amaadi was working as a catechist in his hometown of Aburi, serving under missionary Johannes Dieterle. That year a local man sent a messenger to the mission, indicating a desire to convert to Christianity, along with both of his wives and many children. Dieterle and Samson set out and met this family in the hamlet of Nsekyifo, which he described as a two-hour hike to the west. As they sat in the shade of a grove of oil palm trees—in full view of the entire town—the man had his two wives, each with her children, sit on each side of him. He told Dieterle that one of his wives needed his help. "This woman," he said, "is frequently possessed by the fetish." During these possessions, she articulated that spirit's demand for sacrifices. But since the man had been insufficiently compliant, recently several of her children had begun to be possessed as well. Eleven of his twenty-six children had been killed, he said, and he was willing to listen to God's word, if only his wife and her children would be delivered from possession. Dieterle invited him to come to church on Sunday, but the woman's brother interjected, saying he should baptize her immediately, "because then the fetish would no longer have power over her." Dieterle replied asymmetrically:

> Baptism is no magic formula, and I cannot baptize anyone who has not first received instruction in God's word, and has recognized the depravity in his own heart, but also the love of Jesus Christ, because repentance and faith are prerequisites for entering the community of God and of the Christian church.

The man acquiesced and subsequently began meeting weekly with Samson and attending church, but in his initial response to Dieterle he made clear what these hurdles meant to him:

> He forbade all his people from invoking any fetish, or from receiving medicine from the fetish priest. Rather they would serve God, and if anyone got sick, they would come to [the missionary].[5]

---

5    Johannes Christian Dieterle, "Eine suchende Familie," *HB* 1872, 114–16.

In other words, Dieterle called this man to repent from his sin, but the man responded by agreeing to turn to Dieterle in seeking deliverance from spirit possession. The two men were talking past each other.

This was not merely a case of confusion in translation. Rather, the incident suggests an emerging dynamic of religious reconfiguration, one that recurs not only throughout missionary and ethnographic literature, but also that of contemporary West African Pentecostalisms. According to Rijk van Dijk:

> Deliverance (*ogyee*) [from demonic forces] should be preceded by "breaking" (*obubu*): the spiritual breaking of the bonds that trap people in their past, in their upbringing within the family circle where the ancestors are venerated at shrines through the practices of the shrine priests (*okomfoo*). Name giving, outdooring (a ritual for newborns), initiation, healing and all the other rituals performed at important events in an individual's life may signal the threads that bind that person to the family spirits.[6]

Pentecostal assertions of deliverance and power did not fall out of the sky, but operate in a continuum with received intellectual history.

### THE COLONIAL INTERLUDE

As they matured and grew wealthy as an organization, the Basel Mission grew more jealous for its reputation. Pietist missionaries made their peace with capitalism and imperialism, and they were beginning to see possibilities for fundraising in Britain. Gone were chaotic spiritual experimentations and healings, although this strand of Pietist experience was merely hibernating and would reawaken with the arrival, in the first decade of the twentieth century, of Azusa Street Pentecostalism.[7] In fact, retired Gold Coast Missionary Elias Schrenk, by then stationed back home in Germany, argued against the Pentecostal movement (the *Pfingstbewegung*) as *insufficiently* spiritual: miracles and ecstatic tongues were nothing special, he argued, but a normal part of Christianity in the "Heathen World," and should accordingly not be overstated, as if it were a new thing.[8]

---

    [6]   Rijk van Dijk, "Time and Transcultural Technologies of the Self in the Ghanaian Pentecostal Diaspora," in *Between Babel and Pentecost: Transnational Pentecostalism in Africa and Latin America*, ed. André Corten and Ruth Marshall-Fratani (Bloomington: Indiana University Press, 2001), 224–25.

    [7]   Asamoah-Gyadu convincingly includes Azusa Street's African-American pioneer William Seymour in discussion of founders of African-Initiated Churches: Asamoah-Gyadu, *Contemporary Pentecostal Christianity*, 179.

    [8]   Elias Schrenk, "Geleitwort," foreword to *Erfahrungen in der Pfingstbewegung*, by Heinrich Dallmeyer (Neumünster: G. Ihloff & Co., 1909).

Nevertheless, the long arc of the Basel Mission's spiritual history describes a decline from youthful comfort with states of exception to a progressive need to count, measure, and control. This decline includes a growing identification with empire. Basel contempt for British imperialism began to fade in 1869. In June of that year, the Asante army abducted Fritz and Rosa Ramseyer, along with their infant son Fritz, and Johannes Kühne, from Abetifi, and marched them through the rainforest to the royal city of Kumasi. Like Akropong, Abetifi was an out-of-the-way mountain village, chosen for its elevation and correspondingly healthy climate. Hailing from bilingual families in Neuchâtel in Francophone Switzerland, the Ramseyers had been in the Gold Coast for five years. Kühne, a shipping clerk from Bavaria, had been in Africa for a little more than two and a half years, having arrived on the first voyage of the Basel Mission Trading Company's ship, the *Palme*.[9] Together with another European, the French merchant Marie-Joseph Bonnat, they spent the next four years in the surreal situation of being simultaneously captives and honored guests at King Kofi Karikari's court. They were given an allowance, a house of their own, and some freedom to roam about in the royal city—but were forbidden from leaving, and it was made clear that their lives could be taken at the king's pleasure. They were not allowed to write home, except on a few occasions, and were made to translate diplomatic correspondence and interpret current events. The king was aware of intra-European international politics, and he regularly inquired of European visitors for details about these matters. In December 1870, for instance, the Ramseyers learned about the Franco-Prussian War, which had broken out that summer.[10]

The Ramseyers' captivity was a major factor in the Basel Mission's willingness to support British colonial aims, and the British were happy to use the missionaries' plight to whip up public support for a military adventure of little colonial importance at the time.[11] The actual invasion took place in late 1873 and concluded in January 1874. It consisted of a main body (under Garnet Wolseley) advancing from the Gold Coast protectorate in Fante country, several dozen miles west of Accra, and a flank invasion (under John Glover), approaching Kumasi from the east—a route that took him through the heart of Basel Mission territory.

[9]   Joseph Josenhans, "Die erste Fahrt der 'Palme,'" *HB* 1966, 126.
[10]   Friedrich August Ramseyer and Johannes Kühne, *Vier Jahre in Asante. Tagebücher der Missionare Ramseyer und Kühne*, 2nd ed. (Basel: Missionskomptoir, 1875), 89.
[11]   Alan Lloyd, *The Drums of Kumasi: The Story of the Ashanti Wars* (London: Longmans, 1964), esp. 54–59.

Wolseley fought his way to Kumasi, arriving several days before Glover, only to find the town deserted: in anticipation of the immediate onset of the seasonal rains, which would see the British soldiers subdued by disease, and their supply lines artillery stuck in the mud, the Asante army hid in the forest, refusing Wolseley his satisfaction. As the rains began to arrive, and Karikari continued to stall with one message after another, Wolseley realized he could not win. In frustration, he burnt the palace and retreated to the coast. In the course of these intrigues, King Karikari released the Ramseyers into British custody. Thus, on January 25, a telegram arrived at the Basel Mission home office from London, reading:

> Ramseyer wishes to telegraph hallelujah the Lord has saved us with Bonnat since Friday evening we have been with the English army please tell my brother in Neuchatel to telegraph Akropong.[12]

In contrast to Wolseley's campaign, Glover's was something of a debacle. With a small army of (Muslim) Hausas from Nigeria, Glover had crossed the Volta directly east of Akuapem and marched through Basel Mission towns in Krobo country and in Akropong itself, hoping to raise an indigenous army to join his modest force. Military supplies were stored inside the missionaries' chapel in Odumase.[13] Glover's indigenous forces melted away the closer he got to Kumasi, causing one delay after another. On the other hand, he reserved praise for the Akuapem Christians—the indigenous men associated with the Basel Mission. These men had joined the campaign for domestic reasons, in the interest of demonstrating their loyalty to the Akuapem king. But their valor on the field was a credit to the Basel Mission's home office. In his report to Parliament, Glover expressed his disgust with the Krobo and most of the other indigenous forces under his command but noted "one bright exception to this distressing report of the eastern tribes of the Protectorate."

> Two companies of Christians, one of Akropong and the other of Christiansburgh [sic], numbering about 100 each, under their two captains, accompanied by Bible Readers [Catechists?] of the Basle Mission, attended a morning and evening service of their own daily, a bell ringing them regularly to prayers. In action with the enemy at Adidume, on Christmas Day, they were

---

[12]   BMA D-10.3, 11, item 68.

[13]   Louis Edward Wilson, "The Evolution of Krobo Society: A History from C. 1400 to 1892" (PhD diss., University of California, Los Angeles, 1980), 240.

in the advance, and behaved admirably . . . they have proved themselves the only reliable men of the large native force.[14]

In two ways, the Ramseyers' liberation marked a turning point in the Basel Mission's relationship to the British. First, at the colonial level, the Basel Mission's head missionary in the Gold Coast, Johann Widmann, immediately sought out, and was awarded, a grant-in-aid for the running of the Basel Mission schools. He asked Glover and his Lieutenant Sartorius, who had passed through Akropong, to mention Basel to Wolseley, who was a celebrity in England in 1874. It paid off: on July 19, 1874, Widmann wrote to Basel Mission Inspector (home office) Josenhans, attaching a letter from the governor's office in Cape Coast, which read:

> Sir! I am directed by his Excellency, the Administrator to state, that he is happy to inform you, that the Secretary of State has been pleased to approve a grant of one hundred (£100) pounds per annum to the Basle mission for educational purposes.[15]

What did one hundred pounds mean to the mission? The organization's meticulous annual reports offer numerical context. The colonial grant-in-aid represented 7.8 percent of the African Mission's educational budget, and 1.1 percent of its overall funds. During this same year, indigenous African donations to Basel Mission churches amounted to 1913 francs, or a little less than £76.[16] Taken together, the colonial contribution was helpful, but probably not necessary for the schools' continued operation. It did, however, represent a major change in attitudes to the English. Only fifteen years earlier, in the aftermath of the Mutiny in India, the Basel Mission had emphatically refused government "grants-in-aid" for schools, in order to maintain religious autonomy.[17] Widmann interpreted the 1874 grant as "having something to do with the war."[18]

---

[14] "Report by Captain Glover, R.N., on the conduct of the Deputy Commissioners, Officers, and Men, composing the Expedition Under His Command on the Gold Coast, April 1874," p. 5 [C.-962.], British Parliamentary Papers on the Ashantee Invasion, David M. Rubenstein Rare Book & Manuscript Library.

[15] BMA D-4-26 (1874) Item I-8, July 19, 1874 (Akropong): J. G. Widmann to Basel.

[16] The African mission, which with 228,640.22 Swiss francs claimed nearly a quarter of the Basel Mission's 1874 budget (less than half of India's share; an impressively modest 1.5 percent going to organizational overhead), dedicated 31,913 francs to education, separately itemized as schools, boys' and girls' institutes, and the middle schools and preachers' seminary, and cited an exchange rate of 25.20 francs to the pound. *JB* 1874, 132.

[17] Paul Eppler, *Geschichte der Basler Mission: 1815–1899* (Basel: Verlag der Missionsbuchhandlung, 1900), 166.

[18] BMA D-4-26 (1874) Item I-8, July 19, 1874 (Akropong): J. G. Widmann to Basel.

If the actual amount of money was not great, the grant-in-aid opened the door for closer relations down the road. A bigger, but closely related, development came as the home office used the Ramseyers' story to tap into British private donor networks. And here one may see an indirect embrace of imperialism, as the Mission learned to speak in the register of civilizing mission in speaking to British audiences. As soon as the missionaries were liberated from captivity, their stories, and the lessons they had learned, departed from their control and passed into the hands of the Mission. Inspector Joseph Josenhans wasted no time putting Hermann Gundert, head of the Basel Mission's printing house in Calw near Stuttgart, to work editing Fritz Ramseyer and Kühne's diaries into a book, *Vier Jahre in Asante*, which appeared in English translation later the same year.[19] The publication of these books makes for a fascinating story in its own right, because the editorial sequence—and key discrepancies between the German and English versions—reveals clues as to the Basel Mission's evolving relations with England.

Ramseyer's and Kühne's diaries themselves are rich in detail but do not move much: long periods of everyday life unfolded between a dramatic July 1869 kidnapping from Abetifi, a forced march, nine-month-old baby in arms, into Asante, and their equally dramatic delivery into British hands in January 1874. Ramseyer wrote copiously on Asante society and court intrigues, and in the process his diary became an important source on late precolonial Kumasi.[20] The source diaries were quickly shipped to Basel, where they were copied and sent to Gundert; only the 800-page copy remains in the archives.[21] Gundert was a retired Basel missionary to south India, and a pioneering scholar of Malayalam, a language for which he played a role not unlike Johann Christaller for the

---

[19] Ramseyer and Kühne, *Vier Jahre in Asante*; Friedrich August Ramseyer and Johannes Kühne, *Four Years in Ashantee* (New York: R. Carter & Bros, 1875).

[20] Ramseyer's diary is cited by nearly every twentieth-century historian of precolonial Asante from the 1920s to the present: R. S. Rattray, *Ashanti* (Oxford: Clarendon, 1923), Polly Hill, *The Migrant Cocoa-Farmers of Southern Ghana: A Study in Rural Capitalism* (Cambridge: Cambridge University Press, 1963); Ivor Wilks, *Asante in the Nineteenth Century: The Structure and Evolution of a Political Order* (London: Cambridge University Press, 1975); Eva Meyerowitz, *The Sacred State of the Akan* (London: Faber and Faber, 1951); M. A. Kwamena-Poh, *Government and Politics in the Akuapem State, 1730–1850* Legon History Series (Evanston, Ill.: Northwestern University Press, 1973); T. C. McCaskie, *State and Society in Pre-Colonial Asante*. African Studies Series (Cambridge: Cambridge University Press, 1995).

[21] BMA D-10.7, "Ramseyer's Diary" (Archives of the Basel Mission). In his 1978 finding aid, Jenkins noted: "NB this cannot be the original of Ramseyer's diary from 1869–74 captivity, but it does include more material than the printed German version of the diary, which in turn is much more full than the English printed version." Paul Jenkins, *The Ghana Archive of the Basel Mission, 1828–1918* (Basel: 1978), 58.

Gold Coast language of Twi.[22] Combining Ramseyer's and Kühne's diaries into a single narrative, Gundert devised a means of indicating voice, so that he could organize the story in mostly chronological fashion, while consigning some of the raw ethnographic material to the book's appendices. Gundert appears to have failed to resist the temptation to intervene on occasion, as in an unsigned editorial aside to Ramseyer's description of the Adae cycle of the Asante calendar. This cycle consists of simultaneous six-day and seven-day weeks, which resolve for a forty-two-day month. Ramseyer had needed to clarify the cycle, because otherwise his chronology would not have lined up. The following is added to Ramseyer's description of the cycle: "This way of calculating time is also found among other peoples, for example in Malabar, where doctors divide the mandala into inner rings."[23] This addition could only have been made by Gundert, and indicates the way that editor was reading Ramseyer's journals: less as a record of African savagery than as a witness, however unwilling, of an elaborate civilization in the African interior. Gundert's editorial comment comparing Asante and Malabar calendars may also represent an ongoing German missionary appeal to the Germanophone academic world for recognition as ethnographic scholars.[24]

The German version went to press in Basel in 1875, but the English translation, by a "Mrs. Weitbrecht" was already underway. This was probably Mary Edwards Weitbrecht, who had spent many years in Bengal with her husband John James (also known as Johann Jakob) Weitbrecht of rural Württemberg, a Basel missionary seconded to the Church Missionary Society. Mary, who also went by Martha, returned to Europe after her husband's 1852 death, and edited and translated for various missionary societies thereafter.[25] The translated diary also included a preface, dated December 20, 1874, written by Theodor Christlieb, a theologian in Bonn, and husband of Mary Weitbrecht's daughter Emily.[26] If the edited German version had an intended audience of missionary supporters and German intellectuals, the English version aimed for melodrama: Weitbrecht omitted crucial details from the German version, consistently rendered the Asante as savage as possible, and deleted jokes and other pleasant experiences. Taken together, Weitbrecht's changes combined to make for a very different

[22] Bhadriraju Krishnamurti, *The Dravidian Languages* (New York: Cambridge University Press, 2003), 18, 37, 180.

[23] Ramseyer and Kühne, *Vier Jahre in Asante*, 246.

[24] Erika Eichholzer described Basel missionary linguistics' relationship to Swiss and German ethnography: "Missionary Linguistics on the Gold Coast," in *The Spiritual in the Secular: Missionaries and Knowledge about Africa*, ed. Patrick Harries and David Maxwell (Grand Rapids: Eerdmans, 2012), 72–99.

[25] See Mary Edwards Weitbrecht, *Memoir of the Rev. John James Weitbrecht: Comprehending a History of the Burdwan Mission* (London: James Nisbet, 1854).

[26] Ramseyer and Kühne, *Four Years in Ashantee*, x.

book. The resulting omissions reduced the Asante to unsympathetic brutes. For example, in introducing a lengthy description of the Adae festival (which concludes each forty-two-day calendrical cycle), Ramseyer said in German:

> Wir haben nun allerhand zu lernen, um in dieser wunderlichen Hauptstadt ohne Anstand durchzukommen.

This roughly translates as:

> We now have much to learn, in order to make our way without (knowledge of) etiquette in this wondrous capital city.[27]

But in Weitbrecht's translation, the comment reads:

> We had much to learn in this strange capital.[28]

This kind of selective editing continued throughout. In the German version, the Ramseyers' audience before the king on December 18, 1870, for example, was preceded by the "customary music" [*üblicher Musik*], but in the English version, the "wildest music."[29] Similarly, during an earlier feast, people fell into regaling the missionaries with morbid jokes. As they ate their meal together, "people told of all kinds of Asante pranks," Ramseyer said, "pulled upon visitors, to terrify them." One story that amused the Asante was about how an unidentified British officer had been kept waiting for his audience with the king when the locals paraded past him with a condemned and dying man, as if they had taken a wrong turn. Although such theatrics were clearly not innocent of a menace, the context in which Ramseyer heard the story—storytelling at a feast—makes clear that the perpetrators found it funny, above all else, and were happy to tell the story to the missionaries.

At the end of the evening the missionaries, together with colleagues—whom they knew by name—made their way to their house. On the way a stranger in the street "called out" [*hat nachgerufen*] to the Ramseyers: "Enemies! You are going to be killed!" Upon reaching their home, they gave their companions [*unsern Leuten*] three pots of wine.[30] The menacing catcalls were clearly unnerving, but Ramseyer made it equally clear that hospitality and multiple layers of protocol were involved: they were no more likely to be killed than

---

[27] Ramseyer and Kühne, *Vier Jahre in Asante*, 91.
[28] Ramseyer and Kühne, *Four Years in Ashantee*, 103.
[29] Ramseyer and Kühne, *Vier Jahre in Asante*, 92; Ramseyer and Kühne, *Four Years in Ashantee*, 103.
[30] Ramseyer and Kühne, *Vier Jahre in Asante*, 91.

any other official who was on the king's mind.[31] Mary Weitbrecht, on the other hand, omitted the part about Ramseyer passing out gifts of wine, and reproduced the threat in stronger language, translating *nachgerufen* as "screaming and shouting." Weitbrecht furthermore added a sentence entirely absent in the German: the episode "may be taken as a sample of the cruel tastes of this savage people."[32] Ramseyer had said no such thing.

Taken together, the discrepancies in the translation suggest the Basel Mission had a distinct purpose in choosing to publish the book in English. The German account was meant to conform to the existing genre of Pietist missionary narratives, which were a mixture of devotional encouragement and awakening of God's call to missions among the upcoming generation. The English version, by contrast, was intended to position the mission for inclusion in Britain's colonial program and for fundraising.

Additionally, there are two sections in the English text that do not appear in the German version: the preface, by Theodor Christlieb, and Appendix V, "A word on the politics of the colonial government in the year 1872." The latter consisted of a rebuttal to the English press, two of whose reporters had wondered if their own government had baited King Kofi Karikari to war in a prisoner exchange involving the return to Kumasi of a particularly hotheaded Asante general named Akjampong. In this man, the *Illustrated London News* wrote in 1874,

> They were sending back to Kari-Kari's council the greatest intriguer and the chief of the war officers, which just signified throwing a spark among a heap of shavings. He came to Coomassie at the great death festivities and decided for war.[33]

To the contrary, protested the publishers of the English translation of Ramseyer's journals,

> war was decided upon before Akjampong's arrival in Coomassie. But thus much [sic] is clear from these facts, that *the British Government did not provoke the Ashantee war.*[34]

These italicized words conclude the translated book, and the message is clear: the British had been just in invading Asante. Theodor Christlieb's

---

[31]  McCaskie insists that state violence was highly centralized and formalized; from the middle of the nineteenth century, an execution could only be ordered by the king himself. McCaskie, *State and Society, 201.*

[32]  Ramseyer and Kühne, *Four Years in Ashantee,* 102.

[33]  Illustrated London News, *From Cape Coast to Coomassie: An Illustrated Narrative of the Ashantee War* (1874).

[34]  Ramseyer and Kühne, *Four Years in Ashantee,* 320. Italics original.

preface went further: the military conquest of Asante needed to be followed up by a "holy war," consisting of a second invasion of Asante—this time by missionaries. But not just any missionaries: Christlieb offered Ramseyer's journals to the British public as evidence that the Basel Mission—conflated with "Germany"—was uniquely positioned to initiate this holy war, if only "English liberality" might be relied upon for funding.

> Germany is ready to send into the field the needful, well-qualified soldiers, in the shape of thoroughly educated, persevering, hard-working, frugal missionaries—some of whom have . . . already been dispatched. The indispensable fund for carrying on this holy war amounts to £7,000 for starting, and £700 annually. Is it asking too much if we look for assistance in raising these sums to English liberality?[35]

Certainly, the Basel Mission—which had always dreamed of opening a mission to Asante—had a competitive motivation: they wanted to get to Kumasi before the Wesleyans. However, such an expensive undertaking could only be possible with British donations. *Four Years in Ashantee* was more than a fundraiser for an army of holy warrior missionaries. It was also an articulation of a new kind of thinking—new, that is, to the Basel Mission, who only nine years earlier had described the British barracks at Fort Christiansborg as "Satan's barracks."[36] To its German-speaking donor base, the Basel Mission spoke of salvation from heathenism and forgiveness of sin. But in addressing prospective English subscribers, the Mission offered cold political calculations, a cultural conquest in the name of civilization:

> Assuredly it must be of the greatest importance for the English protectorate . . . even from a merely political point of view to change the kingdom of Ashantee from a wily and cruel enemy, into a peaceful and civilised neighbour.[37]

The Basel Mission used the publication of Ramseyer's journals to assist a concerted fundraising effort underway since shortly after the war. Inspector Josenhans deputed Elias Schrenk, who had recently returned after thirteen years in the Gold Coast, on a speaking tour of England. Schrenk, who in 1861 had accused the English of "blasphem[ing] His name among the heathens" now spent the better part of four years asking them for money and seems to have brought in substantially more money than

[35] Ramseyer and Kühne, *Four Years in Ashantee*, ix.
[36] Joseph Josenhans, "Das Fort von Christiansborg," *HB* 1866, 117.
[37] Ramseyer and Kühne, *Four Years in Ashantee*, ix.

did Widmann's modest grant-in-aid. In one night in Manchester in March 1875, Schrenk raised pledges worth over £600 at an event hosted by the "Ashanti Mission Fund" society; £450 of that amount came from James Boyd Jr.[38] As a wealthy, second-generation textiles industrialist at James Boyd & Sons, this was a man who spun money from cotton yarn machinery lubricated with palm oil, most of which in the 1870s came from West Africa.[39] An interruption to the Gold Coast palm oil trade could shutter Boyd's mill, along with those of many other industrialists in Manchester, Leeds, and elsewhere. If these quirky Germans could deliver a "civilised neighbour," that alone would be worth a good deal more than £450. Indeed, a read of Schrenk's expense reports suggest that he spent most of his time in the northern industrial belt.[40]

To conclude: as late as 1866, the Basel Missionaries in the Gold Coast considered the British Empire to be unchristian, and its coastal forts to be satanic. After three Basel Missionaries were kidnapped by an African king, the mission used the dramatic story to solicit, first, British military assistance in the rescue of their missionaries, and second, thousands of pounds of donations from British private citizens. Having grown dependent on money from an empire the Mission had only a half decade earlier considered to be diabolical, the Basel Mission learned to speak in the register of civilizing missions. Genuine and sustained cross-cultural encounter had collapsed into paternalistic supremacy.

The logic of civilizing mission required its own failure, because missionary tenure in the field could not be justified as long as those to be civilized remained incomplete. The practical outcome, here as elsewhere in Africa, was that for the next generation, the Basel Mission exerted an increasingly patriarchal structure, approaching domination, on its congregations—a paternalism that continued until the First World War, when the missionaries were deported by Britain.[41]

---

[38] BMA D-10.3,12 Folder "Asante Mission 1872–8," item 32: March 16, 1875, James Boyd to Joseph Josenhans.

[39] K. G. Berger and S. M. Martin, "Palm Oil," in *Cambridge World History of Food*, ed. Kenneth Kiple and Kriemhild Coneè Ornelas (Cambridge: Cambridge University Press, 2000), 404; S. O. Aghalino, "British Colonial Policies and the Oil Palm Industry in the Niger Delta Region of Nigeria, 1900–1960," *African Studies Monographs* 21, no. 1 (2000).

[40] BMA D-10.3,12 Folder "Asante Mission 1872–8."

[41] On the Basel Mission's fate in the war, see Elizabeth Wrangham, *Ghana during the First World War: The Colonial Administration of Sir Hugh Clifford* (Durham, N.C.: Carolina Academic Press, 2013), 180–81.

## TRANSCENDING COLONIALISM

Ghanaian biblical hermeneutics, which would come to a full flowering only in the late twentieth century, began early on, long before the colonial interlude, as soon as a quorum of indigenous clergy was equipped, and willing, to talk back to the missionaries. In his study of Pentecostalism in Ghana, Paul Gifford emphasized the ways prosperity preachers in twenty-first-century Accra have seen it as part of their responsibility to correct missionary (including Presbyterian, the indigenous successor church to the Basel Mission) mistakes, as these preachers understand it, in biblical hermeneutics.[42] Gifford quotes prominent Pentecostal pastor Nicholas Duncan-Williams:

> "The traditional and orthodox churches we grew up in held many views which were diametrically opposed to God's word. . . . They preach a doctrine which says in essence—poverty promotes humility. But you all know this is not true. . . . The missionaries erred tragically by not teaching the Africans God's Word and laws regarding sowing and reaping. Thank God he has called us to declare his full counsel to our generation. I preach and teach prosperity like any other doctrine of the Bible."[43]

Asamoah-Gyadu credits some of this change to the forced repatriation of hundreds of thousands of Ghanaian citizens from Nigeria in 1983—people who had previously fled military government in Ghana, and who now brought prosperity-gospel Pentecostalism home; he adds that "the militaristic idiom of the two revolutionary eras in Ghana became part of the hermeneutic of contemporary Pentecostalism."[44] Nevertheless, the Pentecostal insistence that sickness, poverty, disunity, and corruption may be overcome by spiritual power is not new. Something very similar was being expressed nearly two centuries ago, when indigenous people first identified Christian church buildings as sanctuary shrines and missionaries as shrine priests. It was there as Christian congregations, on their knees in prayer, called upon the Lord of Heaven's Armies to drive away the encroaching forces of Asante, and it was there when Nathanael Asare demonstratively ate fish from a sacred river. There is a patricidal quality to the Pentecostal insistence that power and healing had never been seen in Ghana before our day and age. Conversely, as long as observers persist in viewing contemporary West African Pentecostalism as an exotic species, they will continue to be baffled by its success, but then again: the foolishness of God is wiser than human wisdom, and the weakness of God is stronger than human strength.[45]

[42] Paul Gifford, *Ghana's New Christianity*, 46–47.
[43] Paul Gifford, *Ghana's New Christianity*, 46.
[44] Asamoah-Gyadu, *Contemporary Pentecostal Christianity*, 64.
[45] 1 Cor 1:25.

## The Cross and the Machete

By the end of the twentieth century, Ɔkuapemhene (king of Akuapem) Addo Dankwa III was a Christian and member of a Basel Mission-descended church—but he still had to contend with insurrections on the part of the exact same villages as his nineteenth-century namesake Addo Dankwa I. He furthermore addressed these insurrections by way of libations to the ancestors.[46] After nearly two hundred years of Christian history in Akuapem, many (but not all) of the old gods have, if not disappeared, faded into the background. The Danish, the Asante, and the British had all come and gone, the missionaries themselves had departed, and the autonomous Presbyterian Church of Ghana that they left behind was now joined in the capital city of Akropong by a raucous market of Christian churches of several denominations—but ancestral veneration continued unbroken.

Although the situation is anything but settled among Ghanaian Christians, the categories by which these questions are debated differ markedly from the notions of the Basel Missionaries in the nineteenth and early twentieth centuries. As a theology student explained to me with respect to possession by ancestral spirits, "the question is not whether it is happening, but whether it should be happening." In the last half century, as increasing numbers of Christians belonging to churches originating in Europe, including not a few members of the clergy, have made their peace with ancestor veneration (while generally remaining aloof from worship of shrine spirits), further innovations have emerged. Among these are Odwira-week memorial services for the dead among the Presbyterians and liturgical experimentations involving stools, begun in the 1970s by the remarkable Peter Sarpong, Roman Catholic priest (and later archbishop) in Kumasi.[47] In 2014 Ernestina Afriyie, then a teacher at the Akrofi-Christaller Institute in Akropong, a theological and missiological graduate school housed in the same buildings as the Basel Mission's old seminary, did something no one had ever before done as an official representative of a Christian institution: she blessed the king in the formal protocol ritual of Odwira week. Standing before the king's "soul," a youth who himself stood in front of the king, Afriyie pronounced a Christian blessing on the Ɔkuapemhene, then took a mouthful of palm wine, which she blew onto the arms of the youth who then turned to face the king. The latter touched the drops, thus receiving the blessing.[48]

---

[46] Kwame Bediako, *Christianity in Africa: The Renewal of a Non-Western Religion* (Maryknoll, N.Y.: Orbis, 1996), 211ff.

[47] Peter Sarpong, *The Sacred Stools of the Akan* (Tema, Accra: Ghana Pub. Corp., 1971).

[48] Ernestina Afriyie, interview with author, Akropong-Akuapem, October 25, 2015.

The next year, the royal stool was empty: King Addo Dankwa III was dead after forty years in office. As a devout Christian, Addo Dankwa III had always sought to thread the needle of conflicting religious demands, but the delicate balance, which he worked out and which culminated in official church participation in the 2014 rituals, needed revision in his absence. At 2015's Odwira, the so-called traditional spiritual agenda took precedence over the Christian one, as hereditary office holders (ritual guards, musicians, and heads of clans) set about converting the late king into an ancestor. Tension was high in Akropong. Palace elders proclaimed a strict lights-out curfew for nine o'clock at night, so that the ancestors might pass through the town unmolested. Ghanaian state authorities, responding to this "traditional" request, prevailed upon the power company to shut off electricity, and the entire ridge was plunged into darkness.

Over the years, Akropong's Odwira has become one of Ghana's biggest festivals, with hordes of revelers coming up from Accra, many of whom had no connection to the clans at the heart of the events. Makeshift nightclubs and discos sprang up overnight in the narrow strips between the road and the stores; brass bands played Ghanaian highlife or its more recent "hiplife" development, along with thundering dancehall music from Nigeria, Jamaica, England, and America. All week, the noise was incredible—an arms race of loudspeakers—and not the kind of reception appropriate for ancestors.

Protocol was no laughing matter: earlier that week in the palace, on the night in which the Odwira talisman itself appeared (carried by a possessed youth and his retinue), I saw one young showoff add hip-hop moves to an already-acrobatic ritual dance. He did not impress: the executioners tackled him and hauled him away. I was later told they would probably scare him out of his wits and send him home. But a few days later, on the prescribed night in which the late king would be summoned, the stakes were higher. The power grid went down, and the Akrofi-Christaller Institute's large generators remained silent: "we honor the law of the land," a student explained to me as we sat in darkness in the dormitory lounge. The executioners roamed about the town to enforce the darkness, firing their shotguns at houses where a flashlight or candle could be seen through the windows. Around ten, the executioners struck the hostel's gate with drawn machetes, calling out "Yɛn hyia," "do not let us meet." The threat was serious: a violating local might be knifed or named in a curse articulated before the ancestors; a stranger (and there were plenty, some of them staggeringly drunk young men from Accra, in town for the next day's parties) might simply disappear, as had allegedly happened a few years earlier.[49]

---

[49] Joel Dah, interview with author, Akropong-Akuapem, October 22, 2015.

Akropong: Odwira 2015 and the empty stool. Photo by author.

Across the street, another foolhardy youth tried to drive off in his car, and the executioners opened fire and shot the car to pieces. Darkness was important: the king's death represented a tear in the curtain separating the living from the dead. That night represented, in concrete fashion, a state of exception, with, in Walter Benjamin's terms, the separation of lawmaking and law-preserving violence suspended; violence and law approaching total overlap.[50] Agamben called this moment the "threshold," a very dangerous node of responsibility.[51] The late king embodied the authority of the ancestors, in whose name he held the kingdom together, and the night of his ritual passage to the ranks of ancestry may have demonstrated the realistic limits to Christian ability to engage with Odwira.

In an off-limits grove in the forest, the king's white stool was blackened and washed with sacrificial blood. Many years ago, this blood was that of a slave (as appears to have been the fate of the unfortunate Yaa in 1866). These days, sheep's blood was normally used. An old man at the palace told Ernest Nyarko, a theology student writing on Akan sexual ethics, and who spent much of the week kindly explaining things to me, that since this king had spent forty years on the throne, human blood was needed and had been purchased for the

[50] Walter Benjamin, "Critique of Violence," in *Walter Benjamin: Selected Writings*, ed. Marcus Bullock and Michael Jennings (Cambridge, Mass.: Belknap Press of Harvard University Press, 1996).
[51] Agamben, *Homo Sacer*, 66.

Royal Executioners' House, Akropong. Note the liquor bottles (for libations) embedded into the frame. Photo by author, 2019.

purpose. When Nyarko asked the old man why human blood was more efficacious than sheep's blood, the elder turned to the Christian Bible: "Jesus was the king of kings, and when he died, they sent two thieves with him."[52] This reference to the two criminals crucified alongside Jesus constituted an inversion of the biblical story: what to the Romans was a scandal, a ritual shaming—and not at all an honoring—of a man who had identified himself as *I am*, this Ghanaian elder was reconfiguring as a ritual killing to honor the king.[53] Indeed, the logic in the old man's read on Scripture represented a full indigenization of the Christian message, along the lines of so many other spiritual infusions over the centuries. Perhaps the rupture was healed, or was on its way.

In 1990's *Paths in the Rainforest*, Jan Vansina sought to explain the endurance, against continual ruptures, of a social order, a "tradition," in the rainforests of the Congo Basin. Over many centuries, economic and ecological changes challenged the tradition's capacity to absorb innovation. But in response to each external challenge, the tradition proved elastic enough to

[52] Ernest Nyarko, interview with author, Akropong-Akuapem, October 23, 2015.

[53] Joel B. Green and Mark D. Baker, *Recovering the Scandal of the Cross: Atonement in New Testament & Contemporary Contexts* (Downers Grove, Ill.: InterVarsity Press, 2000).

generate solutions from within. This resilience was Vansina's main scholarly point; it also established his basis for understanding the colonial- and missionary-destruction of the system in the Congo's bloody four decades following incorporation as a Belgian colony. The occupiers came not just with guns, but also with Bibles, and these two amounted to a simultaneous assault. While colonial conquest presented the greatest military threat that equatorial Africa had ever encountered, missionaries were simultaneously undermining the legitimacy of the cognitive reality. It is important to observe that on this point, after over two hundred pages of scholarly caution, Vansina transitions to a register of moral judgment. The destruction of the equatorial tradition amounted to an incalculable loss for all of humanity: the precolonial tradition's remarkable achievement at accommodating disasters such as the slave trade "emphasizes that the ability to refuse centralization while maintaining the necessary cohesion among a myriad of autonomous units has been the most original contribution of western Bantu tradition to the institutional history of the world."[54] However, Vansina was wrong to insist on the categorical foreignness of Christianity in the same book in which he had lovingly detailed equatorial Africans' capacity to absorb new ideas.

Ghana is not Congo, but Vansina's argument about the latter offers a way to think about the former. To the degree that men and women of the precolonial and colonial Gold Coast confronted terrible ruptures, whether in their own persons or in the context of a broader societal collapse, their first and most trusted response was to draw on time-tested means of rebalancing and restoring right relations in the seen and unseen worlds alike. They did so in the nineteenth century by fundamentally reconfiguring a foreign god—the Christian Triune God—partially to replace, and partially to redefine, preexisting autochthonous gods. This acquisitive and pragmatic approach to religious change speaks to the power of West African moral imagination.

Or does it? Is it possible that the old primal vision, which prioritized the incorporation of outsiders, and which, nevertheless, excluded many people, was too small? These things are not static, and formerly hospitable people can close their doors to their neighbors. Germany's moral imagination, after all, was a good deal smaller in 1940 than in 1930. To the extent that German ethnic chauvinists, like novelist Gustav Frenssen, a Lutheran pastor turned apostate, flirted with ancient German heathenism, they were abstracting their own human ancestors into an ecological way of thinking, according to which the living could be proud of their racial forebears, who were more or less identical

---

[54] Jan Vansina, *Paths in the Rainforests: Toward a History of Political Tradition in Equatorial Africa* (Madison: University of Wisconsin Press, 1990), 237.

with the soil, but owed them nothing in return.[55] In any case, Nazism had its own patricidal qualities. In 1925, Gustav Neckel asserted that while all religions reflect a common belief in higher powers, "oriental religions" were characterized by "subordinating, deprecating, quivering prostration," in contrast to which Germanic peoples ["Germannen"] cultivated "proud independence."[56]

Post–World War I Basel Missionaries indulged in a bit of patricide as well and were the better off for it. During the four decades prior to the war, the missionaries had compromised themselves with European imperialist Christianity. But these fathers proved themselves unworthy as ancestors, and German theology of the post–World War I years, from Karl Barth to Emil Brunner, was written in the context of a people who had rejected their own fathers. German missiology of the 1920s cannot be understood in any other way than as an attempt to find a foundation for mission in the sudden collapse of an ecclesiology that had served for centuries, and which had secured a peace after confessional conflicts and religious wars in the seventeenth century.[57] In 1928, the organization's new head, Karl Hartenstein—a pastor who had served in an artillery unit on the western front—began comparing contemporary German Christianity ("Heathen-Christians," he called his countrymen, "Heidenchristen") to Hinduism in India. Germans were every bit as needy as those on the other side of the world.

> In guilt and under judgment, we stand in solidarity with all the peoples [*Völker*] among whom we are allowed to work. Standing under the same judgment, they are existentially our neighbors. Before this God all cultural and ecclesiastical barriers are torn down, and we together wait for the new world. Only with this understanding of God and world is real, embracing community possible.[58]

Here in somewhat violent language was the Basel Mission learning to walk away from Christian nationalism. Chronology is important in understanding Hartenstein's intellectual development, because this statement was made after the missionaries' return to the Gold Coast, but before his own experiences there. As of 1928 he was prepared to kill his fathers, but had yet to adopt new ones. However, Hartenstein developed this theological beginning into a pragmatic approach: the missionary "enters these people," he continued, "without

[55] Gustav Frenssen, *Der Glaube der Nordmark* (Stuttgart: G. Truckenmüller, 1936).

[56] Gustav Neckel, *Altgermanische Kultur* (Leipzig: Quelle & Meyer, 1925), 85–86.

[57] John G. Flett, *The Witness of God: The Trinity, Missio Dei, Karl Barth, and the Nature of Christian Community* (Grand Rapids: Eerdmans, 2010).

[58] Karl Hartenstein, *Was hat die Theologie Karl Barths der Mission zu sagen?* (Munich: Kaiser Verlag, 1928), 13–14.

any superiority, in full humility, and with a new goal: the kingdom of God (and not of humanity)." While granting the good intentions of humanitarianism, including much of his mission's educational and economic development projects done during the previous century, Hartenstein firmly and categorically rejected civilizing missions:

> A mission to uplift, however benign, is exclusionary. There will always be some left behind. But the kingdom of God embraces the excluded and the miserable but is not interested in preserving itself. . . . The church is ready to give itself away, to retreat from power and influence. . . . The church must engage in perpetual, fruitful repentance in response to God's revelation of our equality in sin and guilt. For that reason, it is so important that the Church walk the way of the cross.[59]

In practical terms, this meant speaking "substantially more humbly and soberly about our own 'Heathen-Christian' churches." Indeed, it meant viewing the churches everywhere as in need of God's renewal. However, a deeper logic was involved: if the Christian message was alien by its very nature, then there was no such thing as a Christian nation. Accordingly, Germany was every bit the mission field that Africa was. To this eccentric spatial vision, Hartenstein added the element of motion: "give itself away," "retreat," and "perpetual turning." The church was characterized by response, not essence, not by where it was but by where it was going. Hartenstein was thus resolving the German postcolonial crisis by removing from the German church any sense of stability. This was a necessary step, but it was incomplete, because sober ownership of guilt, in the absence of input and fellowship with the victims, can easily collapse into navel-gazing.

Hartenstein was missing half the equation, and the most important half at that: the part about belonging, about allowing oneself to be incorporated into another's family. He himself would visit the Gold Coast two years later, and there he learned what was missing. In 1931 Hartenstein helped dedicate a monument to Samuel Otu in Tekyiman north of Kumasi. Upon his return home, Hartenstein wrote that Germans who had embraced the wrong kinds of fathers (he meant the German empire, but also all the churches who had aligned themselves with nationalism) needed to adopt new fathers. He mentioned a few Ghanaians by name, including Otu.[60] In 1935 Hartenstein

---

[59] Hartenstein, *Was hat die Theologie*, 24–25.
[60] Karl Hartenstein, *Anibue: die "Neue Zeit" auf der Goldküste und unsere Missionsaufgabe* (Stuttgart: Evangelische Missionsverlag, 1932).

published a biography of William Wadé Harris, insisting that Harris' message extended to Germans.[61]

Adopting new fathers was a radical break for the Basel Mission, and it would not have been possible without the trauma of deportation and national humiliation. In that regard, Hartenstein was behaving very much like his compatriots at home, whose spiritual experimentations extended in every direction.[62] Not all German missionaries were behaving this way. Many had nursed their wounds on a dangerous mixture of self-expiation and civilizing mission. Nor was the Basel Mission exempt: some former missionaries became enthusiastic Nazis, including Waldemar Bonsels, beloved children's author (*Maya the Bee*), formerly in Basel Mission service in India. However, if humiliation may have been a necessary condition for so profound a rethinking, it was not, in itself, sufficient. Intellectual change consequent to humiliation is pluripotent.

Shamed people can become generous and compassionate, or they can turn into highly motivated monsters, which is what in fact happened in much of Germany in the 1930s and early 1940s. It all depends on how the humiliation is healed. What the Basel Mission needed was a new encounter with its own message, and that is what happened when the missionaries returned to the Gold Coast, humiliated but finally able to receive Ghanaian Christian leadership. Germany, as a heathen-Christian nation, needed to hear the message in the same way as Africa. More to the point, Germany needed to hear the message *from* Africans. "The day is long gone," Hartenstein wrote several years earlier in 1931 from Accra,

> In which we, in the confidence of our superior culture, our religion, and our knowledge, could go to Africa. The day is gone, in which we could stand among the 'heathens' as their leaders and teachers. Now is a new time, a time to for the missionary to recognize how entangled he is in the spirit of European heathenism, and how . . . spiritually impoverished he is.[63]

Two fundamental assumptions underlie this statement. First, Germany was a mission field. Second and more important, German believers had more in common with African Christians than with their unbelieving countrymen.

---

[61] Karl Hartenstein, "William Wadé Harris, ein schwarzer Prophet," in *Das Buch der deutschen Weltmission*, ed. Julius Richter (Gotha: L. Klotz, 1935), 284–86.

[62] Benjamin Lazier, *God Interrupted: Heresy and the European Imagination between the World Wars* (Princeton: Princeton University Press, 2008).

[63] Hartenstein, *Anibue*, 121.

Hartenstein died young in 1952, but his work was discovered a few years later by one of Barth's final students at the University of Basel: David Jacobus Bosch of South Africa, whose doctorate was supervised by Oscar Cullmann. Bosch, in turn, needed several more years to understand the implications of what he was discovering about the German non-national missiology, eventually calling it a "paradigm-shift" and giving it a name: "post-modern," although *post-imperial* might have been a more accurate term, given what Bosch was trying to do: situate mission at the center of Christian social relations.[64] It is important to observe that Bosch's late-twentieth-century work, which was written against the backdrop of a crumbling apartheid theology, drew substantially on German post-imperial missiology, including Hartenstein.[65]

In 1999, when I began working as an editor in the mission department at InterVarsity Christian Fellowship/USA, most North American missiologists considered Bosch's 1991 magnum opus to be the most important theoretical work in decades. Over the next ten years, I was privileged to meet and work alongside some of the finest Asian, African, and Latin American missiologists. And for that reason, in 2002, when Philip Jenkins published *The Next Christendom*, putting Christian numeric growth in the non-Western world on the radar screen of a general American public to whom the story was unknown and unexpected, I was able to sit in on heated exchanges.[66] Several people in our small but globally active network, especially Africans and South Asians, took great umbrage at Jenkins' analysis, and on one particular point: his use of the word "Christendom" to describe indigenous churches beyond the West. Some of these churches had a valid point: as tiny religious minorities, quite often living under openly hostile local governments, they were not infrequently subject to economic exclusion, extrajudicial violence, forced marriages into Muslim or Hindu communities, and worse. Several of these people communicated to us, as the only Americans they knew, and thus as stand-ins for all of their frustrated dealings with our compatriots, intense distaste at being identified with "Christendom."

---

[64]  David Jacobus Bosch, *Transforming Mission: Paradigm Shifts in Theology of Mission* (Maryknoll, N.Y.: Orbis, 1991). On the problem of Bosch's post-modern nomenclature, see Kirsteen Kim, "Post-Modern Mission," *International Review of Mission* 89, no. 353 (2000).

[65]  Charles Villa-Vicencio, *On Reading Karl Barth in South Africa* (Grand Rapids: Eerdmans, 1988).

[66]  Philip Jenkins, *The Next Christendom: The Coming of Global Christianity* (Oxford: Oxford University Press, 2002).

Jenkins received the pushback graciously, which he incorporated into an October 2002 cover article in the *Atlantic Monthly* (in which he changed his term to *The Next Christianity*). But today I am less convinced of Jenkins' mistake: some of the old Christendom's bad habits have indeed appeared in Ghana, and Nigeria, and elsewhere, as formerly marginalized churches have reached the center of their respective communities, and have taken steps to protect their gains. A Christianity capable of imagining the son of *Onyankopɔn* as an ancestor will be equally capable of spectacular feats of exclusion. In 2016 on its municipal website, the town of Abokobi at the foot of the Akuapem hills included this note:

> All citizens of Abokobi are to a large extent Christians. However, there are inhabitants who are non-Christians and therefore have no right to Abokobi citizenship. Presbyterianism is the only religious practice and activity that is allowed to operate on Abokobi land.[67]

Abokobi is, to be fair, a special case: founded as a Christian town in 1854 after the British bombardment of the Basel Mission's station in Osu by Accra. But the latent potential for violence carried in this statement is chilling.

In his characteristically overwrought travelogue on African religion, V. S. Naipaul paid a visit to a sacred grove in Uganda, where he observed the grove's caretakers' efforts at honoring the ancestors. Key to that effort was the insistence that their shrine remain pure:

> There was a stand of young eucalyptus on that slope. They had been planted ten years before, but it was now accepted that they were a mistake (perhaps because they were foreign), and there was a plan to have them replaced by purely local trees. The topmost line of eucalyptus had been hacked down with a machete, leaving small stumps.[68]

What was found to be impure and foreign had been hacked down with machetes: this was not mere supporting detail. Naipaul saw this Ugandan attempt at restoring ancestor worship as something very dark and ominous. Insistence on purity, religious or otherwise, is rarely far from the appearance of machetes. This is a truth extending beyond Uganda, beyond Germany, Ghana, Asia, the Americas, and elsewhere to the human condition itself: We hate our neighbors, and this hatred is our natural human

---

[67] http://abokobipresby.org/index-3.html, accessed June 28, 2016. As of March 2020, the website is unavailable. Archive.org holds a preserved version from March 4, 2016: https://web.archive.org/web/20160402203611/http://abokobipresby.org/index-3.html.

[68] Naipaul, *The Masque of Africa, 28.*

condition. We cannot live with one another, but history has thrown us together. Our options are exactly two: either we kill one another in honor of our jealous ancestors, or at the risk of their wrath, we dare to become someone else's inheritance.

# Glossary

The following represents two different tasks. On the one hand, it is a simple set of definitions of technical words in various languages. On the other hand, several of these words—such as *heathens*—are weighted down with quite a bit of semantic baggage, necessitating historical nuance to my definitions. Thus, I translate Twi words not according to today's usage, but according to Christaller's dictionary of 1881, and by reference to his Bible, published in stages over the preceding two decades.

Unless otherwise indicated, the entry refers to a word in the Twi language. In Twi, number is usually indicated by prefix and authors of most dictionaries, beginning with Johannes Christaller, have alphabetized words by the first consonant of the root. Thus *afɔre* (sacrifices) appears below under the letter F. Hebrew and Greek entries are alphabetized according to standard romanization.

Bible references in Twi refer to the Christaller/Asante/Opoku translation; some of these words are quite loaded with meaning and have been revised in subsequent translations.[1] Whenever possible, page number references to Christaller's 1881 dictionary are given.[2] While this is no longer the best dictionary, it is quite good and captures language usage close in time to the events

---

[1] J. G. Christaller, *Anyamesɛm anase Kyerɛw Kronkron apãm-dedaw nè apãm-foforo nsɛm wɔ twi kasa mu. The Holy Bible translated from the original tongues into the Tshi-Chwee-language, spoken by the tribes of Akuapem, Akem, Asante, Fante, etc., Gold Coast . . . by J.G. Christaller* (Basel: B. & F.B.S., 1871).

[2] J. G. Christaller, *Dictionary of the Asante and Fante Language Called Tshi (Twi)* (Basel: Printed for the Basel Evangelical Missionary Society, 1881).

at the heart of the present study—including the translation of the Bible by a team led by Christaller himself. When applicable, references to Strong's lexical numbering system are given.[3]

∽

**Alétheia**. Greek: ἀλήθεια. Strong's G225. Truth, lit. un-concealing. Rendered in the Twi Bible as *nokware*. In the Twi Bible, Jesus self-identifies as "nokware" in a complicated formulation. Drawing on philosopher Kwasi Wiredu, McCaskie contrasts *nokware* with *aléthia*, arguing that the former was too wrapped up with duty (social, familial, and other) to develop a speculative tradition that McCaskie viewed as indispensable for dissent; as monopolist of truth, the Asante court was threatened by the introduction of an alternate *nokware* in the form of the Bible.[4]

**bɔne**. Christaller 37. Evil, sin, wickedness. Used in the Twi Bible for multiple words: ἁμαρτία (*hamartia*) and κακός (*kakos*) (Greek) and עָוֹן (*avon*) (Hebrew, Strong's H5771), which is closer to bɔne than the Greek words. The Hebrew notion includes both the sin itself and the punishment, while *hamartia* does not. *Bɔne* may reside in families—see *abusuabɔne*: "a sin hereditary in a family" (Christaller 54).

**ɔbosom**, pl. abosom. Gods, spirits. In contrast with *Onyankopɔn*, the *abosom* were created. In European parlance of the nineteenth century, these deities were called *fetishes*, thus confusing the sentient creature with the amulets used to invoke it. Christaller 42: "tutelar or guardian spirit of a town or family; imaginary spirits, subordinate to God, worshipped or consulted by the negroes, generally called fetishes by the Europeans, though the term fetish would better be restricted to *asuman*, charm, or, to avoid confusion, not be used at all."

**abusua**. Matriclan or more generally, family (especially on the mother's side). Despite the focus on ancestry in family membership, it was possible, by means of ancestral rituals, for an outsider to join an *abusua*. Christaller 54.

**odum**. tree: *chlorophora excelsa*. Often the residence of a spirit. Christaller 98.

**afɔre**. offering, sacrifice (pl. id.). Christaller 133.

---

[3]  James Strong, *The Exhaustive Concordance of the Bible: showing every word of the text of the common English version of the canonical books . . .* (London: Hodder and Stoughton, 1894).

[4]  T. C. McCaskie, *State and Society in Pre-Colonial Asante*, African Studies Series (Cambridge: Cambridge University Press, 1995), 252.

**fetish**. English by way of Portuguese: *feitiço*. This is a complicated and generally unhelpful word and is used here as sparingly as possible, in the recognition that it was in common usage among nineteenth-century Christians in the Gold Coast.

**Gemeinde**. German: congregation, community. In German-speaking Europe, may refer to the local government—akin to the parish. In Ghana, the Basel missionaries restricted the use of the term to the members of the church, including applicants. Smaller congregations were called "outer congregations" (*Außergemeinden*) belonging to a nearby core congregation.

**Gemeindeordnung**. German. Published set of rules regulating communal life (i.e., the indigenous Salem communities, which initially emerged in the 1850s around the missionary chapels).

**hamartia**. Greek: ἁμαρτία, sin. There was no indigenous equivalent in Twi, and thus the missionaries used the word *bɔne*, which spoke of external evil. The missionary message that God, through Jesus, offered forgiveness of sin (*bɔnefafiri*) thus did not communicate: few people felt the need for forgiveness of *bɔne*, but nearly everyone desired protection from and power over the same. One of the major distinctives between indigenous and German biblical hermeneutics centered on this difference. See chapter 6.

**Heiden**. German: heathens. Roughly equivalent to "pagan" in nineteenth-century Basel Mission parlance. From ca. 1840 on, when the Basel Mission gave up on a foray to the pagans and Muslims of the Russian and Persian Caucasus, Muslims were not considered *Heiden*. In the Gold Coast, the Basel Mission initially spoke of Christians and Heathens with little pejorative intent, although this would change by the late century, as the Basel Mission began appropriating British logic of civilization. The word's roots are very old and originally spoke of the land (and thus of indigenous religion) but have long indicated non-Christian.[5] Luther translated "gentiles" (*goyim*) as *Heiden*. The Basel Mission's donor newsletter was the *Heidenbote*, the "Heathen Messenger."

**Heimat**. German: home, homeland; indicates autochthony, always with a spatial component; in Basel Mission annual reports, missionaries' *Heimat* was indicated as the German or Swiss village of birth. According to the logic

---

[5]  Hans-Werner Gensichen, "Heidentum I," in *Theologische Realenzyklopädie*, ed. Gerhard Krause and Gerhard Müller (Berlin: de Gruyter, 1977); Winkler, "Heiden," in *Handwörterbuch des deutschen Aberglaubens*, ed. Hanns Bächtold-Stäubli (Berlin und Leipzig: W. de Gruyter & Co., 1927), 1634–1653; Wolfgang Pfeifer, "Heide," in *Etymologisches Wörterbuch des Deutschen* 1 (a–L), 2nd ed. (Berlin: Akademie Verlag, 1993), 522.

of *Heimat*, a missionary could never become a native, while the tragedy of death in the mission field was partially the tragedy of death far from home. *Heimat* thus describes the limits to German-Ghanaian encounter: a missionary insistence on spatial loyalty elsewhere. See Paul Glen Grant, "Dying German in Ghana: Death, Belonging, and 'Heimat' in the Basel Mission in 19th Century Gold Coast," *Studies in World Christianity* 20, no. 1 (April 2014).

ɔhene. Chief, officer, or king. Christaller 174. Usually as suffix to a proper noun denominating the office. Thus, the *ɔhene* of Akuapem is the *Okuopehene*.

kakos. Greek: κακός (Strong's 2556). Bad, evil. Rendered in the Twi Bible as *bɔne*, as in Matthew 27:24 ("what evil has he done?")

ɔkɔmfo. Sometimes a shrine priest, sometimes the priest's assistant. Christaller 242: "a person who acts, when possessed, as a spirit's mouthpiece."

ɔkra, also spelled *kra* or *ɔkara*. A person's soul, preexisting birth and living beyond death. Christaller's lengthy definition (page 254): "1. *the soul* of man. According to the notions of the natives the kara of a person exists before his birth and may be the soul or spirit of a relation or other person already dead (*cf.* bra, r.3.) that is in heaven or with God and obtains leave to come again into this world (cf. Ababio); when he is thus dismissed in heaven, he takes with him his *errand*, i.e. his *destination* or *future fate* is fixed beforehand; from this the name okara seems to be drawn (*cf.* kra, v. 3. 8.), and the realization of his errand or destiny on earth is then called obra or abra-bo, q.v. The kara, put by God or by the help of a fetish into a child, can be asked while it is yet in the mother's womb (*cf.* fwon). In life the kara is considered partly as the *soul* or *spirit* of a person (*cf.* sunsum, honhom), partly as a separate being, distinct from the person, who protects him (me kra di m'akyi), gives him good or bad advice, causes his undertakings to prosper (pr. 83.) or slights and neglects him (*cf.* okrabiri), and, therefore, in the case of prosperity, receives thanks and thank-offerings like a fetish (*cf.* asumguare). When the person is about to die, the kara leaves him gradually, before he breathes his last, but may be called or drawn back (cf. twe kra). When he has entirely left (whereby the person dies), he is no more called kara, but sesa or osaman.—2. *destiny, fate, lot, luck*; ne kara ye, *he has a good luck* (can be said even of game that escaped the shot of a hunter); ne kra yiye, *happily, luckily*; ne kra nyé = ne ho ade nyé; *cf.* okrabiri."

akyeneboa. Insignia of *abusua* (matriclans) in the Akan world, corresponding with various animal totems. Christaller (p. 282) gives definition of "ape, monkey," making no mention of clans.

ɔman, pl. *aman*. Christaller 294. Generally, a state or political body, but specifically a state or unit within a state organized on military lines. The pluralized *amanaman* is rendered in the Twi Bible for the Hebrew גּוֹיִם (Strong's H1471, *goyim*), as in Psalm 2:1: "Why do the nations rage?"

mogya. Christaller 306: blood. Within the Akan matrilineal societies in Akuapem and to the west, *mogya* represents the female element constituting an individual's personhood, and corresponds to a specific matriclan.

nokware. Christaller 336: truth, truthfulness, faithfulness, honesty. Used in Twi Bible for God's truth—*aletheia*—as in "I am the way the truth and the life" (John 14:6).

Onyame. The high God; generally recognized as equivalent both to the supreme God of the Bible and of the Qur'an. Muslims refer to Mecca as *Nyame-fre-bere*, the "place where God is called."[6] Christaller 342.

Anyamesɛm. Literally *Onyame asɛm*, God's words, the Bible. By naming the Bible thus, the translation team asserted that the book contained the *asɛm* (word, message) of a known but hitherto silent deity. Christaller 343.

Onyankopɔn. Variant of *Onyame*, meaning the creator God. Used 1,930 times in Nkwa Asɛm translation, versus only two times for Onyame. Used for θεός (Theos, Strong's G2316) in Mark 1:1, "Jesus the Messiah, the Son of *Onyankopɔn*. . . ." Christaller 344.

panyar. Portuguese: penhorar, to seize, to arrest, to confiscate. In use in the Accra region long after the departure of the Portuguese; had overtones of enslavement and death.

apesemakahene. The head (*-hene*) of the king's *asafo* (Christaller), his ritual assistants. The opesemakani. Christaller 376.

Sabaoth. Hebrew: צְבָאוֹת also romanized as *tsebaoth*. God the head of heaven's armies. Strong's H6635. Frequently used by Basel Missionaries and indigenous clergy in prayer for power, as in 1869, when Johann Widmann invoked "Lord Sabaoth" to drive away the Asante army.[7]

asafo. plural used as singular. Company, society, association; a division of the men of a township or country, troop, band, gang, host, army. Christaller 403.

Salem. Name given to indigenous settlements surrounding the Christian *asɔredan* structures associated with the Basel Mission, initially in Akropong and expanding throughout the Gold Coast. The origin of the name

6    R. S. Rattray, *Ashanti* (Oxford: Clarendon, 1923), 179, 227.
7    BMA D-1.22 (August 4, 1869), J. G. Widmann to Basel.

is unclear and thus the intent. The settlements predate the name and their organization under missionary leadership (regulated by *Gemeindeordnung* rules). The reference is to Jerusalem. According to J. B. Danquah, the indigenous residents of Kyebi in Akyem Abuakwa referred to that city's Salem as the *"oburoni kurom"* or foreign town, thus designating the Salem residents as outsiders.[8] Ghana's cocoa boom of the early twentieth century was driven by emigrants from the Salems who were seeking a new life as planters. There was thus a generation gap in the experience of the Salem: for the initial settlers, the Salem represented shelter and inclusion—it was thus akin to a sanctuary shrine. To their children, suffering under missionary-imposed *Gemeindeordnung*, the Salem felt like a constriction. The term does not appear in Christaller's dictionary.

**asaman**. Departed spirits, ancestors, also ghosts or apparitions. Translation of φάντασμα in Mark 6:49: "but when they saw [Jesus] walking on the lake, they thought he was a ghost." Christaller 407; Strong's G5326.

**asɛm**. Word, message. Used for λόγος (*logos*, Strong's G3056), as in John 1:1: "In the beginning was *Asɛm* [note the capitalization] and *Asɛm* was with *Onyankopɔn* and *Asɛm* was *Onyankopɔn.*" Christaller 420.

**ɔsɔfoɔ** (pl. asɔfoɔ). Christaller 447: Priest, pastor, missionary. Originally referred to what the missionaries called fetish-priests (and thought of alternately as charlatans or rivals). Used in the Basel Mission's Bible translation for the Greek ἱερεύς (priest) as in Matthew 8:4 ("Go . . . to the priest and present the offering"). Strong's G2409.

**asɔre**. Prayer and worship service. Christaller 451: "common prayer, devotional meeting; divine service; devotional exercise; family worship; public worship."

**asɔredan**. Temple, church building, lit. "house of prayer." Used both for Christian chapels in the Gold Coast and for the biblical temple of Israel. Christaller 452.

**suman**. Christaller 462: "charm, amulet, talisman, worn as a remedy or preservative against evils or mischief, such as diseases and witchcraft, consisting or composed of various things, as feathers, hair, or teeth of various animals, beads, scraps of leather or paper inscribed with mystic characters &c. and tied round some limb or hung about the neck."

---

[8]  J. B. Danquah, *The Akim Abuakwa Handbook* (London: F. Groom, 1928), 90.

**sunsum**. A person's soul; ghost. Translation of *pneuma* (πνεῦμα) in Mark 1:27: "He even gives orders to impure spirits and they obey him." Christaller 464; Strong's G4151.

**Volk**. German: people group, race, language group, ethnicity. The word is significantly stronger than the English *folk*, which is more cultural and mutable. In Basel Mission thought, a *Volk* was defined by language. The early mission in Akuapem was called the Asante mission, with the understanding that all Twi-speakers were part of the same people group. Within Akuapem, the Basel Mission thought of the Guan-speaking minority as not part of the Twi *Volk*, which was a mistake: there were (patrilineal) Guan communities in Akuapem who, by the mid-nineteenth century, had begun speaking Twi, but who remained Guan in the minds of the people of Akuapem. The word has grown more specific over time; Luther variously translated the Greek word *ethnos* as *Volk* or as *Heiden* (heathens); Luther's word choice was inconsistent. By the German nationalist period of the late nineteenth century, the terms had diverged; the core period of the Basel Mission's linguistic work in the Gold Coast fell during this period of transition.

**werɛmpɛ**. Ritual ensemble whose principal responsibility is the ceremony of the same name, by which a deceased chief is invoked to join the ancestors who are the intermediaries between the king and God. Does not appear in Christaller. See Kwasi Ampene and Nana Kwadwo Nyantaki III. *Engaging Modernity: Asante in the Twenty-First Century* (second edition). Ann Arbor: Maize, 2016 (ebook, n.p.): http://dx.doi.org/10.3998/maize .14689915.0001.001.

# Maps

The following maps and details are taken from the Basel Mission's 1857 atlas, produced by Inspector (head) Joseph Josenhans "according to reports" by several named missionaries in Africa and Asia; the maps were drawn by a "topographer" named Rudolf Gross.

Scans are by Paul Grant from a copy held in the special collections of Yale Divinity School Library.

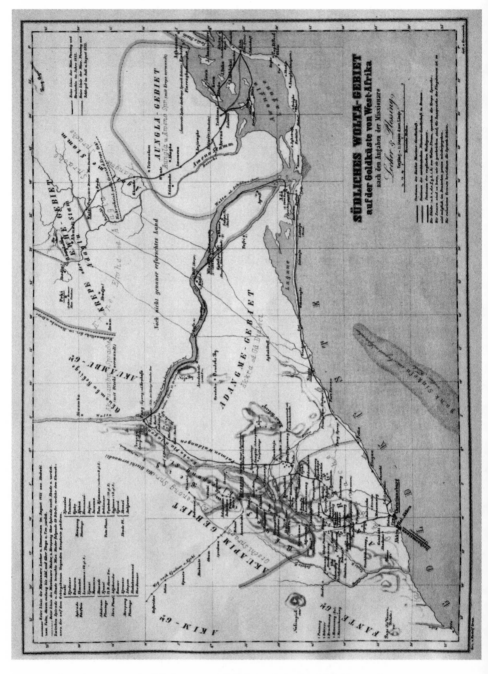

**Southeastern Gold Coast and delta of the Volta River.** Accra is
represented as a cluster of villages, including "Akkra," Usu, and
Christiansborg. Anlo (here "Aungla") is to the east of the Volta;
Akwamu ("Akuambu") to the north.

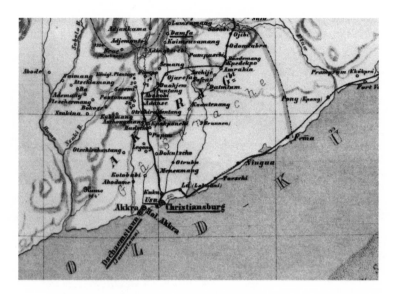

Detail of facing map, centered on the Gã-speaking districts.
On the coast: the cove running between Accra ("Akkra")
and La; including the British (Jamestown; here spelled
"Dschaemstaun"), Dutch ("Hol. Akkra"), and Danish
(Christiansborg) forts. Abokobi is straight north from Accra.

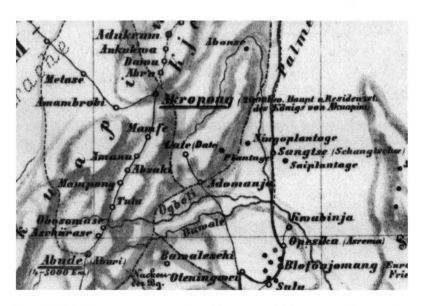

Detail of facing map, centered on the core of Akuapem. The road
between Aburi (here "Abude") through the royal city of Akropong
to Adukrom follows the crest of the Akuapem ridge. Larteh
("Late") is on a parallel ridge to the southeast of Akropong.

**World religions (detail of eastern hemisphere).** Christendom as territorial expanse: prior to the breakthrough in Akuapem, the Basel Mission imagined the process of translation to be irreducibly spatial, with a high degree of overlap between religion, culture, and language.

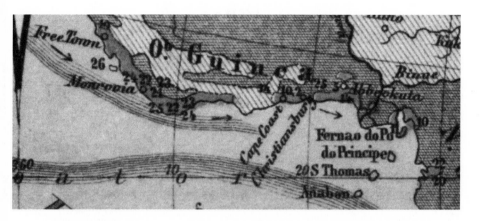

**Detail of facing map.** The religious topography of West Africa. Much of the coastal area is colored as "Protestant" despite this representing only a small part of the population. Areas to the north and west of Cape Coast are inexplicably shaded as Muslim (who were present in small numbers); this is significant because the Basel Mission had previously ceased work among Muslims in Asia.

**Legend of facing map.** The angel is pointing to Matthew 28:18-20 ("Make disciples of all nations"). The Luther Bible the Missionaries were using renders nations (ethnoi) as Völker. Note that only two non-Christian religions are represented: Muslims ("Mohamedaner") and Heathens ("Heiden"). All non-Christian and non-Muslim religions in Africa (and Asia) are subsumed under the latter category.

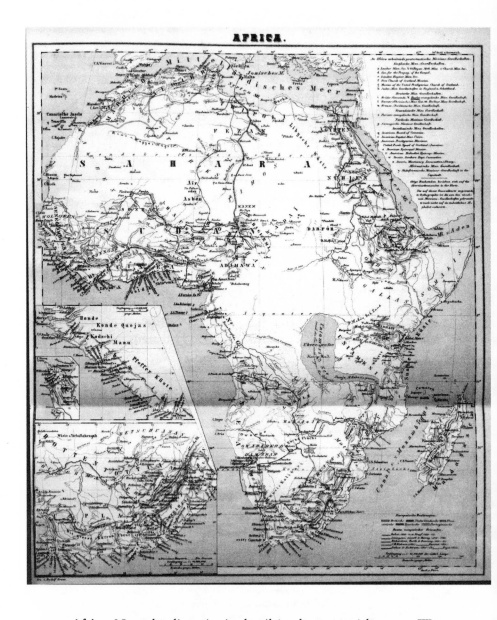

**Africa.** Note the disparity in detail (and accuracy) between West Africa and Equatorial and Great Lakes. The two insets on left are of the Atlantic Coast between Sierra Leone and Liberia (above) and of South Africa (below). The Basel Mission had no presence in South Africa; the map represents the activities of other European and American missionary societies (both Protestant and Catholic). The lines across the Sahara and elsewhere are the "routes of European explorers" rather than established indigenous roads.

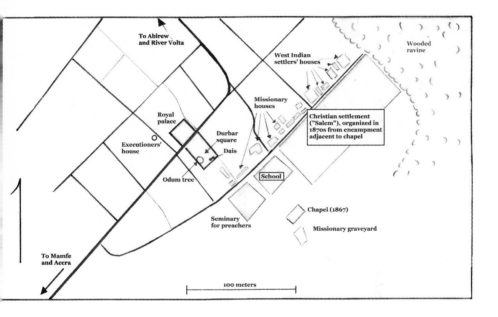

**Akropong around 1880.** The royal palace fronts the main square along the ridgetop road; the site was selected in the eighteenth century for its proximity to an odum tree (see photo on page 263). Hundreds of displaced persons encamped around the chapel upon its inauguration in 1867, effectively designating it an indigenous sanctuary shrine before the missionaries organized the settlement as the "Salem" in the mid-1870s. Map by author.

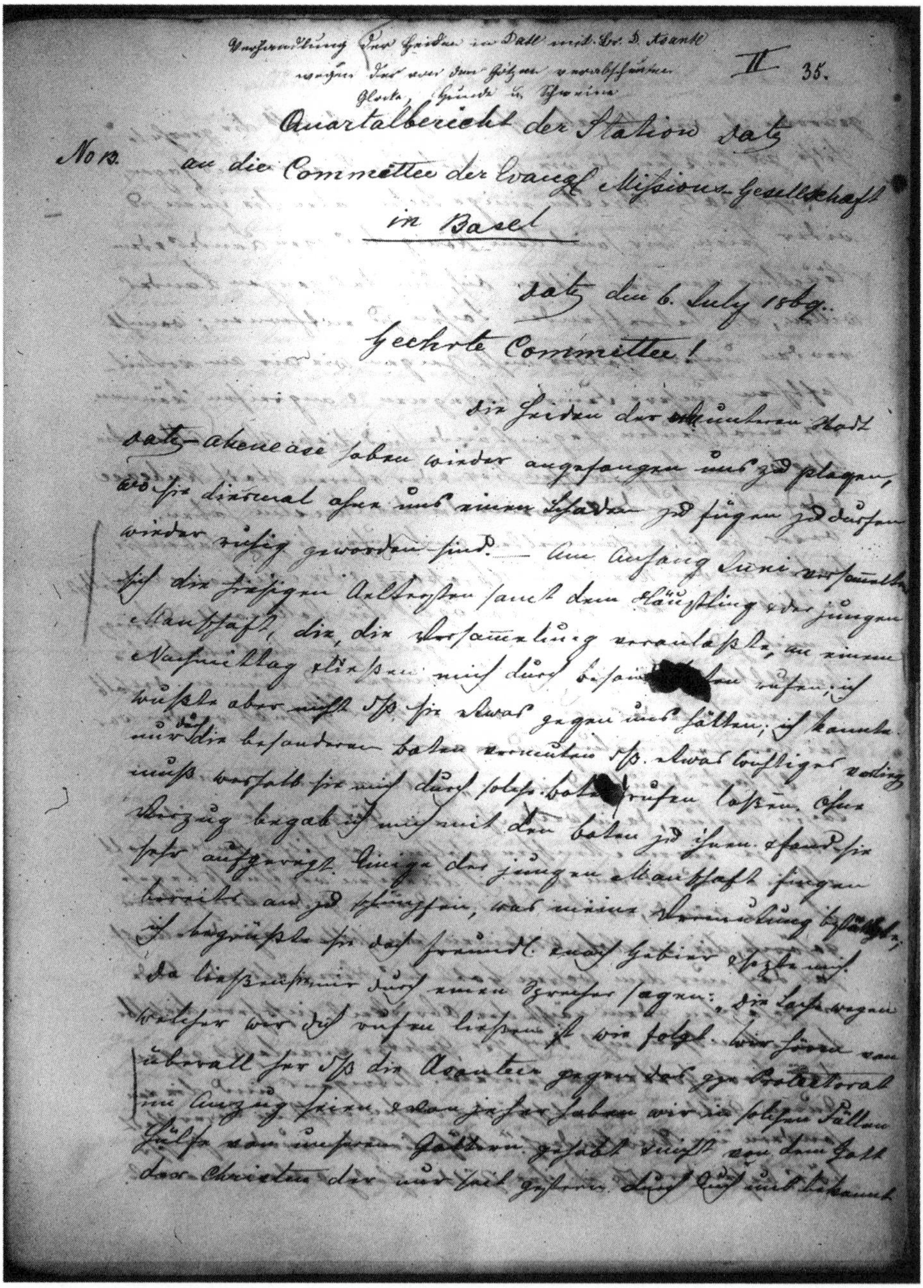
No 12

II 35.

Quartalbericht der Station Date

an die Committee der Evangel. Missions-Gesellschaft

in Basel

Date den 6. July 1869.

Geehrte Committee!

July 6, 1869: David Asante's quarterly report to the Basel Mission home office

# Bibliography

ARCHIVAL SOURCES

Basel Mission Archives, Basel, Switzerland (henceforth BMA)
   Incoming Ghana Correspondence (Series D)
SOAS, University of London, U.K.
   Methodist Missionary Society Archives (MMS)
University of Ghana, Legon
   Furley Collection, Balme Library
Akrofi-Christaller Institute, Akropong, Ghana
   Special Collections, Johannes Zimmermann Library
Yale Divinity School, Special Collections
   International Missionary Council Archives (IMC)
Duke University, Durham, North Carolina
   British Parliamentary Papers on the Ashantee Invasion,
   David M. Rubenstein Rare Book & Manuscript Library

DIGITAL REPOSITORIES

British History Online
   https://www.british-history.ac.uk/
A Collection of the State Papers of John Thurloe. Volume 1, 1638–1653. Edited by
   Thomas Birch. London: Fletcher Gyles 1742.
International Missionary Photography Archive (University of Southern California)
   http://digitallibrary.usc.edu/cdm/landingpage/collection/p15799coll123/
Staatsarchiv des Kantons Basel-Stadt
   http://www.staatsarchiv.bs.ch/archivgut/digitalisiertes-archivgut.html
   Digitalisiertes Archivgut

## Interviews

Afriyie, Ernestina, Akropong-Akuapem, October 25, 2015.
Dah, Joel, Akropong-Akuapem, October 22, 2015.
Nyarko, Ernest, Akropong-Akuapem, October 23, 2015.

## Contemporary Periodicals and Newsletters

*Calwer Missionsblatt*
*The Church Missionary Gleaner*
*Church Missionary Record*
*Deutsche Kolonialzeitung*
*Die Evangelische Heidenbote* (HB)
*Evangelisches Missions-Magazin* (EMM)
*The Gold Coast Leader*
*The Illustrated London News*
*Jahresbericht der Basler Mission* (JB)
*Periodical Accounts relating to the missions of the church of the United Brethren established among the heathen*

## Published and Republished Primary Sources

Asante, David. *Germane Asase so Kristosom terew*. Basel: Verlag der Missionsbuchhandlung, 1875.

———. "Von der Außengemeinde Date." *HB*, 1866, 97–99.

———. *Wiase Abasem mu Nsemma-Nsemma wo Twi kasa mu*. 1874. Basel: Verlag der Missionsbuchhandlung, 1893.

Asare, Nathanael. "Aus der Arbeit eines eingeborenen Missionsarbeiters." *JB*, 1891, 46–47.

Auer, Johann Gottlob. "Predigerseminar." *JB*, 1861, 164–74.

"Aus einem Briefe von Missionar Kugler in Egypten." *Calwer Missions-Blatt* 3, no. 1 (1830), 3–4.

Azu, Noa Akunor Aguae. *Adangbe (Adangme) History*. Translated by Enoch Azu. Accra: Govt. Print Office, 1929.

Barros, João de. "Asia." 1552. In *The Voyages of Cadamosto and Other Documents on Western Africa in the Second Half of the Fifteenth Century*, edited by G. R. Crone, 103–47. London: Hakluyt Society, 1937.

Bellon, Immanuel. "Des weißen Mannes Grab." *HB* 1913, 142.

Blumhardt, Christian Gottlieb. *Versuch einer allgemeinen Missionsgeschichte der Kirche Christi*. 5 vols. Basel: J. G. Neukirch, 1828–1837.

Blumhardt, Johann Christoph. *Handbüchlein der Missionsgeschichte und Missionsgeographie*. Calw: Verlag der Vereinsbuchhandlung, 1844.

———. *Johann Christoph Blumhardt. Briefe*. Volume 1, *Frühe Briefe bis 1838. Texte*. Edited by Dieter Ising. Göttingen: Vandenhoeck & Ruprecht, 1993.

——. *Johann Christoph Blumhardt. Briefe.* Volume 3, *Möttlinger Briefe 1838–1852. Texte.* Edited by Dieter Ising. Göttingen: Vandenhoeck & Ruprecht, 1993.

——. *Johann Christoph Blumhardt. Briefe.* Volume 4, *Möttlinger Briefe 1838–1852. Anmerkungen.* Edited by Dieter Ising. Göttingen: Vandenhoeck & Ruprecht, 1997.

Blumhardt, Johann Christoph, and E. Zuber. *Krankheitsgeschichte der Gottliebin Dittus. Ausführlicher Original-Bericht.* Basel: Brunnen-Verl., 1850.

Bohner, Theodor. *Der Schuhmacher Gottes. Ein deutsches Leben in Afrika.* Frankfurt: Rütten & Loening, 1935.

Bosman, Willem. *A New and Accurate Description of the Coast of Guinea, Divided into the Gold, the Slave, and the Ivory Coasts.* London: Printed for James Knapton and Dan. Midwinter, 1705.

Bowdich, T. Edward. *Mission from Cape Coast Castle to Ashantee: With a Statistical Account of That Kingdom, and Geographical Notices of Other Parts of the Interior of Africa.* London: John Murray, 1819.

"Der Brüdergarten auf der malabarischen Küste." *EMM* 1836, 150–51.

Cardinall, A. W. *The Gold Coast, 1931.* Accra, Gold Coast: Census Office, Government Printer, 1931.

Christaller, J. G. *Anyamesɛm anasɛ Kyerɛw Kronkron apãm-dedaw nè apãm-foforo nsɛm wɔ twi kasa mu. The Holy Bible translated from the original tongues into the Tshi-Chwee-language, spoken by the tribes of Akuapem, Akem, Asante, Fante, etc., Gold Coast . . . by J. G. Christaller.* Basel: B. & F.B.S., 1871.

——. *Dictionary of the Asante and Fante Language Called Tshi (Twi).* Basel: Printed for the Basel Evangelical Missionary Society, 1881.

——. "Einige Sprichwörter der Tschi-Neger." *EMM* 1882, 316–322.

——. *A Grammar of the Asante and Fante Language Called Tshi Based on the Akuapem Dialect with Reference to the Other (Akan and Fante) Dialects.* Basel: Printed for the Basel Evangelical Missionary Society, 1875.

——. *Twi Mmebusɛm, Mpensã-Ahansĩa Mmoaano.* Basel: Evangelisches Missions-Gesellschaft, 1879.

De Marees, Pieter. *Beschryvinghe ende Historische Verhael van het Gout Koninck-rijck van Gunea anders de Gout-Custe de Mina genaemt liggende in het deel van Africa. 1602.* Edited by S. P. L'Honoré Naber. The Hague: M. Nijhoff, 1912.

Dieterle, Johann Christian. "Die Einweihung der neuen Kapelle in Tutu." *HB* 1869, 8.

——. "Georg Schimanek." *HB* 1866, 50.

——. "Eine suchende Familie." *JB* 1872, 114–16.

——. "Der wurmstichige Fetisch." *HB* 1866, 11–12.

Dittrich, August Heinrich, Felician Zaremba, and Heinrich Benz. "Reise nach Tiflis und Georgien, und Aufenthalt daselbst, vom May 1823 bis Febr. 1824." *EMM*, 1824, 460–93.

Dupuis, Joseph. *Journal of a Residence in Ashantee.* London: Henry Colburn, 1824.

Eekhof, Albert. *De Negerpredikant Jacobus Elisa Joannes Capitein, 1717–1747*. The Hague: M. Nijhoff, 1917.

Eisenschmid, David. "Täuflinge auf der Station Kjebi." *HB*, 1866, 64–66.

———. "Zweierlei Sterben." *HB* 1867, 216.

Engmann, Jeremias. "Sein Eifer im Sprachstudium war seine Predigt." *HB* 1913, 120.

Fisch, Rudolf. *Tropische Krankheiten; Anleitung zu ihrer Verhütung und Behandlung für Missionare, Kaufleute, Pflanzer und Beamte*. Basel: Verlag der Missionsbuchhandlung, 1913.

Glover, John. *Ashantee Invasion: Report by Captain Glover, R.N., on the Conduct of the Deputee Commissioners, Officers and Men, Comprising the Expedition under His Command*. Vol. C-962. London: Harrison and Sons, 1874.

Gundert, Hermann. *Die Evangelische Mission: ihre Länder, Völker und Arbeiten*. Stuttgart: Verlag der Vereinsbuchhandlung, 1893.

Harnack, Adolf von. *Die Mission und Ausbreitung des Christentums in den ersten drei Jahrhunderten*. 2nd ed. Leipzig: J. C. Hinrich, 1906.

Hartenstein, Karl. *Anibue: die "Neue Zeit" auf der Goldküste und unsere Missionsaufgabe*. Stuttgart: Evangelische Missionsverlag, 1932.

———. *Was hat die Theologie Karl Barths der Mission zu sagen?* Munich: Kaiser Verlag, 1928.

———. "William Wadé Harris, ein schwarzer Prophet." In *Das Buch der deutschen Weltmission*, edited by Julius Richter, 284–286. Gotha: L. Klotz, 1935.

Heck, Jakob. "Sebastian Lindenmann." *HB* 1866, 61–62.

Illustrated London News. *From Cape Coast to Coomassie: An Illustrated Narrative of the Ashantee War*. 1874.

Isert, Paul Erdmann. *Reise nach Guinea und den caribäischen Inseln in Columbien, in Briefen an seine Freunde beschrieben*. Copenhagen: J. F. Morthorst, 1788.

Josenhans, Joseph. *Atlas der evangelischen Missions-Gesellschaft zu Basel: Nach den Angaben der Missionare Locher u.a. Unter Mitwirkung von Rudolf Gross*. Basel: Missions-Gesellschaft 1857.

———. "Bericht." *JB* 1862, 25–47.

———. "Die erste Fahrt der 'Palme.'" *HB* 1966, 125–29.

———. "Das Fort von Christiansborg." *HB* 1866, 117–18.

———. "Johann Ullrich Lüthy." *HB* 1869, 146–50.

———. *Missionsliederbuch für die Missionsgemeinde und die Arbeiter auf dem Missionsfelde*. Basel: Missions-Gesellschaft, 1879.

———. "Monats-Chronik." *HB* 1866, 165–66.

Kani, Thomas Yaw and Fred M. Agyemang. *Persecution of Kyebi Christians, 1880–1887: An English Translation of "Kyebi Kristofo Taee"*. Translated by Fred M. Agyemang. Accra, Ghana: Synod of the Presbyterian Church of Ghana, Literature Committee, 1975.

Mader, Johann Adam. "Aus dem Jahresbericht der Station Akropong vom Jahr 1876." *JB* 1877, 84–88.

———. "Christenthum und Heidenthum in Akropong." *JB* 1868, 107–8.

———. "Die Einweihung der Jubiläumskirche zu Akropong." *HB* 1869, 42–43.

———. "Der helle Schein in zuvor dunklen Herzen." *HB* 1869, 4–7.

———. "Das Predigerseminar in Akropong." *JB* 1865, 94–96.

Meredith, Henry. *An Account of the Gold Coast of Africa, with a Brief History of the African Company.* London: Longman, Hurst, Rees, Orme, and Brown, 1812.

Mohr, Julie. "Die Kinder des Fetischpriesters." *HB* 1865, 84–85.

"Nachrichten aus West-Afrika." *HB* 1857, 35–39.

Nørregaard, Georg, ed. *Guldkysten: de danske etablissementer i Guinea.* 2nd ed. Volume 8 of *Vore Gamle Tropekolonier,* edited by Johannes Brøndsted. Copenhagen: Fremad, 1968.

Ostertag, Albert. "Die Goldküste und die Basler Mission daselbst," *EMM* 1859, 33–56.

———. "Gottes Gedanken über Afrika" *EMM* 1860, 239–40.

Presbyterian Church of Ghana. *Presbyterian Hymns in Twi, Ga, Dangme and English.* Accra, Ghana: A-Riis Company 2010.

Ramseyer, Friedrich August and Johannes Kühne. *Vier Jahre in Asante. Tagebücher der Missionare Ramseyer und Kühne.* Edited by H. Gundert. 2nd ed. Basel: Missionskomptoir, 1875.

Ramseyer, Friedrich August, and Johannes Kühne. *Four Years in Ashantee.* New York: R. Carter & Bros., 1875.

Rask, Johannes. *A Brief and Truthful Description of a Journey to and from Guinea.* In *Two Views from Christiansborg Castle,* translated and edited by Selena Axelrod Winsnes. Accra: Sub-Saharan Publishers, 2009.

Reindorf, Carl Christian. *The History of the Gold Coast and Asante; Based on Traditions and Historical Facts Comprising a Period of More Than Three Centuries from about 1500 to 1860.* 1889. 2nd ed. Accra: Ghana Universities Press, 1966.

Riis, Andreas. "Die Reise des Missionars in Akropong nach dem Aschantee-Lande im Winter 1839–40." *EMM* 1840, 174–236.

———. "Einige Mittheilungen aus dem Tagebuche des Missionars Andreas Riis." *EMM* 1836, 510–64.

———. "Goldküste in Westafrika." *HB* 1835, Nos. 15–16, 61–65.

Rømer, Ludvig Ferdinand. *A Reliable Account of the Coast of Guinea (1760).* Translated by Selena Axelrod Winsnes. Oxford: Oxford University Press, 2000.

Samson, Edward. *A Short History of Akuapim and Akropong Gold Coast and Autobiography of the Rev. Edward Samson of Aburi, Native Pastor.* Aburi [Ghana], 1908.

Schönfeld, Karl. "Der Heimgang des Missionars Heck in Christiansborg." *HB* 1866, 118–19.

Schrenk, Elias. *Ein Leben im Kampf um Gott.* Basel: Verlag der Missionsbuchhandlung, 1905.

———. "Geleitwort." In *Erfahrungen in der Pfingstbewegung*, by Heinrich Dallmeyer. Neumünster: G. Ihloff & Co., 1909.

Schubert-Christaller, Else. *Missionar J.G. Christaller: Erinnerungen aus seinem Leben.* Stuttgart: Evang. Missionsverlag, 1929.

"Die Station Akropong im letzten Jahrzehnt." *HB* 1877, 67–71.

Stanger, Joseph. "Usu/Accra." *JB* 1850, 206.

Steiner, P. "Land und Leute von Akra." *Deutsche Kolonialzeitung* 2, no. 1–2 (1885), 10–13, 48–53.

Struck, Bernhard. "Geschichliches über die östlichen Tschi-Länder (Goldküste): Aufzeichnungen eines Eingeborenen." *Anthropos* 18 (1923), 465–83.

Tucker, Sarah. *Abbeokuta; or, Sunrise within the Tropics: An Outline of the Origin and Progress of the Yoruba Mission.* London: James Nisbet, 1853.

Warneck, Gustav. *Abriss einer Geschichte der protestantischen Missionen von der Reformation bis auf die Gegenwart.* Berlin: Warneck, 1898.

———. *Die Mission in Bildern aus ihrer Geschichte.* 3rd ed. Gütersloh: Bertelsmann, 1890.

———. *Outline of the History of Protestant Missions from the Reformation to the Present Time.* Edinburgh: James Gemmell, George Bridge, 1884.

Weitbrecht, Mary Edwards. *Memoir of the Rev. John James Weitbrecht: Comprehending a History of the Burdwan Mission.* London: James Nisbet, 1854.

"West-Africa Mission." *Church Missionary Record* 1, no. 1 (January 1830), 1–9.

"West-Afrika. Colonie Sierra Leone." *HB* 1829, 89–91.

Widmann, J. G. (Johann Georg). "Anum und die gefangenen Missionsgeschwister in Westafrika." *HB* 1869, 129–31.

———. "Aus dem letzen Bericht des sel. Miss. Widmann in Akropong," *JB* 1877, 82.

———. "Die Elenden suchen Hilfe." *HB* 1865, 35–36.

———. "Kirchenweihe in Late." *JB* 1859, 111–12.

———. "Mannigfacher Kampf und Sieg." *JB* 1863, 95–96.

———. "Station Akropong." *JB* 1850, 188–201.

Widmann, J. G. (Johann Georg) and Johann Adam Mader. "Der Tod des Königs von Akropong." *HB* 1866, 129–31.

Wulff, Wulff Joseph. *Breve og Dagbogsoptegnelser fra Guldkysten, 1836–1842.* Edited by Carl Behrens. Copenhagen: Nyt Nordisk Forlag, 1917.

Zimmermann, Johannes. "Der Heimgang von Missionar Hetz." *HB* 1866, 133.

———. "Nachruf an den selig vollendeten Miss. Steinhauser." *JB* 1858, 102–3.

SECONDARY SOURCES

Abraham, William. "The Life and Times of Anton Wilhelm Amo." *Transactions of the Historical Society of Ghana* 7 (1964), 60–81.

Abun-Nasr, Sonia. *Afrikaner und Missionar: die Lebensgeschichte von David Asante.* Basel: Schlettwein, 2003.

Ackah, C. A. *Akan Ethics: A Study of the Moral Ideas and the Moral Behaviour of the Akan Tribes of Ghana*. Accra: Ghana Universities Press, 1988.

Addo-Fening, Robert. *Akyem Abuakwa, 1700–1943: From Ofori Panin to Sir Ofori Atta*. Trondheim: Department of History, Norwegian University of Science and Technology, 1997.

Afriyie, Ernestina. "The Theology of the Okuapehene's Odwira: An Illustration of the Engagement of the Gospel among the Akan of Akropong-Akuapem." PhD thesis, Akrofi-Christaller Institute, Akropong, Ghana, 2010.

———. "Taboo." In *Africa Bible Commentary*, edited by Tokunboh Adeyemo, 159. Grand Rapids: Zondervan, 2006.

Agamben, Giorgio. *Homo Sacer: Sovereign Power and Bare Life*. Stanford: Stanford University Press, 1998.

Aghalino, S. O. "British Colonial Policies and the Oil Palm Industry in the Niger Delta Region of Nigeria, 1900–1960." *African Studies Monographs* 21, no. 1 (2000), 19–33.

Ajayi, J. F. Ade. "Nineteenth Century Origins of Nigerian Nationalism." *Journal of the Historical Society of Nigeria* 2, no. 2 (1961), 196–210.

Akyeampong, Emmanuel, and Pashington Obeng. "Spirituality, Gender, and Power in Asante History." *The International Journal of African Historical Studies* 28, no. 3 (1995), 481–508.

Aland, Kurt. "Der Pietismus und die soziale Frage." In *Pietismus und Moderne Welt*, edited by Kurt Aland, 99–137. Witten: Luther-Verlag, 1974.

Allman, Jean Marie, and John Parker. *Tongnaab: The History of a West African God*. Bloomington: Indiana University Press, 2005.

Alt, Karl, ed. *Goethes Faust: in sämtlichen Fassungen mit den Bruchstücken und Entwürfen des Nachlasses*. Berlin: Bong, 1909.

Ampene, Kwasi, and Nana Kwadwo Nyantaki III. *Engaging Modernity: Asante in the Twenty-First Century*. 2nd ed. Ann Arbor: Maize, 2016. http://dx.doi.org/10.3998/maize.14689915.0001.001.

Ansah, J. Kwesi. *The Centenary History of the Larteh Presbyterian Church, 1853–1953*. Larteh, Gold Coast: Larteh Presbyterian Church, 1955.

Anum, Eric. "Collaborative and Interactive Hermeneutics." In *African and European Readers of the Bible in Dialogue: In Quest of a Shared Meaning*, edited by Hans de Wit and Gerald West, 143–65. Leiden: Brill, 2008.

Appiah-Kubi, Kofi. *Man Cures, God Heals: Religion and Medical Practice among the Akans of Ghana*. Totowa, N.J.: Allanheld, Osmun, 1981.

Arhin, Kwame. "Monetization and the Asante State." In *Money Matters: Instability, Values and Social Payments in the Modern History of West African Communities*, edited by Jane I. Guyer, 97–110. Portsmouth, N.H.: Heinemann, 1995.

———. "Rank and Class among the Asante and Fante in the Nineteenth Century." *Africa: Journal of the International African Institute* 53, no. 1 (1983), 2–22.

Arlt, Veit. "Christianity, Imperialism and Culture: The Expansion of the Two Krobo States in Ghana, C. 1830 to 1930." PhD diss., University of Basel, 2005.

Asamoah-Gyadu, J. Kwabena. *Contemporary Pentecostal Christianity: Interpretations from an African Context.* Oxford: Regnum, 2013.

———. "The Church in the African state—The Pentecostal/Charismatic Experience in Ghana." *Journal of African Christian Thought* 1, no. 2 (1998), 51–57.

Atkinson, Roland R. "Old Akyem and the Origins of Akyems Abuakwa and Kotoku 1675–1775." In *West African Culture Dynamics: Archaeological and Historical Perspectives*, edited by B. K. Swartz and Raymond E. Dumett, 350–69. The Hague: Mouton, 1980.

Ault, James. *African Christianity Rising.* DVD. Northampton, Mass.: James Ault Productions, 2013.

Avotri, Solomon K. "The Vernacularization of Scripture and African Beliefs: The Story of the Gerasene Demoniac among the Ewe of West Africa." In *The Bible in Africa: Transactions, Trajectories, and Trends*, edited by Gerald O. West and Musa W. Dube Shomanah, 311–25. Leiden: Brill, 2000.

Awuah-Nyamekye, Samuel. "Belief in Sasa: Its Implications for Flora and Fauna Conservation in Ghana." *Nature and Culture* 7, no. 1 (2012), 1–15.

Aye-Addo, Charles Sarpong. *Akan Christology: An Analysis of the Christologies of John Samuel Pobee and Kwame Bediako in Conversation with the Theology of Karl Barth.* Eugene, Ore.: Pickwick, 2013.

Ayisi, Eric Okyere. "The Basis of Political Authority of the Akwapem Tribes (Eastern Ghana) (Social Change: A Sociological Study)." PhD diss., University of London, 1965.

Bagyire VI, Abiriwhene Otutu. "The Guans: A Preliminary Note." *Ghana Notes and Queries* 7 (1967), 21–24.

Barnes, Andrew E. "The Cross versus the Crescent: Karl Kumm's Missiology." *Islam and Christian–Muslim Relations* 30, no. 4 (2019), 483–503.

Barnes, Sandra. "Shrine Sanctuary and Mission Sanctuary in West Africa." In *Christianity and Social Change in Africa: Essays in Honor of J. D. Y. Peel*, edited by Toyin Falola, 165–83. Durham, N.C.: Carolina Academic Press, 2005.

Barth, Karl. *Protestant Theology in the Nineteenth Century: Its Background & History.* 1952. London: SCM Press, 1972.

Becker, Judith. "Zukunftserwartungen und Missionsimpetus bei Missionsgesellschaften in der ersten Hälfte des 19. Jahrhunderts." In *Geschichtsbewusstsein und Zukunftserwartung in Pietismus und Erweckungsbewegung*, edited by Wolfgang Breul and Jan Carsten Schnurr, 244–70. Arbeiten zur Geschichte des Pietismus. Göttingen: Vandenhoeck & Ruprecht, 2013.

Bediako, Kwame. *Christianity in Africa: The Renewal of a Non-Western Religion.* Maryknoll, N.Y.: Orbis, 1996.

———. *Theology and Identity: The Impact of Culture Upon Christian Thought in the Second Century and in Modern Africa.* Oxford: Regnum, 1992.

———. "The Unique Christ in the Plurality of Religions." In *The Unique Christ in Our Pluralist World*, edited by Bruce J. Nicholls, 47–56. Grand Rapids: Baker, 1994.

Bekele, Girma. *The In-Between People: A Reading of David Bosch through the Lens of Mission History and Contemporary Challenges in Ethiopia.* Eugene, Ore.: Pickwick, 2011.

Benjamin, Walter. "Critique of Violence." In *Walter Benjamin: Selected Writings*, edited by Marcus Bullock and Michael W. Jennings, 236–52. Cambridge, Mass.: Belknap Press of Harvard University Press, 1996.

Berger, K. G., and S. M. Martin. "Palm Oil." In *Cambridge World History of Food*, edited by Kenneth F. Kiple and Kriemhild Coneè Ornelas, 397–411. Cambridge; New York: Cambridge University Press, 2000.

Berry, Sara. *No Condition is Permanent: The Social Dynamics of Agrarian Change in Sub-Saharan Africa.* Madison: University of Wisconsin Press, 1993.

Beuttler, Anne. "Church Discipline Chronicled—a New Source for Basel Mission Historiography." *History in Africa* 42 (June 2015), 109–38.

Boakyewa, Okomfo Ama. "Nana Oparebea and the Akonnedi Shrine: Cultural, Religious and Global Agents." PhD diss., Indiana University, 2014.

Bohnenberger, Karl. "Aus Glauben und Sage." 1904. In *Volkstümliche Überlieferungen in Württemberg: Glaube, Brauch, Heilkunde*, edited by Karl Bohnenberger, 1–26. Stuttgart: Kommissionsverlag Müller & Gräff, 1980.

Bonin, Werner Friedrich. *Die Götter Schwarzafrikas.* Graz: Sammler, 1979.

Bosch, David Jacobus. *Transforming Mission: Paradigm Shifts in Theology of Mission.* Maryknoll, N.Y.: Orbis, 1991.

Brokensha, David. *The Resilient Chieftaincy of Larteh, Ghana.* Ife, Nigeria: Institute of African Studies, University of Ife, 1968.

———. *Social Change at Larteh, Ghana.* Oxford: Clarendon, 1966.

Brown, David. "Anglo-German Rivalry and Krepi Politics 1886–1894." *Transactions of the Historical Society of Ghana* 15, no. 2 (1974), 201–16.

Buschan, Georg. *Das deutsche Volk in Sitte und Brauch: Geburt, Liebe, Hochzeit.* Stuttgart: Union Deutsche Verlagsgesellschaft, 1922.

Busia, K. A. *The Position of the Chief in the Modern Political System of Ashanti.* London: Published for the International African Institute by the Oxford University Press, 1951.

Byer, J. "Geology." In *Akwapim Handbook*, edited by David Brokensha, 2–8. Tema: Ghana Pub. Corp., 1972.

Clark, Christopher M. *Iron Kingdom: The Rise and Downfall of Prussia, 1600–1947.* Cambridge, Mass.: Belknap Press of Harvard University Press, 2006.

Crites, Stephen. *In the Twilight of Christendom: Hegel vs. Kierkegaard on Faith and History.* Chambersburg, Pa.: American Academy of Religion, 1972.

Cross, Whitney R. *The Burned-over District: The Social and Intellectual History of Enthusiastic Religion in Western New York, 1800–1850.* Ithaca: Cornell University Press, 1950.

Crow, Loren D. *The Songs of Ascents (Psalms 120–134): Their Place in Israelite History and Religion.* Atlanta: Scholars Press, 1996.

Curtin, Philip D. *The Image of Africa: British Ideas and Action, 1780–1850.* Madison: University of Wisconsin Press, 1964.

Danquah, J. B. *The Akan Doctrine of God: A Fragment of Gold Coast Ethics and Religion.* London: Lutterworth, 1944.

———. *The Akim Abuakwa Handbook.* London: F. Groom, 1928.

Debrunner, Hans Werner. "Pioneers of Church and Education in Ghana: Danish Chaplains to Guinea, 1661–1850." *Kirkehistoriske Samlinger* 7th series, 4, no. 3 (1962), 373–425.

Deppermann, Klaus. *Der hallesche Pietismus und der preussische Staat unter Friedrich III. (I.).* Göttingen: Vandenhoeck & Ruprecht, 1961.

Douglas, Mary. "No Free Gifts." Foreword to *The Gift: The Form and Reason for Exchange in Archaic Societies,* by Marcel Mauss, vii–xviii. London; New York: Routledge, 1990.

"Ecstasy and Exodus." *The Economist,* January 23, 2016, https://www.economist.com/international/2016/01/23/ecstasy-and-exodus (accessed May 20, 2020).

Eichholzer, Erika. "Missionary Linguistics on the Gold Coast." In *The Spiritual in the Secular: Missionaries and Knowledge about Africa,* edited by Patrick Harries and David Maxwell, 72–99. Grand Rapids: Eerdmans, 2012.

Ellis, Alfred Burdon. *The Tshi-Speaking Peoples of the Gold Coast of West Africa: Their Religion, Manners, Customs, Laws, Languages, Etc.* London: Chapman and Hall, 1887.

Elorm-Donkor, Lord. *Christian Morality in Ghanaian Pentecostalism: A Theological Analysis of Virtue Theory as a Framework for Integrating Christian and Akan Moral Schemes.* Eugene, Ore.: Wipf and Stock, 2017.

Emmer, P. C. *De Nederlandse Slavenhandel, 1500–1850.* 2nd expanded ed. Amsterdam: Arbeiderspers, 2003.

Ephirim-Donkor, Anthony. *The Making of an African King: Patrilineal & Matrilineal Struggle among the Effutu of Ghana.* Trenton, N.J.: Africa World Press, 1998.

Eppler, Paul. *Geschichte der Basler Mission: 1815–1899.* Basel: Verlag der Missionsbuchhandlung, 1900.

Fabian, Johannes. *Out of Our Minds: Reason and Madness in the Exploration of Central Africa.* Berkeley: University of California Press, 2000.

Fatukun, Samson Adetunji. "The Concept of Expiatory Sacrifice in the Early Church and in African Indigenous Religious Traditions." In *African Traditions in the Study of Religion, Diaspora and Gendered Societies,* edited by Ezra Chitando, Afe Adogame, and Bolaji Bateye, 71–81. New York: Routledge, 2016.

Fauvelle-Aymar, François-Xavier. *The Golden Rhinoceros: Histories of the African Middle Ages.* Princeton: Princeton University Press, 2018.

Field, M. J. *Akim-Kotoku: An Oman of the Gold Coast.* London: Crown Agents for the Colonies, 1948.

——. "Spirit Possession in Ghana." In *Spirit Mediumship and Society in Africa,* edited by John Beattie and John Middleton, 3–13. London: Routledge & K. Paul, 1969.

Finneran, Niall. *The Archaeology of Christianity in Africa.* Stroud, Gloucestershire: Tempus, 2002.

Flett, John G. *The Witness of God: The Trinity, Missio Dei, Karl Barth, and the Nature of Christian Community.* Grand Rapids: Eerdmans, 2010.

Fortes, Meyer. "Kinship and Marriage among the Ashanti." In *African Systems of Kinship and Marriage,* edited by A. R. Radcliffe-Brown and Daryll Forde, 252–84. London: Published for the International African Institute by the Oxford University Press, 1950.

——. "Some Reflections on Ancestor Worship in Africa." In *African Systems of Thought; Studies Presented and Discussed at the Third International African Seminar in Salisbury, December, 1960,* edited by Meyer Fortes and G. Dieterlen, 122–42. London: Published for the International African Institute by the Oxford University Press, 1965.

Frempong, M. P. "A History of the Presbyterian Church at Bompata in Asante-Akyem." Translated by E. A. Kyerematen. *Ghana Notes and Queries* 12 (June 1972), 20–23.

Frenssen, Gustav. *Der Glaube der Nordmark.* Stuttgart: G. Truckenmüller, 1936.

Fromont, Cécile. *The Art of Conversion: Christian Visual Culture in the Kingdom of Kongo.* Chapel Hill: University of North Carolina Press, 2014.

Gäbler, Ulrich. "Erweckung in europäischen und im amerikanischen Protestantismus." *Pietismus und Neuzeit* 15 (1989), 24–39.

Gensichen, Hans-Werner. "Heidentum I." In *Theologische Realenzyklopädie,* edited by Gerhard Krause and Gerhard Müller. Berlin: de Gruyter, 1977.

——. *Missionsgeschichte der neueren Zeit.* Göttingen: Vandenhoeck & Ruprecht, 1961.

Geschiere, Peter. *The Modernity of Witchcraft: Politics and the Occult in Postcolonial Africa.* Charlottesville: University Press of Virginia, 1997.

Gestrich, Andreas. "Pietismus und Aberglaube." In *Das Ende der Hexenverfolgung,* edited by Sönke Lorenz and Dieter R. Bauer, 271–83. Stuttgart: F. Steiner, 1995.

Ghana Information Services Department. *Ghana Official Handbook.* Accra: Information Services, 1971.

Gierl, Martin. *Pietismus und Aufklärung: theologische Polemik und die Kommunikationsreform der Wissenschaft am Ende des 17. Jahrhunderts.* Göttingen: Vandenhoeck & Ruprecht, 1997.

Gifford, Paul. *Ghana's New Christianity: Pentecostalism in a Globalizing African Economy.* Bloomington: Indiana University Press, 2004.

Gilbert, Michelle. "The Cracked Pot and the Missing Sheep." *American Ethnologist* 16, no. 2 (1989), 213–29.

———. "Disguising the Pain of Remembering in Akwapim." *Africa* 80, no. 3 (2010), 426–52.

———. "No Condition Is Permanent: Ethnic Construction and the Use of History in Akuapem." *Africa: Journal of the International African Institute* 67, no. 4 (1997), 501–33.

———. "The Sacralized Power of the Akwapim King." In *Religion and Power: Divine Kingship in the Ancient World and Beyond,* Oriental Institute Seminars, edited by Nicole Brisch, 171–90. Chicago: University of Chicago Press, 2008.

Goody, Jack. "Anomie in Ashanti?" *Africa: Journal of the International African Institute* 27, no. 4 (1957), 356–63.

Gómez, Pablo. *The Experiential Caribbean: Creating Knowledge and Healing in the Early Modern Atlantic.* Chapel Hill: University of North Carolina Press, 2017.

Grant, Paul Glen. "Dying German in Ghana: Death, Belonging, and 'Heimat' in the Basel Mission in 19th Century Gold Coast." *Studies in World Christianity* 20, no. 1 (2014), 4–18.

Green, Joel B., and Mark D. Baker. *Recovering the Scandal of the Cross: Atonement in New Testament & Contemporary Contexts.* Downers Grove, Ill.: InterVarsity Press, 2000.

Greene, Sandra E. *Sacred Sites and the Colonial Encounter: A History of Meaning and Memory in Ghana.* Bloomington: Indiana University Press, 2002.

Groves, C. P. *The Planting of Christianity in Africa.* London: Lutterworth, 1948.

Gyekye, Kwame. *Tradition and Modernity: Philosophical Reflections on the African Experience.* New York: Oxford University Press, 1997.

Haenger, Peter. *Sklaverei und Sklavenemanzipation an der Goldküste: ein Beitrag zum Verständnis von sozialen Abhängigkeitsbeziehungen in Westafrika.* Basel: Helbing & Lichtenhahn, 1997.

Halbertal, Moshe. *On Sacrifice.* Princeton: Princeton University Press, 2011.

Haug, Richard. *Johann Christoph Blumhardt: Gestalt und Botschaft.* Metzingen: E. Franz, 1984.

———. *Reich Gottes im Schwabenland: Linien im württembergischen Pietismus.* Metzingen: Franz, 1981.

Henige, David P. *The Chronology of Oral Tradition: Quest for a Chimera.* Oxford: Clarendon, 1974.

Herppich, Birgit. *Pitfalls of Trained Incapacity: The Unintended Effects of Integral Missionary Training in the Basel Mission on Its Early Work in Ghana (1828–1840).* Eugene, Ore.: Wipf and Stock, 2016.

Hill, Polly. *The Migrant Cocoa-Farmers of Southern Ghana: A Study in Rural Capitalism.* Cambridge: Cambridge University Press, 1963.

Horton, Robin. "African Conversion." *Africa* 41, no. 2 (1971), 85–108.

Hubert, Henri, and Marcel Mauss. *Sacrifice: Its Nature and Function.* Translated by W. D. Halls. Chicago: University of Chicago Press, 1964.

Huppenbauer, Hanns Walter. *Königshaus und Missionshaus in Kyebi: Auseinandersetzungen der Basel Missionare mit den Königen von Akyem, 1861–1890.* Affoltern am Albis: Eigenverlag, 2004.

Idowu, E. Bọlaji. *African Traditional Religion: A Definition.* Maryknoll, N.Y.: Orbis, 1973.

Ipsen, Pernille. *Daughters of the Trade: Atlantic Slavers and Interracial Marriage on the Gold Coast.* Philadelphia: University of Pennsylvania Press, 2015.

Ising, Dieter. *Johann Christoph Blumhardt, Life and Work: A New Biography.* Eugene, Ore.: Cascade, 2009.

Jakubowski-Tiessen, Manfred. "Zeit- und Zukunftsdeutungen in Krisenzeiten in Pietismus und Erweckungsbewegung." In *Geschichtsbewusstsein und Zukunftserwartung in Pietismus und Erweckungsbewegung,* edited by Wolfgang Breul and Jan Carsten Schnurr, 175–91. Göttingen: Vandenhoeck & Ruprecht, 2013.

Jay, Nancy B. *Throughout Your Generations Forever: Sacrifice, Religion, and Paternity.* Chicago: University of Chicago Press, 1992.

Jenkins, Paul. "The Basel Mission, the Presbyterian Church, and Ghana since 1918." In Jon Miller, *Missionary Zeal and Institutional Control: Organizational Contradictions in the Basel Mission on the Gold Coast, 1828–1917,* 195–222. Grand Rapids: Eerdmans, 2003.

———. "A Conflict of Faiths at Kukurantumi." *Transactions of the Historical Society of Ghana* 13, no. 2 (1972), 245–56.

———. "Der Skandal fortwährender interkultureller Blindheit." *Zeitschrift für Mission* 23, no. 4 (1997), 224–36.

———. *The Ghana Archive of the Basel Mission, 1828–1918.* Basel, Switzerland: Basel Mission, 1978.

———. "Slavery and Emancipation in the Reports (1868–1900) of a Ghanaian Pastor—Kofi Theophilus Opoku (B. 1842)." Paper presented at the annual meeting of the African Studies Association, San Diego, Calif., November 2015.

———. "Villagers as Missionaries: Wurttemberg Pietism as a 19th Century Missionary Movement." *Missiology* 8, no. 4 (1980), 425–32.

Jenkins, Philip. *The Lost History of Christianity: The Thousand-Year Golden Age of the Church in the Middle East, Africa, and Asia—and How It Died.* New York: HarperCollins, 2008.

———. *The Next Christendom: The Coming of Global Christianity.* Oxford: Oxford University Press, 2002.

Jeyaraj, Daniel. "Die Ordination des ersten protestantischen Pfarrers in Indien 1733." *Zeitschrift für Mission* 23, no. 2 (1997), 105–25.

Jordan, William R. *The Sunflower Forest: Ecological Restoration and the New Communion with Nature.* Berkeley: University of California Press, 2003.

Justesen, Ole, ed. *Danish Sources for the History of Ghana, 1657–1754*. 2 vols. Copenhagen: Det Kongelige Danske Videnskabernes Selskab, 2005.

Kannenberg, Michael. *Verschleierte Uhrtafeln: Endzeiterwartungen im württembergischen Pietismus zwischen 1818 und 1848*. Göttingen: Vandenhoeck & Ruprecht, 2007.

Kapolyo, Joe. "Matthew." In *Africa Bible Commentary*, edited by Tokunboh Adeyemo, 1131–96. Grand Rapids: Zondervan, 2006.

Kierkegaard, Søren. *Kierkegaard's Attack Upon "Christendom."* Translated and edited by Walter Lowrie. Princeton: Princeton University Press, 1946.

Kim, Kirsteen. "Post-Modern Mission." *International Review of Mission* 89, no. 353 (2000), 172–79.

Klingshirn, Agnes. "The Changing Position of Women in Ghana: A Study Based on Empirical Research in Larteh, a Small Town in Southern Ghana." PhD diss., Philipps-Universität Marburg, 1971.

Koehne, Samuel. "Pietism as Societal Solution: The Foundation of the Korntal Brethren." In *Pietism and Community in Europe and North America: 1650–1850*, edited by Jonathan Strom, 329–50. Leiden: Brill, 2010.

Konadu, Kwasi. *The Akan Diaspora in the Americas*. Oxford: Oxford University Press, 2010.

Kpobi, David Nii Anum. *Mission in Chains: The Life, Theology, and Ministry of the Ex-Slave Jacobus E.J. Capitein (1717–1747)*. Zoetermeer, Netherlands: Uitgeverij Boekencentrum, 1993.

———. *Saga of a Slave: Jacobus Capitein of Holland and Elmina*. Accra: Sub-Saharan Publishers, 2001.

Kraemer, Hendrik. *The Christian Message in a Non-Christian World*. London: Published for the International Missionary Council by Edinburgh House Press, 1938.

Krishnamurti, Bhadriraju. *The Dravidian Languages*. New York: Cambridge University Press, 2003.

Kropp Dakubu, M. E. "Foreword." In *Two Views from Christiansborg Castle*, edited by Selena Axelrod Winsnes, 8–11. Accra: Sub-Saharan Publishers, 2009.

———. *Korle Meets the Sea: A Sociolinguistic History of Accra*. New York: Oxford University Press, 1997.

———. "The Portuguese Language on the Gold Coast, 1471–1807." *Ghana Journal of Linguistics* 1, no. 1 (2012), 15–33.

Kuhn, Thomas K. "Diakonie im Schatten des Chiliasmus. Christian Heinrich Zeller (1779–1860) in Beuggen." In *Das «Fromme Basel». Religion in einer Stadt des 19. Jahrhunderts*, edited by Thomas K. Kuhn and Martin Sallmann, 93–110. Basel: Schwabe, 2002.

Kwamena-Poh, M. A. "Church and Change in Akwapem." In *Domestic Rights and Duties in Southern Ghana*, edited by Christine Oppong, 57–67. Legon Family Research Papers. Legon: Institute of African Studies, University of Ghana, 1974.

———. *Government and Politics in the Akuapem State, 1730–1850.* Legon History Series. Evanston, Ill.: Northwestern University Press, 1973.

Labi, Kwame. "Akanization of the Hill Guan Arts." *Research Review of the Institute of African Studies* 18, no. 2 (2002), 1–22.

Lächele, Rainer, ed. *Das Echo Halles: kulturelle Wirkungen des Pietismus.* Tübingen: Biliotheca Academica, 2001.

Lang, Andrew. *The Making of Religion.* 1898. New York: AMS Press, 1968.

Laryea, Philip T. *Ephraim Amu: Nationalist, Poet and Theologian (1899–1995).* Akropong-Akuapem, Ghana: Regnum Africa, 2012.

Law, Robin. "Cowries, Gold, and Dollars: Exchange Rate Instability and Domestic Price Inflation in Dahomey in the Eighteenth and Nineteenth Centuries." In *Money Matters: Instability, Values and Social Payments in the Modern History of West African Communities,* edited by Jane I. Guyer, 53–73. Portsmouth, N.H.: Heinemann, 1995.

Lazier, Benjamin. *God Interrupted: Heresy and the European Imagination between the World Wars.* Princeton: Princeton University Press, 2008.

Lederle, Julia. *Mission und Ökonomie der Jesuiten in Indien: intermediäres Handeln am Beispiel der Malabar-Provinz im 18. Jahrhundert.* Wiesbaden: Harrassowitz, 2009.

Lehmann, Hartmut. "Neupietismus und Säkularisierung. Beobachtungen zum sozialen Umfeld und politischen Hintergrund von Erweckungsbewegung und Gemeinschaftsbewegung." *Pietismus und Neuzeit* 15 (1989), 40–58.

Lenoch, Timothy. "Beneath a Fluid Surface: The Volta Valley, the Dente Shrine and Kete-Krachi, Ghana." Master's thesis, University of Wisconsin-Madison, 2005.

Levack, Brian. "The Decline and End of Witchcraft Prosecutions." In *Witchcraft and Magic in Europe.* Volume 5, *The Eighteenth and Nineteenth Centuries,* by Marijke Gijswijt-Hofstra, Brian Levack, and Roy Porter, 1–94. Philadelphia: University of Pennsylvania Press, 1999.

Li, Anshan. "*Social Protest in the Gold Coast: A Study of the Eastern Province in the Colonial Period.*" PhD diss., University of Toronto, 1993.

Liebau, Heike. *Die indischen Mitarbeiter der Tranquebarmission (1706—1845): Katecheten, Schulmeister, Übersetzer.* Tübingen: Verlag der franckeschen Stiftungen Halle im Max-Niemeyer-Verl., 2008.

Lindberg, Carter. "Introduction." In *The Pietist Theologians: An Introduction to Theology in the Seventeenth and Eighteenth Centuries,* edited by Carter Lindberg, 1–20. Malden, Mass.: Blackwell, 2005.

Lloyd, Alan. *The Drums of Kumasi: The Story of the Ashanti Wars.* London: Longmans, 1964.

Lovejoy, Paul. *Jihād in West Africa During the Age of Revolutions.* Athens: Ohio University Press, 2016.

Manuh, Takyiwaa. "Changes in Marriage and Funeral Exchanges among the Asante: A Case Study from Kona, Afigya-Kwabre." In *Money Matters: Instability, Values and Social Payments in the Modern History of West African Communities*, edited by Jane I. Guyer, 188–202. Social History of Africa. Portsmouth, N.H.: Heinemann, 1995.

Marshall, Ruth. *Political Spiritualities: The Pentecostal Revolution in Nigeria*. Chicago: University of Chicago Press, 2009.

Mbiti, John S. *African Religions & Philosophy*. New York: Praeger, 1969.

McCaskie, T. C. "Accumulation, Wealth and Belief in Asante History. I. To the Close of the Nineteenth Century." *Africa: Journal of the International African Institute* 53, no. 1 (1983), 23–43, 79.

———. "Accumulation: Wealth and Belief in Asante History: II. The Twentieth Century." *Africa: Journal of the International African Institute* 56, no. 1 (1986), 3–23.

———. "Social Rebellion and the Inchoate Rejection of History: Some Reflections on the Career of Opon Asibe Tutu." *Asante Seminar: The Asante Collective Biography Project Bulletin* 4 (February 1976), 34–38.

———. *State and Society in Pre-Colonial Asante*. African Studies Series. Cambridge: Cambridge University Press, 1995.

McEntire, Mark. "Cain and Abel in Africa: An Ethiopian Case Study." In *The Bible in Africa: Transactions, Trajectories, and Trends*, edited by Gerald O. West and Musa W. Dube, 248–59. Leiden: Brill, 2000.

Merton, Robert King. *Social Theory and Social Structure*. Glencoe, Ill.: Free Press, 1957.

Metuh, Emefie Ikenga. *African Religions in Western Conceptual Schemes: The Problem of Interpretation*. Studies in Igbo Religion. Ibadan, Nigeria: Pastoral Institute, Bodija, 1985.

Meyer, Birgit. *Translating the Devil: Religion and Modernity among the Ewe in Ghana*. Trenton, N.J.: Africa World Press, 1999.

Meyerowitz, Eva. *The Akan of Ghana, Their Ancient Beliefs*. London: Faber and Faber, 1958.

———. *Akan Traditions of Origin*. London: Faber and Faber, 1952.

———. *At the Court of an African King*. London: Faber and Faber, 1962.

———. *The Sacred State of the Akan*. London: Faber and Faber, 1951.

Middleton, John. "One Hundred and Fifty Years of Christianity in a Ghanaian Town." *Africa: Journal of the International African Institute* 53, no. 3 (1983), 2–19.

Miller, Jon. *Missionary Zeal and Institutional Control: Organizational Contradictions in the Basel Mission on the Gold Coast, 1828–1917*. Grand Rapids: Eerdmans, 2003.

Mohr, Adam. *Enchanted Calvinism: Labor Migration, Afflicting Spirits, and Christian Therapy in the Presbyterian Church of Ghana*. Rochester, N.Y.: University of Rochester Press, 2013.

———. "Missionary Medicine and Akan Therapeutics: Illness, Health and Healing in Southern Ghana's Basel Mission, 1828–1918." *Journal of Religion in Africa* 39, no. 4 (2009), 429–61.

Montgomery, Robert L. *The Lopsided Spread of Christianity: Toward an Understanding of the Diffusion of Religions.* Westport, Conn.: Praeger, 2002.

Mugambe, Jesse. "A Different World Right Here: The Church within African Theological Imagination." In *A Future for Africa: Critical Essays in Christian Social Imagination*, edited by Emmanuel Katongole, 153–84. Scranton, Pa.: University of Scranton Press, 2005.

Naipaul, V. S. *The Masque of Africa: Glimpses of African Belief.* New York: Alfred A. Knopf, 2010.

Neckel, Gustav. *Altgermanische Kultur.* Leipzig: Quelle & Meyer, 1925.

Newbigin, Lesslie. *Foolishness to the Greeks: The Gospel and Western Culture.* Grand Rapids: Eerdmans, 1986.

Nkansa-Kyeremateng, Kofi. *History, Mission & Achievements: Presbyterian Church, Ghana.* Accra: Sebewie, 1996.

———. *Kwawu Handbook.* Accra: Sebewie, 2000.

———. *The Story of Kwawu.* Accra: Presbyterian Press, 1987.

Nketia, J. H. Kwabena. "Historical Evidence in Ga Religious Music." In *The Historian in Tropical Africa; Studies Presented and Discussed at the Fourth International African Seminar*, edited by Jan Vansina, R. Mauny, and L. V. Thomas, 265–83. London: Published for the International African Institute by the Oxford University Press, 1964.

Obeng, J. Pashington. *Asante Catholicism: Religious and Cultural Reproduction among the Akan of Ghana.* Leiden: Brill, 1996.

Olabimtan, Kehinde. "Wilhelm, Andrew (C.1802 to 1866)." In the *Dictionary of African Christian Biography* http://www.dacb.org/stories/nigeria/wilhelm _andrew.html: 2011.

Olupona, Jacob K. *African Religions: A Very Short Introduction.* New York: Oxford University Press, 2014.

Olupona, Jacob K., and Terry Rey, eds. *Òrìṣà Devotion as World Religion: The Globalization of Yorùbá Religious Culture.* Madison: University of Wisconsin Press, 2008.

Opoku, Kofi Asare. "Communalism and Community in the African Heritage." *International Review of Mission* 79, no. 316 (1990), 487–92.

———. "Training the Priestess at the Akonnedi Shrine." *Research Review of the Institute of African Studies* 6, no. 2 (1970), 34–50.

———. "Riis the Builder." Unpublished manuscript, Akrofi-Christaller Institute, Akropong-Akuapem, Ghana.

Osei-Tutu, Brempong. "Mound Makers and Brass Casters from the Akwapem Ridge." *Journal des Africanistes* 75, no. 2 (2005), 54–63.

Owusu-Ansah, David. *Islamic Talismanic Tradition in Nineteenth-Century Asante.* Lewiston, N.Y.: Edwin Mellen, 1991.

———. *Historical Dictionary of Ghana.* Lanham, Md.: Scarecrow, 2005.

p'Bitek, Okot. *African Religions in Western Scholarship.* Kampala: East African Literature Bureau, 1970.

Painter, Colin. "The Guang and West African Historical Reconstruction." *Ghana Notes and Queries* 9 (November 1966), 58–65.

Parrinder, Geoffrey. *West African Religion: A Study of the Beliefs and Practices of Akan, Ewe, Yoruba, Ibo, and Kindred Peoples.* London: Epworth Press, 1969.

Peel, J. D. Y. *Christianity, Islam, and Orişa Religion: Three Traditions in Comparison and Interaction.* Berkeley: University of California Press, 2016.

———. *Religious Encounter and the Making of the Yoruba.* Bloomington: Indiana University Press, 2000.

Perbi, Akosua Adoma. *A History of Indigenous Slavery in Ghana: From the 15th to the 19th Century.* Accra: Sub-Saharan Publishers, 2004.

Peterson, Derek R. *Creative Writing: Translation, Bookkeeping, and the Work of Imagination in Colonial Kenya.* Portsmouth, N.H.: Heinemann, 2004.

———. *Ethnic Patriotism and the East African Revival: A History of Dissent, c. 1935 to 1972.* Cambridge: Cambridge University Press, 2012.

Pfeifer, Wolfgang. *Etymologisches Wörterbuch des Deutschen 1 (a-L).* 2nd ed. Berlin: Akademie Verlag, 1993.

Pfister, Friedrich. *Schwäbische Volksbraüche: Feste und Sagen.* Augsburg: B. Filser, 1924.

Phillips, John F. V. *Agriculture and Ecology in Africa, a Study of Actual and Potential Development South of the Sahara.* London: Faber and Faber, 1960.

Piggin, Stuart. *Making Evangelical Missionaries 1789–1858: The Social Background, Motives and Training of British Protestant Missionaries to India.* Abingdon: Sutton Courtenay Press, 1984.

Porter, R. "The Crispe Family and the African Trade in the Seventeenth Century." *The Journal of African History* 9, no. 1 (1968), 57–77.

Postma, Johannes. *The Dutch in the Atlantic Slave Trade, 1600–1815.* Cambridge: Cambridge University Press, 1990.

Pugach, Sara Elizabeth Berg. *Africa in Translation: A History of Colonial Linguistics in Germany and Beyond, 1814–1945.* Ann Arbor: University of Michigan Press, 2012.

Quarcoopome, T. N. O. *West African Traditional Religion.* Ibadan, Nigeria: African Universities Press, 1987.

Rattray, R. S. *Ashanti.* Oxford: Clarendon, 1923.

———. *Ashanti Law and Constitution.* Oxford: Clarendon, 1929.

———. *Ashanti Proverbs (the Primitive Ethics of a Savage People).* Oxford: Clarendon, 1916.

———. *Religion & Art in Ashanti.* Oxford: Clarendon, 1927.

Ray, Carina E. *Crossing the Color Line: Race, Sex, and the Contested Politics of Colonialism in Ghana.* Athens: Ohio University Press, 2015.

Renkewitz, Heinz. *Die Losungen. Entstehung und Geschichte eines Andachtsbuches.* 2nd ed. Hamburg: Wittig, 1967.

Rennstich, Karl. "The Understanding of Mission, Civilization and Colonialism in the Basel Mission." In *Missionary Ideologies in the Imperialist Era,* edited by T. Christensen and W. R. Hutchison. Aarhus: Forlaget Aros, 1982.

Robert, Dana L. *Christian Mission: How Christianity Became a World Religion.* Hoboken: Wiley, 2009.

Rodney, Walter. "Gold and Slaves on the Gold Coast." *Transactions of the Historical Society of Ghana* 10 (1969), 13–28.

Sanders, Edith R. "The Hamitic Hypothesis; Its Origin and Functions in Time Perspective." *The Journal of African History* 10, no. 4 (1969), 521–32.

Sanneh, Lamin. *Abolitionists Abroad: American Blacks and the Making of Modern West Africa.* Cambridge, Mass.: Harvard University Press, 1999.

———. *The Crown and the Turban: Muslims and West African Pluralism.* Boulder, Colo.: Westview Press, 1996.

———. *Translating the Message: The Missionary Impact on Culture.* 2nd ed. Maryknoll, N.Y.: Orbis, 2008.

———. *West African Christianity: The Religious Impact.* London: C. Hurst, 1983.

Sarpong, Peter. *Ghana in Retrospect: Some Aspects of Ghanaian Culture.* Tema: Ghana Pub. Corp., 1974.

———. *The Sacred Stools of the Akan.* Tema, Accra: Ghana Pub. Corp., 1971.

Sauter, Gerhard. *Die Theologie des Reiches Gottes beim älteren und jüngeren Blumhardt.* Zürich: Zwingli Verlag, 1962.

Schlatter, W. *Geschichte der Basler Mission: Mit besonderer Berücksichtigung der ungedruckten Quellen.* Volume 1, *Die Heimatgeschichte der Basler Mission.* Basel: Verlag der Missionsbuchhandlung, 1916.

———. *Geschichte der Basler Mission: Mit besonderer Berücksichtigung der ungedruckten Quellen.* Volume 3, *Afrika.* Basel: Verlag der Missionsbuchhandlung, 1916.

Schnakenbourg, Eric. "Sweden and the Atlantic: The Dynamism of Sweden's Colonial Projects in the Eighteenth Century." In *Scandinavian Colonialism and the Rise of Modernity,* edited by Magdalena Naum and Jonas M. Nordin, 229–42. Contributions to Global Historical Archaeology. New York: Springer, 2013.

Schnurr, Jan Carsten. *Weltreiche und Wahrheitszeugen: Geschichtsbilder der protestantischen Erweckungsbewegung in Deutschland, 1815–1848.* Göttingen: Vandenhoeck & Ruprecht, 2011.

Senn, Alfred. "Verhältnis von Mundart und Schriftsprache in der Deutschen Schweiz." *Journal of English and Germanic Philology* 34, no. 1 (1935), 42–58.

Sensbach, Jon F. *Rebecca's Revival: Creating Black Christianity in the Atlantic World.* Cambridge, Mass.: Harvard University Press, 2005.

Shumway, Rebecca. *The Fante and the Transatlantic Slave Trade.* Rochester Studies in African History and the Diaspora. Rochester, N.Y.: University of Rochester Press, 2011.

Sijs, Nicoline van der. "De invloed van de Statenvertaling op de vorming van de Nederlandse standaardtal." In *Leeg en ijdel: de invloed van de Bijbel op het Nederlands*, edited by Nicoline van der Sijs, 39–58. The Hague: Sdu Uitgevers, 2005.

Sill, Ulrike. *Encounters in Quest of Christian Womanhood: The Basel Mission in Pre- and Early Colonial Ghana.* Boston: Brill, 2010.

Smith, Noel. *The Presbyterian Church of Ghana, 1835–1960: A Younger Church in a Changing Society.* Accra: Ghana Universities Press; London: Oxford University Press, 1966.

———. "Protten, Christian (B)." In *Dictionary of African Christian Biography.* https://dacb.org/stories/ghana/protten-cj/, accessed October 25, 2019.

Strong, James. *The Exhaustive Concordance of the Bible: showing every word of the text of the common English version of the canonical books . . .* London: Hodder and Stoughton, 1894.

Stuart, John. *British Missionaries and the End of Empire: East, Central, and Southern Africa, 1939–1964.* Grand Rapids: Eerdmans, 2011.

Sweet, James H. *Domingos Álvares, African Healing, and the Intellectual History of the Atlantic World.* Chapel Hill: University of North Carolina Press, 2011.

Taiwo, Olufemi. "Òrìṣà: a Prolegomenon to a Philosophy of Yorùbá Religion." In *Òrìṣà Devotion as World Religion: The Globalization of Yorùbá Religious Culture*, edited by Jacob K. Olupona and Terry Rey, 84–105. Madison: University of Wisconsin Press, 2008.

Taylor, Charles. *A Secular Age.* Cambridge, Mass.: Belknap Press of Harvard University Press, 2007.

Thornton, John K. *The Kongolese Saint Anthony: Dona Beatriz Kimpa Vita and the Antonian Movement, 1684–1706.* Cambridge: Cambridge University Press, 1998.

Tietjen, Mark A. *Kierkegaard: A Christian Missionary to Christians.* Downers Grove, Ill.: IVP Academic, 2016.

Van Dantzig, Albert. "The Furley Collection: Its Value and Limitations for the Study of Ghana's History." *Paideuma* 33 (1987), 423–32.

Van Dijk, Rijk. "Time and Transcultural Technologies of the Self in the Ghanaian Pentecostal Diaspora." In *Between Babel and Pentecost: Transnational Pentecostalism in Africa and Latin America*, edited by André Corten and Ruth Marshall-Fratani, 216–34. Bloomington: Indiana University Press, 2001.

Vansina, Jan. *De la tradition orale; essai de méthode historique.* Tervuren: Museé royal de l'Afrique centrale, 1961.

———. *Paths in the Rainforests: Toward a History of Political Tradition in Equatorial Africa.* Madison: University of Wisconsin Press, 1990.

Villa-Vicencio, Charles. *On Reading Karl Barth in South Africa*. Grand Rapids: Eerdmans, 1988.

Walls, Andrew. *The Cross-Cultural Process in Christian History: Studies in the Transmission and Appropriation of Faith*. Maryknoll, N.Y.: Orbis, 2002.

———. "The Eighteenth-Century Protestant Missionary Awakening in Its European Context." In *Christian Missions and the Enlightenment*, edited by Brian Stanley, 22–44. Grand Rapids: Eerdmans, 2001.

———. "World Christianity and the Early Church." In *New Day: Essays on World Christianity in Honor of Lamin Sanneh*, edited by Akintunde E. Akinade, 17–30. New York: Peter Lang, 2010.

Wandel, Lee Palmer. *The Eucharist in the Reformation: Incarnation and Liturgy*. New York: Cambridge University Press, 2006.

Warren, Dennis M. *Bibliography and Vocabulary of the Akan (Twi-Fante) Language of Ghana*. Bloomington: Indiana University, 1976.

Weaver, Donna Maier. "Kete-Krachi in the Nineteenth Century: Religious and Commercial Center of the Eastern Asante Borderlands." PhD diss., Northwestern University, 1975.

Weber, Max. *The Protestant Ethic and the Spirit of Capitalism*. 1930. Translated by Talcott Parsons. London: Routledge, 1992.

Weiss, Holger. *Between Accommodation and Revivalism: Muslims, the State, and Society in Ghana from the Precolonial to the Postcolonial Era*. Studia Orientalia 105. Helsinki, Finnish Oriental Society, 2008.

Wendt, Reinhard. *An Indian to the Indians? On the Initial Failure and the Posthumous Success of the Missionary Ferdinand Kittel (1832—1903)*. Wiesbaden: Harrassowitz, 2006.

Werbner, Richard P. *Divination's Grasp: African Encounters with the Almost Said*. Bloomington: Indiana University Press, 2015.

———. *Ritual Passage, Sacred Journey: The Process and Organization of Religious Movement*. Manchester: Manchester University Press, 1989.

White, P. "Centenary of Pentecostalism in Ghana (1917–2017): A Case Study of Christ Apostolic Church International." *HTS Theologiese Studies/Theological Studies* 75, no. 4 (2019), a5185, https://doi.org/10.4102/hts.v75i4.5185.

Wilks, Ivor. *Akwamu 1640-1750: A Study of the Rise and Fall of a West African Empire*. 1958. Trondheim, Norway: Department of History, Norwegian University of Science and Technology, 2001.

———. *Asante in the Nineteenth Century: The Structure and Evolution of a Political Order*. London: Cambridge University Press, 1975.

———. *Forests of Gold: Essays on the Akan and the Kingdom of Asante*. Athens: Ohio University Press, 1993.

———. "The Growth of the Akwapim State: A Study in the Control of Evidence." In *The Historian in Tropical Africa: Studies Presented and Discussed at the Fourth International African Seminar*, edited by Jan Vansina, R. Mauny, and L. V.

Thomas, 390–411. London: Published for the International African Institute by the Oxford University Press, 1964.

———. "Tribal History and Myth." Parts 1 and 2. *Universitas* 2, nos. 3–4 (1956), 84–86; 116–18.

Williamson, Sydney George. *Akan Religion and the Christian Faith: A Comparative Study of the Impact of Two Religions.* Accra: Ghana Universities Press, 1965.

Wilson, Louis Edward. "The Evolution of Krobo Society: A History from c. 1400 to 1892." PhD diss., University of California, Los Angeles, 1980.

Wiltgen, Ralph M. *Gold Coast Mission History, 1471–1880.* Techny, Ill.: Divine Word, 1956.

Wingo, Ajume. "Akan Philosophy of the Person." In The Stanford Encyclopedia of Philosophy (Summer 2017 Edition), edited by Edward N. Zalta, https://plato .stanford.edu/archives/sum2017/entries/akan-person/.

Winkler. "Heiden." In *Handwörterbuch des deutschen Aberglaubens,* edited by Hanns Bächtold-Stäubli. Berlin: de Gruyter, 1927.

Wiredu, Kwasi. "Death and the Afterlife in African Culture." In *Person and Community: Ghanaian Philosophical Studies, I,* edited by Kwasi Wiredu and Kwame Gyekye, 137–52. Washington, D.C.: Council for Research in Values and Philosophy, 1992.

———. "Papa ne Bone." In *Listening to Ourselves: A Multilingual Anthology of African Philosophy,* edited by Chike Jeffers, 158–75. Albany: State University of New York Press, 2013.

———. "Truth and the Akan Language." In *Readings in African Philosophy: An Akan Collection,* edited by Kwame Safro, 187–89. Lanham, Md.: University Press of America, 1995.

Wood, Gillen D'Arcy. *Tambora: The Eruption that Changed the World.* Princeton: Princeton University Press, 2014.

Wrangham, Elizabeth. *Ghana during the First World War: The Colonial Administration of Sir Hugh Clifford.* Durham, N.C.: Carolina Academic Press, 2013.

Yirenkyi, Kwasi. "Transition and the Quest for Identity: A Socio-ethical Study on the Problem of Identity and Political Role of the Ghanaian Clergy in a Modernizing Society." PhD diss., University of Pittsburgh, 1984.

Zachernuk, Philip S. "Of Origins and Colonial Order: Southern Nigerian Historians and the 'Hamitic Hypothesis' C. 1870–1970." *The Journal of African History* 35, no. 3 (1994), 427–55.

Zündel, Friedrich. *Pastor Johann Christoph Blumhardt: An Account of His Life.* 1881. Eugene, Ore.: Cascade, 2010.

# Index

Some African terms beginning with vowels are alphabetized under the first consonant: *asɔfoɔ* under "s."
The open vowel "ɔ" is alphabetized as "o"